Perspectives
on
Writing

Research, Theory, and Practice

Roselmina Indrisano
Boston University
Boston, Massachusetts, USA

James R. Squire
Xerox Corporation, retired
Marlborough, New Hampshire, USA

Editors

INTERNATIONAL
Reading
Association

International Reading Association
800 Barksdale Road, PO Box 8139
Newark, Delaware 19714-8139, USA
www.reading.org

Director of Publications   Joan M. Irwin
Assistant Director of Publications   Jeanette K. Moss
Editor in Chief, Books   Matthew W. Baker
Permissions Editor   Janet S. Parrack
Associate Editor   Tori Mello
Publications Coordinator   Beth Doughty
Association Editor   David K. Roberts
Production Department Manager   Iona Sauscermen
Art Director   Boni Nash
Electronic Publishing Supervisor   Wendy A. Mazur
Electronic Publishing Specialist   Anette Schütz-Ruff
Electronic Publishing Specialist   Cheryl J. Strum
Electronic Publishing Assistant   Jeanine K. McGann

Project Editor   Tori Mello

Library of Congress Cataloging in Publication Data
   Perspectives on writing: research, theory, and practice/Roselmina Indrisano and James R. Squire, editors.
      p.   cm.
   Includes bibliographical references and index.
   1. English language—Rhetoric—Study and teaching.   2. English language—Composition and exercises.   3. Report writing—Study and teaching.   I. Indrisano, Roselmina.   II. Squire, James R.
PE1404.P455   2000   00-026771
808'.042'071—dc21
ISBN 0-87207-268-1

Second Printing, November 2001   Printed in Canada

For
A.I.L.
and
B.L.S.

CONTENTS

Roselmina Indrisano
and James R. Squire

INTRODUCTION

In the concluding sentence of his book *The Sounds of Poetry: A Brief Guide*, Robert Pinsky, Poet Laureate of the United States and Professor of English and Creative Writing at Boston University, writes, "In the particular physical presence of memorable language we can find a reminder of our ability to know and retain knowledge itself: the 'brightness wherein all things come to see' " (p. 116). At a time when long-treasured forms of the printed word—the poem, the essay, the novel—compete with modern technological forms for the time and attention of the young, thoughtful researchers and teachers endeavor to join the advances of the late 20th century with the traditions of centuries past. Perhaps never before in human history has it been more important for scholars to continue to investigate the ways writing is developed and effectively taught, and for teachers to know how to help children and adolescents to appreciate and respond to the written word, to master the craft of writing, and to nurture the imagination. These combined efforts are worthy contributions toward the goal of assuring that future generations will continue to be sustained by the "brightness wherein all things come to see."

This volume brings together the contributions of a group of distinguished researchers and teacher-scholars whose work on the development of writing, the teaching of writing, and the assessment of writing has enriched our understanding and refined our practices. Each chapter presents the significant theory and research related to the topic, the implications of this knowledge for practice, and the directions future researchers might take in extending understanding and refining practice. In a sense, each chapter is a microcosm of a cycle that began early in the 20th century and that endures into the 21st century .

Part One is concerned with the development of writing. The framework for the book is found in the first chapter, wherein John R. Hayes presents a theoretical model of writing that is informed by scholarship in both cognitive and affective domains. In the next two chapters, Anne Haas Dyson and Judith A. Schickedanz focus on the youngest learners. Dyson's chapter is a lyrical reminder of the primacy of oral language in the development of reading and writing. Schickedanz's chapter is a thoughtful discussion of two critical aspects of emergent writing: narrative discourse development and the development of alphabetic, phonological, and orthographic knowledge. The ways in which basic literacy emerges from a variety of experiences of the young child seem particularly significant for educators at all levels.

In the final chapter of this section, Arthur N. Applebee describes the current status of writing instruction within the context of the models of writing that have influenced teaching and assessment. At the conclusion of his chapter, Applebee presents a convincing case for the development of alternative models of the developmental process.

Part Two addresses what is known about the relationship of writing to reading, and to the ways in which readers effectively respond to informational prose. Such knowledge is important in view of the fact that reading instruction, particularly in the early years, has been concerned primarily with narrative. In the intermediate years and beyond, it is the knowledge that is gained through reading informational prose that provides students with the linguistic and conceptual knowledge on which successful learning from text depends. Judith A. Langer and Sheila Flihan explore the history of research on the relationships between reading and writing, and the ways these relationships affect learning and inform instruction. They conclude their chapter with a vision for future research that draws on scholarship from a variety of disciplines. In her insightful chapter on response to informative prose, Bonnie B. Armbruster reports the major studies of students' ability to respond to text, the potential benefits of writing to learn, and the instructional practices validated by research in this area.

Competence in writing is grounded in language and literacy development, broadly construed. Upon this foundation rest the knowledge and abilities required of effective writers, the focus of Part Three. Dale D. Johnson's chapter on vocabulary begins with an examination of the notion of *word*, and continues with a review of classic and contemporary studies of vocabulary development. The chapter concludes with a discussion of the influences of vocabulary on writing and suggestions for educators who wish to help their students gain access to the words that bring ideas to reality.

The chapter by Richard E. Hodges is an exemplar of the power of the writer to stimulate the full continuum of response, from the afferent to the efferent. The technical aspects of writing—spelling, punctuation, and handwriting—are elegantly described within the context of the mental processes that allow writers to learn and use these conventions. Historical, theoretical, and research insights provide the basis for a discussion of informed practice.

In Part Four, the focus is on classroom practice, but the previous chapters' pattern of describing the research and theory that informs instruction continues. Richard T. Vacca and Jo Anne L. Vacca address writing across the curriculum by inviting the reader to observe two learners in different classrooms as they learn both expressive and transactional types of writing. The authors conclude their chapter with a general discussion of instructional principles and activities to support writing across the curriculum.

The urban intermediate classroom is the focus of the chapter by James Flood and Diane Lapp. Following a detailed discussion of critical factors affecting writing development and instruction, the authors introduce their Center-Activity Rotation System, a plan for improving classroom instruction through the effective use of grouping practices and learning centers, including those that afford experiences with technology. Technology is the theme of the last chapter in this section in which Colette Daiute addresses writing and communication technologies. This chapter must, of necessity, be more speculative than the others because the theory and research that inform practice are still in the emergent stages.

Assessment is the focus of Part Five, in which Robert C. Calfee describes the state of writing assessment and the increasingly important portfolio form of assessment. Through the lens of novice-expert, purpose-audience, and scope, the author examines three aspects of portfolios: activity, assessment, and authenticity. The chapter concludes with a proposal that is informed by the author's long and fruitful experience working with teachers in school settings. Calfee describes a model of portfolio assessment specifically designed to improve instructional practice and inform policy makers.

As suggested in the afterword, one of the constant concerns of teachers is the need for classroom conditions that permit them to implement the promising ideas suggested in the literature on writing. In this light, Edmund J. Farrell and Julie M. Jensen review the literature on class size—beginning with a study that was published nearly a half-century ago—and conclude that although the findings of the full body of research are mixed, the pioneer study on class size "will continue to remind teachers of the wide discrepancy between what is and what might be." A recent resolution on class-size reduction passed by the International Reading Association concludes this section, and a final commentary on the text is offered by the editors. Because this volume could not include chapters by all the scholars and researchers who have made substantial contributions to the research, theory, and practice of writing, the annotated bibliography prepared by Sarah E. Dietrich and Margaret Harrington that ends this volume includes references to this body of work.

In a recent presentation to a Boston University audience composed of members of an educational honor society, Robert Pinsky, whose words were cited at the beginning of this introduction, spoke eloquently of the art of teaching, "the transmission of the timeless treasures of humanity." Inspired by this vision, and on behalf of the writers of this text, we offer this volume to the profession, with gratitude to our colleagues, the authors of these chapters; to Tori Mello, our editor; to Elizabeth Bayerl and Patricia Glazer, our doctoral assistants; and to Joan Irwin, Director of Publications of the International Reading Association, our wise and constant guide.

Reference

R. Pinsky. (1998). *The sounds of poetry: A brief guide.* New York: Farrar, Straus & Giroux.

PART ONE

THE DEVELOPMENT OF WRITING

John R. Hayes
Carnegie Mellon University

CHAPTER ONE

A New Framework for Understanding Cognition and Affect in Writing

Alan Newell (1990) described science as a process of approximation. One theory will replace another if it is seen as providing a better description of currently available data (pp. 13–14). Nearly 15 years have passed since the Hayes-Flower model of the writing process first appeared in 1980. Since that time a great many studies relevant to writing have been carried out and there has been considerable discussion about what a model of writing should include. My purpose here is to present a new framework for the study of writing—a framework that can provide a better description of current empirical findings than the 1980 model, and one that can, I hope, be useful for interpreting a wider range of writing activities than was encompassed in the 1980 model.

This writing framework is not intended to describe all major aspects of writing in detail. Rather, it is like a building that is being designed and constructed at the same time. Some parts have begun to take definite shape and are beginning to be usable. Other parts are actively being designed and still others have barely been sketched. The relations among the parts—the flow of traffic, the centers of activity—although essential to the

From Levy, C.M., & Ransdell, S. (Eds.). (1996). *The science of writing*. Mahwah, NJ: Lawrence Erlbaum Associates. Reprinted with permission of Lawrence Erlbaum Associates.

successful functioning of the whole building, are not yet clearly envisioned. In the same way, the new framework includes parts that are fairly well developed—a model of revision that has already been successfully applied, as well as clearly structured models of planning and of text production. At the same time, other parts (such as the social and physical environments), through recognized as essential, are described only through incomplete and unorganized lists of observations and phenomena—the materials from which specific models may eventually be constructed.

My objective in presenting this framework is to provide a structure that can be useful for suggesting lines of research and for relating writing phenomena one to another. The framework is intended to be added to and modified as more is learned.

The 1980 Model

The original Hayes-Flower (1980) writing model owes a great deal to cognitive psychology and, in particular, to Herbert Simon. Simon's influence was quite direct. At the time Flower and I began our work on composition, I had been collaborating with Simon on a series of protocol studies exploring the processes by which people come to understand written problem texts. This research produced cognitive process models of two aspects of written text comprehension. The first, called UNDERSTAND, described the processes by which people build representations when reading a text (Hayes & Simon, 1974; Simon & Hayes, 1976), and the second, called ATTEND, characterized the processes by which people decide what is most important in the text (Hayes, Waterman, & Robinson, 1977). It was natural to extend the use of the protocol analysis technique and cognitive process models to written composition.

Figure 1 (see page 8) shows the Hayes-Flower model as it was originally proposed (Hayes & Flower, 1980). Figure 2 (see page 9) is a redrawing of the original model for purposes of graphic clarity. It is intended to better depict the intended relations in the original rather than as a substantive modification. In the redrawing, memory has been moved to indicate that it interacts with all three cognitive writing processes (*planning, translating,* and *revision*) and not just with planning—as some readers were led to believe. The names of the writing processes have been changed to

Figure 1. The Hayes-Flower Model Proposed in 1980

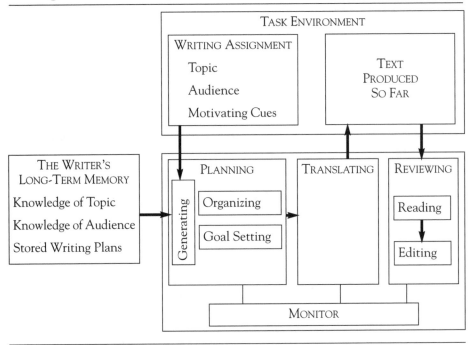

those in more current use. Certain graphic conventions have been clarified. The boxes have been resized to avoid any unintended implication of differences in the relative importance of the processes. Arrows indicate the transfer of information. The process-subprocess relation has been indicated by including subprocesses within superprocesses. In the 1980 model, this convention for designating subprocesses was not consistently followed. In particular, in the original version, the monitor appeared as a box parallel in status to the three writing process boxes. Its relation to each process box was symbolized by undirected lines connecting it to the process boxes. As is apparent in the 1980 paper (pp. 19–20), the monitor was viewed as a process controlling the subprocesses: planning, sentence generation, and revising. Thus, in Figure 2, the monitor is shown as containing the writing subprocesses.

The model, as Figures 1 and 2 indicate, had three major components. First is *the task environment*; it includes all those factors influencing the writing task that lie outside of the writer's skin. We saw the task environment as including both social factors, such as a teacher's writing assignment, as well

Figure 2. The Hayes-Flower Model (1980) Redrawn for Clarification

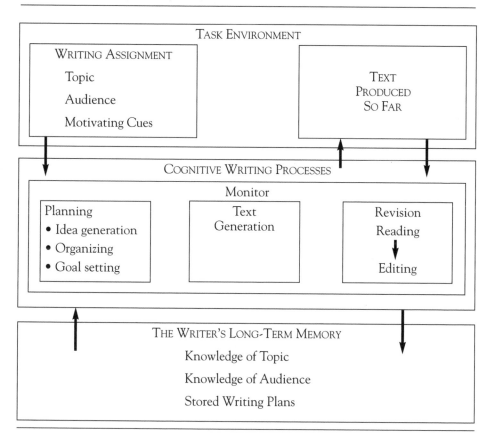

as physical ones such as the text the writer had produced so far. The second component consisted of the cognitive processes involved in writing. These included planning (deciding what to say and how to say it), translating (called text generation in Figure 2, turning plans into written text), and revision (improving existing text). The third component was the writer's long-term memory, which included knowledge of topic, audience, and genre.

General Organization of the New Model

Figure 3 (see page 10) shows the general organization of the new model. This model has two major components: the task environment and the individual. The task environment consists of a social component, which

Figure 3. The General Organization of the New Model

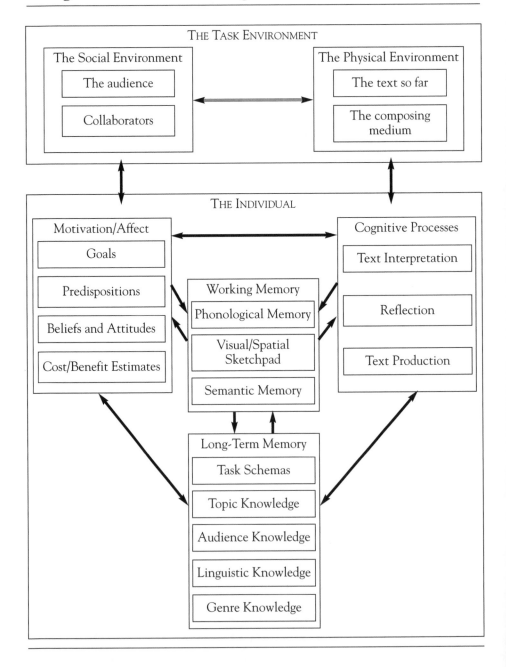

includes the audience, the social environment, and other texts that the writer may read while writing, and a physical component, which includes the text that the writer has produced so far and a writing medium such as a word processor. The individual incorporates *motivation and affect, cognitive processes, working memory,* and *long-term memory.*

In the new model, I group cognition, affect, and memory together as aspects of the individual; I depict the social and physical environments together as constituting the task environment. Thus, rather than a social-cognitive model, the new model could be described as an individual-environmental model.

In what follows, I will say more about modeling the individual aspects of writing than about the social ones. This is because I am a psychologist and not a sociologist or a cultural historian. It does not mean that I believe any of these areas is unimportant. Rather, I believe that each of the components is absolutely essential for the full understanding of writing. Indeed, writing depends on an appropriate combination of cognitive, affective, social, and physical conditions if it is to happen at all. Writing is a communicative act that requires a social context and a medium. It is a generative activity requiring motivation, and it is an intellectual activity requiring cognitive processes and memory. No theory can be complete that does not include all of these components.

There are four major differences between the old model and the new: First, and most important, is the emphasis on the central role of working memory in writing. Second, the model includes visual-spatial as well as linguistic representations. Scientific journals, schoolbooks, magazines, newspapers, ads, and instruction manuals often include graphs, tables, or pictures that are essential for understanding the message of the text. If we want to understand many of the texts that we encounter every day, it is essential to understand their visual and spatial features. Third, a significant place is reserved for motivation and affect in the framework. As I will show, there is ample evidence that motivation and affect play central roles in writing processes. Finally, the cognitive process section of the model has undergone a major reorganization. Revision has been replaced by text interpretation; planning has been subsumed under the more general category, reflection; translation has been subsumed under a more general text production process.

The Task Environment

The Social Environment

Writing is primarily a social activity. We write mostly to communicate with other humans. But the act of writing is not social just because of its communicative purpose. It is also social because it is a social artifact that is carried out in a social setting. What we write, how we write, and who we write to is shaped by social convention and by our history of social interaction. Our schools and our friends require us to write. We write differently to a familiar audience than to an audience of strangers. The genres in which we write were invented by other writers and the phrases we write often reflect phrases earlier writers have written. Thus, our culture provides the words, images, and forms from which we fashion text. Cultural differences matter. Some social classes write more than others (Heath, 1983). Japanese write very different business letters than Americans. Further, immediate social surroundings matter. Nelson (1988) found that college students' writing efforts often have to compete with the demands of other courses and with the hurly burly of student life. Freedman (1987) found that efforts to get students to critique each others' writing failed because they violated students' social norms about criticizing each other in the presence of a teacher.

Although the cultural and social factors that influence writing are pervasive, the research devoted to their study is still young. Many studies are, as they should be, exploratory in character and many make use of case study or ethnographic methods. Some areas, because of their practical importance, are especially active. For example, considerable attention is now being devoted to collaborative writing both in school and in the workplace. In school settings, collaborative writing is of primary interest as a method for teaching writing skills. In a particularly well-designed study, O'Donnell, Dansereau, Rocklin, Lambiote, Hythecker, and Larson (1985) showed that collaborative writing experience can lead to improvement in subsequent individual writing performances. In workplace settings, collaboration is of interest because many texts must be produced by work groups. The collaborative processes in these groups deserve special attention because, as Hutchins (1995) showed for navigation, the output of group action depends on both the properties of the group and those of the individuals in the group. Schriver (in press) made similar observations in extensive case studies of collaboration in document design groups working both in school and industry.

Other research areas that are particularly active are socialization of writing in academic disciplines (Greene, 1991; Haas, 1987; Velez, 1994), classroom ethnography (Freedman, 1987; Sperling, 1991), sociology of scientific writing (Bazerman, 1988; Blakeslee, 1992; Myers, 1985), and workplace literacy (Hull, 1993).

Research on the social environment is essential for a complete understanding of writing. I hope that the current enthusiasm for investigating social factors in writing will lead to a strong empirical research tradition parallel to those in speech communication and social psychology. It would be regrettable if antiempirical sentiments expressed in some quarters had the effect of curtailing progress in this area.

The Physical Environment

In the 1980 model, we noted that a very important part of the task environment is the text the writer has produced so far. During the composition of any but the shortest passages, writers will reread what they have written apparently to help shape what they write next. Thus, writing modifies its own task environment. However, writing is not the only task that reshapes its task environment. Other creative tasks that produce an integrated product cumulatively such as graphic design, computer programming, and painting have this property as well.

Since 1980, increasing attention has been devoted to the writing medium as an important part of the task environment. In large part, this is the result of computer-based innovations in communication such as word processing, e-mail, the World Wide Web, and so on. Studies comparing writing using pen and paper to writing using a word processor have revealed effects of the medium on writing processes such as planning and editing. For example, Gould and Grischowsky (1984) found that writers were less effective at editing when that activity was carried out using a word processor rather than hard copy. Haas and Hayes (1986) found searching for information on-line was strongly influenced by screen size.

Haas (1987) found that undergraduate writers planned less before writing when they used a word processor rather than pen and paper.

Variations in the composing medium often lead to changes in the ease of accessing some of the processes that support writing. For example, on the one hand, when we are writing with a word processor, including crude sketches in the text or drawing arrows from one part of the text to another is more difficult than it would be if we were writing with pencil and paper. On the other hand, word processors make it much easier to move blocks of text from one place to another, or experiment with fonts and check spelling. The point is not that one medium is better than another, although perhaps such a case could be made, but rather that writing processes are influenced, and sometimes strongly influenced, by the writing medium itself.

As already noted, when writers are composing with pen and paper, they frequently review the first part of the sentence they are composing before writing the rest of the sentence (Kaufer, Hayes, & Flower, 1986). However, when writers are composing with a dictating machine, the process of reviewing the current sentence is much less frequent (Schilperoord, in press). It is plausible to believe that the difference in frequency is due to the difference in the difficulty of reviewing a sentence in the two media. When writing with pen and paper, reviewing involves little more than an eye movement. When composing with a dictating machine, however, reviewing requires stopping the machine, rewinding it to find the beginning of the sentence, and then replaying the appropriate part.

The writing medium can influence more than cognitive processes. Studies of e-mail communication have revealed interesting social consequences of the media used. For example, Sproull and Kiesler (1986) suggested that marked lapses in politeness occurring in some e-mail messages (called flaming) may be attributed to the relative anonymity the medium provides the communicator.

Such studies remind us that we can gain a broader perspective on writing processes by exploring other writing media and other ways of creating messages (such as dictation, sign language, and telegraphy) that do not directly involve making marks on paper. By observing differences in process due to variations in the media, we can better understand writing processes in general.

The Individual

In this section I discuss the components of the model that I have represented as aspects of the individual writer: working memory, motivation and affect, cognitive processes, and long-term memory. I will attend to both visual and verbal modes of communication.

Working Memory

The 1980 model devoted relatively little attention to working memory. The present model assumes that all of the processes have access to working memory and carry out all nonautomated activities in working memory. The central location of working memory in Figure 3 is intended to symbolize its central importance in the activity of writing. To describe working memory in writing, I draw heavily on Baddeley's (1986) general model of working memory. In Baddeley's model, working memory is a limited resource that is drawn on both for storing information and for carrying out cognitive processes. Structurally, working memory consists of a central executive together with two specialized memories: a "phonological loop" and a visual-spatial "sketchpad." The phonological loop stores phonologically coded information and the sketchpad stores visually or spatially coded information. Baddeley and Lewis (1981) likened the phonological loop to an inner voice that continually repeats the information to be retained (e.g., telephone numbers of the digits in a memory span test). The central executive serves such cognitive tasks as mental arithmetic, logical reasoning, and semantic verification. In Baddeley's (1986) model, the central executive also performs a number of control functions in addition to its storage and processing functions. These functions include retrieving information from long-term memory and managing tasks not fully automated or that require problem solving or decision making. In the writing model, I represent planning and decision making as part of the reflection process rather than as part of working memory. Further, I specifically include a semantic store in working memory because, as I discuss later, it is useful for describing text generation. Otherwise, working memory in the writing model is identical to Baddeley's model of working memory.

Useful experimental techniques have been developed for identifying the nature of the representations active in working memory. In particular, tasks that make use of phonologic representations such as the memory span task are seriously interfered with when the individual is required to repeat an arbitrary syllable (e.g., la, la, la, etc.). This procedure is called *articulatory suppression*. Similarly, tasks that make use of visual/spatial representation such as interpreting spatial direction are interfered with when the individual is required to engage in spatial tracking tasks (e.g., monitoring the position of a visual or auditory target). These techniques could be useful for identifying the roles of visual and phonological representations in reading and writing tasks.

Motivation

Few doubt that motivation is important in writing. However, motivation does not have a comfortable place in current social-cognitive models. The relatively low salience of motivational concerns in cognitive theorizing is in striking contrast to earlier behaviorist thinking, which provided an explicit and prominent theoretical role to motivation (see, for example, Hull, 1943). Hilgard (1987) believed that cognitive theorists have not attended to motivation because their information-processing models are not formulated in terms of physiological processes. It is these processes that give rise to the basic drives.

I find this explanation unconvincing for the following reason: Cognitive psychologists have been interested in human performance in areas such as reading, problem solving, and memory. The motivations underlying such performances have never been adequately accounted for by the behaviorists or by anyone else in terms of basic drives. Cognitive psychology's failure to account fully for motivation in these complex areas of human behavior is not unique.

Actually, cognitive psychologists, following the lead of the Gestalt psychologists, took an important step in accounting for the effects of motivation by recognizing that much activity is goal directed. Powerful problem-solving mechanisms such as means-ends analysis and hill climbing are built on this recognition (see Hayes, 1989, Chapter 2). Despite the success of such mechanisms in providing insight into a number of important behaviors, much more needs to be understood about motivation and affect. In the following section, I discuss four areas that I believe are of special importance for writing.

1. The Nature of Motivation in Writing. Motivation is manifest, not only in relatively short-term responses to immediate goals, but also in long-term predispositions to engage in certain types of activities. For example, Finn and Cox (1992) found that teachers' ratings of fourth-grade students for engagement in educational activities correlated strongly with the achievement scores of those students in the first three grades. Hayes, Schriver, Hill, and Hatch (1990) found that students who had been admitted to college as "basic" writers engaged much less in a computer-based activity designed to improve their writing skills than did "average" and "honors" students. In particular, the basic students attended fewer training sessions than did the average and honors students. Further, when basic students did attend training sessions, they spent less time attending to the instructional materials than did the average and honors students.

Research by Dweck (1986) suggests that the individual's beliefs about the causes of successful performance are one source of such long term predispositions. Dweck compared students who believed that successful performance depended on innate and unchangeable intelligence with those who believed that successful performance depended on acquirable skills. She found that these two groups of students responded very differently to failure. The first group tended to hide failure and to avoid those situations in which failure was experienced. In contrast, the second group responded to failure by asking for help and by working harder. One can imagine that if students believe that writing is a gift and experience failure, they might well form a long-term negative disposition to avoid writing.

Palmquist and Young (1992) explored in college students the relation between the belief that writing is a gift, on the one hand, and the presence of writing anxiety, on the other. They found that students who believed strongly that writing is a gift had significantly higher levels of writing anxiety and significantly lower self-assessments of their ability as writers than other students.

2. Interaction Among Goals. Activities that are successfully characterized by means-end analysis typically have a single dominant goal. In writing, there are many situations, however, that involve multiple goals which interact with each other to determine the course of action. For example, the college students described by Nelson (1988) had goals to write papers for their classes but often those goals were set aside because of competition with other goals. If a writer has a goal, that does not mean the goal will necessarily lead to action.

Writers typically have more than one goal when they write (Flower & Hayes, 1980). For example, they may want both to convey content and also to create a good impression of themselves, or they may want to convey information clearly but not to write a text that is too long, or they may want to satisfy a first audience but not offend a second. Van der Mast (1996) studied experts writing policy documents for the Dutch government. He found that writers employ explicit linguistic strategies for creating texts that are ambiguous about issues on which members of the audience have conflicting interests. In all of these cases, the text will be shaped by the writer's need to achieve a balance among competing goals.

3. Choice Among Methods. Even for situations in which the goals are specified, motivational factors can additionally influence action by influencing strategy selection. If a person wants to get from one place to another or to compute the answer to an arithmetic problem, the person can still make choices about what strategies should be used to reach that goal. Siegler, Adolph, and Lemaire (1995) studied strategy choice in a variety of situations. In one situation, infants who had just learned to walk were trying to reach their mothers on the other side of a ramp. To reach her, the infants could traverse the ramp by walking, or by crawling forward or backward, prone or supine. Siegler et al. found that experienced infants chose their strategy on the basis of the steepness of the slope, choosing to walk when the slope was small but choosing other strategies when the slope was large.

In a second study, Siegler et al. studied the choice of strategy for solving arithmetic problems among elderly people. Participants could solve problems by retrieving the answers from memory, by pencil-and-paper calculation, or by calculator. Siegler et al. found that the choice of strategy depended on the difficulty of the problem. The more difficult the problem, the more likely it was that the participants would use the calculator.

Thus, motivation may be seen as shaping the course of action through a kind of cost-benefit mechanism. Even when the overall goal of an activity is fixed, individuals will select the means that, in the current environment, is least costly or least likely to lead to error. This mechanism appears to shape overt as well as reflective actions. In a recent study by Kenton O'Hara (in press) at the University of Cardiff, participants were asked to solve a puzzle using a computer interface. The experimenter manipulated the interface so that it was either easy or difficult to make moves. At first, individuals using the difficult interface spent more time between trials than those using the easier interface. However, with practice, those using the hard interface rapidly decreased their time between trials until they were responding more quickly than those with the easy interface.

In another study, O'Hara compared two groups who had practiced for five trials either on the hard or the easy interface. Both groups were then transferred to a third interface. Those trained on the hard interface solved problems in fewer steps and with shorter solution times than those trained on the easy interface. O'Hara's results suggest that:

- people who use the hard interface reflect more before making a move about what move is most likely to lead to solution,
- they do so because the cost of reflection is more likely to be outweighed by its benefits—a reduction in the number of steps to solution—when the cost of each step is high, and
- increased reflection leads to increased learning and improved performance in solving the problems.

The studies of Siegler et al. (1995) and O'Hara (1996) indicate that changes in the task environment can have significant impact on the costs of both overt and reflective activities and an thereby influence the way in which tasks are carried out. In the case of writing, changes in the writing media such as those already discussed can influence the cognitive processes involved in carrying out writing tasks. Designers of word processing systems and other writing media should understand that system characteristics can have significant impact on writing processes.

4. Affective Responses in Reading and Writing. Earlier I mentioned that students who believe both that they are poor writers and that writing is a gift are likely to experience writing anxiety. Reading and writing have a number of other affective consequences as well.

Schriver (1995) studied reader's affective responses to manuals for consumer electronic products such as video cassette recorders and telephone answering machines. In a first study, she asked 201 consumer electronic customers where they placed the blame when they had difficulty understanding the instructions for electronic products they bought: on the manual, on the machine, on the manufacturer, or on themselves. Across both genders and across all age groups (from under 20 to over 60), readers blamed themselves for more than half of the problems they experienced. In a second study Schriver collected thinking-aloud protocols from 35 participants as they were using manuals to help them carry out typical tasks with consumer electronics products. Analysis of the comments that the participants made as they worked, again indicated that they blamed themselves for their difficulties in more than half of the cases (52%).

Schriver found that people were right in about a third of the cases in which people blamed themselves. They had misread or misused the manual. However, in two thirds of the cases, the manual was clearly at fault. The information was either unintelligible, missing, or incorrectly indexed. The tendency of people to blame themselves when they read poorly designed instructional texts may well lead them to believe they are not competent readers of such materials and therefore make them reluctant to read it. We should very seriously consider whether a comparable problem exists in students reading school texts.

Note that people respond effectively not just to the linguistic aspects of a text but to the graphic features as well. Wright, Creighton, and Threlfall (1982), Redish (1993), and Schriver (1996) all noted that if a text is unappealing in appearance, then people frequently decide not to read it.

A developing body of research indicates that the act of writing about stress related topics can have important affective consequences. A number of researchers in the field of health psychology have conducted studies on the use of writing to reduce stress. In a typical study, a group of people subject to stress (e.g., unemployed people, or students entering college) are divided at random into experimental and control groups. Both groups are asked to write for about 20 minutes on each of 3 to 5 days. The experimental group is asked to write about a stress-related topic, for example, "Getting laid off" or "Coming to college." The control group is asked to write on a neutral topic such as "What I did today." Then the groups are compared on some stress-related variables such as doctor visits, immune levels, or symptoms of depression. Pennebaker and Beall (1986) found that participants asked to write about traumatic experiences showed a significant drop in health center visits as compared to control groups. Greenberg and Stone (1992) found similar results. Pennebaker, Kiecolt-Glaser, and Glaser (1988) found that experimental participants showed enhanced immune function after the last day of writing compared to controls.

These results are still controversial. Some researchers have failed to find positive effects of writing on mental health. Further, when writing is compared with face-to-face discussion, the effects of discussion are usually found to be more powerful.

Cognitive Processes

There is a fairly popular view in the field of literacy studies in the United States that social/cultural studies are "in" and cognitive studies are "out." Many feel it is no longer appropriate to do cognitive analyses of writing. Comments such as "We've done cognition" are pronounced with a certain finality.

There are two reasonable arguments that might lead to abandoning cognitive studies of writing. First, one might argue that all there is to know has already been learned about the relation of writing to topic knowledge, to language structure, to working memory capacity, and so on, and, therefore, no further investigations are necessary. However, this argument would not be easy to defend. Second, one might argue that all of the issues that can be investigated through cognitive measures such as working memory capacity or reading level are better or more conveniently studied through social factors such as race, class, or gender. The validity of this position certainly has not been demonstrated nor is it likely to be.

The real reason for the current rejection of cognitive methods is an unfortunate tendency to faddishness that has plagued English studies in the United States, the locus of much research on writing, though certainly not all or necessarily the best work. It is a sort of professional "7-year itch," a kind of collective attention deficit that has nothing to do with scientific progress. Just as we would think a carpenter foolish who said, "Now that I have discovered the hammer I am never going to use my saw again" so we should regard a literacy researcher who says, "Now that I have discovered social methods, I am never going to use cognitive ones again." Our research problems are difficult. We need all available tools, both social and cognitive. Let's not hobble ourselves by following a misguided fad.

In this model, I propose that the primary cognitive functions involved in writing are text interpretation, reflection, and text production.

Text interpretation is a function that creates internal representations from linguistic and graphic inputs. Cognitive processes that accomplish this function include reading, listening, and scanning graphics. *Reflection* is an activity that operates on internal representations to produce other internal representations. Cognitive processes that accomplish reflection include problem solving, decision making, and inferencing. *Text production* is a function that takes internal representations in the context of the task environment and produces written, spoken, or graphic output. It was important to include spoken language in a writing model because spoken language can provide useful inputs to the writing process in the form of content information and editorial comment. In the case of dictation, speech is the output medium for the composing process. Further, for many writers, the process of planning written sentences appears to be carried out, either vocally or subvocally, in the medium of speech.

I assume that the cognitive processes involved in writing are not bound solely to writing but are shared with other activities. For example, I assume that the text-interpreting activities involved in writing overlap with those involved in reading novels and understanding maps; that the reflective activities involved in writing overlap with those involved in solving mystery stories and arithmetic puzzles; and that the text-producing activities involved in writing overlap those used in ordinary conversation and drawing. In addition, I assume that working memory and long-term memory resources are freely shared among both cognitive and motivational processes involved in writing.

Replacing Revision With Reading

Hayes, Flower, Schriver, Stratman, and Carey (1987) reported an extensive series of studies of revision in expert and not so expert adults. These studies led to the model of revision shown in Figure 4. Central to this model is the evaluation function—a process that is responsible for the detection and diagnosis of text problems. We postulated that this

Figure 4. The Revision Process

(From Hayes et al., 1987. Reprinted with permission of Cambridge University Press.)

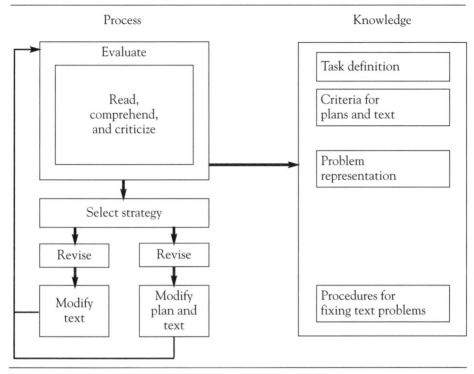

evaluation function was similar to the process of reading comprehension as described by Just and Carpenter (1980).

Figure 5 (see page 24) shows an adaptation of the Just-Carpenter model for our tasks. The important feature of this model is that it shows reading comprehension as a process of constructing a representation of the text's meaning by integrating many sources of knowledge—from knowledge of word patterns and grammatical structures to factual knowledge and beliefs about the writer's intent. Also represented in Figure 5 is the observation that when we read to comprehend, we do not attend much to text problems. That is, we try to form a clear internal representation of the text's message but we are rarely concerned with stylistic issues. When we have problems in comprehending a text, we try to solve those problems and then, most usually, forget them. Consequently, when readers are reading for comprehension, their retrospective reports about text difficulty tend to be very incomplete. However, when we read to revise, we treat the text quite dif-

Figure 5. Cognitive Processes in Reading to Comprehend Text

(From Hayes et al., 1987. Reprinted with permission of Cambridge University Press.)

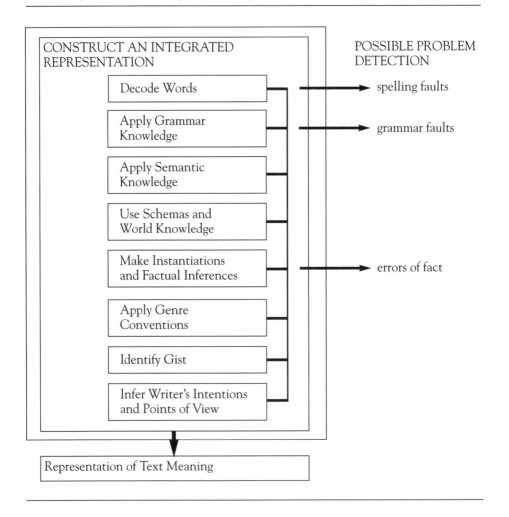

ferently. We are still concerned with the text's message, but now we are also concerned with bad diction, wordiness, and poor organization—features of the text that we may not have attended to when we were reading for comprehension. In revision tasks, people read not only to represent the text's meaning but more importantly they read to identify text problems. With the extra goal of detecting problems, the reviser reads quite differently than does the reader who is simply reading for comprehension, seeing not only problems in the text but also opportunities for improvement that do not necessarily stem from problems. Our model for reading to evaluate a text is shown in Figure 6.

Our model of revision, then, had a form of reading built in. Before it was constructed, I was concerned that revision did not seem to fit comfortably as a basic process in the writing model. Recognizing that the revision

Figure 6. Cognitive Processes in Reading to Evaluate Text
(From Hayes, et al. 1987. Reprinted with permission of Cambridge University Press.)

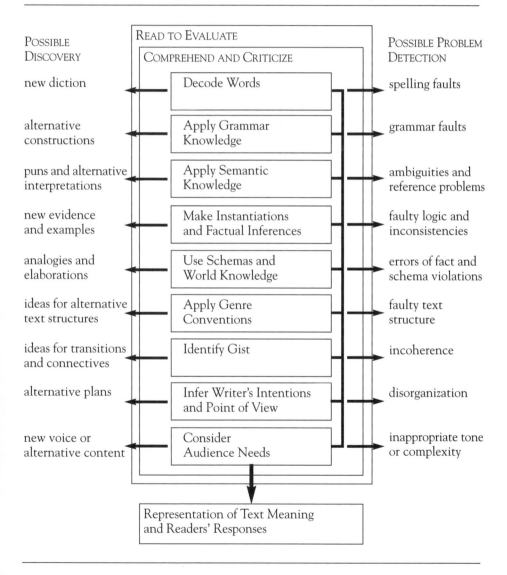

model included reading as a subpart suggested that revision would more naturally be thought of as a composite of more basic processes, in particular, a composite of text interpretation, reflection, and text production.

To understand revision, it is not enough to identify the underlying processes involved. It is also necessary to understand the control structure that determines how these processes are invoked and sequenced. I propose the following provisional model for that control structure. First, the control structure for revision is a task schema. By task schema I mean a package of knowledge, acquired through practice, that is useful for performing the task and is retrieved as a unit when cues indicating the relevance of the schema are perceived. This package of knowledge might be thought of as a set of productions—that is, condition-action rules—that mutually activate each other. People's knowledge of arithmetic shows evidence of being organized in task schemas for solving particular classes of problems. A person may hear just the first few words of a problem (e.g., "A river boat...") and be able to retrieve the problem category ("river current" problems), the nature of the information to be provided (the speed of the boat upstream and downstream), the question to be asked (What would the boat's speed be in still water?) and the kinds of mathematical procedures needed to find the answer.

The control structure for revision is a task schema that might include some or all of the following:

- A goal: to improve the text.
- An expected set of activities to be performed: evaluative reading, problem solving, text production.
- Attentional subgoals: what to pay attention to in the text being revised, what errors to avoid.
- Templates and criteria for quality: criteria for parallelism, dictation, and so on.
- Strategies for fixing specific classes of text problems.

Figure 7 suggests how the components of the revision process might be organized.

The following example illustrates how this model may be applied. In a protocol study, Hayes, Flower, Schriver, Stratman, and Carey (1987)

Figure 7. A Model of Revision

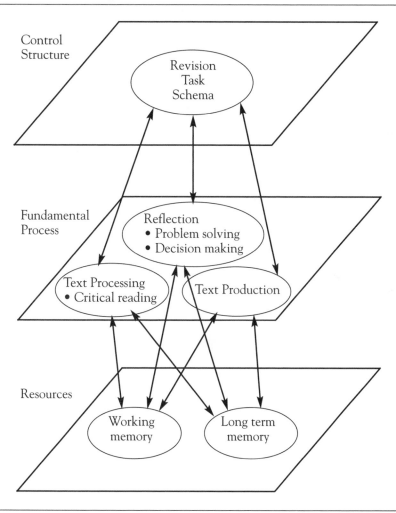

Control Structure

Revision Task Schema

Fundamental Process

Reflection
- Problem solving
- Decision making

Text Processing
- Critical reading

Text Production

Resources

Working memory

Long term memory

observed that college freshmen tended to focus their revision activities on problems at or below the sentence level but that more experienced writers attended both to local and global problems. There are a number of reasons one might propose to account for this failure to revise globally. First, the writer's basic revision processes may be inadequate. For example, the reading process may fail to detect global problems. Second, as Bereiter and Scardamalia (1987) suggested, the writer may lack sufficient working memory to coordinate the basic revision processes. For example, the writer may see the global problems in the text but may be unable to keep the problems in focus while trying to fix them. Third, the writer's task schema may be at fault. For example, as Wallace and Hayes (1991) hypothesized, the control structures of freshman writers simply many not include the goal to attend to global problems.

To test the control structure hypothesis, Wallace and Hayes (1991) designed 8 minutes of instruction that demonstrated the difference between global and local revision, and urged students to revise both globally and locally. The authors reasoned that 8 minutes of instruction might modify the control structure by changing students' definition of the revision task but would be unlikely to cause changes in the basic revision processes or in the functioning of working memory. Wallace and Hayes (1991) then compared revisions produced by a group of freshmen who had received the instruction, the experimental group, with those of a control group that had been instructed simply to make the original text better. The experimental group out-performed the control group both in number of global revisions and in the holistically assessed quality of the revision. These results suggest two conclusions: First, the control structure for revision can be modified by a brief instructional prompt. Second, the control structure plays an important role in determining the nature and quality of revision performance.

Reading as a Central Process in Writing

As discussed previously, reading to evaluate the text is a central component of revision. Poor text evaluation skills, such as Hayes et al. (1987) report, must surely lead to poor revisions. In addition to reading to evaluate, two other kinds of reading play important roles in writing: *reading source texts* and *reading to define tasks*.

Reading Source Texts. Usually, we think of source texts as providing writers with content, that is, with topic information that any competent reader would infer from the source text. However, if writers are not competent readers, if they oversimplify or misunderstand the source texts, their own texts that interpret or summarize those source texts are likely to suffer. For example, Zasloff (1984) studied a group of student writers who were asked to summarize an essay with the form "Others hold Position A but I hold Position B." Some of the students misread the essay to mean that the author held Position A. As a result, these students received very poor grades for their written summaries. Spivey (1984) found that students who wrote more adequate summaries tended to score better on reading tests than did students who wrote less adequate summaries. Chenoweth (1995) found that nonnative speakers of English had particular difficulty in identifying the main points of an essay, suggesting that these students may not be responding appropriately to textual cues that indicate the relative importance of information.

However, the reading of source texts is not simply an activity that provides readers with topic knowledge. Readers may form at lease three different representations when they read: a representation of the topic discussed, a representation of the writer's persona, and a representation of the text as a spatial display.

Representations of the Writer's Persona. In addition to forming a representation of the topic of the text, readers may also form another and quite different representation as they read—a representation of the writer's personality. Hatch, Hill, and Hayes (1993) asked judges to read college application essays and to identify personality traits of the authors. They found that the judges showed substantial agreement in the personality traits they attributed to the authors. In a second study, Hatch et al. (1993) found that these personality judgments predicted whether or not college admission personnel would vote to admit the author of the application essay to college. Thus, for these texts at least, the reader's representation of the author appeared to play an important role in the functioning of the text. Finally, Hatch et al. (1993) showed that readers' judgments of the writer's personality could be influenced in predictable ways by modifying the style of the text in ways that left the content substantially unchanged. For example, in one of the texts, a student described a play that she and her friends had produced. When that text was modified by replacing the word "we" with the word "I," there was a sharp reduction in judgments of the author as "likable" and "sensitive to others."

Hill (1992) asked undergraduates to rate the personality traits of writers who would write pro or con essays on a controversial topic (legalization of drugs). He found that the ratings were far more positive for the writer who agreed with the rater's own position than for the writer who did not. Schriver, Hayes, and Steffy (1994) asked primary and secondary school students to make judgments about the text, the graphics, and the author of drug education brochures. They found that the students often perceived the writers as people who would not be credible communicators. For example, students characterized the writers as people who got their information from books rather than from experience, and as people who were different from themselves in age and social class.

These results suggest that the reader's representation of the author can play an important role in the way readers respond to a text. Indeed, in some cases, the acceptance of a writer's argument may depend more on how the writer comes across as a person than on the logical quality of the argument itself.

Representations of the Text as a Spatial Display. Even when texts consist simply of sequences of sentences without any obvious graphic features such as pictures, tables, and graphs, they still have important spatial features. For example, Rothkopf (1971) found that individuals reading from multiple printed texts showed significant incidental memory for the spatial location in the text of information they read. Readers showed better than chance recall of where the information was located both on the page and within the text. Haas and Hayes (1986) found that readers formed a less precise spatial image of the text when they read one page at a time from a computer screen than from a two-page spread in hardcopy. In addition, they provided evidence linking readers spatial images of the text to their success in searching for information in the text.

Bond and Hayes (1984) asked readers to paragraph text passages from which the original paragraphing marks had been removed. In one condition, the original texts were otherwise unchanged; in other conditions, the original texts were degraded by replacing categories of words (e.g., nouns) with Xs. In the most extreme condition, all of the words were replaced with Xs. The result was that readers showed greatest agreement in paragraphing with the undegraded texts. However, they still showed significant agreement even when all of the words had been replaced by Xs. To account for their data, Bond and Hayes (1984) proposed a model of paragraphing that included both linguistic and spatial features of the text.

Reading to Understand the Task. Reading to understand the writing task is another important function that reading serves for the writer. It is a specialized reading genre that shapes writers' interpretation of writing tasks in school and at work. Success in carrying out this activity in school seems to depend on skill in interpreting terms such as "describe," "argue," and "interpret." In many school writing tasks, and possibly in other writing tasks as well, a text is judged inadequate because the writer has done the wrong task. For example, when assigned to analyze an article, students often respond by summarizing it. Chenoweth (1995) reported a study of this sort of reading in which students were shown exam questions together with an answer a student had written in response to the question. The task was to select one of four items of advice about how to improve the answer. Teachers and students differed systematically in the answers they chose. Students tended to prefer the suggestion to improve the mechanics. In contrast, teachers preferred the suggestion to make the answer more responsive to the question.

Reading, then, takes on a central role in the new model. It is seen as contributing to writing performance in three distinct ways: reading for comprehension, reading to define the writing task, and reading to revise. The quality of writers' texts often depends on their ability to read in these three ways.

From Planning to Reflection

In the 1980 model, planning played a prominent role in our thinking about writing and about writing pedagogy. Indeed, planning was the only reflective process that was explicitly included in that model. Since that time, consideration of the available data has convinced me that other reflective processes should be included in the model and that they are organized as follows: problem solving (including planning), decision making, and inferencing.

Problem Solving. People engage in problem solving when they want to achieve a goal but do not know as yet what steps will achieve it. Problem solving is an activity of putting together a sequence of steps to reach a goal. In writing, problem solving constitutes a substantial part of any but the most routine composing activities. It may take the form of chaining together a sequence of phrases to form a sentence or of claims to form an argument. It may involve constructing a graph to make a point or it may involve creating a plan for an essay or a book.

In cognitive science, planning is treated as one of several problem solving methods (see Hayes, 1989). Chapter 2 [of the original volume, Levy & Randsell, *The Science of Writing*, 1996] presents a theoretical treatment of planning processes in adults together with a taxonomy of these planning processes and a critical review of some of the literature on planning in writing. The most important conclusion we drew from this review was that although several studies showed strong positive correlations between the time spent planning and the quality of the texts, these correlations were confounded with time on task. When time on task was taken into account, the correlations between planning and text quality were generally nonsignificant. These observations do not suggest that planning is unimportant, but they do suggest that we placed too much emphasis on planning in the 1980 model.

Writers, especially student writers, are often required to do writing tasks for which they do not yet have a fully adequate task schema. When this occurs, writers must rely on their general problem-solving and decision-making skills to manage the writing task. It is in such cases that writers engage in process planning described by Hayes and Nash [Chapter 2 in original volume].

Decision Making. People engage in decision making when they evaluate alternatives to choose among them. Like problem solving, decision making is also an important component of all but the most routine writing tasks. Many writing tasks are ill-defined problems. that is, they are problems that cannot be solved unless the writer makes a number of *gap-filling* decisions (Reitman, 1964). For example, if students are asked to write an essay on a controversial topic, they will have to make decisions about what perspective to take, what sources to read, what points to emphasize, how to order those points, how to deal with conflicting views, and so on. In fact, the writers have so many gap-filling decisions to make in writing such an essay that if two students were to submit the same essay, there would be a strong presumption of plagiarism.

If gap-filling decisions are especially important for creating first drafts, evaluative decisions are especially important for revision. When revising, writers must decide whether or not the text is adequate on a variety of dimensions including diction, tone, clarity, effect on audience, and so on. For example, they must answer questions such as "Is this graph clear?", "Is this language appropriate for teenagers?", and "Is this phrase better than that one?"

Difficult writing tasks often require writers to do a substantial amount of problem solving or decision making. Document design tasks may require the designer to produce alternative designs that satisfy complex sets of spatial and linguistic constraints and then to evaluate the relative merits of the designs. As yet, though, relatively little research has been devoted to the complex problem solving and decision making processes that go on in writing.

Inferencing. Inferencing is a process by which new information is derived from old. It may or may not be goal directed, and it may be conscious or unconscious. Inferencing is important in both reading and writing. For example, as Braddock (1992) pointed out, readers often infer the main point of a paragraph when that point is not explicitly stated in the text. Similarly, writers often make inferences about the knowledge and interests of their audiences. Clearly, inferencing is an important process that allows readers and writers to make useful extensions of available information. However, in some cases, readers may extend given information in surprising ways. For example, Stein (1992), studying a phenomenon of "elaboration," found that readers may draw inferences from reading that are both idiosyncratic and consequential.

Stein asked readers to imagine themselves as jurors, to read transcripts of a murder trial, and to make judgments as to the degree of guilt of the defendant in the trial. The case involved a fight between a victim who was stabbed to death by the defendant after the victim had threatened the defendant with a razor. In debriefing, participants revealed that their decisions had been influenced by idiosyncratic representations of the crime situation. For example, one participant, who voted for acquittal on the basis of self defense, had represented the defendant as being unable to avoid the victim because his escape routes were cut off by brick walls. In fact, the trial transcript said nothing about walls. Another participant, who voted for first-degree murder, thought that stabbing was far too strong a response to being threatened with a razor. When asked to draw the razor, she represented a small disposable safety razor, a type that might cause a nick but certainly not a fatal wound.

Notice that there appears to be a strong visual/spatial component in these representations. The fact that the first participant was making inferences about spatial locations of people and objects suggests that his representation included a mental image of the scene. Similarly, the second participant's description of the size and shape of the razor also suggests a mental image. The presence of a visual-spatial component is consistent with the reports of a number of the other participants in Stein's study. For example, one participant reported that the bar mentioned in the transcript (but not described) looked like one with which he was familiar.

If visual representations play an important role in reflecting about texts, as Stein's observations suggest, we need to be alert to the functional properties of these representations. Studies by Paivio (1971) and Bower (1972) indicate that visual and verbal inputs are represented in different ways in memory. Further, studies indicate that these differences in representation can influence the way in which people use the inputs in making inferences and in solving problems. For example, Santa (1977) showed participants a display and asked them to say whether or not it had the same elements as a display they had studied earlier. In some cases, the displays showed an array of geometrical figures and in other cases, an array of names of geometrical figures. He found that some matching problems were easier with visual/spatial input but that others were easier with verbal input indicating that the visual and verbal representations were being processed differently. In a study of physics problem solving, Larkin and Simon (1987) found that visual-spatial inputs were sometimes better than verbal inputs because the visual inputs supported powerful visual inference procedures but the verbal inputs did not. Clearly, if we are to understand how tests are understood and how they are best designed, we have to attend both their verbal and their visual features.

Although reflective processes may be carried on for extended periods without input or output, they are often interleaved with input and output processes. For example, in library research, individuals may alternate between reading paragraphs and summarizing them, and, in brainstorming, individuals may alternate between generating ideas and writing them down.

Text Production

Kaufer, Hayes, and Flower (1986) conducted series of studies of competent and advance adult writers that provided several insights into the processes involved in text generation. Protocol data revealed that writers produce text not in whole sentences but, rather, in sentence parts. Sentence parts were identified either by a pause of two or more seconds or by a grammatical discontinuity indicating that the current language represents a revision of earlier language. On average, writers produced about three sentence parts for each sentence of the final text. The average length of these parts was 7.3 words for competent writers and 11.2 words for advanced writers. However, variability in the size of sentence parts was large. In some cases, a sentence part might consist of a single word. In other cases, the same writer might produce a sentence part that consisted of several clauses or a whole sentence.

Generally, sentences were composed from left to right with more than 90% of sentence parts being added at the leading edge of the sentence—that is, the word farthest from the beginning of the sentence that has been produced so far. Writers frequently reread the sentence produced so far, prior to adding a sentence part to an incomplete sentence. About a third of the sentence parts ended at clause boundaries, which is more than would be expected by chance. When sentence parts are produced, they are evaluated and may be rejected either for semantic or syntactic problems. When a sentence part is accepted, writers often appear to search for an appropriate meaning for the next part in the sentence. Thus, the content of the sentence may not be fully determined before the writer begins to produce syntactically complete sentence parts. Kaufer et al. also provided evidence indicating that sentence production was about equally facilitated by prior knowledge of a sentence's meaning and prior knowledge of its grammatical structure. Further, they found that these two facilitative effects, knowledge of syntax and semantics, were independent of each other.

In what follows, I propose a provisional model of text production that draws heavily on the theoretical ideas and empirical results of Kaufer et al. According to this model, text is produced as follows: Cues from the writing plan and from the text produced so far are used to retrieve a package of semantic content. This content is stored in working memory but not in the articulatory buffer. (This may correspond to what Garrett, 1976, described as the "message level" in his model of speech production.) A surface form to express this content is then constructed and stored in the articulatory buffer. Garrett's (1980) observations on "word exchange" errors (e.g., "the room to my door" for "the door to my room") suggest that the construction process may sometimes operate on more than one clause at a time (p. 193). When all of the content is expressed or when the capacity limit of the articulatory buffer is reached, the sentence part is articulated either vocally or subvocally. If all of the current content has been expressed, then the writer may show evidence of searching for new content. If the articulated sentence part is positively evaluated, then it is written down and the process is repeated. If it is rejected, a new sentence part is constructed and evaluated.

As studies of pausing during composing have indicated (Matsuhashi, 1981; Schilperoord, in press), working memory demands are especially high following clause boundaries. Thus, the limit of the articulatory buffer is more likely to be exceeded at clause boundaries than at other places. For this reason, the model predicts that sentence parts will also be somewhat more likely to end at clause boundaries than at other places. In addition, experience in writing and, more generally, experience with language should reduce the amount of memory required for constructing sentence parts from content. Therefore, writers who have more language and writing experience should write longer sentence parts than other writers.

The following hypotheses may be derived from this model:

1. Secondary tasks that involve the phonological loop, such as the continuous repetition of a syllable string, should interfere seriously with text production. In particular, such secondary tasks will reduce the rate at which text is produced, the average length of the sentence parts produced, and the cohesion of the text that is produced.

2. The length of sentence parts produced should increase as the writer's experience with the language increases. For example, writers who are learning a new language would be expected to produce short sentence parts. (Observations by Friedlander, 1987, on Chinese students writing in English provide some support for this hypothesis.)

Long-Term Memory

Writing simply would not be possible if writers did not have long-term memories in which to store their knowledge of vocabulary grammar, genre, topic, audience, and so on. I will discuss three topics: task schemas, knowledge of audience, and the impact of extended practice as they relate to LTM.

Task Schemas. Task schemas, such as the schema for revision already discussed, are packages of information stored in long-term memory that specify how to carry out a particular task. Typically, task schemas will include information about the goals of the task, the processes to be used in accomplishing the task, the sequencing of those processes, and criteria for evaluating the success of the task. Adults may be expected to have schemas for tasks such as reading graphs, writing business letters, reading a textbook, editing, and so on.

Task schemas are usually activated by environmental stimuli. For example, the editing schema may be triggered by a misspelled word. However, schemas may also be activated by reflection. For example, thinking about a topic may remind us that we have failed to credit the work of a colleague in a paper and thus trigger revision.

Knowledge of Audience. When people are writing to friends or acquaintances, they can draw on a history of personal interaction to decide what to say and how to say it. However, when writers address audiences they do not know personally, they have no such experience to rely on. Writers are sometimes urged to role-play the audience, that is "get inside the skin" of the audience and to try to experience the message as the audience would. To do so would be quite a complex representational act. Protocols of people who are writing for an audience of strangers rarely reveal this sort of complex representation of the audience. Rather, what one sees are not very frequent occasions in which the writer considers whether or not a particular text feature is appropriate for the audience. For example, the writer may say of a teenage audience, "I wonder if this is too racy for them?" or of a child audience "Will they know this word?" When writers show evidence of considering the audience at all, they appear to consider them in a limited and one-dimensional way.

Observations such as these, together with the traditional belief that experts have difficulty writing for novices, led Hayes, Schriver, Spilka, and Blaustein (1986) to hypothesize that writers may use themselves as their primary model for the audience. That is, for example, that they will judge a text unclear for the audience if and only if it is unclear for them.

To explore this hypothesis, Hayes et al. (1986) asked participants to read a difficult text and to underline parts of the text that would be unclear to another reader. Participants in the experimental condition were given information immediately prior to making judgments of difficulty that clarified a number of points in the text. Participants in the control condition were not given this information. The result was that compared to participants in the control condition, the experimental participants were significantly less likely to identify those points that had been clarified for them as being unclear for others. The participants, then, did appear to be using themselves as models for the imagined reader.

If writers do use themselves as models for the audience, it is easy to understand why experts have trouble writing clear instructions for novices. Writing clear instructions has been a major practical problem for the consumer electronics industry where engineers often write user manuals. Swaney, Janik, Bond, & Hayes (1991) showed that the clarity of instruction manuals could be improved significantly by providing writers with think-aloud protocols of real users trying to use the manuals. This technique, called Protocol-Aided Revision, allowed writers to supplement the knowledge that they would ordinarily use to model the audience with data reflecting the responses of audience members.

Schriver (1987) showed that exposure to user protocols can provide writers with knowledge about readers that is generalizable to new readers and new genre. Schriver constructed a sequence of 10 lessons in which readers first predicted reader difficulties with a passage from a computer manual and then read a protocol of a person trying to use the manual. Using a pre–post paradigm, she showed that students who completed these lessons were significantly better at anticipating readers' difficulties with popular science texts than were controls who received traditional training in anticipating audiences' needs.

The Impact of Extensive Practice. In addition to topic knowledge and audience knowledge, writing practice provides people with other sorts of knowledge that are useful in writing. For example, with increased experience, writers may acquire more effective writing strategies, more refined standards for evaluating text, more facility with specific genre, and so on. Indeed, writing experience is widely assumed to be essential for the development of high levels of writing skill.

The literature on expert performance provides some useful insights into the relation of practice and writing skill. In a landmark study, Chase and Simon (1973) provided evidence that skill in chess depends on a very large store of knowledge of chess patterns. They estimated that a grand master chess player had at least 50,000 chess patterns stored in memory. They noted that chess players typically take 10 years or more to acquire such chess knowledge. Following this lead, Hayes (1985) conducted biographical studies to determine if famous composers also required long periods of practice before they began to produce the works for which they were famous. He examined the lives of 76 composers to determine when each had begun the serious practice of music. He then determined how long after this beginning date each of the composer's major works had been written. (A major work was defined as one for which at least five independent recordings were available.)

Hayes found that almost none of the major works were written in the first 10 years after the beginning of practice. From about 10 to 20 years after the beginning of practice, there was a rapid increase in the production of major works. From 20 years to about 45 years, productivity remained fairly stable at about one work every 3 years. Hayes then carried out a parallel study in which he examined the lives of 131 painters. In this case, the criterion of a major work was inclusion in one of a set of general histories of art. The results for the painters were quite similar to those for the composers. Wishbow (1988) conducted a parallel study of 66 English and American poets, defining a major work as one included in the *Norton Anthology of Poetry*. Her results closely paralleled those found for composers and painters.

These three studies indicate that even very talented individuals require a long period of practice before they can produce notable works of music, art, or poetry. Many years of practice may also be required to attain expert performance in any of the genres of writing.

Conclusions

The new writing framework I have presented here is intended to provide a more accurate and more comprehensive description of available observation than was provided by the Hayes-Flower (1980) model. The major changes in focus in the new framework are: greater attention to the role of working memory in writing, inclusion of the visual-spatial dimension, the integration of motivation and affect with the cognitive processes, and a reorganization of the cognitive processes which places greater emphasis on the function of text interpretation processes in writing.

In addition, the new framework includes new and more specific models of planning, text production, and revision and proposes a number of testable hypotheses about writing processes.

I hope that the new framework provides a clearer and more comprehensive description of writing processes than did the earlier model. However, it will have served its function if it stimulates new research and discussion.

Acknowledgments

The author wishes to express thanks to Karen A. Schriver for her many critical readings of this manuscript and for her extensive help in its preparation. The author is also greatly indebted to Michael Levy, Sarah Ransdell, Gert Rijlaarsdam, and Eliza Beth Littleton for many helpful comments. In addition, the author would like to recognize the stimulating discussions and collegial support provided by his many friends at the Center for Language and Communication, University of Utrecht, where much of this manuscript was written.

References
Baddeley, A.D. (1986). *Working memory*. Oxford, UK: Oxford University Press.
Baddeley, A.D., & Lewis, V.J. (1981). Inner active processing in reading: The inner voice, the inner ear and the inner eye. In A.M. Lesgold & C.A. Perfetti (Eds.), *Interactive processes in reading* (pp. 107–129). Hillsdale, NJ: Erlbaum.
Bazerman, C. (1988). *Shaping written knowledge: The genre and activity of the experimental article in science*. Madison, WI: University of Wisconsin Press.

Bereiter, C., & Scardamalia, M. (1987). *The psychology of written composition*. Hillsdale, NJ: Erlbaum.

Blakeslee, A.M. (1992). *Investing scientific discourse: Dimensions of rhetorical knowledge in physics*. Unpublished doctoral dissertation, Carnegie Mellon University.

Bond, S., & Hayes, J.R. (1984). Cues people use to paragraph text. *Research in the Teaching of English, 18*, 147–167.

Bower, G.H. (1972). Mental imagery and associative learning. In L. Gregg (Ed.), *Cognition in learning and memory*. New York: Wiley.

Braddock., R. (1992). The frequency and placement of topic sentences in expository prose. *Research in the Teaching of English, 8*, 287–302.

Chase, W., & Simon, H.A. (1973). Perception in chess. *Cognitive Psychology, 4*, 55–81.

Chenoweth, A. (1995, March). *Recognizing the role of reading in writing*. Paper presented at the College Composition and Communication Conference, Washington, DC.

Dweck, C. (1986). Motivational processes affecting learning. *American Psychologist, 41*, 1040–1048.

Finn, J.D., & Cox, D. (1992). Participation and withdrawal among fourth-grade pupils. *American Educational Research Journal, 29*(1), 141–162.

Flower, L.S., & Hayes, J.R. (1980a). The cognition of discovery: Defining a rhetorical problem. *College Composition and Communication, 31*, 21–32.

Flower, L.S., & Hayes, J.R. (1980b) The dynamics of composing: Making plans and juggling constraints. In L.W. Gregg & E.R. Steinberg (Eds.), *Cognitive processes in writing* (pp. 31–50). Hillsdale, NJ: Erlbaum.

Freedman, S.W. (1987). *Peer response groups in two ninth-grade classrooms* (Tech. Rep. No. 12). Berkeley, CA: University of California, Center for the Study of Writing.

Friedlander, A. (1987). *The writer stumbles: Constraints on composing in English as a second language*. Unpublished doctoral dissertation, Carnegie Mellon University.

Garrett, M.F. (1976). Syntactic processes in sentence production. In R.J. Wales & E. Walker (Eds.), *New approaches to language mechanisms* (pp. 231–255). Amsterdam: North Holland.

Garrett, M.F. (1980). Levels of processing in sentence production. In B. Butterworth (Ed.), *Language production: Vol. 2. Speech and talk*. New York: Academic Press.

Gould, J.D., & Grischkowsky, N. (1984). Doing the same work hard copy and with CRT terminals. *Human Factors, 26*, 323–337.

Greenberg, M.A., & Stone, A.A. (1992). Writing about disclosed versus undisclosed traumas: Immediate and long-term effects on mood and health. *Journal of Personality and Social Psychology, 63*, 75–84.

Greene, S. (1991). *Writing from sources: Authority in text and task* (Tech. Rep. No. 55). Berkeley, CA: University of California, Center for the Study of Writing.

Haas, C. (1987). *How the writing medium shapes the writing process: Studies of writers composing with pen and paper and with word processing*. Unpublished doctoral dissertation, Carnegie Mellon University.

Haas, C., & Hayes, J.R. (1986). What did I just say? Reading problems in writing with the machine. *Research in the Teaching of English, 20*, 22–35.

Hatch, J., Hill, C., & Hayes, J.R. (1993). When the messenger is the message: Readers' impressions of writers. *Written Communication, 10*(4), 569–598.

Hayes, J.R. (1985). Three problems in teaching general skills. In S. Chipman, J. Segal, & R. Glaser (Eds.), *Thinking and learning skills*. Hillsdale, NJ: Erlbaum.

Hayes, J.R. (1989). *The complete problem solver* (2nd ed.). Hillsdale, NJ: Erlbaum.

Hayes, J.R., & Flower, L.S. (1980). Identifying the organization of writing processes. In L. Gregg & E.R. Steinberg (Eds.), *Cognitive processes in writing* (pp. 3–30). Hillsdale, NJ: Lawrence Erlbaum Associates.

Hayes, J.R., Flower, L.S., Schriver, K.A., Stratman, J., & Carey, L. (1987). Cognitive processes in revision. In S. Rosenberg (Ed.), *Advances in applied psycholinguistics: Vol. 2. Reading, writing, and language processing* (pp. 176–240). New York: Cambridge University Press.

Hayes, J.R., & Nash, J.G. (1996). On the value of planning in writing. In C.M. Levy & S.E. Ransdell (Eds.), *The science of writing: Theories, methods and applications*. Mahwah, NJ: Erlbaum.

Hayes, J.R., Schriver, K.A., Hill, C., & Hatch, J. (1990). *Seeing problems with text: How students' engagement makes a difference* (Final report of Project 3, Study 17). Pittsburgh, PA: Center for the Study of Writing, Carnegie Mellon University.

Hayes, J.R., Schriver, K.A., Spilka, R., & Blaustein, A. (1986). *If it's clear to me, it must be clear to them*. Paper presented at the College Composition and Communication Conference, New Orleans, LA.

Hayes, J.R., & Simon H.A. (1974). Understanding written problem instructions. In L.W. Gregg (Ed.), *Knowledge and cognition*. Hillsdale, NJ: Erlbaum.

Hayes, J. R., Waterman, D., & Robinson, S. (1977). Identifying the relevant aspects of a problem text. *Cognitive Science, 1*, 297–313.

Heath, S.B. (1983). *Ways with words: Language, life, and work in communities and classrooms*. New York: Cambridge University Press.

Hilgard, E.R. (1987). *Psychology in America: A historical survey*. New York: Harcourt Brace Jovanovich.

Hill, C. (1992). *Thinking through controversy: The effect of writing on the argument evaluation processes of first-year college students*. Unpublished doctoral dissertation, Carnegie Mellon University.

Hull, C.L. (1943). *Principles of behavior*. New York: Appleton Century Crofts.

Hull, G. (1993). Hearing other voices: A critical assessment of popular views on literacy and work. *Harvard Educational Review, 63*(1), 20–49.

Hutchins, E. (1995). *Cognition in the wild*. Cambridge, MA: MIT Press.

Just, M.A., & Carpenter, P.A. (1980). A theory of reading: From eye fixations to comprehension. *Psychological Review, 87*, 329–354.

Kaufer, D.S., Hayes, J.R., and Flower, L.S. (1986). Composing written sentences. *Research in the Teaching of English, 20*, 121–140.

Larkin, J.E., & Simon, H.A. (1987). Why a diagram is (sometimes) worth ten thousand words. *Cognitive Science, 11*, 65–99.

Matsuhashi, A. (1981). Pausing and planning: The tempo of written discourse production. *Research in the Teaching of English, 15*, 113–134.

Myers, G. (1985a). The social construction of two biologists' proposals. *Written Communication, 2*, 219–245.

Myers, G. (1985b). Text as knowledge claims: The social construction of two biologists' proposals. *Written Communication, 2*, 219–245.

Nelson, J. (1988). *Examining the practices that shape student writing: Two studies of college freshmen writing across disciplines.* Unpublished doctoral dissertation, Carnegie Mellon University.

Newell, A. (1990). *United theories of cognition.* Cambridge, MA: Harvard University Press.

O'Donnell, A.M., Dansereau, D.F., Rocklin, T., Lambiote, J.G., Hythecker, V.I. & Larson, C.O. (1985). Cooperative writing: Direct effects and transfer. *Written Communication, 2*(3), 307–315.

O'Hara, K. (1966). Cost of operations affects planfulness of problem-solving.

Paivio, A. (1971). *Imagery and verbal processes.* New York: Holt, Rinehart, and Winston.

Palmquist, M., & Young, R. (1992). The notion of giftedness and student expectations about writing. *Written Communication, 9*(1), 137–168.

Pennebaker, J.W., & Beall, S.K. (1986). Confronting a traumatic event: Toward an understanding of inhibition and disease. *Journal of Abnormal Psychology, 95*(3), 274–281.

Pennebaker, J.W., Kiecolt-Glaser, R. (1988). Disclosure of traumas and immune function: Health implications for psychotherapy. *Journal of Consulting and Clinical Psychology, 56*, 239–245.

Redish, J. (1993). Understanding readers. In C.M. Barnum & S. Carliner (Eds.), *Techniques for technical communicators* (pp. 14–41). New York: Macmillan.

Reitman, W.R. (1964). Heuristic decision procedures, open constraints, and the structure of ill-defined problems. In M.W. Shelley & G.L. Bryan (Eds.), *Human judgment and optimality.* New York: Wiley.

Rothkopf, E.Z. (1971). Incidental memory for location of information in text. *Journal of Verbal Learning and Verbal Behavior, 10*, 608–613.

Santa, J.L. (1977). Spatial transformations of words and pictures. *Journal of Experimental Psychology: Human Learning and Memory, 3*, 418–427.

Schilperoord, J. (1996). *It's about time: Temporal aspects of cognitive processes in text production.* Unpublished doctoral dissertation, Utrecht University.

Schriver, K.A. (1987). *Teaching writers to anticipate the reader's needs: Empirically based instruction.* Unpublished doctoral dissertation, Carnegie Mellon University.

Schriver, K.A. (1995, June). *Document design as rhetorical action.* Belle van Zuylen Lecture Series, Netherlands: University of Utrecht (available from Faculteitsbureau, Kromme Nieuwegracht 46, 3512 H.J. Utrecht).

Schriver, K.A. (1996). *Dynamics in document design.* New York: Wiley.

Schriver, K.A., Hayes, J.R., & Steffy, A. (1994). Designing drug education literature: A real audience speaks back. *Briefs on Writing, 1*(1), 1–4. Berkeley, University of California, National Center for the Study of Writing and Literacy.

Siegler, R.S., Adolph, K., & Lemaire, P. (1995). *Strategy choices across the lifespan.* Paper presented at the Carnegie Symposium on Cognition: Implicit Memory and Metacognition.

Simon, H.A., & Hayes, J.R. (1976). The understanding process: Problem isomorphs. *Cognitive Psychology, 8*, 165–190.

A New Framework for Understanding Cognition and Affect

Sperling, M. (1991). *High school English and the teacher-student writing conference: Fine tuned duets in the ensemble of the classroom.* (Occasional Paper No. 26). Berkeley, CA: University of California, Center for the Study of Writing.

Spivey, N.N. (1984). *Discourse synthesis: Constructing texts in reading and writing* (Outstanding Dissertation Monograph Series). Newark, DE: International Reading Association.

Sproull, L., & Kiesler, S. (1986). Reducing social context cues: Electronic mail in organization communication. *Management Science, 32,* 1492–1512.

Stein, V. (1992). *How we begin to remember: Elaboration, task and the transformation of knowledge.* Unpublished doctoral dissertation, Carnegie Mellon University.

Swaney, J., Janik, C., Bond, S., & Hayes, J.R. (1991). Editing for comprehension: Improving the process through reading protocols. In E.R. Steinberg (Ed.), *Plain language: Principles and practice.* Detroit, MI: Wayne State University Press.

van der Mast, N.P. (1996). Adjusting target figures downwards: On the collaborative writing of policy documents in the Dutch government. In M. Sharples & T. van der Geest (Eds.), *The new writing environment: Writers at work in a world of technology.* London: Springer Verlag.

Velez, L. (1994). *Interpreting and writing in the laboratory: A study of novice biologists as novice rhetors.* Unpublished doctoral dissertation, Carnegie Mellon University.

Wallace, D.L., & Hayes, J.R. (1991). Redefining revision for freshmen. *Research in the Teaching of English, 25,* 54–66.

Wishbow, N. (1988). *Studies of creativity in poets.* Unpublished doctoral dissertation, Carnegie Mellon University.

Wright, P., Creighton, P., & Threlfall, S.M. (1982). Some factors determining when instructions will be read. *Ergonomics, 25,* 225–237.

Zasloff, T. (1984). *Diagnosing student writing: Problems encountered by college freshmen.* Unpublished doctoral dissertation, Carnegie Mellon University.

Anne Haas Dyson
University of California, Berkeley

CHAPTER TWO

Writing and the Sea of Voices: Oral Language In, Around, and About Writing

I learned that
space is a good place
to be if I lovd [lived]
in that place I would
died Srey [Sorry] Ms. Rita
Oh Precious
You DoNe iT
Srey [Sorry] Boys AND girls

On its own, isolated on an expanse of paper, the above text makes little sense. To construct that sense, readers would no doubt be helped if I provided the "sea of talk" on which the writing floated. That metaphor of the sea of talk was suggested by James Britton more than 25 years ago. In his words,

> All that the children write, your response [as educator] to what they write, their response to each other, all this takes place afloat upon a sea of talk. Talk is what provides the links between you and them and what they write, between what they have written and each other. (1970, p. 29)

That is, children, like the author of the "Precious" text mentioned earlier, generate their ideas and sustain their written voices through talk with others.

In the years since Britton offered his metaphor, researchers have worked to understand more fully the relation between talk and writing. Paradoxically, through these efforts, child writers have become more firmly anchored to sociocultural contexts, and the sea of talk has been channeled carefully—grounded, in fact, within dyadic encounters, literacy events, and cultural practices.

And yet, the notion of floating writing that so captured Britton's imagination is making a comeback, although the sea is no longer so tranquil. In its recent manifestations, writing does not so much float on a sea of talk as mediate a sea of voices; the individual writer is not only supported by, but also struggling against, the currents of the never-ending human conversation.

In this chapter I consider the transformations of Britton's sea of talk. In order to keep afloat myself, I will take along with me 6-year-old Denise, the playful author who, quite literally, raised her oral and written voice to a space child named Precious.

The Solidification of the Sea: Functions, Dyads, and Events

My decision to ground this discussion not only in theoretical constructs, but also in data excerpts from an ongoing study involving Denise, reflects a major theoretical and methodological turn in language studies. That turn, beginning most notably in the late 1960s, was away from the study of language as an abstraction and toward consideration of everyday speech—and writing—as concrete "utterances" (Bakhtin, 1986).

The reasons given for this turn are complex and diverse, among them new technological possibilities (particularly the tape recorder) and new theoretical challenges as well. For example, in response to Chomskian generative grammar based on edited written sentences, some socially oriented linguists analyzed the messiness of conversational speech (Chafe, 1982), while others offered performance rules for speech in diverse cultural contexts (Hymes, 1972); developmentally oriented linguists explored how young children acquired complex linguistic rules (Brown, 1973), and suggested functional needs that organized biological possibilities for language (Halliday, 1973).

This observational turn in language studies yielded rich concepts for analytically examining the sea of talk and, more specifically, for studying how speech functioned during composing and how that functioning was linked to social relationships and cultural life. These efforts added theoretical layers of grounded, useful detail for language arts researchers and educators.

The Functions of Talk: Listening to the Young

Influenced by those who documented the functions of children's speech, like Halliday (1973) and Tough (1977), researchers developed coding schemes to describe the functions of speech during early writing (e.g., Dyson, 1983; Graves, 1979). Although older children and adults may write silently, young children, still developing the use of inner speech (Vygotsky, 1962), are typically quite audible writers. To illustrate, following is an excerpt from the child talk that accompanied the "Precious" text:

> Denise and Vanessa, both first graders, are sitting side by side, working on their "What I Learned About Space" pieces. They are to proceed quietly, because their teacher, Rita, is working intently with the rest of the class. Denise has written "I learned," apologized (in writing) for using the word *died* (a word Vanessa said she was not supposed to be using), and now focuses on Precious, the space robot she made:

> Denise: I'm gonna write, "Oh Precious." Precious, she got on my nerves.... "Oh Precious. You done it. You done it. Oh Precious, you done it." I would say it in a mean voice. "OH PRECIOUS! YOU DONE IT! I'm GONNA (unclear) YOU! YOU DONE IT!"
>
> Vanessa: Write it in big ol' letters!
>
> Denise: (does so and then reads) "OH PRECIOUS! YOU DONE IT!"
>
> Rita: Denise! Be quiet!

> Denise looks startled, mildly embarrassed, and then smiles and writes *Sre [sorry] boys and girls* (i.e., sorry I disturbed you).

As Denise composes, her talk reveals and sustains the social relationships within which writing takes shape; in this case those relationships involve Denise with her space child, her best friend, her teacher, and her class. Moreover, her talk serves as a kind of "recruiting area" (Britton, 1970, p. 29) for the representational aspects of writing, and also as a regulator, helping her (and others) plan, encode, monitor, orchestrate, and evaluate her written efforts:

"I'm gonna write, 'Oh Precious,'" Denise planned.

"Write it in big ol' letters," suggested Vanessa, who had some notion of how to encode spoken meanness in written graphics.

Talk's self-regulatory function—its role in helping individuals control and organize their own behavior (Vygotsky, 1962)—has received much research attention. Children less sophisticated than Denise may use print as a kind of prop (Dyson, 1983)—an interesting phenomenon to be explored, talked about (for instance, "This is my Mama's name"), and used in varied kinds of social, often playful activity (such as playing post office or school).

As they gain a functional understanding of print as a means of recalling instead of only representing messages (Luria, 1983), children's speech both reveals and supports their efforts to act on this understanding. From early attempts to differentiate one squiggle—or one letter—from another by more familiar means (color, shape, size, physical context), children may turn their attention to sound itself (Clay, 1975; Ferreiro & Teberosky, 1982; Read, 1986). Their speech thus becomes raw material and a tool with which to manipulate this material (Dyson, 1983). Child observers thus can hear the more spontaneous activity of speaking literally becoming the more "volitional" (Vygotsky, 1962; 1987, p. 204), more deliberate, act of rendering meaning through drawing speech.

In the following excerpt, also of Denise and her friend Vanessa, the use of speech to manipulate speech is very evident:

Denise is writing about her Thanksgiving Day, but she is struggling with the spelling of that holiday.

Vanessa: You don't gotta spell the whole thing, just sound it out like you can, girl.... 'Cause that word...is long.

Denise, however, finds the word displayed in the classroom. She then uses self-regulatory speech, orally rereading, monitoring, and planning her words.

Denise: "For Thanksgiving" (reading), I (writing) had, went (planning)... How do you spell *went*?

Vanessa: W—(pauses, walks to a pocket-chart word bank and brings back *want* for her friend)

Denise: Read the back [of the card].

Vanessa: "I want a red pencil" (reading)—oh, that's *want*. (Retrieves another card.) This has got to be it.

Denise: That's *with*.

Vanessa: Where is *went*?

Denise: I just got to sound it out! I just got to sound it out!

Denise does so, listening to the sounds as she pronounces the word slowly. She continues on, writing "for Thanksgiving I wet [went] to Hace hez [Chucky Cheese]," sounding out the name of that restaurant with Vanessa's help, and then she adds "and I sow [saw]."

Denise: I just gotta put one thing and you know what it's gonna be!

Vanessa: My name, or your name, [and] I love you....

Denise gives Vanessa her writing book so that Vanessa can write her own name.

Denise: If you sign Wenona [another child's name] I'm gonna be mad at you.

Vanessa: OK.

A logical question raised by Denise's speech is, How do children learn to use oral language in these ways? The answer to this question helps solidify those seaworthy links between writers and others and to organize these links into patterns of talk.

Dyads: Scaffolding Reflective Behavior

Inspired both by a newly available book of Vygotskian theory (Vygotsky, 1934/1978) and based on research on parent/child interaction in language learning (e.g., Cross, 1975), in the 1980s researchers added to a focus on students and their texts a consideration of dyadic encounters between students and teachers about their texts.

From this perspective, children's self-regulatory speech during writing is linked to the responsive, regulating talk of adult guides or other experts. During writing, these guides "loan" children their consciousness about language and language use (Bruner, 1986, p. 175); they thus negotiate the developmental gap—the "zone of proximal development" (Vygotsky, 1934/1978, p. 84)—helping children to choose, encode, and reflect on their written choices. In pedagogical discussions of writing, there are many visions of children as "apprentice" journalists, novel writers, and researchers, getting responsive help from adults and from each other as well (e.g., Graves, 1983; Rogoff, 1994).

In these "scaffolding" interactions, teachers, like their caregiver counterparts (Ninio & Bruner, 1978), orally support children's language. Scaffolding is central to an oft-recommended instructional activity—"writing conferences." In these conferences, teachers respond to child writers in ways that they hope children will respond, in time, to their own and each other's written efforts. Building from the pedagogical work of Graves (1983), Sowers suggested that such conferences revolve around "versions of reflect (what was it [the reported experience] really like?), expand (what else is important to add [to your text about that experience]?), and select (what is most important?)" (1982, p. 87; 1985).

Denise's teacher, Rita, responded to her children and their writing both individually as they wrote and in whole-class sharing sessions. Her responses to children grappling with encoding are reflected quite clearly in the earlier interactions of Vanessa and Denise (for example, their trips to check the word bank, their admonishments to sound out words as best they could). Rita also responded to her children with queries about text clarity and informativeness, and she encouraged her children to talk to each other in this way. For example, Rita instructed her class, "If you just say to me, 'Oh yeah, I love the holidays; I had a good time,' I'm gonna come back to you and ask 'What was a good time?' You can do that for each other."

Despite the usefulness of the scaffolding metaphor, and its predictable routines and contingent responses, thoughtful observers questioned the heavy emphasis on dyadic scaffolds. After all, unlike the middle class caregivers and their singular charges studied in language-development research, teachers have 20 to 30 children or more, and those children do not necessarily share sociocultural background with their teachers. What kinds of assumptions about teacher-student relationships and about textual structures and functions undergird the recommended talk during conferences? Do all students share these assumptions? Are there other kinds of helpful teacher-student talk about writing (Delpit, 1988; Gray, 1987; Reyes, 1991; Walker, 1992)? What about the children themselves—do they help each other only by revoicing their teachers' words (Daiute, 1989; Dyson, 1989)?

To address these questions, researchers and educators needed to step back from those dyadic encounters between teachers and children and to allow both teachers and children complex histories and roles in diverse institutions (families, classrooms, schools, communities). In the 1980s and 1990s, this stepping back was aided by Vygotskian interpretations that stress the sociocultural nature of intellectual thought and, moreover, by ethnographic perspectives on language and literacy in communities and, particularly, by the construct of the event.

Events: Supporting Community Participation

Like all oral interaction, the responsive talk of guiding teachers is itself organized within, and constitutive of, social activity or "events." In fact, as Barton (1994) points out, activities involving oral language provide the context for most instances of print use: "Even in the most seemingly literate of environments, such as a court of law, a schoolroom, or a university office, most of the conventions of how to act and what to do [with and through texts] are passed on orally" (p. 90). Informal interactions, collaborative work sessions, and formal meetings are all occasions for the generation, development, presentation, and revision of ideas encoded in diverse media, including print—and they are also occasions that reveal and sustain participants' social relationships.

These occasions for use of and talk about print—whether in family or government agency—are literacy events (Basso, 1974; Heath, 1983). Like speech events (Hymes, 1972), *literacy events* are energized by particular purposes, characterized by certain ways of relating to other participants, and marked by expected moods, possible and anticipated oral interactions, and also by expected text topics and structures. Many scholars have investigated the diverse ways in which such events are organized within the interactional patterns and cultural values—the events—of everyday life (e.g., Heath, 1983; Philips, 1975).

Learning Within Events. The shift from dyadic encounters to literacy events entails a rethinking of oral/written configurations and their relationship to learning to write. In *dyadic instructional encounters*, social relationships are primarily helpful ones, in which more expert others (or perhaps collaborative peers) help learners write; the goal is that the learner internalizes the oral guidance so that gradually those others can withdraw.

In *events*, there may be many participants with diverse roles, not all of which are explicitly helpful. In fact, even the most expert writers are not necessarily aware of the assumptions about purposes, relationships, and structural features that guide their efforts (Applebee, 1996; Freedman & Medway, 1994). Further, social participants in events do not disappear and leave writers "alone"; rather, over time social relationships change, as do the nature of the learner's participation and perhaps the nature of the event itself.

From this perspective, learning to produce different kinds of texts or genres requires many opportunities to participate orally in the social spheres—the interrelated literacy events—within which such genres matter, and learning itself can happen in many ways: listening to and observing others talk about and use text, receiving explicit instruction, engaging in the event alongside more expert and responsive others, and gaining feedback from participants (who are not necessarily helpers) in an audience role.

Ethnographic researchers have illustrated the oral and written configurations—the complex events—within which people use, and learn to use, print. For example, in many cultural contexts, children may collaborate orally to compose a written letter with their parents. However, across letter-writing events, literacy expertise may be distributed quite differently among child and adult participants because of their respective knowledge of written graphics, genre conventions, audience expectations, and linguistic code (control over a standard language). These differences may engender nontraditional family dynamics (for instance, children guiding adults), thus, they may have ramifications for both social and language learning (Schieffelin & Cochran-Smith, 1984; Vasquez, Pease-Alvarez, & Shannon, 1994).

A related illustration is provided by Kalman's (1996) study of the work life of Mexican scribes. The scribes earn their livelihood composing letters for clients who come to them for assistance in varied legal, workplace, and family matters. Because the distribution of relevant expertise varies between scribes and clients, the scribes' composing events entail complex oral negotiating. In Kalman's words, "Any use of writing and written texts implies understanding how convention, purpose, knowledge, and power are negotiated to produce a particular piece of writing" (p. 215). Moreover, given new social circumstances for writing such as new institutional contexts or new relationships, any "expert" can become a "novice."

Classroom Events. Classrooms, too, are kinds of communities within which conventions, purposes, knowledge, and power are negotiated. In these communities, suggest Moll and Whitmore (1993), the basic organizational unit for learning is not the dyadic zone of proximal development but the "collective" zone, formulated by diverse events in varied units of study. Participating in this zone entails the interactive use of both oral and written language to make decisions about topics for study, resources to consult, and issues to analyze, as well as more text-focused decisions involving planning, encoding, and evaluating text.

Children's talk about and use of text is guided, then, not only by scaffolding interactions but also by their evolving understanding of event purposes, social relations, and textual expectations—understanding gained from and negotiated by oral participation. Over school years, as the curriculum differentiates into disciplines, children's participation in literacy events and their associated genres becomes a means for participation in and development of disciplinary knowledge (Applebee, 1996; Freedman & Medway, 1994).

Some researchers have focused attention on the interplay between the nature of teacher-organized talk, teacher-student relationships, and student writing (e.g., Applebee, 1996; Gutierrez, 1992; Losey, 1997; Nystrand, 1996; Sperling & Woodlief, 1997). A consistent finding of such work is that the "default" teacher-student interaction pattern, to use Cazden's term (1988, p. 53), predominates in classrooms, providing minimal support for student composing. As Cazden discusses, to enact this familiar interactional rhythm, teachers ask testing questions, students provide minimal responses, and teachers evaluate those responses. This interactional mode is very well suited to "assembling factual information" that can be provided in "short answers" (p. 50)—but not well suited to interactively guided composing in which ideas are exchanged, elaborated, and integrated.

For example, Gutierrez (1992) examined composing lessons in elementary classrooms serving primarily immigrant Latino children. Although all classrooms offered writing opportunities to children, the way those opportunities were realized varied strikingly, and an important factor in that variation was the nature of classroom talk. In classrooms in which talk about writing was predominantly teacher controlled (with the teacher giving directions, asking known information questions, and evaluating student understanding of *the* way to do a task), students had limited opportunities to generate or elaborate their ideas; to draw from their own experiences and linguistic resources; to adopt the multiple roles of author, reader, and critic; or even to grasp the purpose of a writing task. For instance, teaching children "brainstorming" as a singular task to be done "correctly" may allow them little sense of what they are doing, or why, or how, as a purpose-driven, socially organized event, brainstorming might be linked to other events in some larger endeavor.

Although they did not use words like "collective zones" or "literacy events," members of an urban teachers' study group (Dyson, with Bennett et al., 1997)—all experienced primary teachers—described and enacted such zones and events. The teachers valued highly social activities allowing child participants many potential avenues to negotiate social participation and symbol use in classroom settings. For example, in her second-grade classroom, teacher Jill Walker orchestrated a series of events involving Arnold Lobel's well-known characters, Frog and Toad. In one event, the children chose partners, play-acted a Frog and Toad story, and wrote improvised lines. They negotiated character roles, generated dialogue, reflected on (and argued about) chosen dialogue lines and potential spellings, studied books to see how to format dialogue, and watched the clock so that they did not "squabble" over whose turn it was to type on the classroom computer. Although Jill's interactions with her students scaffolded their efforts, so too did the children's own interactions and their understanding of the familiar activity of role play. (For extended discussions of play and writing, see Daiute, 1989, 1993.)

I will now return to Denise's space text. As composer, Denise was supported in part by her understanding of familiar classroom reporting activities. For example, she and her classmates made use of the teacher-modeled opening line "I learned that" when they planned what they would tell their parents about space, and also when they reported to each other facts they had learned recently—both oral events linked to the assigned written report. Still, this description of classroom events does not adequately account for Denise's text, which flows over the boundaries of those official events. A more adequate account requires some theoretical wave-making in this too peaceful sea of talk.

Making Waves: Unofficial Events and Critical Practices

At this point, Britton's fluid sea of talk may seem quite organized: writers' talk is channeled by functional use and dyadic encounters within literacy events, which are interrelated within institutional, including disciplinary, contexts. And yet, that sea of talk is not, in fact, so easily contained. In any institution, talk mediates participants' social and cultural identities that are not subsumed by—and potentially in conflict with—social roles in officially sanctioned events. By examining unofficial events and considering critical practices, I begin to make some waves in that peaceful sea.

Unofficial Events: Complicating Agendas

There are always official, as well as unofficial, networks of social organization (Goffman, 1963). In classroom communities, children simultaneously participate in official and unofficial events (for instance, those governed by their relationships with other children). Moreover, their interactions in these events are shaped by the repertoire of genres or familiar ways of using language they bring from other institutions, including their homes, churches, the popular media, and the local peer cultures themselves (Dyson, 1989, 1993; Gilmore, 1983; Heath, 1983; Sola & Bennett, 1985).

For example, readers may recall Denise's and Vanessa's shared assumption that Denise would write Vanessa's name and "I love you"—certainly not an official expectation of a student's essay about "My Thanksgiving," but very much an unofficial expectation of these best friends and "fake sisters." Moreover, if Denise had violated those expectations, Vanessa—not her teacher, Rita—would have corrected her.

In an urban arts magnet school, I examined the role of unofficial relationships and peer talk in children's literacy learning (Dyson, 1989). Children's earliest "texts" were woven through the use of many available symbolic resources or media; their talk and drawing carried much of the functional work of representing, reflecting on, and sharing texts. Influenced by official writing events (and official expectations) for writing, the children's social, playful, and reflective talk about each other's drawing began to engulf their writing as well, helping print become a legitimate object of attention.

Moreover, peer relationships themselves—linked to the values and concerns of unofficial worlds—began to be mediated through writing. Children began to use peers as characters in their stories and to plan to include certain words or actions to amuse or tease them. Like Denise and Vanessa, they began to manipulate the elements (and thereby the words) of written language in order to manipulate the oral responses of others to their efforts.

Such anticipated responses, and the oral interaction through which they are realized, may conflict with the dominant interactional patterns of official school events, as illustrated in another urban study site (Dyson, 1993). Consistent with a Bakhtinian perspective, the social responses anticipated and desired were an integral aspect of the genres—or types of textual "utterances" (Bakhtin, 1986, p. 60)—the children composed. For example, sometimes the focal children (in this study, all African American) recalled experiences watching popular media stories or listed well-known celebrities; the desired social response seemed to be "Oh yeah, I saw that [know that] too." Often these were not texts that lent themselves well to conference-type oral "reflection," or "expansion," because recalling a shared experience—not explicitly communicating a unique experience—was the goal.

The children also composed artful stories, frequently drawing from their oral expressive resources (that is, features of verbal art, which highlight the musical and image-creating properties of language; see Tannen,

1989). Even first graders initiated revisions of these texts; familiarity with popular genres often guided their efforts to make words rhyme, phrases rhythmic, dialogue fast-paced, and images funny. Given their anticipation of a performance, with its associated pleasures, given and received, children might take help from those in "collaborator" or "teacher" roles, but not from those regarded as "audience" (event roles often combined in writing pedagogy).

Educators, like all language users, are not always aware of their own assumptions about appropriate social roles and textual structures in literacy events. The diversity of children's social agendas underscores the importance of careful teacher observation of peer talk during composing time. In his study in an urban site serving mainly Chinese American and immigrant students, Lee (1997) provides a clear illustration of this need. He reveals how low peer status could severely limit immigrant children's access to peer assistance (including help with translating) and, more generally, to the social guidance and social energy peer talk potentially provides.

Further, the diversity of child agendas also suggests the need for teacher-student discourse that allows space for and expects student elaboration and explanation of their own work. Such discourse helps teachers enact "permeable" curricula in which they allow for students' social and linguistic knowledge, for class members to learn from each other, and for their own "loaning of consciousness" to their students; in this loaning, teachers provide vocabulary and analytic talk that allows unexpected knowledge and unanticipated agendas consideration in the classroom "collective zone" (Dyson, 1993).

Unanticipated agendas provide insight into the social, developmental, and textual sense of Denise's writing that opens this chapter. As she was completing a textual world, she also was participating in different social worlds, themselves linked to different aspects of her sociocultural identity; for example, she was a student saying "what she learned," an irritated mother of her robot child "Precious" (and Vanessa's playful sister), and a dutiful child and a polite human being, apologizing for forgetting where she was. Thus, her text mediated—provided a substantive form for, but also shaped—her actions in diverse official and unofficial spheres, with their respective space and time dimensions and textual resources. Denise appropriated "I learned that" from the official world, "YOU DONE IT!" from unofficial ones, and the conversational "sorrys" from general conventions of politeness in and out of school. The resulting oral and written excursions into varied space and time structures (unexpected shifts of tense and author stance) are common in young children's writing (Dyson, 1989); they reflect the multiple textual and social worlds negotiated in a composing act.

This attention to Denise orienting and re-orienting herself in a swirling sea of talk—swallowing its words, becoming a part of the sea even as she moves within it—prepares the way for the final construct to be considered herein, that of critical practices.

Critical Practice: Questioning Agendas

As the language philosopher Bakhtin explains, the words we appropriate as our own—those we swallow, so to speak—always "taste" of the situational and relational contexts in which they were learned (1981, p. 293). Thus, learning social roles, cultural values, and power relations is an integral aspect of learning language, oral or written. The very words, genres, and vernaculars that allow us to express ourselves also express us—they position us in a social and political world. For example, Denise's word *precious* was resisted by the boys with whom she and Vanessa were supposed to design a planet. "Every planet name [the girls] came up with had *precious* in it," said Samuel, one of the boys in the class, in explaining his group's failure to collaborate.

The dyadic scaffolds and interactive events within which children learn to compose do not necessarily help them reflect on ideological assumptions (such as perceptions of "girl words"). For some scholars, the word *practice*, in contrast to the word *event*, highlights the ideological aspects of literacy use (see especially Street, 1995). *Critical literacy* practices involve talk that helps participants reflect on given words—and potentially change their ways of acting on and with those words in given social worlds.

Building on the critical pedagogy of Freire (1970), literacy educators in diverse settings have studied the kinds of interactions that support such reflection. During traditional writing conference events, interaction is organized around individuals and their writing; response flows between teacher and/or peers on the one hand and the writer on the other. During critical literacy practices, the interactional dynamic is different. Writer, teacher, peers—all may respond to each other. Points of difference and agreement are viewed not only as developmental gaps in writing skill, but also as potential sociopolitical gaps to be articulated and examined.

For example, in an urban primary school, teacher Kristin Stringfield promoted critical reflection through an Author's Theater activity in which children acted out their composed texts (studied in Dyson, 1997). Many of these texts were based on the popular media, especially superhero stories, whose ideologically charged content such as gender roles and physical power generated many sociopolitical gaps. For example, children's different perceptions of who could be a superhero or a victim, or even of the value of superhero stories themselves, were initially visible in children's giggles, sour faces, scrunched noses, and cries of "that's not fair," in response to a peer's Author's Theater presentation. By helping the children articulate these views—by lending them her own analytic vocabulary for comparing texts—Stringfield helped the children link interrelated issues of gender, race, and power to authors' decisions about details of character and plot— that is, about how they would revoice words appropriated from the media.

In related work, Moss (1989) describes her efforts to help secondary students articulate their pleasures in and reservations about what she terms the "un/popular" fictions of teenage romance stories and comic book adventures; in so doing, she reveals the complex authorial processes—decisions about the portrayal of love, power, and gender roles—that lie behind a seemingly simplistic text. And, in a powerful piece, poet June Jordan (1988) describes her African American college students' talk about writing—especially their talk about the kind of talk in writing—as she helped them "separate themselves from their own activity [their own speech]" and to reflect on the "historical dimensions" of the negative evaluations they had appropriated uncritically about African American vernaculars (Freire, 1970, p. 80). (For a moving analysis of critical literacy as enacted in an adult women's writing group, see Heller, 1997.)

The message undergirding these educators' critical practices is that appropriating words, stories, genres, and linguistic codes involves more than being situationally appropriate or communicatively competent in language events (Hymes, 1972). The appropriation of words and the deliberate decision to use them or not in particular ways involves decisions about being itself, about who authors want to be as they orient themselves among others in a sea of voices. Becoming aware of how textual options link to social and ideological alternatives is dependent on interaction with others positioned differently in the sea.

The Sea of Voices

The scholarship reviewed in this chapter initially makes Britton's sea of talk more socially organized and then disrupts that order, providing more interactional crosscurrents, more ideological waves. As Britton anticipated, the social relationships—the dyadic links and interactive events—realized through talk allow writers a sense of direction and purpose, as well as supportive others to help them on their way. However, those helpful relationships, steeped in societal beliefs and values, also channel writing in ways that may constrain us as members of a particular gender, ethnic group, social class, discipline, or other constructed category. And yet, it is in the socially lively, sometimes turbulent, sea of voices that new discursive routes may form as old ones come together, move apart, or intertwine in fresh ways (for an interesting discussion of this idea, see Gilyard, 1996).

Further, writers do more than recruit ideas from that sea—they swallow its very words. Indeed, for Bakhtin (1986, p. 62), most written genres have been formed by "absorb[ing] and digest[ing]" simpler, usually oral, genres such as dialogue. Thus, our written voices are quite literally linked to the oral voices of others. Sometimes our appropriated words slip away from us, not because of a writing skill problem per se, but because of our socio-ideological positioning—we may not anticipate the meanings others may find in our words.

For young children, the social, ideological, and textual complexities of the sea of voices can result in awkward texts, such as Denise's space report. But, on occasion, when given time and ideological space (for instance, different perspectives or orientations to subject matter) and the support of at least some familiar social waters (such as events), even the youngest of writers can position themselves quite skillfully amid the sea. To illustrate, I offer, in closing, another of Denise's texts, this one written during a study unit about freedom and slavery.

The freedom and slavery unit is a regular one in local schools—I have witnessed many such units. But Rita's was different in its fullness of voices—voices singing, orating, reading, and in dialogue, often accompanied by, guided by, or stimulated by written texts. For example, she consulted an adult's reference book about the African American artist Jacob Lawrence as she showed the children slides of his well-known paintings of Harriet Tubman's life. She interwove commentary on Lawrence's artistic style with a telling of Tubman's own story as imagined by the artist. Lawrence is famous for his drawing of hands, Rita told them, and Harriet Tubman had strong hands. Because of her strength, Tubman had to chop wood, haul water, and plow, but "she was not gonna give in," even though, as Rita told her students, she would be beaten if she were caught running away.

Before, during, and after the study of Lawrence and his paintings, Rita played and taught the children the words to Pete Seeger's version of "Follow the Drinking Gourd"; she also played albums by, shared a video about, and discussed the artistic skill of the vocal group Sweet Honey in the Rock: "Do you want your freedom?" one of the group sings. "Oh yeah," echo the other singers, joined by the voices of Rita and the children.

In small collaborative groups, the children discussed and made posters about what freedom and slavery meant, historically and in their own lives. Denise, who is African American, told her group that she had been a slave for 3 months. "I'm just playing," she told me later when I asked her about it—a serious kind of play in which one imagines a different self, takes a different angle on a word and a world.

With the rest of the class, Denise listened to (and chose to read with Vanessa) Faith Ringgold's *Aunt Harriet and the Underground Railroad* (1992), whose own text appropriates songs and, moreover, features a young girl like Denise who finds contemporary meaning in historical time. Denise also memorized Eloise Greenfield's (1978) poem about Harriet Tubman, which, as Rita pointed out, uses a kind of written talk to "break the rules" about how written language is supposed to sound—and rule breaking is sometimes a good thing to do:

Harriet Tubman...

Didn't come in this world to be no slave
And wasn't going to stay one either....

She ran to the woods and she ran through the woods
With the slave catchers right behind her

And she kept on going 'til she got to the North
Where those mean men couldn't find her

Nineteen times she went back South
To get the three hundred others
She ran for her freedom nineteen times...

All this singing, poem reciting, picture drawing, story reading, and talking created a collective zone of voices down, around, and about writing. Children who were African American, Asian American, and European American could position themselves differently in their own writing of texts—as sharers of facts, commentators on social evils, or story tellers—and in those stories they could be distant narrators or first-person participants.

In her own story, Denise began as a third-person narrator but, through dialogue, also became a first-person participant. As her story illustrates, she had not only learned from and with other voices, she also had appropriated those other voices to express herself. In reading her text, readers may hear echoes of many others, among them Ringgold, Greenfield, Seeger, her teacher Rita, and Denise herself.

Aunt Harriet wasnt a slave
for Log. She was born a
Slave. She ran back to
sav 300 PePal. She said
We Are going To be free.
But I will follow The Drinking GorD North.
We did it Said HarrieT
yes yes yes yes yes yes
But WhaT if he beats us?
Cit [Can't.] We are SafE now.

It was speech that linked Denise's spoken words to her written ones, in all the texts shared herein. It was speech too—in the form of social dialogue—that invited her into the literate activities of her classroom worlds, be they official or unofficial. It was and is critical dialogue that will help Denise understand the literary, social, and political ramifications of her chosen genres, plots, characters, and words. And, of course, it is the words themselves—with their complex links to a diversity of sources, oral and written, and to a diversity of perspectives—that will keep her, us, and all our students active forces in the dialogic currents of the times.

References

Applebee, A. (1996). *Curriculum as conversation: Transforming traditions of teaching and learning*. Chicago: University of Chicago Press.

Bakhtin, M. (1981). Discourse in the novel. In C. Emerson & M. Holquist (Eds.), *The dialogic imagination: Four essays by M. Bakhtin* (pp. 259–422). Austin, TX: University of Texas Press.

Bakhtin, M. (1986). *Speech genres and other late essays*. Austin, TX: University of Texas Press.

Barton, D. (1994). *Literacy: An introduction to the ecology of written language*. London: Blackwell.

Basso, K. (1974). The ethnography of writing. In R. Bauman & J. Sherzer (Eds.), *Explorations in the ethnography of speaking* (pp. 425–432). Cambridge, UK: Cambridge University Press.

Britton, J. (1970). *Language and learning*. Harmondsworth, Middlesex, UK: Penguin.

Brown, R. (1973). *A first language: The early stages*. Cambridge, MA: Harvard University Press.

Bruner, J. (1986). *Actual minds, possible worlds*. Cambridge, MA: Harvard University Press.

Cazden, C. (1988). *Classroom discourse: The language of teaching and learning*. Portsmouth, NH: Heinemann.

Chafe, W. (1982). Integration and involvement in speaking, writing, and oral literature. In D. Tannen (Ed.), *Spoken and written language: Exploring orality and literacy* (pp. 35–53). Norwood, NJ: Ablex.

Clay, M. (1975). *What did I write?* Auckland, NZ: Heinemann.

Cross, T. (1975). Some relationships between mothers and linguistic levels in accelerated children. *Papers and reports on child language development* (Vol. 10). Stanford, CA: Stanford University.

Daiute, C. (1989). Play as thought: Thinking strategies of young writers. *Harvard Educational Review, 59*, 1–23.

Daiute, C. (Ed.). (1993). *The development of literacy through social interaction*. San Francisco: Jossey-Bass.

Delpit, L. (1988). The silenced dialogue: Power and pedagogy in educating other people's children. *Harvard Educational Review, 58*, 280–298.

Dyson, A.H. (1983). The role of oral language in early writing processes. *Research in the Teaching of English, 17*, 1–30.

Dyson, A.H. (1989). *Multiple worlds of child writers: Friends learning to write*. New York: Teachers College Press.

Dyson, A.H. (1993). *Social worlds of children learning to write in an urban primary school*. New York: Teachers College Press.

Dyson, A.H. (1997). *Writing superheroes: Contemporary childhood, popular culture, and classroom literacy*. New York: Teachers College Press.

Dyson, A.H. (with A. Bennett, W. Brooks, J. Garcia, C. Howard-McBride, J. Malekzadeh, C. Pancho, L. Rogers, L. Rosenkrantz, E. Scarboro, K. Stringfield, J. Walker, & E. Yee). (1997). *What differences does difference make? Teacher perspectives on diversity, literacy, and the urban primary school.* Urbana, IL: National Council of Teachers of English.

Ferreiro, E., & Teberosky, A. (1982). *Literacy before schooling.* Portsmouth, NH: Heinemann.

Freedman, A., & Medway, P. (Eds.). (1994). *Learning and teaching genre.* Portsmouth, NH: Boynton/Cook.

Freire, P. (1970). *Pedagogy of the oppressed.* New York: Continuum.

Gilmore, P. (1983). Spelling "Mississippi": Recontextualizing a literacy-related speech event. *Anthropology & Education Quarterly, 14,* 235–256.

Gilyard, K. (1996). *Let's flip the script: An African American discourse on language, literature, and learning.* Detroit, MI: Wayne State University Press.

Goffman, E. (1961). *Asylums: Essays on the social situation of mental patients and other inmates.* Chicago: Aldine Press.

Graves, D. (1979). Let children show us how to help them write. *Visible Language, 13,* 16–28.

Graves, D.H. (1983). *Writing: Teachers and children at work.* Portsmouth, NH: Heinemann.

Gray, B. (1987). How natural is "natural" language teaching: Employing wholistic methodology in the classroom. *Australian Journal of Early Childhood, 12,* 3–19.

Greenfield, E. (1978). *Honey I love.* New York: Harper & Row.

Guttierez, K. (1992). A comparison of instructional contexts in writing process classrooms with Latino children. *Education in Urban Society, 24,* 244–262.

Halliday, M. (1973). *Explorations in the functions of language.* London: Edward Arnold.

Heath, S.B. (1983). *Ways with words: Language, life and work in communities and classrooms.* Cambridge, UK: Cambridge University Press.

Heller, C. (1997). *Until we are strong together.* New York: Teachers College Press.

Hymes, D. (1972). Models of the interaction of language and social life. In J.J. Gumperz & D. Hymes (Eds.), *Directions in sociolinguistics* (pp. 35–71). New York: Holt, Rinehart & Winston.

Jordan, J. (1988). Nobody means more to me than you and the future life of Willie Jordan. *Harvard Educational Review, 58,* 363–374.

Kalman, J. (1996). Joint composition: The collaborative letter writing of a scribe and his client in Mexico. *Written Communication, 13,* 190–220.

Lee, P. (1997). *Constructing social and linguistic identities: Exploring competence, social goals, and peer interactions within the writing curriculum of a 4th grade ESL classroom.* Unpublished doctoral dissertation, University of California, Berkeley, CA.

Losey, K. (1997). *Listen to the silences: Mexican American interaction in the composition classroom and the community.* Norwood, NJ: Ablex.

Luria, A. (1983). The development of writing in the child. In M. Marlew (Ed.), *The psychology of written language* (pp. 237–277). New York: John Wiley.

Moll, L., & Whitmore, K. (1993). Vygotsky in classroom practice: Moving from individual transmission to social transaction. In E. Forman, N. Minick, & C.A. Stone

(Eds.), *Contexts for learning: Sociocultural dynamics in children's development* (pp. 19–42). New York: Oxford University Press.

Moss, G. (1989). *Un/popular fictions*. London: Virago.

Ninio, A., & Bruner, J. (1978). The achievement and antecedents of labeling. *Journal of Child Language, 5*, 1–15.

Nystrand, M. (with A. Gamoran, R. Kachur, & C. Prendergast). (1996). *Opening dialogue: Understanding the dynamics of language and learning in the English classroom.* New York: Teachers College Press.

Philips, S. (1975). Literacy as a mode of communication on the Warm Springs Indian Reservation. In E.H. Lenneberg & E. Lenneberg (Eds.), *Foundations of language development* (pp. 367–381). New York: Academic Press; Paris: UNESCO.

Read, C. (1986). *Children's creative spelling*. London: Routledge.

Reyes, M. de la Luz. (1991). A process approach to literacy using dialogue journals and literature logs with second language learners. *Research in the Teaching of English, 25*, 291–312.

Ringgold, F. (1992). *Aunt Harriet's underground railroad in the sky*. New York: Crown.

Rogoff, B. (1994). Developing understanding of the idea of communities of learners. *Mind, Culture, and Activity: An International Journal, 1*, 209–229.

Schieffelin, B., & Cochran-Smith, M. (1984). Learning to read culturally: Literacy before schooling. In H. Goelman, A.A. Oberg, & F. Smith (Eds.), *Awakening to literacy* (pp. 3–23). Portsmouth, NH: Heineman.

Sola, M., & Bennett, A. (1985). The struggle for voice: Narrative, literacy, and consciousness in an East Harlem School. *Journal of Education, 167*, 88–110.

Sowers, S. (1982). Reflect, expand, select: Three responses in the writing conference. In T. Newkirk & N. Atwell (Eds.), *Understanding writing: Ways of observing, learning, & teaching* (pp. 47–56). Chelmsford, MA: Northeast Regional Exchange.

Sowers, S. (1985). Learning to write in a workshop: A study in grades one through four. In M.F. Whiteman (Ed.), *Advances in writing research (Vol. 1): Children's early writing development* (pp. 297–342). Norwood, NJ: Ablex.

Sperling, M., & Woodlief, L. (1997). Two classrooms, two writing communities. *Research in the Teaching of English, 31*, 235–239.

Street, B. (1995). *Social literacies: Critical approaches to literacy in development, ethnography, and education*. London: Longman.

Tough, J. (1977). *Teaching and learning*. London: Ward Lock Educational.

Walker, E.V.S. (1992). Falling asleep and failure among African-American students: Rethinking assumptions about process teaching. *Theory into Practice, 31*, 321–328.

Vasquez, O., Pease-Alvarez, L., & Shannon, S. (1994). *Pushing boundaries: Language and culture in a Mexicano community*. New York: Cambridge University Press.

Vygotsky, L.S. (1962). *Thought and language*. Cambridge, MA: MIT Press.

Vygotsky, L.S. (1978). *Mind in society: The development of higher psychological processes.* (M. Cole, V. John-Steiner, S. Scribner, & E. Souberman, Eds. and Trans.). Cambridge, MA: Harvard University Press. (Original work published 1934)

Vygotsky, L.S. (1987). *L.S. Vygotsky, collected works: Volume 1, Problems of general psychology*. New York: Plenum Books.

Judith A. Schickedanz
Boston University

CHAPTER THREE

Emergent Writing: A Discussion of the Sources of Our Knowledge

In learning to write, children gradually master several diverse systems of behavior. This chapter focuses on the sources of our understanding of two aspects of emergent writing—narrative discourse development and the development of alphabetic, phonological, and orthographic knowledge. Research in these areas has developed differently and therefore illustrates different conceptions of where and how one needs to look for explanations about development and its variations. After an initial period of normative research (i.e., maturationist), researchers probing the development of narrative in children have approached their investigations using a Vygotskian social-interaction framework (Vygotsky, 1978). In contrast, researchers investigating the development of preschool children's alphabetic, phonological, and orthographic knowledge have rarely sought data at the level of social interaction. Working within a cognitive developmentalist (Piagetian) or nativist (maturationist) framework, these researchers have tended instead to use tasks to elicit children's behavior and to analyze behavior in terms of an ideal prototype.

Nativists and Piagetian cognitive developmentalists attribute variations in development primarily to differences in what the child takes to his or her experiences. In Piaget's theory, the internal processes of assimilation, accommodation, and equilibration regulate learning and determine how quickly the child constructs knowledge. The environment provides opportunities for the child to create meaning (knowledge), but little variation in eventual outcomes is expected or predicted, given the assumption that knowledge acquisition results primarily from the structure imposed on the environment by the child.

Social interactionists (Vygotskians) recognize variations in the timetable for milestone attainment. Within scaffolded experiences some children have a cognitive reach that is quite far from the limits of their own independent action, while the reach of other children extends only a bit beyond their current independent range, regardless of the support an adult provides. A child's reach when aided—the child's zone of proximal development—along with both the frequency and quality of a child's scaffolded experiences, determines the timetable of a child's learning.

Vygotskian theory predicts variation in the content and form of the knowledge constructed, because virtually all learning, regardless of the domain of knowledge, is thought to begin in social interactions. Even those parts of the world that are directly observable and presumably subject to physical laws originate in social interaction, according to this theory, although variations in physical or logical-mathematical knowledge are certainly more constrained than knowledge in areas that are more purely social.

The Development of Narrative in Young Children

Research on the development of narrative began with efforts to chart the developmental course of children's narrative productions. The descriptive methodology used initially was typical of research designed to establish norms. Researchers did not search for links between experience and child behavior, given that both the form of the behavior and the timetable for its expression are attributed primarily to child-related characteristics in maturationist theory. The theoretical framework for considering this area of development, and thus the methodology used to study it, began to shift toward social interaction in the 1980s. Understanding of the links between socialization of the child by the parent, with respect to narrative content and form, and the subsequent content and form of the child's later narratives, became the primary focus of much of the research. Age-related patterns continued to be of interest, although within a social interaction framework, normative patterns and departures from them are accounted for by both individual differences and variations in children's experiences.

A Brief Review of the Descriptive Research

The first studies of narrative skill were analyses of stories dictated by children (Pitcher & Prelinger, 1963). A plotted narrative framework (see Todorov, 1969, in Leondar, 1979, p. 176) was used to establish developmental milestones. In order to chart the course of narrative development in children as young as $2^1/_2$ years of age, researchers developed schemes that were sensitive to small changes in skill (Botvin & Sutton-Smith, 1977; Stein, 1988). The scheme developed by Botvin and Sutton-Smith (1977, pp. 379–381) contains seven levels. Level 1 narratives consist of a series of unrelated events (see Wanda's story in Table 1). At Level 2, stories contain a focal event dyad (for instance a disruption event and a related action event), without any events between the initial and final terms of the dyad (see Watson's story in Table 1).

Level 3 narratives contain intervening events (see Tracy's story). Level 4 narratives have more than one episode, but no events intervening between the dyad events in each episode. Level 5 narratives have two or more well-developed episodes, but lack the embedding found at Level 6. Level 7 narratives contain "a subordination of plots within plots" (Botvin & Sutton-Smith, p. 381).

Botvin and Sutton-Smith found that nine of ten 3- and 4-year-olds created Level 1 narratives. Out of ten 5-year-olds, only one created a Level 1 narrative. Two children created a Level 2 narrative, six created a Level 3 narrative, and one created a Level 4 narrative. By age 7, Level 1 and 2 narratives had completely disappeared, and plotted narratives (such as goal-based episodes) had begun to appear.

Similar results have been obtained by other researchers, regardless of whether they asked children to tell a story (Benson, 1993; Leondar, 1979), or elicited narratives with a wordless picture book (Berman, 1988). With the picture book task, Berman (1988) found that only one of thirty

Table 1. Stories Produced by Children
Ages 2 to 5 Years Old

"A bus. He went up a hill. He crashed. He down. He went down in the water and he swammed. He went round and round and round and round. He crashed in a mountain. Then he went up in the air and crashed."

Dale, 2 years, 5 months (p. 30)

"Baby cried. Baby hurt his eyes. The baby broke his eye. Then he got it all fixed."

Watson, 2 years, 9 months (p. 34)

"Once there was a car and it broke. It went up a hill and got broke. Then a different car came. The other car made the car go. And it went right home."

Name unknown, 2 years, 10 months (Leondar, 1979, p. 180)

"Once there was a little girl. She ate too many raisins. She got sick. The doctor had to come. And they had to stick a needle in her. She cried. Then he had to listen to her heart. And then he had to give her some pills. Then he had to go home to his little girl. Then she had to eat lunch. Then she got better. Then she could have someone to play with. Then that child that was playing with her slept for the night. Then she had to eat breakfast with her daddy and mommy. Then she had to go to school."

Thecla, 3 years, 7 months (p. 68)

"Once a mouse opened a door into his house from playing on the snow. He had hot coffee and then he had lunch and then he had dinner—three sandwiches and some coffee. He read the paper and then he go to bed."

Kent, 4 years, 10 months (p. 82)

"There was a boy named Johnny Hong Kong and finally he grew up and went to school and after that all he ever did was sit all day and think. He hardly ever went to the bathroom. And he thought every day and every thought he thought up his head got bigger and bigger. One day it got so big he had to go live up in the attic with trunks and winter clothes. So his mother bought some goldfish and let them live in his head—he swallowed them—and every time he thought, a fish would eat it up until he was even so he never thought again, and he felt much better."

Tracy, 5 years, 8 months (p. 133)

"Little girl took a walk in the woods, got a butterfly. She let it go. She said, 'How are you doing?' She started running. She kept a little stone. She saw a little girl and she had a jacket on. She was blindfolded. She untied it. Then she said, 'All right, I'm going home.' She looked at a book. She started running. She put lipstick all over the window sill (cleaned it off afterwards). She saw a little bear and he had a scratch on his paw and she bandaged it up. And that's the end of the story."

Wanda, 5 years, 8 months (p.150)

From Pitcher, E.G., & Prelinger, E. (1963). *Children tell stories: An analysis of fantasy.* Madison, CT: International Universities Press. Reprinted with the permission of International Universities Press.

3- and 4-year-olds mentioned the main character's goal—that he was searching for the frog—while half the 5-year-olds and all the 7-year-olds mentioned it.

Age trends with respect to children's ability to orient a listener to their narratives also were studied (Menig-Peterson & McCabe, 1978; Trabasso et al., 1984; Trabasso & Nickels, 1992). Although the proportion of total orientation comments to event-action comments has been found to be similar across all ages, older children include more comments at the beginning of a narrative than do younger children who are more likely to insert them as they go along. Older and younger children also provide different types of orientation information. Younger children are explicit about props and the sequence of actions—what is there and when something happened—but they are less explicit than older children about the participants, about where actions take place, and especially about why a character carries out an action.

The child's awareness that characters' actions can be accounted for in terms of motives and goals (mental states) appears at around 5 or 5$^1/_2$ years of age. Children can sequence events using both script knowledge (Nelson, 1988) and knowledge of physical causation (Baillargeon, 1994) several years before they can understand psychological causation. The emergence of psychological causation is thought to depend on the development in children of a representational theory of mind (Wellman & Bartsch, 1994). Three-year-olds do not yet conceive of thoughts as representations of reality, but as direct percepts of reality. By age 4$^1/_2$, when children have achieved the insight that thoughts are representational, they realize, for example, that false beliefs can occur, that one's thoughts can change from one time to another, and that knowledge can arise from several different sources (for example, from direct experience or from having been told about something) (Welch-Ross, 1997).

One hypothesis about the development of a representational theory of mind is that it is prompted, in part, by discussions with parents about how people feel and about how feelings are related to human action (Dunn, Brown, Slomkowski, Tesla, & Youngblade, 1991). This hypothesis is consistent with a social interactionist rather than a maturationist or cognitive-developmental theoretical framework (Peterson & McCabe, 1994). Research on early socialization about feelings illustrates the shift in developmental psychology research toward a Vygotskian theory of development. The study of narrative development itself has shifted from descriptive (or normative) research to research focusing on the social construction of narrative. This research converges with work done by linguists who have sought to understand differences in narrative style in terms of culture and social class (Gee, 1985, 1986), although research by developmental psychologists has tended to focus more on variations in development that are due to differences in parental skill in scaffolding a specific kind of narrative, rather than on the socialization of different styles of narrative.

The Social Construction of Narrative Discourse

In the following discussion, two possible sources of variation in children's narrative development are highlighted: (1) differences among parents with respect to their skill in scaffolding narrative performances, and (2) differences found across cultures and social classes, with respect to what is to be included or emphasized in a narrative, and what style or form a narrative is to take.

Differences in Parental Skill in Scaffolding Children's Personal Narrative Productions

Parents begin talking with their children about past events at around 18 to 20 months of age (Fivush, 1991; Hudson, 1990; Miller, Wiley, Fung, & Liang, 1997; Nelson, 1993; Sperry & Sperry, 1996). At first, parents pose questions to the child about past experiences but get few answers. Thus, the parent actually provides the information about what happened in these early collaborations (Fivush, 1991). Between 24 and 28 months of age, children are more responsive to parental questions about past events, but are not able to produce complete and coherent narratives on their own. Sometime between 27 and 30 months, children begin to initiate somewhat coherent conversations about past experiences (Fivush, 1991). (See transcripts of conversations from three age levels in Table 2.)

Parents differ in their approach to prompting children's recall of past events. Elaborative or "topic extending" parents provide informative comments, especially when their children fail to respond to a query (Peterson

Table 2. Parental Scaffolding of Autobiographical Memory in a 21- to 27-Month-Old Child

21 months

Mother:	Did you see Aunt Gail and Uncle Tim last week?
Child:	Yes, yes, Uncle Tim.
Mother:	What did we do with Aunt Gail and Uncle Tim?
Child:	Said bye-bye.
Mother:	You said bye-bye to Aunt Gail and Uncle Tim?
Child:	Yes, go in car, in car.
Mother:	In the car?
Child:	Yes, Tim went in the car.
Mother:	Tim went in the car?
Child:	Aunt Gail went with Uncle Tim.
Mother:	Aunt Gail was with Uncle Tim in the car? Right. Do you remember what else you did with Aunt Gail and Uncle Tim?
Child:	(No response.)
Mother:	Did we go eat?
Child:	(No response.)
Mother:	What did we have to eat?
Child:	(unintelligible) Chair.
Mother:	Rachel sat in a chair? Did Aunt Gail sit next to you?
Child:	Yes.
Mother:	What did she read to you?
Child:	Ernie and Bert book?
Mother:	The Ernie and Bert book?
Child:	Yeah.
Mother:	She read that to you?
Child:	Yeah.
Mother:	Yeah, did you eat hamburger?
Child:	Yeah.

(conversation continues for a few more turns)

24 months

Mother:	Did you like the apartment at the beach?
Child:	Yeah. And I have fun in the, in the, in the water.
Mother:	You had fun in the water?
Child:	Yeah. I come to the ocean.
Mother:	You went to the ocean.
Child:	Yeah.
Mother:	Did you play in the ocean?
Child:	And my sandals off.
Mother:	You took your sandals off?

(continued)

Schickedanz

Table 2. Parental Scaffolding of Autobiographical Memory in a 21- to 27-Month-Old Child (continued)

Child:	And my jamas off.
Mother:	And your jamas off. And what did you wear to the beach?
Child:	I wear hot cocoa shirt.
Mother:	Oh, your cocoa shirt, yeah, and your bathing suit?
Child:	Yeah. And my cocoa shirt.
Mother:	Yeah. Did you walk on the beach?
Child:	Yeah.
Mother:	Who went to the beach?
Child:	Mommy and Daddy.
Mother:	Did you play in the sand?
Child:	Build sand castles.
Mother:	Yeah. And did you go in the water?
Child:	(No response).
Mother:	Who went in the water with you?
Child:	Daddy and Mommy.
Mother:	Right. Did the big waves splash you?
Child:	Yeah.

27 months

Child:	Do you remember the waves, Mommy?
Mother:	Do I remember the waves? What about the waves?
Child:	I go in the waves and I build a sand castle. And do you remember we swimmed? I swimmed in the waves and we did it again. Did we play again?
Mother:	Yeah, so let's see, you went in the waves and you built sand castles and we did that together?
Child:	Yeah.
Mother:	Yeah. I remember those waves. Did you like the beach?
Child:	I cried.
Mother:	You cried?
Child:	Yeah.
Mother:	Why?
Child:	I cried I want to go to the beach.
Mother:	We went together, didn't we?
Child:	No.
Mother:	Who went to the beach?
Child:	Grandma Pat.
Mother:	Grandma Pat was there.
Child:	A big wave come and (unintelligible) my beach chair and hat. Do you remember my beach hat?
Mother:	Yeah. The waves came to your beach chair and your hat, right? (pp. 180–181)

From Hudson, J.A. (1990). The emergence of autobiographical memory in mother-child conversation. In R. Fivush & J.A. Hudson (Eds.), *Knowing and remembering in young children* (pp. 166–196). New York: Cambridge University Press. Reprinted with permission of Cambridge University Press.

& McCabe, 1992). In the conversations provided in Table 2, the mother follows up her question, "What did you have to eat?" by asking, "Did you eat hamburger?" She does not repeat, "What did you have to eat?"

Parents using a repetitive approach proceed differently:

Mother: Do you remember when we went to Disneyland?

Child: Yeah.

Mother: Do you remember Disneyland? (long pause) Do you remember that? Who did we go to Disneyland with? Who did we see down there?

Child: What?

Mother: You can't remember? (Fivush, 1991, p. 63).

Here, the mother tries to prompt the child's memory of Disneyland with a second question ("Who did we go to Disneyland with?"), rather than with information about who was present at an event. The non-elaborative parent also gives up quickly when the child cannot recall the information. In contrast, an elaborative parent tends to provide more and more information, even if he or she must tell most of the narrative.

Differences in the tendency to provide elaborative versus repetitive prompts are correlated with different tendencies to stick to a topic. Peterson and McCabe (1994) found that, on average, middle-class parents provided about 13 utterances per narrative elicitation. The range, however, was enormous (4 to 37 prompts in one study of mothers and their $2^1/_2$- to 3-year-old children). Parents exhibiting an elaborative style of scaffolding narrative production tend to stick to a topic, while mothers using a repetitive style of interaction tend to switch topics, perhaps in search of something the child can talk about. But switching topics rarely works, given that young children have difficulty recalling experiences without considerable help from adults. No wonder, then, that in interactions with parents who use a repetitive style, a number of topics are raised although few if any are explored in depth (Peterson, Jesso, & McCabe, 1999).

Parental styles of eliciting personal narratives are correlated with various child outcomes. Those $2^1/_2$-year-olds whose parents routinely elaborate and extend conversation on a topic about a past experience produce longer personal narratives 1 year later. Children whose parents use a repetitive approach progress little (McCabe & Peterson, 1991; Peterson et al., 1999).

Parental stress on causal connectives also is correlated with the child's use of causal connectives 1 year later. Similarly, children whose parents use more orienting comments in discourse about past events when they are 2½ years old use more orienting comments themselves 1 year later (Fivush, 1991).

These close associations between what parents stress and what children later include in their narratives do not seem to result from initial differences in children. Parental styles of eliciting personal narratives (elaborative versus repetitive) are stable across siblings of various ages (Haden, 1998). Intervention studies (for example, Peterson et al., 1999), as well as studies using a time-lagged methodology indicate that parental styles are apparent in parents' speech before specific features appear in their children's narratives.

In a time-lagged methodology study (Peterson & McCabe, 1992, 1994), one child's (Helen's) mother prompted mostly for contextual information—the who, where, and when of the events—while the other child's (Cathy's) mother included as many prompts for "what happened" as for context. Between 27 and 33 months of age, the two girls made about the same number of orientation comments, although Cathy specified "when" more often than Helen. At age 3, however, it was Helen who provided more of every kind of orienting comment. Additionally, by age 3, the girls' narratives were structured differently: fifteen percent of Helen's narratives were of the "leapfrog" kind (for instance out of spatial/temporal order, as described by Applebee, 1977), while only 5% of Cathy's were this type. Five percent of Cathy's narratives ended at a high point (Labov, 1972), and 15% fit the classic pattern of a problem followed by actions to resolve it, while not a single one of Helen's narratives ended at a high point or fit the classic (story grammar) narrative pattern. Similar correlations between mothers' scaffolding (26 to 31 months) and the child's later narratives (32 to 37 months) were found in 10 other mother-child dyads participating in the same longitudinal study.

Cultural and Social Class Differences in the Socialization of Narrative

The content and form of narrative discourse varies across cultures and social class. For example, Minami and McCabe (1991) found a succinct style in Japanese children's narratives, which they attributed to the influence of exposure to haiku, a literary form in which the number of sylla-bles per verse is limited. Scollon and Scollon (1984) have reported that Athabascan students tend to relate details that are important to their lives, and to leave out other details, with the result that their narratives do not take the elaborated form typically used to judge the adequacy of children's narratives. Gee (1985, 1986) has extensively discussed differences in the organization of narrative within oral versus literate traditions.

Kwon (1999) has suggested that children from different cultures prob-ably include different balances between evaluative and contextual com-ments, both in their personal narratives and in their discussions of stories. Kwon bases this hypothesis on Jeong's (1996) finding that Korean mothers often locate specific relationships between their child and the stories they read to him or her, as if stories are to serve as sources of lessons on how children should behave. Jeong (1999) suspects that Korean mothers stress moral lessons more than other mothers, and that Korean children would, as a consequence of this socialization, make more evaluative interpreta-tions than other children, and also relate stories more specifically to them-selves. Research designed to probe for these differences between Korean children and children with other cultural backgrounds has not been con-ducted, although knowledge about differences of this kind, if they exist, would be useful.

Content comparisons have been the subject of a series of studies on the narrative development of children living in two working-class and one middle-class European American communities (Burger & Miller, 1999; Miller & Sperry, 1988). Although no social class differences were found in the proportion of referential versus evaluative utterances, differences were found in the content of evaluative utterances and in the modes that chil-dren use to express emotional content (such as evaluative utterances). Chil-dren and parents in the poorer of the two working-class communities pro-duced far more negative evaluative comments than did children and parents in the other working-class group or in the middle-class group, and middle-class children and parents produced the fewest negative comments of all.

The forms used to talk about negative emotions also differed in these three communities. Working-class children and parents used negative verbs (hit, punch, smash, knock), negative attributions (fraidy cat, yucky), and expletives far more than did the middle-class children and parents, and used emotion-state words (*happy, sad, excited, surprised, angry*) far less. The researchers characterized these differences in modes of talking as differences on a "continuum of linguistic resources for conveying affect, with dramatic language on the one end and psychological language on the other" (Burger & Miller, 1999, p. 169). Interestingly, when children and parents conveyed positive emotion content, working-class children used as many emotion-state terms as middle-class children.

Differences of this kind, found in early personal narratives, are likely to affect the negative or positive content of stories children later write, as well as the kind of language they use to convey this content. These differences might affect narrative coherence judgments, given that emotion-state words explicitly indicate feelings and motives, while these must be inferred from action verbs and attributions. Different school assignments ("Write about an experience that was very important to you" versus "Write about the best thing that ever happened to you") would be expected to lead to different judgments about the child's linguistic resources and narrative skill.

Consequences of a Social Interactionist Research Framework

As these examples of research in narrative development illustrate, a social interactionist research framework is basically "child sparing." In other words, it is likely to lead to fewer false deficit judgments about achieved competence or the child's potential for achieving competence than are maturationist or cognitive-developmental frameworks. A focus on social interaction provides data on several possible sources of variation, including (1) characteristics of the individual child, (2) parental skill in scaffolding children's early narrative productions, (3) cultural and social class differences in narrative content and form, and (4) differences relating to task demands (for example, personal narratives versus retellings of stories).

Research on the Development of Children's Alphabetic, Phonological, and Orthographic Knowledge

Maturationist or cognitive-developmental frameworks have prevailed in much of the research on the early development of children's alphabetic, phonological, and orthographic knowledge. Knowledge about language at this level differs in kind from knowledge about language at the discourse level, with the latter known to be more vulnerable to variations related to culture and social class (Schieffelin & Eisenberg, 1984). Nevertheless, it is doubtful that this knowledge originates solely or primarily in autonomous child-environment interactions, or that variations in development are attributable only, or even primarily, to child characteristics. In any perceptually based domain of knowledge, where there are specific and relatively narrow constraints on variation, the second source of variation (parental scaffolding skill) in the list provided earlier still must be accounted for. The third and fourth sources no doubt also come into play, although perhaps not to the same extent, because rather narrow constraints on variations must be observed within a system of writing if the system is to be accessed. But various meanings about how the writing system works are conveyed to children by adults as they scaffold children's learning of this "technical" knowledge, and these meanings can be expected to vary in terms of their helpfulness.

General Age Trends in Young Children's Understanding of Word Creation in an Alphabetic Writing System

A child's first idea about word making is usually that words should bear some physical resemblance to the object being signified. Children usually select a quantifiable aspect of an object and match it to quantifiable aspects of their marks. Ferreiro and Teberosky (1982) observed this strategy in 4- and 5-year-olds. For example, when asked to write *bear*, one child said that the word would need to be bigger (longer) than the word he had written for *duck*, "because it is a name that is bigger than duck" (the name of an animal bigger than a duck) (p. 180). Another child instructed an adult to write his name "longer" one day than it had been written the day before, explaining, "yesterday was my birthday." (p. 184)

Levin and Tolchinsky-Landsmann (1989) also found that the number of marks used by children sometimes varied systematically with the size of the object (for instance, more marks for larger than for smaller objects), and also that the marks themselves were sometimes selected because they resembled the shape of a object (round letters were selected for a round object). Children sometimes even captured an attribute, such as length, by spacing letters farther apart.

Following use of this initial, physical relationship approach to word creation, children often copy the sequence of marks they observe that others use to denote an object or person (Schickedanz, 1990). Because children who use this approach have not yet acquired the "generating principle"—the understanding that the same small set of letters can be rearranged to create many different words (Clay, 1975)—they believe that each word is a completely unique design—that its marks are not to be found in any other word. Three-year-olds, for example, often claim that any word beginning with the first letter of their name is their name. Even though children at this age understand that writing is arbitrary (or that words do not capture physical characterics of the objects or persons they represent), they do not understand that a small set of graphemes is used to spell all words.

After children understand the generating principle, two new word-creation strategies are seen: a syllabic strategy and a visual rule strategy (Harste, Burke, & Woodward, 1981; Ferreiro & Teberosky, 1982; Schickedanz, 1990). The syllabic strategy involves the use of one mark to represent each syllable. Marks may be selected without regard for letter-sound associations; in fact, marks may be scribbles rather than alphabet letters or even approximations of them. Words created with a visual rule strategy look like words, but are not because letter selection is based on visual rules (for example, "Don't make words too long or too short" or "Use a variety of symbols rather than many of just one"), rather than on an analysis of the sound structure of words (Ferreiro & Teberosky, 1982).

Ages reported for mock word production vary across studies; some researchers have reported observations in middle-class children who were between $3^{1}/_{2}$ to $4^{1}/_{2}$ years of age (Schickedanz, 1990), while others have reported observations of 4- and 5-year-olds (Dyson, 1985; Ferreiro & Teberosky, 1982; Kamler & Kilarr, 1983; Sulzby, 1985).

Following the syllabic and mock word approaches, children begin to segment phonemes within words and to code what they hear. At first, children's knowledge of letter names guides their mapping of specific letters onto specific sounds (Thompson, Fletcher-Flinn, & Cottrell, 1999;

Treiman, Tincoff, & Richmond-Welty, 1997). Because this strategy does not allow for the mapping of graphemes to all sounds and because children lack familiarity with standard English spelling conventions, early spellings depart from standard spellings, which is why they are called *invented.*

Researchers working in the United States have found explicit phonemic awareness to be absent in many children until 6 or 7 years of age—until sometime during first grade (e.g., Liberman, Shankweiler, Liberman, Fowler, & Fisher, 1977). However, the age at which phonemic-based spelling appears varies enormously in different populations. In the children studied by Read (1975), explicit awareness of phonemes appeared at about 3 years of age. In another study, a child produced one sample of phonemic-based spelling at about 4½ years of age, and the approach dominated his writing by age 5 (Schickedanz, 1990). A child in Kamler and Kilarr's (1983) study invented a spelling when she was 5½ years old. None of Dyson's (1985) three kindergarten children (5½ years of age) invented spellings. Some of Sulzby's (1985) kindergarten children (5 years, 4 months at the beginning of the study) did. (See also Dyson, Chapter Two in this volume.) The children studied by Ferreiro and Teberosky (1982) were 6 years old when they began inventing spellings, although some children in this study never progressed beyond syllabic-based coding.

Finally, children progress to an orthographic phase in which multi-letter units, including morphographs, begin to guide spelling (Ehri, 1994). This phase can begin at 4 or 5 years of age in children who learn to read early (Schickedanz, 1990); it appears much later, usually by the end of second grade, in the more typical child (Juel, 1983; Leslie & Thimke, 1986).

Learning Processes: Social Construction or Autonomous Child Discoveries?

Theorists must try to explain how children move from one word-creation strategy to another, and why different children achieve a given level at quite different ages. Cognitive developmentalists explain changes in cognition in terms of conflicts that arise between a child's current understandings and experiences in the environment. Although "the environment" includes social behavior of others, this is viewed very much as an object existing apart from the child, something for the child to observe. Social interaction as a mediator of the child's discoveries is not stressed.

For example, Ferreiro and Teberosky (1982) explain the waning of a child's tendency to string together letters to create mock words to "block-ages" created by children's increasing knowledge of stable strings (or sight words). Ferreiro and Teberosky also describe the "fundamental evolutionary moment" when a child "discovers the need for an analysis that goes beyond the syllable" because of a conflict between the syllabic hypothesis (one of the child's conceptions) and "the minimum quantity of graphic characters rule" used to create letter strings (another of the child's conceptions) and a conflict "between graphic strings provided by the environment and the reading of these strings according to the syllabic hypothesis" (p. 204); in other words, print and speech do not match. According to Ferreiro and Teberosky,

> Children have developed two very important ideas which they resist leaving behind...that a certain number of letters are necessary for something to be readable (reinforced by the new notion that writing something means representing progressively the sound segments of the name), and that each letter represents one of the syllables that compose the name. The environment has provided a stock of letters, a series of sound equivalents for some of them...and a series of stable strings, the most important of which is undoubtedly the child's own name....When the environment does not provide this information, one of the occasions for conflict is missing. (pp. 207–208)

Ferreiro and Teberosky do not explain how the child acquires the insight that "writing means representing progressively the sound segments" (p. 207). We see here a conception of the child as an independent and autonomous learner, and of writing as a cultural object. Though the word *culture* here acknowledges that writing is a social invention, the use of the word *object* is interesting. This object, like other physical objects, is presumably "out there" for the child to observe and explore. A distinction between the contexts in which this object and physical objects, as well as substances such as water, sand, blocks, and toy cars are explored seems not to have been made to any extent.

A contrast may be observed between the Piagetian view and a social construction view seen in the approach to data collection used by Gundlach,

McLane, Stott, and McNamee (1985). Data were collected from parental interviews and also from direct observations of parent-child interactions. The following sample is from a parent interview:

> In late March, his mother reported that Jeremy had been spending a lot of time playing with his magnetic letters, which were kept on the refrigerator door. He would ask his mother how to spell words.... Sometimes he arranged them in small groups of 3–7 letters and asked his mother what they spelled. She would sound out "words" such as X-M-R-E-O-U-A or F-D-L-P-A, which Jeremy found very amusing.... Not long after this, his mother observed that he "often asked how to spell words." (pp. 16–17)

In May, Jeremy and his mother participated in another episode. This time, at Jeremy's request, they played "homework." A transcript of an interaction follows:

Mother:	What word do you want to spell?
Jeremy:	*Ball.*
Mother:	Okay. What letter do you think it starts with?
Jeremy:	*B.*
Mother:	Can you write *B*?
Jeremy:	I'll write small *b*. That's easier. (Writes *b*.)
Mother:	Very good. What do you think has an "ah" sound for the next letter?
Jeremy:	*I?*
Mother:	No.
Jeremy:	*E?*
Mother:	That does sound like it, but the letter you use for ball is *A*.
Jeremy:	(Writes capital *A*.)
Mother:	Very good. Now what has the "LL" sound?
Jeremy:	(No hesitation.) *L.*
Mother:	Right! Can you write that?
Jeremy:	No. You do it. I did all these other letters. Now you have to do some.
Mother:	All right. (She writes an *L*.) Now you can write another right next to it.
Jeremy:	Okay. (Writes an *O*.)

Mother:	That's not an *L*.
Jeremy:	(Laughs wickedly. Great delight at the trick he has played.)
Mother:	Do you want to read a story now?
Jeremy:	Yes.

It is instructive to compare a parental report from Dyson's (1985) research to this interaction between Jeremy and his mother. The parents are responding to questions posed by Dyson during an interview:

| Mom: | Lots of times she'll bring books to me and ask, "What does this spell?" |
| Dad: | Or, she'll write with letters and ask, "What does this spell?" She wants to know if it is a word. I tell her it is nothing. |

Jeremy's mother led him to see that his letter strings were "nothing" (i.e., not actual words), rather than tell him "it is nothing." What difference might this make? We can ask the same question about the difference between Jeremy's mother's approach to providing the spelling of *ball,* and Dyson's report of her own response to her case-study children's requests for spelling. When Vivi, a 5-year-old, asked Dyson how to spell *for,* Dyson reports that she "spelled *for,* which Vivi copied." A minute later, Vivi asked how to spell *too.* Dyson reports that she "spelled *too,* which Vivi copied" (p. 115–116). With another child, Dyson says, "At Tracy's request, I had just written *swimming pool* on a slip of paper that already contained *Mom* and *Valentine*" (p. 86).

What might be the different consequences to a child's learning from involvement in the process of sounding out words and thinking about how the sounds should be represented by letters versus being supplied with written spellings, unaccompanied by any modeling of the sounding-out or letter-selection processes? Why might adults adopt one approach versus the other? For example, with respect to content of parent-child interactions in these situations, might the native language of the parent, along with the parent's skill in the second language the child is acquiring, influence the parent's approach?

It is interesting, in this regard, that in our laboratory preschool at Boston University there is a reluctance among Chinese parents to sound out English words for their children, in response to the children's requests for spellings, because the parents think that their pronunciation does not provide an accurate model. It would be interesting to learn whether this reluctance is also influenced by the fact that Chinese is not an alphabetic language. That is, might parents whose native writing system is logographic tend to think that the process of getting to sound-letter correspondences in an alphabetic language is basically a matter of first noticing similarities and differences within the spellings of sight words, and then using these patterns as a basis for appreciating the sound differences among the words?

For the most part, studies of progress in young children's alphabetic, phonological, and orthographic knowledge have not focused on data that can answer these questions. Cognitive developmentalist (Piagetian) theory explains development and its variations as consequences of conflicts in the child's own thinking.

The final chapter in Marie Clay's (1987) book, *Writing Begins at Home*, is titled, "How Can a Parent Help?" The title suggests that a child has the capacity to strike out very much on his or her own, leaving parents to wonder if there might be some small way in which they can help a largely self-propelled child. But Clay's specific suggestions for parents include parent-child collaboration: "Have your child work alongside you when you are writing—letters, shopping lists, filling out forms, or when siblings are being helped with their homework.... Encourage children to add their 'bit'...to the letters you write to relatives" (Clay, 1987, p. 50). What might we have learned about development in this domain of emergent literacy had researchers worked from inside the interactions making up such collaborations, rather than working outside, collecting children's writing products or eliciting writing samples using tasks designed to obtain a snapshot of current levels of knowledge?

Clay (1993) has alluded to the potential value of information about the social mediation of this knowledge:

What is not clear from the reports...is whether the shift to conventional spelling occurs simply as a result of teachers fostering large quantities of writing...or whether additional factors...are necessary to bring about the conventionalization of spelling.... I suspect...the teacher, in interaction with the young writer, has something to do with some of the shifts that occur. I am always wary of statements which imply the naturalness or inevitability of learning something as complex as the spelling of English. Undoubtedly children can invent for themselves something like written English, but not all children will invent it. Knowing what helps the successful ones to make the necessary shifts for themselves will help teachers to assist the unresponsive or confused children. (p. 263)

Although I suspect that children have a better chance of inventing some spelling knowledge for themselves (see Thompson et al., 1999, and Treiman et al., 1997) than of inventing the alphabetic principle, Clay's caution is a good one. Knowing more about the details and incidence of interactions would help illuminate the question of how to help "unresponsive or confused" children, not only those of school age but in preschool as well. These differences in young children do not seem to be due simply to individual differences in children. For example, the Chinese children in the preschool we studied seem quite confused when teachers attempt to answer their spelling questions by sounding out words, or by suggesting that they do this, during word-spelling collaborations; when asked, "What letter do you think that word might start with?", the child is likely to say quickly, "I don't know," even when the child has extensive letter-name knowledge. Of course, lack of insight in these matters is fairly common among all preschoolers, although in this particular preschool, it is quite common for children who are native speakers of English to acquire alphabetic insight by 4 or $4^{1}/_{2}$ years of age. However, it is difficult to induce this insight in some non-native speakers of English at this same age, especially those whose native languages are not alphabetic. Yet once they pass this obstacle (accomplished by the teachers' persistence in sounding out words), these children often zoom ahead and begin to read and write in both English and their native language by 5 or $5^{1}/_{2}$ years of age.

I suspect that if we studied this area of emergent literacy at the interaction level, we would find that children do not invent the alphabetic principle themselves and that different rates of acquisition are closely correlated with what transpires in adult-child interactions. There would, of course, be variations among children who experience virtually the same set of social circumstances, with some showing more precociousness than others. However, the tendency to attribute variations in developmental timetables and variations in paths of development, primarily to child characteristics, would undoubtedly diminish. Research conducted within a

Vygotskian framework would certainly provide a more complete picture of the processes involved during the emergent phase of acquiring this aspect of literacy knowledge, and would surely be more "child sparing" than a constructivist approach.

References

Baillargeon, R. (1994). Physical reasoning in young infants: Seeking explanations for impossible events. *British Journal of Developmental Psychology, 12,* 9–33.

Benson, M.S. (1993). The structure of four- and five-year-olds' narratives in pretend play and storytelling. *First Language, 13,* 203–223.

Berman, R.A. (1988). On the ability to relate events in narrative. *Discourse Processes, 11,* 469–497.

Botvin, G.J., & Sutton-Smith, B. (1977). The development of structural complexity in children's fantasy narratives. *Developmental Psychology, 13*(4), 377–388.

Burger, L.K., & Miller, P.J. (1999). Early talk about the past revisited: Affect in working-class and middle-class children's co-narrations. *Journal of Child Language, 26*(1), 133–162.

Clay, M.M. (1975). *What did I write?* Auckland, NZ: Heinemann.

Clay, M.M. (1983). On getting a theory of writing. In B.M. Kroll & G. Wells (Eds.), *Explorations in the development of writing* (pp. 259–284). New York: John Wiley & Sons.

Clay, M.M. (1987). *Writing begins at home.* Portsmouth, NH: Heinemann.

Dunn, J., Brown, J., Slomkowski, C., Tesla, C., & Youngblade, L. (1991). Young children's understanding of other people's feelings and beliefs: Individual differences and their antecedents. *Child Development, 62,* 1352–1366.

Dyson, A.H. (1985). Individual differences in emerging writing. In M. Farr (Ed.), *Advances in writing research: Vol. 4. Children's early writing development* (pp. 59–125). Norwood, NJ: Ablex.

Ehri, L.C. (1994). Development of the ability to read words: Update. In R.B. Ruddell, M.R. Ruddell, & H. Singer (Eds.), *Theoretical models and processes of reading* (4th ed., pp. 323–359). Newark, DE: International Reading Association.

Ferreiro, E., & Teberosky, A. (1982). *Literacy before schooling.* Portsmouth, NH: Heinemann.

Fivush, R. (1991). The social construction of personal narratives. *Merrill-Palmer Quarterly, 37*(1), 59–81.

Gee, J.P. (1985). The narrativization of experience in the oral style. *Journal of Education, 167*(1), 9–35.

Gee, J.P. (1986). Units in the production of narrative discourse. *Discourse Processes, 9,* 391–422.

Gundlach, R., McLane, J.B., Stott, F.M., & McNamee, G.D. (1985). The social foundations of children's early writing. In M. Farr (Ed.), *Advances in writing research: Vol. 1. Children's early writing development* (pp. 1–58). Norwood, NJ: Ablex.

Haden, C.A. (1998). Reminiscing with different children: Relating maternal stylistic consistency and sibling similarity in talk about the past. *Developmental Psychology*, *34*(1), 99–114.

Harste, J.C., Burke, C.L., & Woodward, V.A. (1981). *Children, their language and world: Initial encounters with print* (Final report of the National Institute of Education Project, No. NIE-G-79-0132). Bloomington, IN: Indiana University.

Hudson, J. (1990). The emergence of autobiographical memory in mother-child conversations. In R. Fivush & J.A. Hudson (Eds.), *Knowing and remembering* (pp. 166–196). Cambridge, UK: Cambridge University Press.

Jeong, M. (1996). *The influence of home and school reading experiences on young children's emergent reading stances and response to children's books.* Unpublished doctoral dissertation, University of California at Berkeley.

Juel, C. (1983). The development and use of mediated word identification. *Reading Research Quarterly, 18*, 306–327.

Kamler, B., & Kilarr, G. (1983). Looking at what children can do. In B.M. Kroll & G. Wells (Eds.), *Explorations in the development of writing* (pp. 177–208). New York: John Wiley & Sons.

Kwon, G. (1999). Case studies of interaction between young Korean children and their mothers during story-reading time. *International Journal of Early Childhood Education, 4*, 25–49.

Labov, W. (1972). *Language in the inner city.* Philadelphia: University of Pennsylvania Press.

Leondar, B. (1979). Hatching plots: Genesis of storymaking. In D. Perkins & B. Leondar (Eds.), *The arts and cognition* (pp. 172–191). Baltimore: Johns Hopkins University Press.

Leslie, L., & Thomke, B. (1986). The use of orthographic knowledge in beginning reading. *Journal of Reading Behavior, 18*, 229–241.

Levin, I., & Tolchinsky-Landsmann, L. (1989). Becoming literate: Referential and phonetic strategies in early reading and writing. *International Journal of Behavioral Development*, 369–384.

Liberman, I.Y., Shankweiler, D., Liberman, A.M., Fowler, C., & Fischer, F.W. (1977). Phonetic segmentation and recoding in the beginning reader. In A.S. Reber & D.L. Scarborough (Eds.), *Toward a psychology of reading* (pp. 207–225). Hillsdale, NJ: Erlbaum.

McCabe, A., & Peterson, C. (1991). Getting the story: A longitudinal study of parental styles in eliciting oral personal narratives and developing narrative skill. In A. McCabe & C. Peterson (Eds.), *Developing narrative structure* (pp. 217–253). Hillsdale, NJ: Erlbaum.

Menig-Peterson, C.L., & McCabe, A. (1978). Children's orientation of a listener to the context of their narratives. *Developmental Psychology, 14*, 582–592.

Miller, P.J., & Sperry, L. (1988). Early talk about the past: The origins of conversational stories of personal experience. *Journal of Child Language, 15*, 293–315.

Miller, P.J., Wiley, A.R., Fung, H., & Liang, C. (1997). Personal storytelling as a medium of socialization in Chinese and American families. *Child Development, 68*(3), 557–568.

Minami, M. (1996). Japanese preschool children's narrative development. *First Language, 16*, 339–363.

Minami, M., & McCabe, A. (1991). Haiku as a discourse regulation device: A stanza analysis of Japanese children's personal narratives. *Language in Society, 20*, 577–599.

Nelson, K. (1988). The ontogeny of memory for real world events. In U. Neisser & E. Winograd (Eds.), *Remembering reconsidered: Ecological and traditional approaches to memory* (pp. 177–282). New York: Cambridge University Press.

Nelson, K. (1993). The psychological and social origins of autobiographical memory. *Psychological Science, 4*(1), 7–14.

Peterson, C.L., Jesso, B., & McCabe, A. (1999). Encouraging narratives in preschoolers: An intervention study. *Journal of Child Language, 26*, 49–97.

Peterson, C.L., & McCabe, A. (1992). Parental styles of narrative elicitation: Effect on children's narrative structure and content. *First Language, 12*, 299–321.

Peterson, C.L., & McCabe, A. (1994). A social interactionist account of developing decontextualized narrative skill. *Developmental Psychology, 30*(6), 937–948.

Pitcher, E.G., & Prelinger, E. (1963). *Children tell stories.* New York: International Universities Press.

Read, C. (1975). *Children's categorization of speech sounds in English.* Urbana, IL: National Council of Teachers of English.

Schickedanz, J. (1990). *Adam's righting revolutions.* Portsmouth, NH: Heinemann.

Schieffelin, B.B., & Eisenberg, A.R. (1984). Cultural variation in children's conversations. In R.L. Schiefellbusch & J. Picker (Eds.), *The acquisition of communicative competence* (pp. 378–420). Baltimore: University Park Press.

Scollon, R., & Scollon, S.B.K. (1984). Cooking it up and boiling it down: Abstracts in Athabascan children's story retellings. In D. Tannen (Ed.), *Coherence in spoken and written discourse* (pp. 173–200). Norwood, NJ: Ablex.

Sperry, L.L., & Sperry, D.E. (1996). The early development of narrative skills. *Cognitive Development, 11*, 443–4665.

Stein, N.L. (1988). The development of children's storytelling skill. In M. Franklin & S.S. Barten (Eds.), *Child language: A reader* (pp. 282–295). New York: Oxford University Press.

Sulzby, E. (1985). Kindergarteners as writers and readers. In M. Farr (Ed.), *Advances in writing research: Vol. 1. Children's early writing development* (pp. 127–199). Norwood, NJ: Ablex.

Thompson, G.B., Fletcher-Flinn, C.M., & Cottrell, D.S. (1999). Learning correspondences between letters and phonemes without explicit instruction. *Applied Psycholinguistics, 20*, 21–50.

Trabasso, T., & Nickels, M. (1992). The development of goal plans of action in the narration of a picture story. *Discourse Processes, 15*, 249–275.

Trabasso, T., Secco, T., & van den Broek, P. (1984). Causal cohesion and story coherence. In H. Mandl, N.L. Stein, & T. Trabasso (Eds.), *Learning and comprehension of text* (pp. 83–111). Hillsdale, NJ: Erlbaum.

Treiman, R., Tincoff, R., & Richmond-Welty, E.D. (1997). Beyond zebra: Preschoolers' knowledge about letters. *Applied Psycholinguistics, 18*, 391–409.

Vygotsky, L.S. (1978). *Mind in society: The development of higher psychological processes.* (M. Cole, V. John-Steiner, S. Scribner, & E. Souberman, Eds. and Trans.). Cambridge, MA: Harvard University Press. (Original work published 1934)

Welch-Ross, M.K. (1997). Mother-child participation in conversation about the past: Relationships to preschoolers' theory of mind. *Developmental Psychology, 33*(4), 618–629.

Wellman, H.M., & Bartsch, K. (1994). Before belief: Children's early psychological theory. In C. Lewis & P. Mitchell (Eds.), *Children's early understanding of mind* (pp. 331–354). Hillsdale, NJ: Erlbaum.

Arthur N. Applebee
University at Albany
Center on English Learning and Achievement

CHAPTER FOUR

Alternative Models of Writing Development

The elementary and secondary school curriculum in writing has always been a somewhat precarious affair, dependent on implicit models of the interrelationships among reading, writing, and oral language, as well as on assumptions about the nature of writing ability itself. During much of the 19th century, the teaching of writing focused on penmanship and little else. Later, writing instruction was often postponed until the middle and upper grades, when students have presumably achieved basic literacy in reading (Applebee, 1974).

In this chapter, I will review the current status of writing instruction in schools and discuss alternative models of the developmental process that have influenced how writing is taught, suggesting that no model is fully adequate as a guide to curriculum, instruction, and assessment.

Writing in U.S. Schools

The last thorough examination of the status of writing in the school curriculum in the United States was the National Study of Writing in the Secondary School (Applebee, 1981, 1984). Replicating and extending James Britton's work in the United Kingdom (Britton, Burgess, Martin, McLeod, & Rosen, 1975), the study found that the curriculum in writing was narrow in scope and problematic in execution. In general, students wrote infrequently within a narrow range of genres for limited purposes. In fact, although students were expected to put pencil to paper some 44% of the time, only about 3% of classwork and homework involved composing original text. Instead, most of the "writing" that students did, across English and other subjects, involved writing without composing: fill-in-the-blank and completion exercises, direct translation, or other work in which the text was constructed by the teacher or textbook and the student supplied missing information that was, typically, judged as right or wrong. When more extended writing was required, it tended to be similarly limited in scope. The typical assignment was a first-and-final draft, begun in class and completed for homework, and requiring a page or less of writing. Topics for these assignments usually were constructed to test previous learning rather than to convince, inform, or entertain a naive audience.

English classes were most likely to include some imaginative writing (primarily story writing) as part of the curriculum. Both the amount of writing and the level of abstraction expected (moving from simple reporting of events toward analysis and theorizing) also increased somewhat in the upper grades compared with the lower grades. Within this broad pattern, there were some consistent variations by grade and subject. Assignments that required some extended writing were most common in English classes, but in total, students wrote more for their other subjects combined than they did for English. Thus, although English is usually seen as the locus of instruction for the development of writing abilities, students' experiences in their other subjects play a significant role in learning to write.

Although no recent comprehensive survey is available, the responses to background items that have been included as part of the periodic writing assessments given by the National Assessment of Educational Progress (NAEP) suggest that there have been some changes in recent years. In particular, the NAEP results at grades 4, 8, and 12 indicate that teachers are spending more time on writing instruction than they have in the past, with perhaps somewhat more attention to a wider variety of genres. On the 1998 assessment (Greenwald, Persky, Campbell, and Mazzeo, 1999; additional data available at http://nces.ed.gov/nationsreportcard/tables), for example, twelfth-grade students reported some regular (at least monthly) attention to persuasive writing, analysis or interpretation, report or summary writing, and story or narrative writing. Grade 4 students were asked fewer questions in the assessment, but reported regular journal writing and story or report writing.

By 1998, 57% or more of the teachers also were reporting that writing process instruction and integrated reading and writing were central to their teaching, and at least another 51% reported similar emphasis on grammar or skill-based instruction. Rather than treating writing process approaches and skill-based instruction as in opposition to one another, all but a handful of the teachers surveyed reported some emphasis on both. Teacher reports were available only for fourth- and eighth-grade instruction, but student reports at grades 4, 8, and 12 similarly suggest more use of writing process activities than the Applebee (1981) study had found. The 1998 NAEP assessment also found that attention to spelling, grammar, and punctuation exercises was highest in the lower grades and for low achieving students within each grade.

Alternative Models of Writing Development

The phrase "writing development" is ambiguous in an interesting way: it can refer to the ordinary developmental course of learning to write, or to the systematic (or less so) curriculum or program of instruction for developing those skills. This ambiguity, or conflation, is also present in most attempts at specifying appropriate curricular sequences or emphases. Discussions of writing development have had many different starting points, but they can be roughly categorized as emphasizing purposes for writing, fluency and writing conventions, the structure of the final product, or strategic knowledge—each of which implies a different emphasis in curriculum and assessment.

Purposes for Writing

Britton et al.'s (1975) *Development of Writing Abilities* provides a good example of an emphasis on purposes for writing. Reporting on a study of the uses of writing in secondary schools in the United Kingdom, Britton and his colleagues offered both a survey of the kinds of writing students were being asked to do and a taxonomy whose internal structure suggested a way to think about the relationships among different kinds of writing. At its most basic, Britton's model suggests that learning to write is a process of learning an increasingly diverse array of uses of language in general and writing in particular. At the core of this model is what Britton called *expressive* uses of language. Expressive language is the relatively informal language of everyday use, of gossip among friends who share a common context and frame of reference. It has the developed form neither of story nor of exposition, but instead moves back and forth easily among both. The expressive is also the language of intimacy and of infancy; in Britton's system, it is the first genre of language use to emerge out of the reciprocity (Bruner, 1968) between infant and caregiver.

Britton argues that other uses of language develop as differentiations from the expressive, and are characterized by formal structure that allows language users to communicate for new purposes with increasingly distant audiences with whom they share fewer initial understandings. As language becomes increasingly formalized, it takes on new purposes—to persuade, to inform, to entertain—rather than simply to explore the shared understandings that are characteristic of the expressive. As new uses of language develop, however, the expressive does not disappear. It remains the primary means of coming to understand new experiences, as a language of the working group as well as the language of self-exploration. In Britton's argument, the expressive becomes an important tool for learning—the genre in which a learner explores and assimilates new ideas and experiences, whether working alone or with groups of peers.

Britton's model has other features important to understanding the development of writing abilities. One is a sharp distinction between the language of the world (*transactional* in his terminology) and the language of literature (*poetic* in his terminology). He argues that these involve very different techniques of formalization: those of exposition, which lead ultimately to the formalizations of mathematics and symbolic logic, and those of storytelling, which lead instead to the layered meanings of the most sophisticated literature. Like Bruner (1986), Rosenblatt (1978), and Langer (1995), Britton argues that these two techniques lead to different yet complementary ways of making sense of the world. Each in turn has its own range of special genres and a developmental trajectory that involves developing competency in the use of an increasing range of genres and structural devices. (Note that I am simplifying Britton's argument here. In fact,

he distinguishes between the symbolic techniques represented by the poetic and transactional, and the participant [expository] and spectator [lit-
erary] roles that each text invites. A given text will be treated as either participant or spectator by a given reader at a given time, whereas poetic and
transactional techniques can be [and usually are] mixed within a text.)

Grounding their work in a diverse sample of school writing, Britton et
al. (1975) also laid out a developmental continuum within transactional
writing. This continuum, drawing from the work of Moffett (1968), is
based on the distance from immediate experience, beginning with simple
reporting of ongoing events (as in a sports commentary), moving through
report and analysis to theorizing. The developmental hypothesis implicit
in these categories would predict that expressive writing would dominate
in a child's earlier years, with a gradual movement toward the more abstract forms of transactional writing and literary writing in later years
(Britton et al., 1975). Instead, as in Applebee's (1981, 1984) studies in
the United States, Britton found that curricular goals "did not include
the fostering of writing that reflects independent thinking; rather, attention was directed towards classificatory writing which reflects information
in the form in which both teacher and textbook present it" (p. 197).

In spite of the disappointing portrait of what was going on in schools,
Britton's model has been used widely in the study of writing in the English-
speaking world (see also Durst & Newell, 1989). Its strengths include its
grounding in actual samples of student writing and its emphasis on the
overall purpose of the writing, thus focusing attention on the effectiveness of the writing as a whole instead of on its parts. Criticisms of the
model have focused on the sharp dichotomy that is drawn between literary
and expository writing, and the emphasis on the expressive as the primary
matrix out of which other uses of language develop (Durst & Newell, 1989;
Newkirk, 1987, 1989).

These criticisms aside, Britton's approach illustrates the conflation
that is inevitable in discussions of the "natural" development of writing
abilities. As he and his colleagues argued in discussing their results, the
patterns that were observed can only be understood as a reflection of the
aims of the curricula the students experienced. To a very large extent, they
learned what they were taught in the order in which they were taught it.
Britton's study, like others that have followed (for example, Applebee,

1981), is more successful as an assessment of the balance (or lack thereof) in the curriculum than it is as a study of the developmental course of writing skills.

A number of other studies have looked more closely at the development of children's skills when writing for different purposes. Langer (1986), in an extensive study that examined the relationship between reading and writing development, explored children's knowledge of story and report genres at ages 8, 11, and 14. She found that even at age 8, the children differentiated clearly between storytelling and exposition, but in general had a more developed repertoire of storytelling devices available to them. Between ages 8 and 14, their stories became richer and more fully elaborated, but there was little change in overall structure; for reports, on the other hand, there was a rapid growth of structural devices during this age span. Langer argued that this difference in the developmental trajectory stemmed from the children's out-of-school experiences, which involved considerable contact with stories similar to those read in school, but less contact with the forms of exposition with which schools typically deal. (See also Langer and Flihan, Chapter Five in this volume.)

Applebee (1978) explicitly set out to examine development within the poetic dimension of Britton's model. These studies, which involved a diverse range of tasks and a wide age range, demonstrated that children as young as 2 had a clear sense of story as a separate use of language, and that between ages 2 and 5 children learned to use a variety of formal and structural devices in their storytelling. In later years, students' writing about literature showed many of the developments that Britton had predicted for transactional writing in general, as students became increasingly competent at analysis and generalization.

Studies that have examined early forms of expository writing also have found a range of genres available to even very young children. Newkirk (1987, 1989), for example, provides an inventory of types that begins with labels and lists and moves through ordered paragraphs; he argues that the variety of forms he found calls into question Britton's emphasis on the expressive as the developmental matrix out of which other forms of writing are differentiated.

Assessing Mastery of Diverse Purposes for Writing. The major approach to assessment of mastery of diverse purposes is primary trait scoring, developed by Richard Lloyd-Jones and Carl Klaus for the NAEP (see also Lloyd-Jones, 1977). Primary trait assessment in its initial formulations focused on the specific approach that a writer might take to be successful on a specific writing task; every task required its own unique scoring guide. Over the years as primary trait approaches were used more widely, they evolved into a more generic approach which recognized the similarities in approach within broad uses or purposes. The basic question addressed in scoring, however, remained, Did the writer successfully accomplish the purpose of this task? To ensure that raters maintained this focus, scoring guidelines usually instructed raters to ignore errors in conventions of written language, and to focus on overall rhetorical effectiveness.

The Development of Fluency and Control of Written Language

If Britton's work focuses on the diverse purposes for writing, many other studies have focused on more limited aspects of writing development—on fluency irrespective of purpose, or on the subskills or components that are believed to contribute to such fluency. There is a long tradition of research, for example, that has looked at the development of syntactic structures in students' writing. Dating as far back as the 1920s, such studies have reflected changing emphases in the larger field of linguistics, moving from Latinate school grammars to structural to transformational analyses of writing development. One of the most extensive studies in this tradition was Walter Loban's (1976) longitudinal analysis of oral and written language development. For this study, Loban followed a representative sample of 211 Oakland, California, students for 13 years, from kindergarten through grade 12. Oral language samples were gathered every year, complemented by writing samples from grades 3 through 12 and a variety of other measures (including teachers' ratings of achievement, IQ scores, and reading, listening, and language measures). Loban's analyses focused primarily on syntax; he found that factors that characterized language development included the use of longer communication units (sentences), greater elaboration of subject and predicate, more embedding (from analyses of grammatical transformations), greater use of adjectival dependent clauses, more use of dependent clauses of all kinds, greater variety and depth of vocabulary, and greater use of tentativeness (supposition, hypotheses, conjecture, and conditional statements) (Loban, 1976). Written and oral language seemed to develop in parallel, although in many analyses trends observed in written language occurred approximately 1 year after they were observed in similar analyses of oral language samples.

The attempt to find a developmental sequence of syntactic structures appropriate for the teaching of school writing eventually failed. As Kellogg Hunt (1965) notes in the conclusion of his own study of grammatical structures written at grades 4, 8, and 12, the structures he studied "are virtually all used by fourth graders and are used often enough and successfully enough to indicate that fourth graders command them. The study provides no justification for teaching some structures early and others late" (p. 155). Other investigators pushed these conclusions further, arguing that by the time children enter school, they are already competent in the grammatical structures of English. Rather than the accumulation of new structures, what seems to develop during the school years is students' ability to manage an increasing degree of structural complexity—that is, to include more structures effectively within a single sentence.

This sense of writing development as learning to combine a variety of structures within a single linguistic unit led to a related line of research on transformational sentence combining. Researchers at a variety of grade levels developed sentence combining curricula and sought to demonstrate that these eventually led to growth in writing abilities. Early versions of these programs (Mellon, 1969) began with explicit teaching of specific "transformations" drawn from then-current systems of transformational grammar; later versions relied on nontechnical cues (for instance "Join these sentences using 'although'") or invited students to combine sentences in any way that would make the resulting writing more effective. Initial studies demonstrated that sentence combining practice did in fact lead to the use of more complex syntax, though gains in overall writing quality were less clear (Daiker, Kerek, & Morenberg, 1985; Hillocks, 1986). As a result of these studies, a variety of sentence-combining curricula were developed, and sentence manipulation exercises became a standard part of more general writing textbooks.

The aspects of fluency and control that can and have been examined are almost limitless. In addition to features of syntax and punctuation, these include the development of cohesion and cohesive harmony (Cameron, Lee, Webster, & Monroe, 1995; Crowhurst, 1987; Halliday & Hasan, 1976; Irwin, 1988; Rentel & King, 1983;); rhetorical strategies (Beach & Anson, 1988); spelling (Read, 1975); and vocabulary (Breland et al., 1987).

Assessing Fluency and Control of Written Language. Models of writing that emphasize fluency and control of written language have led to a wide variety of approaches to writing assessment. At the level of the essay as a whole, Paul Diederich at Educational Testing Service developed holistic (or general impression) scoring methods that sought to achieve a synthesis among the many different components of fluency and control, including vocabulary, punctuation, spelling, and organization (Diederich, 1974). On the other hand, many approaches to assessment have focused on the individual components. T-unit length, for example, essentially a measure of the degree of embedding and syntactic complexity, has become a widely used measure in studies of first- and second-language learning. Various schemes for analyzing specific spelling, punctuation, and usage errors also have been proposed, though in practice, patterns of errors have been too topic specific to be very useful as achievement measures (NAEP, 1975). More successful have been multiple choice or short answer measures, in which content can be controlled. Such measures have been used widely as part of standardized achievement tests, IQ measures, and college entrance or placement examinations (Breland et al., 1987). Even simple number of words has been used as a rough measure of fluency, because essay length tends to correlate highly with other ratings of overall writing quality (Bereiter & Scardamalia, 1987).

Structural Knowledge

Just as there is a long tradition of viewing writing development in terms of fluency and control of written language, there is an equally long tradition of viewing writing development as the learning of larger structural patterns. This has had many variations over the past 100 years, varying from an emphasis on alternative models of paragraph development (compare-contrast, comment and elaboration) to the study or imitation of models to the learning of larger patterns such as the structure of the five-paragraph theme. All these approaches share a focus on conventional structures that students must master, whether through the analysis of what others have written, through the study of abstract rules, or through writing and revision.

The emphasis on larger structural patterns in writing is usually traced to Alexander Bain (1866). From Bain comes both a belief in the value of patterns derived from the writings of the "masters" of vernacular literature and the beginnings of a prescriptive tradition in the study of writing and of grammar. Bain's broad patterns—description, narration, exposition, oratory (persuasion), and poetry—have provided a guiding structure for composition programs for nearly 150 years. The categories are limited and overlapping, however, having little direct relation to the ways in which writing is structured in out-of-school contexts. Britton's analysis of the uses of writing was in part an attempt to correct these distortions.

Other writers have questioned the value of traditional schoolbook advice about essay structure. Braddock (1974), for example, studied the usefulness of advice to begin each paragraph with a topic sentence, and found that only 13% of the paragraphs in published prose followed this prescription. (Fewer than half the paragraphs in his sample even had a topic sentence in the textbook sense.) Meade and Ellis (1970) similarly examined the use of composition-textbook prescriptions on approaches to paragraph development (for example, cause-effect, chronology, definition, comparison), and likewise found little correspondence between the traditional axioms and the structure of published prose.

Some studies have looked at how students actually come to master more complex prose structures. Langer (1986), in her study of 8- to 14-year-olds, found that new organizing patterns (such as causal structures) appeared first as lower level structures in limited contexts that students could handle more easily, and only with age and experience became central organizing structures for a whole essay. Development also was marked by a wider repertoire of organizing devices and deeper elaboration of the writing as a whole. Durst (1984) found similar processes at work in the writing of eleventh-grade students as they struggled with the new demands of analytic writing as opposed to report writing. In a retrospective analysis of three students' writing from grade 3 through the end of high school, Durst found the students' writing shaped by rigid formula (for lab reports and book reports, for example) that initially helped them master new forms but eventually seemed to limit their continuing growth as effective writers.

More recent attention to children's mastery of structural patterns has come from heightened interest in genre as a theoretical concept. In the United States, this has stemmed from treatments of genre as an inherently shifting and fluid response to particular social and cultural contexts (Miller, 1984). In this tradition, genres can be modified as well as mastered. In Australia, however, another tradition of genre theory has developed, emphasizing the importance of particular genres to success in academic as well as out-of-school contexts. Australian genre theory, which merges a version of Michael Halliday's systemic linguistics with a strong concern for social justice, emphasizes the explication of the characteristics of the genres of schooling, and of power, so that they can be mastered by all students (Cope & Kalantzis, 1993; Halliday & Martin, 1993). This approach begins with a detailed linguistic analysis of the genres of each of the school subjects, in order to isolate the structural features characteristic of each genre (which differ markedly from one school subject to another). These features become the basis of a new literacy curriculum that emphasizes the grammars (or text structures) of the genres that are central to each discipline.

Assessment of Structural Knowledge. Assessment of structural knowledge has usually taken the form of ratings of "organization" or "use of appropriate evidence or detail." Such scales are a prominent part of most analytic rating schemes, as well as of Diederich's (1974) holistic rating procedures. Like other parts of such scales, they have typically been highly correlated with ratings of other dimensions, rather than yielding independent information about students' writing development. (Diederich suggests that the separate scales in his system are best used as a way to socialize teams of examiners to a common standard; experienced raters can move directly to the final "holistic" score without completing the separate subscales.) Alternatively, there have been some multiple choice measures of structural knowledge, usually requiring students to specify the most effective order of sentences in paragraphs, or to choose among alternative paragraph structures (see Godshalk, Swineford, & Coffman, 1966).

Strategic Knowledge

The approaches discussed so far have treated writing development as a function of what writers produce—that is, of the success of their "products." Another important tradition has sought to explain development in terms of the strategies or "processes" that the writer uses to create those products (Hairston, 1982). Emig's (1971) study of the composing processes of twelfth graders is usually taken as the start of this tradition, and it was followed quickly by a number of studies that treated writing as something that evolved over time, usually through a recursive cycle of generating ideas, drafting, revising, editing, and sharing. (For reviews of this work, see Hillocks, 1986.) Emig's description of composing processes was opportunistic and atheoretical, but it was followed by more systematic explorations. One of the most comprehensive of these was proposed by Linda Flower and John R. Hayes (1980; Hayes & Flower, 1980) within a cognitive problem-solving paradigm. Though this model lacked an explicitly developmental dimension, Flower and Hayes and their students at Carnegie Mellon University used it to guide a long and careful series of studies contrasting novice and expert writers at the college level. (See Hayes, Chapter One in this volume.)

A second series of studies, by Carl Bereiter and Marlene Scardamalia (1987), focused on the development of writing processes in school-age children. These studies delineated two quite different approaches to writing, one that Bereiter and Scardamalia called *knowledge telling* and a second that they called *knowledge transforming*. In these studies, knowledge-telling strategies enabled writers to efficiently "tell what they know" about a topic, an appropriate approach to the limited kinds of tasks that dominate school writing assignments. On the other hand, knowledge-transforming strategies went beyond knowledge telling to allow for the development of new ideas within the process of composing, as writers rethought previous knowledge and ideas and found appropriate ways to present the new understandings.

Other scholars concerned with the development of strategic processes in younger writers have focused their attention on particular components of the process (prewriting, revising, editing) or on meaning-making strategies that may be more general than simply writing. For example, in the study discussed earlier, Langer (1986) used both think-aloud protocols and retrospective reports to examine the writing and reading processes of her 8-, 11-, and 14-year-olds. Looking at strategic processes from a variety of perspectives (reasoning operations, monitoring behaviors, meaning-making strategies, and sources of knowledge drawn upon), she found that individuals were consistent in their use of such processes across both reading and writing, and across story and report tasks. Based on these results, Langer suggested that students were deploying a set of common cognitive and linguistic resources in approaching these tasks. On the other hand, the patterns in which these resources were deployed varied with the task and showed clear development with age. Overall, the 8-year-olds were more restricted in the strategies they deployed and less able to reflect forward or back on their ideas.

Other research relating strategic processes to types of writing has similarly found that, faced with different tasks, writers deploy their cognitive and linguistic resources in different ways (Durst, 1987; Newell, 1984).

Assessment of Strategic Processes. The concern with writing processes has had a widespread effect on teachers' beliefs and on the writing curriculum. As noted earlier, the majority of teachers in the 1998 NAEP assessment of writing claimed writing processes had a "central" role in their teaching (http://nces.ed.gov/nationsreportcard/tables). Writing processes are also a major feature in the *Standards for the English Language Arts* developed by the National Council of Teachers of English and the International Reading Association (1996). Writing textbooks from major publishers also now give extensive attention to strategic processes, usually presented as discrete "steps" in the writing process.

Attempts to assess students' development of strategic processes have been less successful. The NAEP has experimented with assessments of revision strategies at least since 1974 (NAEP, 1977) but has been unable to find a format that leads students to make extensive revision. Similarly, some NAEP assessments have provided opportunities for students to make use of prewriting strategies, but relatively few students make use of these opportunities (see also Greenwald et al., 1999). Given the complex nature of writing, these attempts may in fact be wrong-headed. Writers are most likely to make extensive use of prewriting or revision strategies with tasks that are particularly new and difficult. On-demand assessments, on the other hand, are likely to present relatively contained and familiar tasks for which little overt use of composing strategies will be needed. In the end, the best assessment of the effectiveness of strategic processes may be the quality of the writing that is produced.

The one widely used set of measures that can be seen as related to strategic processes involves editing. The College Board has used a variety of multiple choice and interlinear editing exercises to assess writing ability (Godshalk, Swineford, & Coffman, 1966), and has recently reintroduced them as a measure of writing skills on the Scholastic Aptitude Test. Such tasks, however, also can be seen as part of the tradition of concern with fluency and the avoidance of error.

Toward a Broader Model: Writing as Participation in Social Action

At present, writing development remains ill-defined and difficult to assess. It is confounded with language development more generally, as well as with the development of content knowledge in particular domains. (Even the best writers will write unsuccessfully in a completely unfamiliar domain.) Indeed, performance on most of the components of writing achievement varies with topic and type of writing: vocabulary, syntactical patterns, fluency, patterns of errors, organizing structures, and even writing processes will all vary from one topic or type of writing to another.

At the same time, any particular topic will be redefined by each individual writer in ways that make it difficult to array specific topics along a developmental scale. (A topic such as "An interesting person" can lead, for example, to a well-written paragraph by a fourth-grade student, a short story by a twelfth grader, and a *New Yorker* profile by a professional writer.) Different models of development have led to a wide variety of measures of writing ability, but each measure is limited in its own way, and the patterns of intercorrelations among them are at best modest. The most reliable measures of writing ability are based on multiple-choice measures of limited skills; those with the greatest face validity require extensive socialization of raters to a common standard that is difficult to explain and to replicate in other contexts. The limits of all of these approaches were evident in an international study of written composition, which found it impossible to develop agreed-upon definitions of writing quality across countries and cultures (Purves, 1992). Even within the United States, "development," with a few notable exceptions (Delpit, 1995; Dyson, 1989, 1993; Gee, 1996; Heath, 1983), has meant the development of mainstream, middle-class students.

The models discussed so far have treated writing development outside the contexts within which that development occurs. Britton et al. (1975), for example, delineate a variety of uses of writing that occur across the full range of school subjects, with no attention to how a particular use (such as report writing) may differ in history class versus mathematics, for instance. And this is equally true of studies of fluency, structure, and strategic processes. A second dimension of Britton's analysis does, however, give somewhat more attention to the social dimension of writing. Focusing on the audience for student writing, Britton posits a continuum that begins with writing for oneself, passes through a variety of school-specific audiences (such as writing to be graded or assessed), and ends with writing for a wider unknown audience. Again, there is an implicit developmental model inherent in this category system, but one that was foiled by the domination of school writing by writing for assessment purposes. A variety of other studies have looked at students' developing sense of audience, often in the context of broader skills of social cognition (see Bonk, 1990, for a review).

Recent work in writing, however, moves beyond simple notions of audience to a broader consideration of the social contexts within which writing occurs and develops. In these contexts, writers negotiate their place within the many communities of which they are a part, with a variety of resources and competing demands. Dyson (1989, 1993; see also Chapter Two of this volume), for example, in her ethnographies of primary grade children learning to write, has described the complicated interplay among previous experiences, uses of writing, uses of other symbol systems, peer relationships, and the goals and orientation of the teacher. Children in different classrooms learn to write in different ways, and children in the same classroom show great variations in the strategies they use and the genres they prefer as they negotiate their roles with their teacher and their peers. In such contexts, the children develop a sense of the many different uses that writing can serve, and a growing repertoire of strategies for orchestrating what they write. In a later article, Dyson (1995) has argued explicitly that children's differentiation of ways of using language is linked directly to their differentiation of their own place within the social world. Heath (1983), Gee (1996), and Delpit (1995) have made clear how closely tied such knowledge is to the social and cultural contexts within which students grow up.

At the other end of the developmental spectrum, a number of authors have explored the challenges facing writers at the undergraduate and graduate levels. McCarthy (1987) and Geissler (1994) have examined the conflicting demands encountered by college freshmen in a variety of disciplines. Herrington (1985) has similarly analyzed the experiences of students in two advanced courses in chemical engineering, finding that expectations for writing were very different even within this relatively specialized context. Berkenkotter, Huckin, and Ackerman (1988) traced the gradual enculturation of "Nate" into the doctoral program in rhetoric at Carnegie Mellon University. What each of these studies makes clear is that in order to write well in these new contexts, these already-accomplished writers have to learn a great deal about the particular demands of their new situations. In each case, they serve a kind of apprenticeship during which they come to understand not only the appropriate rhetorical forms, but also the underlying issues that make writing interesting and arguments effective. They learn, in fact, how to participate within the new contexts in which they find themselves. Stuart Greene (1994, 1995) has described this process as one of learning how to assume the role of *authorship* within a new context, a role which a writer can only assume by learning how to speak with authority within the disciplinary tradition.

The notion of effective participation in important domains offers another way to think about the development of writing ability, as well as a way to bring together some of the diverse emphases in previous models of writing development (see also Hicks, 1997). If students are to participate effectively in a domain, they must learn how to take action within that domain: how to *do* science, for example, not simply to learn *about* it. Taking action within a domain involves learning the genres that structure it as well as all of the kinds of knowledge previously discussed—fluency, appropriate uses of language, structural knowledge, and strategic processes. It also requires, however, knowledge of content and procedures appropriate to the domain—that is, knowledge of what is interesting and important and relevant in order to partake in the ongoing conversation about significant ideas. This notion of an ongoing conversation, which involves reading and writing as well as speech, combined with contemporary voices as well as those from the past, provides a way to think about the curriculum as a whole as well as about the curriculum in writing. If we want students to participate in important conversations, then we must help them write in ways appropriate to those conversations. And we must judge their development as writers in terms of their ability to participate with increasing effectiveness in an increasingly wide array of culturally significant domains for conversation (Applebee, 1996). We may also need to pay more attention to the goals and expectations that students bring to these conversations—the factors that shape how and whether they will choose to engage with the topics we may proffer (Durst, 1999).

Judging writing ability in terms of ability to participate effectively in curricular conversations does not simplify the problem of describing writing development, but it may reorient it in productive ways. Effective participation requires all the features of writing development that have been explored out of context—fluency, structure, purpose, and strategic knowledge—but it also requires expertise within a domain. The effective participant will be the person who can use writing to make his or her own contribution to the conversation, who can write with authority in ways that others will find interesting and convincing. Because there are many such conversations that are important in our social and cultural world, writing development may in turn become a matter of developing a voice in a wider array of conversations and learning to make one's contribution in increasingly powerful and effective ways.

Author Notes

Preparation of this chapter was supported in part by the Research and Development Centers Program (award No. R305A60005) administered by the Office of Educational Research and Improvement, U.S. Department of Education. However, the contents do not necessarily represent the positions or policies of the sponsoring agencies.

I would like to thank Mary Adler for her help in gathering materials for this chapter.

References

Applebee, A.N. (1974). *Tradition and reform in the teaching of English: A history.* Urbana, IL: National Council of Teachers of English.

Applebee, A.N. (1978). *The child's concept of story: Ages two to seventeen.* Chicago: University of Chicago Press.

Applebee, A.N. (1981). *Writing in the secondary school: English and the content areas* (Research Monograph 21). Urbana, IL: National Council of Teachers of English.

Applebee, A.N. (1984). *Contexts for learning to write: Studies of secondary school instruction.* Norwood, NJ: Ablex.

Applebee, A.N. (1996). *Curriculum as conversation: Transforming traditions of teaching and learning.* Chicago: University of Chicago Press.

Bain, A. (1866). *English composition and rhetoric: A manual.* London: Longmans, Green.

Beach, R., & Anson, C.M. (1988). The pragmatics of memo writing: Developmental differences in the use of rhetorical strategies. *Written Communication, 5*(2), 157–183.

Bereiter, C., & Scardamalia, M. (1987). *The psychology of written composition.* Mahwah, NJ: Erlbaum.

Berkenkotter, C., Huckin, T., & Ackerman, J. (1988). Conventions, conversations, and the writer: Case study of a student in a rhetoric Ph.D. program. *Research in the Teaching of English, 22*(1), 9–44.

Bonk, C.J. (1990). A synthesis of social cognition and writing research. *Written Communication, 7*(1), 136–163.

Braddock, R. (1974). The frequency and placement of topic sentences in expository prose. *Research in the Teaching of English, 8,* 287–302.

Breland, H.M., Camp, R., Jones, R.J., Morris, M.M., & Rock, D. (1987). *Assessing writing skill.* New York: College Entrance Examination Board.

Britton, J.N., Burgess, T., Martin, N., McLeod, A., & Rosen, H. (1975). *The development of writing abilities (11–18).* London: MacMillan Educational for the Schools Council.

Bruner, J.S. (1968). *Processes of cognitive growth: Infancy.* Worcester, MA: Clark University Press.

Bruner, J.S. (1986). *Actual minds, possible worlds.* Cambridge, MA: Harvard University Press.

Cameron, C.A., Lee, K., Webster, S., & Monroe, K. (1995). Text cohesion in children's narrative writing. *Applied Psycholinguistics, 16*(3), 257–269.

Cope, B., & Kalantzis, M. (Eds.). (1993). *The powers of literacy: A genre approach to teaching writing.* Pittsburgh, PA: University of Pittsburgh Press.

Crowhurst, M. (1987). Cohesion in argument and narration at three grade levels. *Research in the Teaching of English, 21*(2), 185–201.

Daiker, D.A., Kerek, A., & Morenberg, M. (Eds.). (1985). *Sentence combining: A rhetorical perspective.* Carbondale, IL: Southern Illinois University Press.

Delpit, L. (1995). *Other people's children: Cultural conflict in the classroom.* New York: The New Press.

Diederich, P. (1974). *Measuring growth in English.* Urbana, IL: National Council of Teachers of English.

Durst, R.K. (1984). The development of analytic writing. In A.N. Applebee (Ed.), *Contexts for learning to write* (pp. 79–102). Norwood, NJ: Ablex.

Durst, R.K. (1987). Cognitive and linguistic demands of analytic writing. *Research in the Teaching of English, 21*(4), 347–376.

Durst, R.K. (1999). *Collision course: Conflict, negotiation, and learning in college composition.* Urbana, IL, National Council of Teachers of English.

Durst, R.K., & Newell, G.E. (1989). The uses of function: James Britton's category system and research on writing. *Review of Educational Reseach, 59*(4), 375–394.

Dyson, A.H. (1989). *Multiple worlds of child writers: Friends learning to write.* New York: Teachers College Press.

Dyson, A.H. (1993). *Social worlds of children learning to write in an urban primary school.* New York: Teachers College Press.

Dyson, A.H. (1995). Writing children: Reinventing the development of childhood literacy. *Written Communication, 12*(1), 4–46.

Emig, J. (1971). *The composing processes of twelfth graders* (Research Monograph 13). Urbana, IL: National Council of Teachers of English.

Flower, L.S., & Hayes, J.R. (1980). The dynamics of composing: Making plans and juggling constraints. In L.W. Gregg & E.R. Steinberg (Eds.), *Cognitive processes in writing* (pp. 31–50). Mahwah, NJ: Erlbaum.

Gee, J.P. (1996). *Social linguistics and literacies: Ideology in discourses* (2nd ed.). Bristol, PA: Taylor & Francis.

Geisler, C. (1994). *Academic literacy and the nature of expertise.* Mahwah, NJ: Erlbaum.

Godshalk, F.I., Swineford, F., & Coffman, W.E. (1966). *The measurement of writing ability.* New York: College Entrance Examination Board.

Greene, S. (1994). Constructing a voice from other voices: A sociocognitive perspective on the development of authorship in a beginning writing classroom. In K.H. Pogner (Ed.), *Odense working papers in language and communication* (pp. 11–40). Odense, Denmark: Institute of Language and Communication, Odense University.

Greene, S. (1995). Making sense of my own ideas: The problems of authorship in a beginning writing classroom. *Written Communication, 12*(2), 186–218.

Greenwald, E.A., Persky, H.R., Campbell, J.R., & Mazzeo, J. (1999). *NAEP 1998 writing report card.* Washington, DC: National Center for Education Statistics, U.S. Department of Education.

Hairston, M. (1982). The winds of change: Thomas Kuhn and the revolution in the teaching of writing. *College Composition and Communication, 33*(1), 76–88.

Halliday, M.A.K., & Hasan, R. (1976). *Cohesion in English.* London: Longman.

Halliday, M.A.K., & Martin, J.R. (1993). *Writing science: Literacy and discursive power.* Pittsburgh, PA: University of Pittsburgh Press.

Hayes, J.R. (1996). A new framework for understanding cognition and affect in writing. In C.M. Levy & S. Ransdell (Eds.), *The science of writing: Theories, methods, individual differences, and applications* (pp. 1–27). Mahwah, NJ: Erlbaum.

Hayes, J.R., & Flower, L. (1980). Identifying the organization of writing processes. In L. Gregg & E. Steinberg (Eds.), *Cognitive processes in writing* (pp. 3–30). Mahwah, NJ: Erlbaum.

Heath, S.B. (1983). *Ways with words.* New York: Cambridge University Press.

Herrington, A. (1985). Writing in academic settings: A study of the contexts for writing in two college chemical engineering courses. *Research in the Teaching of English, 19*(4), 331–361.

Hicks, D. (1997). Working through discourse genres in school. *Research in the Teaching of English, 31*(4), 459–485.

Hillocks, G., Jr. (1986). *Research on written composition.* Urbana, IL: National Conference on Research in English.

Hunt, K.W. (1965). *Grammatical structures written at three grade levels* (Research Monograph 3). Urbana, IL: National Council of Teachers of English.

Irwin, J.W. (1988). Linguistic cohesion and the developing reader/writer. *Topics in Language Disorders, 8*(3), 14–23.

Langer, J.A. (1986). *Children reading and writing: Structures and strategies.* Norwood, NJ: Ablex.

Langer, J.A. (1995). *Envisioning literature: Literary understanding and literature instruction.* New York: Teachers College Press; Newark, DE: International Reading Association.

Lloyd-Jones, R. (1977). Primary trait scoring. In C.R. Cooper & L. Odell (Eds.), *Evaluating writing: Describing, measuring, judging* (pp. 33–66). Urbana, IL: National Council of Teachers of English.

Loban, W. (1976). *Language development: Kindergarten through grade twelve* (Research Report 18). Urbana, IL: National Council of Teachers of English.

McCarthy, L.P. (1987). A stranger in strange lands: A college student writing accross the curriculum. *Research in the Teaching of English, 21*(3), 233–265.

Meade, R.A., & Ellis, W.G. (1970). Paragraph development in the modern age of rhetoric. *English Journal, 59*, 219–226.

Mellon, J. (1969). *Transformational sentence combining: A method for enhancing the development of syntactic fluency in English composition* (Research Monograph 10). Urbana, IL: National Council of Teachers of English.

Miller, C.R. (1984). Genre as social action. *Quarterly Journal of Speech, 70*, 151–167.

Moffett, J. (1968). *Teaching the universe of discourse.* Boston: Houghton Mifflin.

National Assessment of Educational Progress. (1975). *Writing mechanics, 1969–1974* (Writing Report 05-W-01). Washington, DC: U.S. Government Printing Office.

National Assessment of Educational Progress. (1977). *Write/rewrite: An assessment of revision skills* (Writing Report 05-W-04). Washington, DC: U.S. Government Printing Office.

National Council of Teachers of English & International Reading Association. (1996). *Standards for the English language arts.* Urbana, IL, & Newark, DE: Authors.

Newell, G. (1984). Learning from writing in two content areas: A study/protocol analysis of writing to learn. *Research in the Teaching of English, 18*(3), 265–287.

Newkirk, T. (1987). The non-narrative writing of young children. *Research in the Teaching of English, 21*(2), 121–144.

Newkirk, T. (1989). *More than stories: The range of children's writing.* Portsmouth, NH: Heinemann.

Purves, A.C. (1992). Reflections on research and assessment in written composition. *Research in the Teaching of English, 26*(1), 108–122.

Read, C. (1975). *Children's categorization of speech sounds in English* (Research Monograph 17). Urbana, IL: National Council of Teachers of English.

Rentel, V., & King, M. (1983). Present at the beginning. In P. Mosenthal, L. Tamor, & S.A. Walmsley (Eds.), *Research on writing: Principles and methods* (pp. 139–176). New York: Longman.

Rosenblatt, L.M. (1978). *The reader, the text, the poem: The transactional theory of the literary work.* Carbondale, IL: Southern Illinois University Press.

PART TWO

WRITING AND READING
RELATIONSHIPS

Judith A. Langer and Sheila Flihan
University at Albany
Center on English Learning and Achievement

CHAPTER FIVE

Writing and Reading Relationships: Constructive Tasks

Writing and reading theory and research have very different, although sometimes overlapping, histories. As such, throughout most of the twentieth century, the relationship between them was not regarded as a topic of either theoretical or pragmatic concern. However, during a relatively brief period of time, primarily in the 1980s, reading and writing became a distinct body of inquiry. This research grew from separate bodies of scholarship and focused on separate aspects of education as well as on different grade levels.

This small but intense body of scholarship and research into the interrelationships between writing and reading also focused on ways in which those relationships might affect learning and inform instruction. It was initially motivated and shaped by extensive research on cognitive processes in the separate fields of writing and reading, primarily from a constructivist perspective. Here, both writing and reading were linked to language and communication as well as to reasoning. A concomitant wave of research into the social dimensions of writing and reading, with an eye to their actual functions and uses, moved the target of theory and research toward contextualized practice within real life and real school situations. As a result, one route of scholarship began to examine literacy or, rather, literate acts as they serve social and communicative uses, with a concomitant shift in the focus of inquiry away from writing and reading relationships and toward the ways in which they function in the contexts of life, both in and outside the classroom.

As the object of inquiry became more contextualized, similarities and differences in the writing and reading processes and the ways in which reading and writing develop, affect each other, and relate to learning and schooling became less focal. They did not, however, become less important. We will review these changes and close the chapter with a call for a renewed yet somewhat changed research focus on the uses of reading and writing and the ways in which reading and writing interact in relation to the contexts and social relations in which they are embedded. Informed by past as well as current knowledge from the perspectives of sociocognitive, sociohistorical, and critical theory as well as psychology, linguistics, anthropology, and English, this renewed focus will examine ways in which reading and writing function in the development and communication of ideas and understandings in the social, private, and internal worlds of people and groups.

A Brief History of Writing and Reading Research

Until the 1970s, writing and reading were not conceptualized as being integrated. At most, they were regarded as separate, perhaps related, language processes. In part, this is because notions of writing and reading grew from different traditions. Taking a historical look back, one sees a conceptual and disciplinary schism between scholarship in writing and reading. They have been shaped by different scholars with different backgrounds and training. Writing, as an academic subject, is deeply rooted in classic Aristotelian rhetoric. Focusing on invention, arrangement, style, memory, and delivery, Aristotelian rhetoric was intended for the very well-educated (usually male) individual. It "dominated course work in American colleges during the eighteenth century and was modeled after the curriculum already taught in English universities" (Langer & Allington, 1992, p. 688). By the 1800s the work of Campbell (1776/1963) and Blair's (1783/1965) belles-lettres view of rhetoric became widespread in the

United States, "bringing appreciation of the art of writing into the commonplace tradition" (Langer & Allington, 1992, p. 688). While rhetoric continued to emphasize grammar, diction, and word choice, there was a new focus on the functions of discourse and the study of literary models. Toward the end of the nineteenth century, these traditional notions of writing were challenged by practical, functional views of writing and by the progressive movement. The work of Carpenter, Baker, and Scott (1903) and Dewey (1915), calling for experiential student-centered education, became influential, but it did not replace traditional notions of and approaches to writing. Writing remained rooted in rhetoric through the 1940s, 1950s, and 1960s, but the emphasis shifted among classic Aristotelian views, expressionist views, and the new rhetoric.

Interest in writing processes grew in the 1970s and 1980s. Work in the fields of language and cognition (Anderson & Bower, 1973; Chafe, 1970; Chomsky, 1965; Fillmore, 1968; Rumelhart, 1975; Schank & Ableson, 1977; Searle, 1969; Tulving, 1972; Winograd, 1972) led to a research emphasis on the relationships among writing processes, the learner, and the text (Bereiter & Scardamalia, 1982; Emig, 1971; Flower & Hayes, 1980; Hillocks, 1972). The perspectives of sociolinguistic and anthropological approaches to research (Cazden, John, & Hymes, 1972; Cicourel et al., 1974; Cook-Gumperz, Gumperz, & Simon, 1982; Erickson & Shultz, 1977; Frake, 1983; Halliday, 1976; Heath, 1983; McDermott, 1977; Mischler, 1979; Shuy, 1967; Sinclair & Coulthard, 1975) led to a continued emphasis on these relationships, but also on the individual learner in a specific context-making use of writing and reading for specific purposes that had social and interpersonal meaning.

The early history of reading follows a different course. "Tradition in reading curriculum relied on British notions of primary instruction (for method), on religion (for content), and by the later 1800s on scientific experiments (for theory)" (Langer & Allington, 1992, p. 694). Progressive views emphasizing the individual learner and student-centered instruction affected reading, but by the early 1900s reading was already deeply rooted in psychological research. In fact, "the combined effects of the expanding scientific research base and the application of management principles to the organization of schools seemed to overwhelm the influence of the progressive reading educators" (Langer & Allington, 1992, p. 695).

Reading research, curriculum, and instruction continued to be shaped by associationist and behaviorist psychology through the 1940s, 1950s and 1960s. During this time reading also was influenced by research and theory in language and concept development (e.g., Bloom, 1971; Bruner, 1960, 1966; Inhelder & Piaget, 1958), linguistics (e.g., Bloomfield, 1942; Fries, 1963), and psycholinguistics (e.g., Goodman, 1967; Smith, 1971). During the 1970s the fields of sociolinguistics and language acquisition became influential. Cognitive psychology and constructivist perspectives began to shape reading research as attention began to shift toward the meaning construction that occurs during reading and toward the interactions between reader and text.

Due to their different beginnings, research traditionally approached writing and reading as distinct areas of exploration. The 1980s marked a change in focus. Research began to examine the relationships between writing and reading as cognitive and social processes. Throughout the last decade, research has maintained its interest in writing and reading as separate but interdependent and interrelated acts, while interest in literacy has grown steadily.

Distinctions are now made between "literacy as the act of writing and reading and literacy as a way of thinking and speaking" (Langer, 1987). Language is a tool, and literacy is "culturally based...involves the higher intellectual skills appropriate to the culture, and is learned by children as they interact with families and communities" (Langer, 1987, p. 2). Langer's sociocognitive view of literacy is fully compatible with the distinction Collins (1995) makes between "a universalist or autonomous literacy, seen as a general, uniform set of techniques and uses of language, with identifiable stages and clear consequences for culture and cognition, and relativist or situated literacies, seen as diverse, historically and culturally variable practices with texts" (pp. 75–76). In light of these expanded views, literacy research has a broader scope. Although the skills, processes, and interplay of reading and writing remain important, they are much less distinct. Therefore, the central focus of research on literacy examines reading and writing as they are embedded in social and cultural contexts. Influenced by the field of anthropology and the methods of ethnographic research, literacy studies now explore how, when, where, by whom, and for what purposes reading and writing are used.

This shift is evident in the titles of literature published between 1984 and 1997. The titles of reports and books published by National Council of Teachers of English, International Reading Association, and nine major journals in the fields of education, reading, and English were searched using descriptors such as "reading and writing," "writing and reading," and "literacy." This search yielded 164 titles. Seventy-three percent of these titles contain the word *literacy*. Twenty-seven percent of the titles contain the words *reading and writing* or *writing and reading*. Interestingly, 82% of the publications with the word *literacy* in the title were published between 1990 and 1997; only 18% were published between 1984 and 1989. Publications with the words *reading and writing* or *writing and reading* in the title seem more evenly distributed, with 43% published between 1984 and 1989 and 57% published between 1990 and 1997.

Writing and Reading Relationships

Writing and reading have long been considered to be related activities. Along with listening and speaking, they have been treated by educators as essential components of the English language arts "pie," at least since the National Conference on Research in English charter in 1932 (Petty, 1983). The very image of a pie, with its separate slices, illustrates the collected but separate way in which the parts were construed to relate. However, a large and extremely influential body of research from a constructivist perspective (Anderson, Spiro, & Montague, 1977; Bereiter & Scardamalia, 1982; Hayes & Flower, 1980; Spiro, Bruce, & Brewer, 1980) indicates that reading and writing development are characterized by gradually more sophisticated rule-governed representations, and that the learner is an active problem solver who is influenced by background knowledge, text, and context. An accompanying and eventually equally influential body of work, primarily from a sociolinguistic, sociocultural, and sociohistorical perspective (Chafe, 1970; Cook-Gumperz, & Gumperz, 1981; Halliday, 1975; Heath, 1983; Scribner & Cole, 1981; Stubbs, 1980; Vygotsky, 1934/1978, 1934/1986) permitted consideration of ways in which life's experiences as well as the uses and functions of writing and reading affect both the acts of writing and reading and how they relate.

As early as the 1960s, during the period of extensive interdisciplinary research into language and thought spearheaded by the Center for Cognitive Studies at Harvard University (see Brown & Bellugi, 1964; Bruner, Goodnow, & Austin, 1956; Weir, 1962), writing and reading were regarded as related language processes. In his important longitudinal study of students' reading and writing development across grades 4, 6, and 9, Loban (1963) indicated strong relationships between reading and writing as measured by test scores. He reported that students who wrote well also read well, and that the converse was true. Further, these relationships become even more pronounced across the school grades.

In 1983, Stotsky published a review of correlational and experimental studies that investigated reading and writing relationships. Her much-cited synthesis spans approximately 50 years, from the beginning of the 1930s to 1981. Studies correlational to that time showed that "better writers tend to be better readers (of their own writing as well as of other reading material), that better writers tend to read more than poorer writers, and that better readers tend to produce more syntactically mature writing than poorer readers" (p. 636). With regard to instruction Stotsky reported, "Studies that sought to improve writing by providing reading experiences in place of grammar study or additional writing practice found that these experiences were as beneficial as, or more beneficial than, grammar study or extra writing practice. Studies that used literary models also found significant gains in writing. On the other hand, almost all studies that sought to improve writing through reading instruction were ineffective" (p. 636). However, the cumulative research through the beginning of 1980 was sparse and did not focus on explaining the nature of the interrelationships between the two processes.

A number of scholars contributed toward a growing conception of reading and writing relationships by focusing on students' engagement in the tasks, describing how from the early years, children use signs and symbols (both those in their environment and those they invent) to gain and convey meaning, even as they are first acquiring the conventionally accepted codes (Bissex, 1980; Clay, 1975; Read, 1971). Wittrock (1983) considered the generative nature of both domains; DeFord (1981) noted the supporting and interactive nature of the processes as they occur in primary classrooms; and Goodman and Goodman (1983) described relationships between the two based on the pragmatic functions of each. Through efforts to communicate through writing and reading, students gradually adopt both symbols and conventions of use. Eckhoff (1983) found that the second-grade students she studied tended to imitate the style and structure of the basals used for reading instruction, which affected the organizational structures and linguistic complexity of the students' writing. Chall and Jacobs (1983) conducted a study of writing and reading development among poor children, based on test scores similar to the National Assessment of Educational Progress. Although reading and writing scores in grades 2 and 3 were good, the authors noted a deceleration in proficiency gains beginning in grades 4 and 5 and continuing through grade 7. Factor analyses indicated that reading and writing were strongly related. Together, this work suggested that the two domains do have an impact on each other, with implications for enhancing learning. The work suggested a need to better understand the underlying processes of writing and reading and how they relate to each other.

Writing and Reading Processes: Similarities and Differences

Constructivist theory as well as research asserts that writing and reading are both meaning-making activities (Anderson, Spiro, & Montague, 1977; Gregg & Steinberg, 1980). When people write and read, meaning is continually in a state of becoming. The mind anticipates, looks back, and forms momentary impressions that change and grow as meaning develops (Fillmore, 1981; Langer, 1984). Language, syntax, and structure are all at play as texts develop in the mind and on paper. Because writing and reading involve the development of meaning, both are conceptualized as composing activities in the sense that both involve planning, generating, and revising meaning—which occur recursively throughout the meaning-building process as a person's text world or envisionment grows. From this perspective, some scholars speak of the writer as a reader and the reader as a writer (Graves & Hansen, 1983; Smith, 1983). According to Smith (1983) reading like a writer allows one to actually become a writer. When reading like a writer, in addition to making meaning of the text, the reader takes in and learns from the author's style and use of conventions. Thus, when reading like a writer, the reader uses the author's text as a model for texts that he or she will eventually write.

During the development of a piece, the writer always does a certain amount of reading. And, further, writers often try to place themselves in the shoes of their audience, the readers, in order to check the comprehensibility of their presentation from the reader's perspective. In a similar manner, the reader also has been considered a writer in that the reader's mind races ahead to anticipate (and thus create) not only the message, but also the structure and presentational style of a piece; words are thought of as well as ideas in ways in which they might appear (Bereiter & Scardamalia, 1982; Flower & Hayes, 1980). Thus, a reader's text can be compared with an author's text, and be revised when needed. This sense of writing as reading provides a sense of personal engagement to the reading experience. Readers also sometimes place themselves in the shoes of the author in order to gain a personal or cultural perspective that enriches their own responses or interpretation (Purves, 1993).

Tierney and Pearson (1983) argued that both readers and writers compose meaning. They described planning, drafting, aligning, revising, and monitoring as essential characteristics of the effective composing process. Further, they saw "these acts of composing as involving continuous, recurring, and recursive transactions among readers and writers, their respective inner selves, and their perceptions of each other's goals and desires" (p. 578). They distinguished their conception from earlier notions of reading and writing relationships in a number of ways, including treating the two domains as multimodal processes and considering the inner as well as social selves of the writer and reader. Tierney (1985), in a later description of this model, suggests that purpose also plays a role: "Both reading and writing are tools in accordance with the purposes they serve; they cannot be extracted from context" (p. 115).

Both domains also were considered similar composing activities in that writers and readers use similar kinds of knowledge (Aulls, 1985; Flood & Lapp, 1987; Kucer, 1987) in the act of making their meanings: knowledge about language, knowledge about content, knowledge about genre conventions, knowledge about organization and structure, knowledge of pragmatics (in this case about the appropriate use of other kinds of knowledge in relation to the activity—the author's purpose for having written the piece, or the writer's or reader's own purposes for having taken up that act of writing or reading), and knowledge about interaction (especially between reader and author). Rubin and Hansen (1986) suggested that different types of knowledge that can be tapped through reading instruction might transfer to writing instruction: informational knowledge, structural knowledge, transactional knowledge, aesthetic knowledge, and process knowledge. Flower (1988) adds knowledge of purpose to the list. She asks how writers come by their sense of purpose, how (or whether) readers are affected by the rhetorical structure woven by writers, and how individual purposes interact with context and convention in the creation and interpretation of a text. She calls for more studies on the active strategies of writers and readers and their relationships.

Researchers also have pointed to specific differences between writing and reading. In her study of children reading and writing, Langer (1986a) found that although reading and writing are cognitively related efforts with regard to meaning making, they are markedly different with regard to activity, strategy, and purpose. Children also differ across ages with regard to the variety of approaches that they use and the behaviors they exhibit while reading or writing.

For a study of third, sixth, and ninth graders' reading and writing of stories and reports, Langer (1986a) developed a procedure for analyzing the knowledge sources, reasoning operations, monitoring behaviors, and specific strategies used during the course of meaning construction before, during, and after reading and writing. She found that although the same reasoning behaviors are called on when reading and writing for meaning, the patterns of each category showed differences between writing and reading. Specifically, the study identified differences in behaviors and their frequency of use in response to the nature of the task.

The study also revealed that when reading and writing, students' dominant concern was with the meanings they were developing. There are stable and consistent approaches to envisionment building that emerged, as evidenced in the students' focus on ideas, content, product, and refinement of meaning. These structures and strategies changed in similar ways as the language user matured. However, "underlying this overall focus were such differences as a slightly higher concern with bottom-up issues such as mechanics, syntax, text, and lexical choices when writing as compared to reading" (Langer, 1986a, p. 94). Also, when students wrote they were more aware of and concerned with the strategies they used to get at meaning. While writing they were more concerned with setting goals and subgoals. When reading, on the other hand, the students focused more on content and validation of the text worlds they were developing.

Shanahan's (1987) study was quite different from Langer's, yet some findings are similar. He used four reading measures and eight writing measures to study the magnitude and nature of the reading and writing relationship, and to estimate the amount of overlap that exists between the components of writing and reading used in his study of second- and fifth-grade students' writing and reading. His findings suggest that the "idea that reading and writing are identical in terms of underlying knowledge, does not appear to be true" (p. 98). Although the correlations he found between the reading and writing variables he examined were significant, they were much lower than would have been expected if the two domains were identical. Shanahan concludes that, "In fact, the correlations are low enough that it would be unwise to expect automatic improvements to derive from the combination of reading and writing or from the replacement of one with the other" (p. 98).

Webster and Ammon (1994) used a Piagetian framework to explore the relationship between cognitive scores (specific classification and seriation tasks) and specific reading and writing tasks at the elementary level. In interpreting the generally low correlations, the authors concluded that "facility with the relevant cognitive skill is necessary but not sufficient" (p. 101) for a high level of performance in writing and reading. Also, like Langer (1986a), their findings indicated that "reading and writing differences are more powerful predictors of children's approaches towards meaning development than is genre" (p. 104).

Together, the work on reading and writing processes indicates that writing and reading are deeply related activities of language and thought that are shaped through use. The structures and strategies that writers and readers use to organize, remember, and present their ideas are generally the same in writing and reading. However, the structure of the message and the strategies used to formulate and organize it are driven by purpose and therefore different.

Writing and Reading Relationships
With Regard to Instruction

Researchers and scholars interested in writing and reading connections also have considered ways in which the two, conceptualized as related composing processes, might implicate various uses of language and thought and thereby affect students' learning. Specifically, research began to examine how the processes of reading and writing are related in actual practice. Researchers also looked at the ways in which students' knowledge of writing and reading processes can influence and support reading and writing respectively in the classroom. They also studied the kinds of classroom contexts and instructional activities that might foster reading and writing as mutually beneficial activities.

When approached as similar, related composing processes rather than as isolated skills and behaviors, writing and reading can influence and support the development of reading, writing, and thinking (Squire, 1983). Writers incorporate what they have learned about language, structure, and style from the texts they have encountered as readers. They also reflect on their knowledge of texts they have read and experiences they have had as a way of generating and synthesizing ideas for writing. In becoming familiar with and gaining experience in writing and reading texts even first graders can "develop a sense of authorship that helps them in either composing process" (Graves & Hansen, 1983, p. 182).

The experience and knowledge that is shared between reading and writing can strengthen a writer's ability to read and a reader's ability to write (Blatt & Rosen, 1987; Butler & Turbill, 1984; Rubin & Hansen, 1986; Shanahan & Lomax, 1986). In a study that compared the interactive model, the reading-to-write model, and the writing-to-read model of the writing and reading relationship (Shanahan & Lomax, 1986), writing samples from 256 second graders and 251 first graders were examined with regard to specific reading and writing dimensions. Analyses showed that the students' work at both grade levels was best described by the interactive model of the reading and writing relationship, which suggests the transfer of knowledge between the two processes.

This transfer and sharing of knowledge also is demonstrated in a study of fifth graders sharing their poetry as well as the work of published authors (Comstock, 1992). Over time, students began borrowing literary techniques, such as the use of imagery and repetition, from each other. They also began to look to their surroundings for ideas that might prompt them to write. Blatt and Rosen's (1987) account of a young child's ability to call on her experience as a listener and reader of fairy tales as she wrote her own also demonstrates this transfer of knowledge between writing and reading. She was able to create a tale that included a protagonist, an antagonist, and a conflict and began with "Once upon a time," much like all the tales with which she was familiar (p. 123).

It seems that "reading and writing intersect in natural ways when literate persons are actively using reading and writing to learn" (Hanson et al., 1991, p. 58). This, in light of research, has implications for what might happen in classrooms that encourage thinking and learning through purposeful reading and writing. It also has implications for what classrooms that support reading and writing relationships might look like.

To begin, research tells us that successful instruction in both reading and writing can begin in the earliest grades (Butler & Turbill, 1984; Clay, 1985; Graves & Hansen, 1983; Shanahan & Lomax, 1986), and are best learned when not taught in isolation from each other (Blatt & Rosen, 1987; Butler & Turbill, 1984; Sternglass, 1987). Even though it is possible for instruction in writing to improve students' reading comprehension of informational texts (Raphael, Kirschner, & Englert, 1988), to affect overall learning, instruction does best to focus on both reading and writing (Ferris & Snyder, 1986; Shanahan, 1984). Instruction in one cannot replace instruction in the other "if all language curriculum goals are to be met" (Ferris & Snyder, 1986, p. 755).

In the classroom, students do best with frequent and extended opportunities to read and write (Blatt & Rosen, 1987; Butler & Turbill, 1984; Hanson et al., 1991; Rubin & Hansen, 1986) and when exposed to a body of literature that represents a variety of genres, topics, and styles (Blatt & Rosen, 1987; Butler & Turbill, 1984; Comstock, 1992). Providing students with choice in what they read and write and are encouraged to read and write, and allowing opportunities to write about topics and ideas that interest them and with which they are familiar positively affects their attitudes toward learning (Hanson et al., 1991; Rubin & Hansen, 1986).

Teachers most successfully support their students' reading and writing development when they create a variety of learning contexts, such as cooperative learning groups and peer dyads, in which discussion and instructional scaffolding support students' needs (Hiebert, 1991). Within these contexts teachers help students explore their understandings by providing them with ample opportunities to consider personal responses to the texts they compose and to make links between their prior experiences and what they are reading and writing. Students share their ideas and insights and feel that they will be accepted by members of the classroom community (Blatt & Rosen, 1987; Butler & Turbill, 1984; Comstock, 1992; Graves & Hansen, 1983; Hanson et al., 1991; Rubin & Hansen, 1986; Sternglass, 1987).

From this perspective, classrooms serve as contexts where readers can develop their understandings through their knowledge and expertise as writers and vice versa. Instruction that encourages meaning making through reading and writing is based on an understanding of reading and writing as related composing processes. In the classroom, "a failure to recognize that composing and comprehending are process-oriented thinking skills which are basically interrelated...impedes our efforts not only to teach children to read and write, but our efforts to teach them how to think" (Squire, 1983, p. 581).

Writing and Reading as Related to Thinking, Conceptualizing, and Communicating Knowledge

Moving beyond an examination of the ways in which writing and reading are related is research that examines how reading and writing, as processes, are used to conceptualize and communicate thoughts and ideas. This research looks at the "synergism" (Tierney, 1992, p. 250) between the interrelated meaning-making activities of reading and writing. During these activities it is the "interplay of mind and text that brings about new interpretations, reformulations of ideas, and new learnings" (Langer, 1986a, pp. 2–3).

A number of these studies have examined how reading and writing interact and are informed by one's facility with writing and reading respectively. In addition to demonstrating that children's writing is influenced heavily by their reading experiences, DeFord's (1981) observations of first graders indicate that "there is a supportive, interactive relationship between the reading and writing processes. Children learn about how to become writers from reading as well as how to become readers. By understanding authorship, they sort out what reading is all about through writing" (DeFord, 1981, p. 657). A sense of authorship can lead to the development of critical literacy in which the reader/writer moves past simply understanding the content of the text or using it as a model to be imitated and begins to question, test, shape, and reshape it (Flower, 1990).

Greene (1992) expands on this notion of learning to become a writer through reading by introducing the metaphor of mining as a means of exploring how writers read when they have an eye toward authoring their own texts. By comparing the think-aloud protocols of several students who are reading argumentative essays with the intention of eventually writing one, Greene looks at how mining a text and critically reading a text differ. Mining is "fueled by three key strategies that can inform reading: reconstructing context, inferring or imposing structure, and seeing choices in language.... [Using these strategies], a reader can begin to make informed guesses about how to use the ideas or discourse features of a given text in light of his or her goals as a writer" (Greene, 1992, p. 155). When mining, a sense of authorship guides the reader. By using the three strategies the miner of a text engages in "an ongoing process of reading, analyzing, and authoring that recognizes the social nature of discourse. Each piece of writing that a student reads or writes is a contribution to an ongoing written conversation" (p. 158). Conversely, critical readers engage in a search for meaning by breaking down isolated texts. Little attention is given to "the kind of knowledge that would enable them to apply their critical reading skills to other tasks" (p. 159).

Questions about how a sense of authorship can guide reading also are encountered by studies examining how writers create new texts of their own from multiple sources, which may include the texts they are reading presently as well as their own prior knowledge. Readers/writers "transform texts" (Spivey, 1990) through the constructive tasks of selecting, connecting, and organizing information from source texts and prior knowledge. This incorporation of prior knowledge is what Stein (1990) refers to as *elaboration*. This cognitive process is "the principle means by which information from memory is combined with source text material in the reading process" (p. 146). Elaborations during reading create a "pool of ideas from which to draw during the writing process" (p. 147).

Whether referred to as reading to write (Flower, 1990; Stein, 1990) or composing from sources (McGinley, 1992; Spivey, 1990; Spivey & King, 1989), the readers/writers are involved in processes of reading and writing that are so integrated

> that boundaries between the two processes tend to blur. When writers compose from sources, reading and writing processes blend, making it difficult, if not impossible, to distinguish what is being done for purposes of reading from what is being done for purposes of writing...we often cannot say whether a writer performs a certain operation to make meaning of the text that is read or to make meaning for the text that is being written. (Spivey, 1990, p. 258)

Creating new texts in this way is a complex and recursive process (McGinley, 1992) in which context (for example, task, setting, or prior experience of reader/writer), one's expertise as a reader, and his or her ability to use strategies play important roles (Flower, 1990; McGinley, 1992; Spivey, 1990; Spivey & King, 1989; Stein, 1990).

Research also has considered the effects of reading and writing on thinking and how different types of writing tasks shape thinking and learning. It suggests that "reading and writing in combination are more likely to prompt critical thinking than when reading is separated from writing or when reading is combined with knowledge activation or answering questions" (Tierney et al., 1989, p. 134). Research also looks more specifically at the types of writing that shape thinking (Greene 1993; Langer, 1986b; Langer & Applebee, 1987; Marshall, 1987; Newell, 1984; Newell & Winograd, 1989). In the content areas, essay writing was found to be more beneficial than answering questions or taking notes regardless of students' prior knowledge (Newell, 1984). Students involved in note-taking and responding to study questions seem to concentrate on remembering and regurgitating specific information from the text. Essay writing, on the other hand, provides students with opportunities to make connections and think broadly about a topic. These studies indicate that "the greatest variety of reasoning operations occur during essay writing, suggesting that this type of activity provides time for students to think most flexibly as they develop their ideas" (Langer & Applebee, 1987, p. 100).

Langer & Flihan

These findings are supported by Marshall's (1987) examination of the relationship between writing and the understanding of literature. By looking at the effects of restricted writing, personal analytic writing, and formal analytic writing, he found that restricted writing (like responding to short answer questions) may actually hinder students' understanding of literary texts because such tasks fail to provide students with an opportunity to explore and elaborate on possible interpretations.

Similarly, Greene (1993) studied the ways in which problem-based essays and report-writing assignments shaped history students' thinking as they attempted to compose from multiple sources. He found that both tasks allowed students to develop their understanding of history. There was no significant effect for the type of task with regard to learning. However, "[d]ifferent tasks of writing encouraged students not only to think about historical issues differently but also to supply different patterns of organization in writing about these issues. Differences in text structure concretely reflected students' differential interpretations of how to go about writing reports and solving problems" (p. 72).

Clearly, the focus of research has shifted. Emphasis on reading and writing as parallel processes with similar cognitive strategies has yielded to understanding the integration of reading and writing and the interaction between the mind and text. Within this body of research, process and purpose remain focal. Also, the effects of grade and ability level on reading and writing persist as areas of concern. Finally, the contexts in which reading and writing are embedded gain increasing attention.

Writing and Reading as Literacy Events

As sociolinguistic, sociocultural, and anthropological perspectives became more influential during the 1970s and 1980s, new ways of thinking, talking, and learning about literacy took hold. There was growing interest in the interactions surrounding text and the ways in which interactions between and among individuals, who they are, and why they are writing and reading influence meaning making. Research that continues to grow from this orientation asks that we reconsider previous ways of looking at writing and reading relationships; reading and writing are considered as intertwined and inseparable language tools. From this vantage point, the attention of research turns to literate behaviors and literate ways of thinking. Here, literacy means the ability to manipulate the language and thought involved when people make sense in a variety of situations; it involves ways of thinking that are learned in the many contexts of life (Langer, 1987, 1995). The functions and uses of oral, written, and spoken language as well as the images and other semiotic meaning-bearing devices encountered and used in the variety of everyday life experiences (John-Steiner, 1995; New London Group, 1996) are the focus of an expanded view of literacy. Research from this perspective has focused on the ways in which adolescents, adults, and even very young children use language to construct meaning within particular social and cultural communities (Dyson, 1989, 1992; Heath, 1983; Scribner & Cole, 1981; Teale & Sulzby, 1986). Within this body of research the literacy event is "a conceptual tool useful in examining within particular communities of modern society the actual forms and functions of oral and literate traditions and co-existing relationships between spoken and written language" (Heath, 1988, p. 350). Research observes the ongoing activities that make up literacy events occurring in the classroom and in the community at large (for instance the home or workplace). Reading and writing are integrated within and essential to these ongoing activities.

Langer (1997) describes 8 years of research that investigated how individuals in school and in school-like settings think and reason when they are engaged with literature and how classroom interactions may foster literacy development. She found that "envisionment-building" literature classes invite students to be members of a social community in which they can share their ideas and differences with others and "expect those differences to move their own thinking toward more individually rich, but never singular interpretations" (p. 10).

This research also showed that a collaborative, broad-based literature activity such as story writing or telling provided individuals of diverse ages and linguistic and cultural backgrounds with opportunities to "become aware of and discuss language and discourse differences as well as to learn English literacy. Despite their ages, be they 2 or 42 years old, the subjects were members of a language- and literacy-rich environment where they learned to talk about and control features of language and form—where the literature that was sought and valued was their own" (p. 9).

Students in the envisionment-building classroom and those involved in the broad-based activity are constantly and simultaneously involved in listening, discussing, reading, and writing, but reading and writing are not viewed as separate in time or purpose. Furthermore, reading and writing "are never regarded as skills, activities, or ends in themselves, but as tools of language" (Langer, 1995, p. 140).

Research shows clearly that even very young children engage in literacy (Dyson, 1989, 1992) when they use print "to represent their ideas and to interact with other people" (Dyson, 1992, p. 4). Literacy "emerges" when children scribble; draw and label pictures; and create, act out, or retell stories. During these times children are engaged in literate behaviors that are essential parts of the language development process (Teale & Sulzby, 1986).

Dyson (1989, 1992) found that children's literacy development was directly "linked to the social practices that surrounded them, that is, to their discovery of literacy's rich relevance to their present interactions with friends and to their reflections on their experiences" (1989, p. 276). Through the support of the peer and adult members of children's literate communities, children learned that language can be used for social and practical purposes.

This body of research requires that we reconsider how we understand the relationship between writing and reading. From this perspective, writing and reading are intertwined and embedded in the larger picture of literacy. It also moves us to reflect on what counts as literacy. Finally, it asks that we take a closer look at the ways in which literacy is developed and demonstrated at home, work, and school.

In thinking about literacy as universalist, autonomous (Collins, 1995; Street, 1993), or schooled (Cook-Gumperz, 1986), what counts are those behaviors, practices, skills, or tasks that are traditionally associated with reading and writing. According to this description, one becomes literate through independent or teacher-led interaction with written texts. One's level of literacy and the resultant label of literate or illiterate is determined through the testing and measuring of these skills. Literacy then is assumed to be a standardized, institutional notion that exists and is identified independently of a social or cultural context. Moreover, this notion of literacy is often the basis by which schools and society determine one's intellect, educability, and potential contribution to and earning power in the workforce.

Heath (1983) found that some children, as members of particular communities, are accustomed to and participate in literate ways of thinking and behaving that may not be incorporated into or reflected in the children's classrooms. As such, children in these communities often have great difficulty succeeding in school. In her study, teachers helped children from three communities narrow the gaps between their home and community literacy experiences and those of school. Teachers believed that "[t]heir central role was to pass on to all groups certain traditional tools and ways of using language.... Children had to reformulate to different degrees their home habits of handling knowledge and their ways of talking about knowledge" (pp. 354–355).

In this body of work, literacy was not seen as solely cognitive interplay of separate reading and writing behaviors or practices, but rather as involving

> manipulation of the language and thought we engage in when we make sense and convey ideas in a variety of situations; it involves ways of thinking, which we learn in the many contexts of our lives. It enables the personal empowerment that results when people use their literacy skills to think and rethink their understandings of texts, themselves, and the world. It gives importance to individuals and the oral and written texts they create and encounter, and calls upon as well as fosters the kinds of language and thought that mark good and sharp thinking. (Langer, 1995, p. 1)

The studies focused on ways in which reading and writing can be used as tools to make sense of the world and to express thoughts that demonstrate and convey literate knowledge and understanding.

Future Directions

Where do educators go from here? A new set of issues has been brought to the table by a variety of writers who take, for example, a feminist perspective (Belenky et al., 1986; Brodkey, 1989; Fetterly, 1978; Gilligan, 1982; Minnich, 1990; Solsken, 1993) or a cultural perspective (Ferdman, 1990; Hakuta, 1986; Street, 1984; Valencia, 1991; Weber, 1991; Wong-Fillmore, 1992). These writers emphasize issues of power (Apple, 1982; Bordieu & Passeron, 1977; Cope & Kalantzis, 1993; Freire, 1972; Halliday

& Martin, 1993), self (Giroux, 1983; Rockhill, 1993, Rose, 1989), and more recently authorship (Rabinowitz & Smith, 1997), which further complicate our notions of writing and reading relationships in important ways. They force us to consider the connections between literacy and the ways in which we place ourselves in relation to the literacy experience. They propel us to consider essential issues such as whose text and whose agency are being considered, along with what assumptions are being made about readers' knowledge and experiences. The next logical step is for researchers to look at how readers and writers, as both individuals and members of a variety of groups, approach reading and writing as constructive tasks that are embedded in life's situations. More precisely, research needs to refocus on the ways in which reading and writing develop and influence each other while constantly being affected by the social, cultural, and political contexts in which they are enacted. This will require consideration of genres. For example, if genres are the products of socially developed conventions that foster communicability within groups of people, as the variety of groups considered to fall within the purview of the educational sphere changes to include the variety of students who populate both our schools and the world, so too will our understandings of the constructions of these genres need to change so that we might recognize, value, and teach them. So too, will we need to study the inevitable genre changes as the groups themselves change over time.

A number of school and classroom-based research agendas are called for. First, careful "teaching and learning" studies are needed of situated (Brown, Collins, & Draguid, 1989; Greeno, 1997) and activity-based learning events from the perspectives of the diverse students and teachers who make up the classes; the nature of the discourse groups they form, communicate within, and learn from; and the ways in which the students learn, as well as the literacy skills and knowledge they develop in these settings. Of course student learning will need to be considered in relation to the ways in which particular tasks and group dynamics affect various aspects of literacy learning, including the degree to which these are learned and how available they are for use in new situations. A careful look will need to be taken at the particular skills and knowledge students learn in these situations, the additional kinds of support that might be needed based on students' knowledge and needs, and how these can be linked coherently in ways that are most supportive of students' growing literacy abilities. Teaching and learning studies also will need to focus on particular ways in which diversity can be used to advantage in diverse classrooms as a way to help all students gain from the experiences of others and use what they already know in new literacy learning.

Another set of studies will need to focus on the curriculum. First, the curriculum will need to be studied in terms of what it includes and excludes in skills as well as content, and ways in which skills are linked. The tools of learning and uses of literacy have been changing rapidly in our present-day society, calling us to revisit the guidelines meant to structure and provide coherence to student coursework. Here studies will need to focus on the literacy knowledge students bring to school with them that is not recognized as such (for example, computers as well as graphic imagery or the ability to manipulate language in culturally or socially sanctioned ways, such as rap music), as well as the varieties of literate knowledge they will need to successfully live their lives as participants in our changing society. Research also needs to focus on what gets read, when, and how. Although issues of the canon tend to become politicized, an orchestrated body of research should focus not only on what works are to be included and what others will be optional, but also on the ways in which particular combinations of texts can be used to stimulate more complex thinking and higher literacy (Applebee, 1996; see also Applebee, Chapter Four in this volume). Further, studies of the curriculum will need to investigate the role curriculum can play in helping all students maintain a sense of self-worth and learning, yet meet their differential needs as learners, with the end goal of maximum proficiency for all.

Finally, as classrooms change and students learn to become literate participants in particular social, political, and cultural contexts within their school environments, it will be necessary to explore the ways in which the variety of texts they encounter and create through writing and reading relate to their developing literate selves and the strategies they use to explore and achieve life's possibilities.

References

Anderson, J., & Bower, G. (1973). *Human associative memory*. Washington, DC: Winston.

Anderson, R.C., Spiro, R.J., & Montague, W.E. (1977). *Schooling and the acquisition of knowledge*. Hillsdale, NJ: Erlbaum.

Apple, M.W. (1982). *Education and power*. Boston: Routledge and Kegan Paul.

Applebee, A.N. (1996). *Curriculum as conversation*. Chicago: University of Chicago Press.

Aulls, M.W. (1985, Fall). Understanding the relationship between reading and writing. *Educational Horizons*, 39–44.

Belenky, M.F., Clinchy, B.M., Goldberger, N.R., & Tarule, J.M. (1986). *Women's ways of knowing: The development of self, voice, and mind*. New York: Basic Books.

Bereiter, C., & Scardamalia, M. (1982). From conversation to composition. In R. Glaser (Ed.), *Advances in instructional psychology (Vol. 2)*. Hillsdale, NJ: Erlbaum.

Bissex, G.L. (1980). *GNYS AT WRK: A child learns to write and read*. Cambridge, MA: Harvard University Press.

Blair, H. (1965). *Lectures on rhetoric and belles lettres*. Carbondale, IL: Southern Illinois University Press. (Original work published 1783)

Blatt, G., & Rosen, L.M. (1987). Writing: A window on children and their reading. *English Quarterly, 20*(2), 121–130.

Bloom, B.S. (1971). Mastery learning and its implications for curriculum development. In E.W. Eisner (Ed.), *Confronting curriculum reform*. Boston: Little, Brown.

Bloomfield, L.J. (1942). Linguistics in reading. *Elementary English Review, 19*(4), 125–130, 183–186.

Bordieu, P., & Passeron, J.C. (1977). *Reproduction in education, society, & culture*. Beverly Hills, CA: Sage.

Brodkey, L. (1989). On the subject of class and gender in "The Literacy Letters." *College English, 51*, 125–141.

Brown, J.S., Collins A., & Draguid, P. (1989). Situated cognition and the culture of learning. *Educational Researcher, 18*, 34–42.

Brown, R.W., & Bellugi, U. (1964). Three processes in the child's acquisition of syntax. *Harvard Educational Review, 34*, 133–151.

Bruner, J.S. (1960). *The process of education*. Cambridge, MA: Harvard University Press.

Bruner, J.S. (1966). *Toward a theory of instruction*. Cambridge, MA: Belknap–Harvard University Press.

Bruner, J.S., Goodnow, J.J., & Austin, B.A. (1956). *A study in thinking*. New York: Wiley.

Butler, A., & Turbill, J. (1984). *Towards a reading-writing classroom*. Rozelle, Australia: Primary English Teaching Association.

Campbell, G. (1963). *The philosophy of rhetoric*. Carbondale, IL: Southern Illinois University Press. (Original work published 1776)

Carpenter, G.R., Baker, F.T., & Scott, F.N. (1903). *The teaching of English in the elementary and secondary schools*. New York: Longmans, Green.

Cazden, C.B., John, V.P., & Hymes, D. (Eds.). (1972). *Functions of language in the classroom*. New York: Teachers College Press.

Chafe, W. (1970). *The meaning and structure of language*. Chicago: University of Chicago Press.

Chall, J.S., & Jacobs, V.A. (1983). Writing and reading in the elementary grades: Developmental trends among low SES children. *Language Arts, 60*(5), 617–626.

Chomsky, N. (1965). *Aspects of a theory of syntax*. Cambridge, MA: MIT Press.

Ciroucel, A.V. et al., (1974). *Language use and school performance.* New York: Academic Press.

Clay, M.M. (1975). *What did I write? Beginning writing behavior.* Auckland, NZ: Heinemann.

Clay, M.M. (1985). *The early detection of reading difficulties.* Auckland, NZ: Heinemann.

Collins, J. (1995). Literacy and literacies. *Annual Review of Anthropology, 24,* 75–93.

Comstock, M. (1992). Poetry and process: The reading/writing connection. *Language Arts,* 69(4), 261–267.

Cook-Gumperz, J.J. (1986). *The social construction of literacy.* New York: Cambridge University Press.

Cook-Gumperz, J.J., & Gumperz, J. (1981). From oral to written culture. In M. Whitman (Ed.), *Variations in writing.* Hillsdale, NJ: Erlbaum.

Cook-Gumperz, J.J., Gumperz, J., & Simon, H.D. (1982). *Final report on school/home ethnography project.* Berkeley, CA: University of California.

Cope, B., & Kalantzis, M. (Eds.). (1993). *The powers of literacy: A genre approach to teaching writing.* Pittsburgh, PA: University of Pittsburgh Press.

DeFord, D.E. (1981). Literacy: Reading, writing, and other essentials. *Language Arts,* 58(6), 652–658.

Dewey, J. (1915). *The school and society.* Chicago: Chicago University Press.

Dyson, A.H. (1989). *Multiple worlds of child writers: Friends learning to write.* New York: Teachers College Press.

Dyson, A.H. (1992). *The social worlds of children learning to write in an urban primary school.* New York: Teachers College Press.

Eckhoff, B. (1983). How reading affects children's writing. *Language Arts,* 60(6), 607–616.

Emig, J. (1971). *The composing process of twelfth graders* (Research report No. 13). Urbana, IL: National Council of Teachers of English.

Erickson, F., & Schultz, J. (1977). When is a context? *Quarterly Newsletter for Comparative Human Development,* 1(2), 5–10.

Ferdman, B.M. (1990). Literacy and cultural identity. *Harvard Education Review,* 60(2), 181–204.

Ferris, J.A., & Snyder, G. (1986). Writing as an influence on reading. *Journal of Reading,* 29(8), 751–756.

Fetterley, J. (1978). *The resisting reader: A feminist approach to American fiction.* Bloomington, IN: Indiana University Press.

Fillmore, C.J. (1968). *The case for case: Universals in linguistic theory.* New York: Rinehart & Winston.

Fillmore, C.J. (1981). *Ideal readers and real readers* (Proceedings of the 32nd Georgetown University Round Table Conference). Washington, DC: Department of Linguistics, Georgetown University.

Flood, J., & Lapp, D. (1987). Reading and writing relations: Assumptions and directions. In J. Squire (Ed.), *The dynamics of language learning* (pp. 9–26). Urbana, IL: National Conference in Research in English.

Flower, L. (1988). The construction of purpose in writing and reading. *College English,* 50(5), 528–550.

Flower, L. (1990). The role of task representation in reading-to-write. In L.S. Flower, J. Ackerman, M.J. Kantz, K. McCormick, & W.C. Peck (Eds.), *Reading-to-write: Exploring a cognitive and social process*. New York: Oxford University Press.

Flower, L.S., & Hayes, J.R. (1980). The cognition of discovery: Defining a rhetorical problem. *College Composition and Communication, 31*(1), 21–32.

Frake, C. (1983). Did literacy cause the great cognitive divide? *American Ethnologist, 10,* 368–371.

Freire, P. (1972). *Pedagogy of the oppressed*. London: Penguin.

Fries, C.C. (1963). *Linguistics and reading*. New York: Holt, Rinehart and Winston.

Gilligan, C. (1982). *In a different voice: Psychological theory and women's development*. Cambridge, MA: Harvard University Press.

Giroux, H.A. (1983). *Theory and resistance in education*. South Hadley, MA: Bergin & Garvey.

Goodman, K.S. (1967). Reading: A psycholinguistic guessing game. *Journal of the Reading Specialist, 6*(4), 126–135.

Goodman, K., & Goodman, Y. (1983). Reading and writing relationships: Pragmatic functions. *Language Arts, 60*(5), 590–599.

Graves, D., & Hansen, J. (1983). The author's chair. *Language Arts, 60*(2), 176–183.

Greene, S. (1992). Mining texts in reading to write. *Journal of Advanced Composition, 12,* 151–170.

Greene, S. (1993). The role of task in the development of academic thinking through reading and writing in a college history course. *Research in the Teaching of English, 27,* 46–75.

Greeno, J. (1997). Response: On claims that answer the wrong question. *Educational Researcher, 26*(1) 5–17.

Gregg, L.W., & Steinberg, E.R. (Eds.). (1980). *Cognitive processes in writing*. Hillsdale, NJ: Erlbaum.

Hakuta, K. (1986). *Mirror of language*. New York: Basic Books.

Halliday, M.A.K. (1976). *Learning how to mean*. New York: Elsevier N. Holland.

Halliday, M.A.K., & Martin, J.R. (1993). *Writing science: Literacy and discursive power*. Pittsburgh, PA: University of Pittsburgh Press.

Hanson, R., Prentice, W., Bartkowiak, M., Berthouex, S., Dreifuerst, L., Jacobson, C., & Welter, P. (1991). Reading/writing relationships: Implications for teachers. *Journal of the Wisconsin State Reading Association, 35*(1), 57–63.

Hayes, J.R., & Flower, L. (1980). Identifying the organization of writing processes. In L.W. Gregg & E.R. Steinberg (Eds.), *Cognitive processes in writing*. Hillsdale, NJ: Erlbaum.

Heath, S.B. (1983). *Ways with words: Language, life and work in communities and classrooms*. New York: Cambridge University Press.

Heath, S.B. (1988). Protean shapes in literacy events ever shifting oral and literate traditions. In E.R. Kintgen, B.M. Kroll, & M. Rose (Eds.), *Perspectives on literacy* (pp. 348–370). Carbondale, IL: Southern Illinois University Press.

Hiebert, E.H. (1991). Literacy contexts and literacy processes: Research directions. *Language Arts, 68*(2), 134–139.

Hillocks, G. (1972). *Alternatives in English*. Urbana, IL: ERIC.

Inhelder, B., & Piaget, J. (1958). *The growth of logical thinking from childhood to adolescence.* London: Routledge & Kegan Paul.

John-Steiner, V. (1995). Cognitive pluralism: A sociocultural approach. *Mind, Culture, and Activity, 2*(1), 2–11.

Kucer, S.B. (1987). The cognitive base of reading and writing. In J. Squire (Ed.), *The dynamics of language learning* (pp. 27–51). Urbana, IL: National Conference in Research in English.

Lakoff, G. (1971). On generative semantics. In D.D. Steinberg & L.A. Jakobovits (Eds.), *Semantics: An interdisciplinary reader in philosophy, linguistics, and psychology* (pp. 232–296). Cambridge, UK: Cambridge University Press.

Langer, J.A. (1984). Levels of questioning: An alternative view. In R. Freedle (Ed.), *Cognitive and linguistic analyses of standardized test performance.* Norwood, NJ: Ablex.

Langer, J.A. (1986a). *Children reading and writing: Structures and strategies.* Norwood, NJ: Ablex.

Langer, J.A. (1986b). Learning through writing: Study skills in the content areas. *Journal of Reading, 29,* 400–406.

Langer, J.A. (1987). *Language, literacy, and culture: Issues of society and schooling.* Norwood, NJ: Ablex.

Langer, J.A. (1995). *Envisioning literature: Literary understanding and literature instruction.* New York: Teachers College Press; Newark, DE: International Reading Association.

Langer, J.A. (1997). Thinking and doing literature: An 8-year study. *English Journal, 87*(2), 16–22.

Langer, J.A., & Allington, R. (1992). Curriculum research in writing and reading. In P.W. Jackson (Ed.), *Handbook of research on curriculum* (pp. 687–725). New York: Macmillan.

Langer, J.A., & Applebee, A.N. (1987). *How writing shapes thinking: A study of teaching and learning.* Urbana, IL: National Council of Teachers of English.

Leont'ev, A.N. (1981). The problem of activity in psychology. In J.V. Wertsch (Ed.), *The concept of activity in Soviet psychology* (pp. 37–71). Armonk, NY: Sharpe.

Loban, W. (1963). *The language of elementary school children (Research Report 1).* Urbana, IL: National Council of Teachers of English.

Marshall, J.D. (1987). The effects of writing on students' understanding of literary texts. *Research in the Teaching of English, 21*(1), 30–63.

McDermott, R.P. (1977). Social relations as context for learning in schools. *Harvard Educational Review, 47,* 198–213.

McGinley, W. (1992). The role of reading and writing while composing from sources. *Reading Research Quarterly, 27,* 226–248.

Minnich, E.K. (1990). *Transforming knowledge.* Philadelphia, PA: Temple University Press.

Mischler, E. (1979). Meaning in context: Is there any other kind? *Harvard Education Review, 49,* 1–19.

Newell, G.E. (1984). Learning from writing in two content areas: A case study/protocol analysis. *Research in the Teaching of English, 18,* 265–287.

Newell, G.E., & Winograd, P. (1989). The effects of writing on learning from expository text. *Written Communication*, 6(2), 196–217.

New London Group. (1996). A pedagogy of multiliteracies: Designing social futures. *Harvard Education Review*, 66(1), 60–92.

Petty, W.T. (1983). *A history of the National Conference on Research in English*. Urbana, IL: National Council of Teachers of English.

Purves, A.C. (1993). *Toward a revaluation of reader response and school literature* (Report Series 1.8). Albany, NY: National Research Center on the Teaching and Learning of Literature, University at Albany.

Rabinowitz, P., & Smith, M. (1997). *Authorizing readers*. New York: Teachers College Press.

Raphael, T.E., Kirschner, B.W., & Englert, C.S. (1988). Expository writing program: Making connections between reading and writing. *The Reading Teacher, 41*, 790–795.

Read, C.C. (1971). Pre-school children's knowledge of English phonology. *Harvard Educational Review, 41*, 1–34.

Rockhill, K. (1993). Gender, language, and the politics of literacy. In B. Street (Ed.), *Cross-cultural approaches to literacy* (pp. 156–175). New York: Cambridge University Press.

Rose, M. (1989). *Lives on the boundary*. New York: The Free Press.

Rubin, A., & Hansen, J. (1986). Reading and writing: How are the first two "R's" related? In J. Orasanu (Ed.), *Reading comprehension: From research to practice*. Hillsdale, NJ: Erlbaum.

Rumelhart, D.E. (1975). Notes on a schema for stories. In D.G. Bobrow & A.M. Collins (Eds.), *Representation and understanding: Studies in cognitive science*. New York: Academic Press.

Schank, R.C., & Abelson, R.P. (1977). *Scripts, plans, goals, and understanding*. New York: John Wiley & Sons

Scribner, S., & Cole, M. (1981). *The psychology of literacy*. Cambridge, MA: Harvard University Press.

Searle, J. (1969). *Speech acts: An essay on the philosophy of language*. London: Cambridge University Press.

Shanahan, T. (1984). The nature of the reading-writing relation: An exploratory multivariate analysis. *Journal of Educational Psychology*, 76(3), 466–477.

Shanahan, T. (1987). The shared knowledge of reading and writing. *Reading Psychology: An International Quarterly, 8*, 93–102.

Shanahan, T., & Lomax, R. (1986). An analysis and comparison of theoretical models of the reading-writing relationship. *Journal of Educational Psychology*, 78(2), 116–123.

Shuy, R. (1967). *Discovering American dialects*. Champaign, IL: National Council of Teachers of English.

Sinclair, J.M., & Coulthard, R.M. (1975). *Towards an analysis of discourse*. London: Oxford University Press.

Smith, F. (1971). *Understanding reading*. New York: Holt, Rinehart & Winston.

Smith, F. (1983). Reading like a writer. *Language Arts*, 60(5), 58–567.

Solsken, J.W. (1993). *Literacy, gender and work in families and school.* Norwood, NJ: Ablex.

Spiro, R.J., Bruce, B.C., & Brewer, W.F. (1980). *Theoretical issues in reading comprehension: Perspectives from cognitive psychology, linguistics, artificial intelligence and education.* Hillsdale, NJ: Erlbaum.

Spivey, N.N. (1990). Transforming texts: Constructive processes in reading and writing. *Written Communication, 7*(2), 256–287.

Spivey, N.N. & King, J.R. (1989). Readers as writers composing from sources. *Reading Research Quarterly, 24,* 7–26.

Squire, J.R. (1983). Composing and comprehending: Two sides of the same basic process. *Language Arts, 60*(5), 581–589.

Stein, V. (1990). Elaboration: Using what you know. In L. Flower, V. Stein, J. Ackerman, M.J. Kantz, K. McCormick, & W. Peck (Eds.), *Reading to write: Exploring a cognitive and social process.* New York: Oxford University Press.

Sternglass, M. (1987). Instructional implications of three conceptual models of reading writing relationships. *English Quarterly, 20*(3), 184–193.

Stotsky, S. (1983). Research on reading /writing relationships: A synthesis and suggested directions. *Language Arts, 60*(5), 627–642.

Street, B. (1984). *Literacy in theory and practice.* New York: Cambridge University Press.

Street, B. (1993). The new literacy studies, guest editorial. *Journal of Research in Reading, 16*(2), 81–97.

Stubbs, M. (1980). *Language and literacy: The socio-linguistics of reading and writing.* London: Routledge & Kegan Paul.

Teale, W.H., & Sulzby, E. (1986). Introduction: Emergent literacy as a perspective for examining how young children become writers and readers. In W.H. Teale & E. Sulzby (Eds.), *Emergent literacy: Writing and reading* (pp. vii–xxv). Norwood, NJ: Ablex.

Tierney, R.J. (1985). Reading writing relationships: A glimpse at some facets. *Reading Canada Lecture, 3*(2), 109–116.

Tierney, R.J. (1992). Ongoing research and new directions. In J.W. Irwin & M.A. Doyle (Eds.), *Reading/writing connections: Learning from research* (pp. 246–259). Newark, DE: International Reading Association.

Tierney, R.J., O'Flahaven, J.F., McGinley, W., & Soter A. (1989). The effects of reading and writing upon thinking critically. *Reading Research Quarterly, 24,* 134–173.

Tierney, R.J., & Pearson, P.D. (1983). Toward a composing model of reading. *Language Arts, 60*(5), 568–580.

Tulving, E. (1972). Episodic and semantic memory. In E. Tulving & W. Donaldson (Eds.), *Organization of memory* (pp. 382–404). New York: Academic Press.

Valencia, R.R. (Ed.). (1991). *Chicano school failure and success: Research and policy analysis for the 1990's.* London: Falmer Press.

Vygotsky, L.S. (1978). *Mind in society: The development of higher psychological processes.* (M. Cole, V. John-Steiner, S. Scribner, & E. Souberman, Eds. and Trans.). Cambridge, MA: Harvard University Press. (Original work published 1934)

Vygotsky, L.S. (1986). *Thought and language* (A. Kozalin, Trans.). Cambridge, MA: Harvard University Press. (original work published 1934)

Weber, R.M. (1991). Linguistic diversity and reading in American society. In R. Barr, M.L. Kamil, P. Mosenthal, & P.D. Pearson (Eds.), *Handbook of reading research* (Vol. 2, pp. 97–19). White Plains, NY: Longman.

Webster, L., & Ammon, P. (1994). Linking written language to cognitive development: Reading, writing, and concrete operations. *Research in the Teaching of English, 28*(1), 89–109.

Weir, R. (1962). *Language in the crib*. The Hague: Mouton.

Winograd, T. (1972). *Understanding natural language*. Edinburgh, Scotland: Edinburgh University Press.

Wittrock, M.C. (1983). Writing and the teaching of reading. *Language Arts, 60*(5), 600–606.

Wong-Fillmore, J. (1992). Against our best interest: The attempt to sabotage bilingual education. In J. Crawford (Ed.), *Language loyalties: A source book on the official English controversy* (pp. 648–685). Chicago: University of Chicago Press.

Bonnie B. Armbruster

University of Illinois at Urbana-Champaign

CHAPTER SIX

Responding to Informative Prose

For the sake of simplicity, *informative prose* is defined here as prose written to explain or convey information. Informative prose is known commonly as *nonfiction*; *exposition* and *expository text* are other synonyms. Informative prose constitutes much of what is read in the classroom, the workplace, and other walks of life. Written responses to informative prose can take the form of exposition, narration, persuasion, or poetry, and the responses can vary in length from a phrase or sentence to a book. The topic of responding to informative prose is potentially vast, although research on the topic is still rather limited. The research reviewed in this chapter has investigated primarily school-like informative prose (typically excerpts from textbooks or articles from magazines) with response types limited essentially to exposition ranging in length from a phrase to an essay or report.

Why is responding to informative text important? The past two decades have seen an increased interest in both practitioner and research communities about writing in response to informative prose. This interest is based on the assumption that writing facilitates thinking and learning. Writing has been touted as a "mode of learning" (Emig, 1977, p. 122), and "a powerful tool for the enhancement of thinking and learning" (Tierney & Shanahan, 1991, p. 272). The consensus in education about the value of writing is reflected in the following comment:

There is no question that students should write. Without exception, it seems, reports and studies dealing with educational quality in recent years have advocated more writing, at every phase of learning.... It seems inconceivable that any suggestion to have students write less would be taken seriously, so powerful is the current belief that composing lies at the center of learning. (Gage, 1986, p. 8)

This interest in what has been called "writing-to-learn" is reflected in K–12 classrooms in the movement toward whole language, integrated language arts, integrated curricula, and writing in the content areas. Similarly, colleges and universities have invested heavily in a movement toward writing across the curriculum (WAC). In the research community, too, writing-to-learn currently receives a great deal of attention. From his assessment of the trends in reading education through the ERIC/RCS database for educational research, Smith (1990) notes that "entries about writing as a response to reading, writing across the curriculum, and writing to learn indicate that *writing* may be the single most used term today in our professional discussions" (p. 680). Given the prevalence of writing-to-learn in the curriculum and in the profession of reading education, it is important to see what research has to say about it.

This chapter addresses three questions related to responding to informative prose: (1) What writing do students do in response to informative prose? (2) What effect does writing in response to informative prose have on learning? and (3) What methods have been developed to teach students to write in response to informative prose? Of course, these questions are not the only ones that could have been addressed. Given space limitations in this chapter, however, only these three questions will be discussed. In keeping with tradition, the final section of the chapter will address future directions for research on responding to informative prose.

What Writing Do Students Do in Response to Informative Prose?

Information about the writing that students do has come from two main sources: The National Study of Writing in the Secondary School (Applebee, 1984a) and reports from the National Assessments for Educational Progress (NAEP). This research reveals something about the amount and time middle school and high school students spend writing and the type of writing they do. Although these studies do not specifically investigate writing in response to informative prose, the results have implications for such writing.

Applebee (1984a) conducted a large-scale, multiyear investigation involving a U.S. national survey and case studies of secondary schools and individual students. Among his conclusions were the following:

1. Secondary students are not required to do much writing. Typical school writing assignments require a response of less than one paragraph, and students spend only about 3% of their high school time (in class or for homework) writing pieces that are a paragraph or longer in length.

2. The purpose of the writing assignments is usually to evaluate student learning. In their writing, students are expected to summarize or analyze material presented in a textbook or by a teacher rather than synthesize or extend learning for themselves.

Data from three NAEP studies over a 10-year period will be presented. The report on writing from the 1988 NAEP study (Applebee, Langer, Mullis, Jenkins, & Foertsch, 1990) addresses the questions of amount of writing, time spent writing, and type of writing done in grades 8 and 12. The research included surveys of eighth- and twelfth-grade students regarding writing in English or language arts class and of eighth-grade teachers of English or language arts. Less than two-thirds of eighth and twelfth graders reported being asked to write one or two paragraphs at least once a week, while only one-third claimed to write one- or two-page papers at least once a week. About half the twelfth-grade students reported writing no more than two school papers during the previous 6 weeks, while only about 20% reported writing five or more papers in that time frame. Information on time spent writing comes from surveys of eighth-grade teachers; over half (58%) of teachers reported that they expected their students to spend an hour or less on their writing assignments each week.

Regarding the type of writing, the NAEP survey categories that seem most closely associated with responding to informative text are (a) reports or summaries and (b) analytic or interpretive essays or themes. It seems likely that at least some of these reports, summaries, and essays were written in response to informative prose, probably textbooks. Sixty-one percent of eighth graders and 54% of twelfth graders claimed that reports or summaries were assigned at least once or twice a month. Forty-six percent of eighth graders and 60% of twelfth graders reported writing requiring analysis or interpretation at least once or twice a month.

The report on writing from the 1992 NAEP (Applebee, Langer, Mullis, Latham, & Gentile, 1994) indicates some change from the previous report. In 1992, students at both eighth- and twelfth-grade levels reported doing a somewhat greater amount of writing for their English or language arts classes. This change is particularly evident in the writing of longer pieces, with twelfth graders reporting a requirement to write three or more pages at least monthly, which increased rather dramatically from 40% in 1988 to 64% in 1992. Eighth-grade teachers reported a similar trend toward increased writing requirements. Teachers' responses to the question of how much time they expected students to spend each week on writing assignments also increased from the earlier report, with 64% of teachers reporting that they expected their students to spend 1 to 2 hours on their writing assignments. The 1992 reports also showed differences regarding types of writing assignments. In 1992, 78% of eighth graders and 82% of twelfth graders claimed to write reports or summaries at least monthly, while 66% of eighth graders and 84% of twelfth graders reported writing analytic or interpretive essays or themes at least monthly.

Student data from the 1998 NAEP writing assessment (http://nces.ed.gov/nationsreportcard/site/home.asp) are very similar to the 1992 data. (Unfortunately, 1998 data from teachers were not available at the time of writing.) In 1998, 61% of twelfth graders and 48% of eighth graders reported writing three or more pages at least monthly. Regarding type of writing, 81% of twelfth graders and 79% of eighth graders claimed to write reports or summaries at least monthly, while 85% of twelfth graders and 73% of eighth graders reported writing analytic or interpretive essays or themes at least monthly. The figure for analytic or interpretive writing by eighth graders represents a 7% increase over the1992 figure (from 66% to 73%).

Although the National Study of Writing and the NAEP studies focus on writing at the secondary level, there is evidence that the situation is similar in elementary schools (Applebee, 1984b). For example, Applebee says of elementary schools, "Students do little extended writing, and when they do, it tends to involve a process of recitation rather than reasoning" (1984b, p. 590). Likewise, from her review of studies of writing at the elementary level, Rosaen (1990) concludes that typical assignments require factual recall and reduce writing to "knowledge telling."

Reflecting on their several reports from the NAEP, Langer and Applebee (1987) summarize the situation well when they state, "Put simply, in the whole range of academic course work, American children do not write frequently enough, and the reading and writing tasks they are given do not require them to think deeply enough" (p. 4). However, Langer and Applebee reached that conclusion more than a decade ago. As the 1992 NAEP report suggests, the situation may be improving. (See also Applebee, Chapter Four in this volume.)

What Effect Does Writing in Response to Informative Prose Have on Learning?

There are many types of learning, to use Rumelhart and Norman's (1981) terms, ranging from *accretion* (the incorporation of new information into existing knowledge structures) to *knowledge restructuring* (the creation of new knowledge structures). As Schumacher and Nash (1991) observe, most studies of writing-to-learn have looked at learning as accretion, using predominantly reproductive measures of learning such as recall, short answer, or multiple-choice tasks. The majority of the research on writing-to-learn as accretion has investigated the effect of writing in response to single texts on learning information from that text. Other research has examined writing in response to multiple informative texts, often called discourse synthesis. Both research areas are summarized in this section.

Writing-to-Learn From Single Texts

Among the writing tasks associated with informative prose are traditional studying strategies such as question answering, notetaking, and summarizing. These strategies are designed specifically to increase memory for information contained in particular text selections. In the domain of studying strategies, the simplest form of writing is responding to adjunct or inserted questions accompanying informative prose. Adjunct questions are questions provided before or after the target text, while inserted questions are questions embedded within the target text. A vast amount of research has been conducted on adjunct and inserted questions, and several excellent reviews of this research exist (see Anderson & Biddle, 1975; Cook & Mayer, 1983; Faw & Waller, 1976). The research has revealed that different types of question answering strategies result in different learning outcomes. For example, of particular relevance here are the general findings that (a) writing in response to short answer questions is more effective than answering multiple choice questions, (b) writing answers is more effective than simply answering questions mentally, and (c) "meaningful" and "higher order" postquestions are more facilitative of recall than lower level questions in other positions relative to the text. In other words, in answering questions about text, some writing is better than none, and writing answers to questions requiring thought after reading is better than writing answers to factual questions during reading.

Another common studying strategy is notetaking, or writing information about a text in either verbatim or paraphrase form. Reviews of notetaking studies (see Ackerman, 1993; Alvermann & Moore, 1991; Anderson & Armbruster, 1984; Cook & Mayer, 1983) reveal mixed results, but generally support notetaking as an effective way to enhance learning accretion.

Summarizing is often included among recommended strategies to improve text comprehension and memory (see Pressley, Johnson, Symons, McGoldrick, & Kurita, 1989). However, few studies support summarizing as an effective studying strategy (Ackerman, 1993; Anderson & Armbruster, 1984) unless subjects have received some instruction in how to write summaries. A notable exception is a study by Wittrock and Alesandrini (1990) designed as one of many tests of Wittrock's well-known model of generative learning (see, for example, Wittrock, 1990). Briefly, Wittrock's model states that comprehension and learning are facilitated when learners generate two types of relationships: (1) among the ideas in the text, and (2) between the text and the learner's knowledge and experience.

In the Wittrock and Alesandrini (1990) study, college students studied a 50-paragraph informative text under one of three treatments—two that were designed to promote generative learning and one read-only control. In the first generative treatment, students were asked to write one- or two-sentence summaries after each paragraph, with the stipulation that the summaries should be in the student's own words, avoiding any terminology from the paragraph. Students in the second generative condition were asked to pause after each paragraph to write an analogy—a statement connecting the information just read with the learner's prior knowledge. Both of these treatments were designed to prompt the learner to make connections between text ideas and between the text and their prior knowledge and experience. On a test of recall of literal information, students who wrote summaries or analogies outperformed students who simply read and reread the text. These results support the notion that stimulating generative processes through activities such as writing paraphrase summaries or analogies can enhance learning, at least as assessed by a reproductive measure.

Adults in the Wittrock and Alesandrini study were able to write effective paragraph summaries with no more than a simple direction to write the summary in their own words. Children, however, do not summarize text effectively without instruction (see Brown & Day, 1983). If children receive instruction in how to write summaries, though, they can improve reproductive learning from reading informative prose. A number of studies have shown that with summarization training, children who summarize the text they read perform better than those who do not on two types of knowledge accretion measures: free recall and answering specific short answer or multiple choice questions (Armbruster, Anderson, & Ostertag, 1987; Bean & Steenwyk, 1984; Berkowitz, 1986; Brown, Day, & Jones, 1983; Rinehart, Stahl, & Erickson, 1986; Taylor, 1982; Taylor & Beach, 1984).

Also within the tradition of studying strategies is a study by Hayes (1987). High school students read and recalled a target text and then read a sequence of topically related passages while responding in writing to each by either paraphrasing, formulating questions, comparing and contrasting, or completing matching exercises or worksheets. Finally, students recalled the target text again. Both writing questions and writing compare-contrast statements resulted in the recall of more new information from the target text, while writing questions resulted in greater recall of more superordinate information. Hayes concluded that the type of written response to reading influences the degree of active manipulation and transformation of text material.

Armbruster

In sum, research on studying strategies involving writing has shown that writing that requires manipulation of the content of informative prose (for example, through generative strategies such as those posited by Wittrock) tends to improve later recall, but the type of improvement is closely related to the type of manipulation required by the writing task.

Studying strategies all involve relatively simple writing tasks. Other research has investigated the effect of more complex types of writing on learning by accretion. Most often, the more complex writing was an analytic essay written about single texts. Some key studies in this tradition are summarized in the following paragraphs.

Newell (1984) examined the effect of three types of "school writing tasks" (answering study questions, notetaking, and essay writing) on high school students' learning from science and social studies textbooks as measured by passage recall, organization of passage knowledge, and concept application. In an attempt to show relationships between the writing process and the outcome measures, Newell also investigated the operations of writing and learning that the subjects were able to verbalize during composing-aloud protocols. The results included the finding of differing profiles of writing process scores and differing learning outcomes, depending on the writing task. For example, essay writing, which was most effective in aiding passage recall (but was not effective on the other measures), also produced more writing and learning operations overall. Newell concluded that composing a coherent text (the analytic essay) involved more extensive thought and consideration of passage content than did the more fragmentary activities of notetaking and question answering.

Newell and Winograd (1989) report on an extended analysis of the data from Newell's (1984) earlier study. In this extension, the effects of essay writing, notetaking, and question answering on recall of specific text elements (content and relationships) and on recall of the theme were examined; in addition, the effects of prior passage-specific knowledge and level of importance of information in the passage were investigated. The results indicated that the effect of writing on learning is extremely complex and is influenced by factors such as prior knowledge and the level of information in the passage, as well as by the nature of the writing task. The study extended and corroborated Newell's earlier finding that analytic essay writing entails the complex manipulation of more passage information, thus resulting in greater recall of the passage and more coherent representations of the theme of the passage.

In a study by Durst (1989), high school students read two passages from a history textbook and wrote, while composing aloud, either a summary or analytic essay about each passage. The composing-aloud protocols were scored for various metacognitive strategies (or monitoring operations) and the time at which the monitoring occurred. The two writing tasks resulted in different types and amounts of monitoring operations. When writing analytic essays, students attended to figuring out the demands of the writing task, examining their own understanding of the content, and evaluating the effectiveness of their own writing strategies. When writing summaries, however, students did far less reflecting on content, monitoring their writing strategies, and regulating their thinking.

Tierney, Soter, O'Flahavan, and McGinley (1989) investigated the effects of writing with and without reading on critical thinking. College undergraduates were asked to explore a topic through one of various types of activities, including reading alone, writing alone, or either activity in combination with questions or a knowledge activation activity. After these activities, the students wrote a letter to the editor about the topic and responded to debriefing questions about the task. Three main findings emerged from the study. First, responses to the debriefing questions revealed that students used different reasoning operations depending on whether they were reading, writing, or answering questions. Second, students who both wrote and read appeared to be more engaged in the task of writing, including pursuing ideas, answering questions, and judging their own ideas and those of the author. Finally, students who wrote in conjunction with reading appeared to use more sophisticated reasoning operations than students who were engaged in only reading or writing.

Penrose (1992) asked college students to think aloud as they either wrote a report about or studied for a test on two informative articles. The think-aloud protocols were analyzed for cognitive operations, and all writing that the students did for either task was analyzed for "writing activity," or type of writing produced. Compared to the writing task, the studying task resulted in significantly higher scores on simple recall and on application items. The cognitive operations in which students engaged were found to vary with type of passage and with their interpretation of the task more than with the task itself. For example, students assumed a more active or constructive approach for the more abstract passage than for the fact-based passage. Also, students varied their writing activities and cognitive operations depending on how they interpreted the demands of the assigned task. By pointing out the important interactions of task, text, and learner variables, Penrose's study highlighted the complexity of the writing-learning connection.

In a study of writing and learning among secondary students (part of the larger study by Langer and Applebee reported in this chapter), Langer (1986) found that, compared to answering questions and notetaking, writing essays in conjunction with reading informative prose resulted in a focus on larger issues and topics, as reflected in her measure of topic-related knowledge. Langer concluded that essay writing encouraged students to engage in more conceptually complex thought than did the other types of writing. Langer and Applebee (1987) reported on a large-scale, 3-year project that investigated the relationship between writing and content learning in secondary schools. The part of the research of most concern here consisted of three experimental studies of learning from writing. The researchers collected think-aloud protocols as students completed a variety of classroom and experimental writing tasks. General conclusions from the three studies of learning from writing included the following:

1. "Writing assists learning" (p. 135). Writing activities of many kinds lead to better learning than activities involving reading only.
2. [W]riting is not writing is not writing" (p. 135). In other words, when students engage in different types of writing tasks, they focus on different kinds of information, they reflect about that information in different ways, and they acquire different amounts and kinds of knowledge.

In sum, the general conclusion from a growing number of research studies is that different types of writing tasks done in conjunction with reading informative prose involve different kinds of cognitive processes, thus resulting in different kinds of learning. The relationship among reading, writing, and learning, however, is extremely complex and is influenced not only by the type of writing task, but also by the type of prose read and by learner variables such as prior knowledge of the topic and interpretation of the writing task. (See Langer and Flihan, Chapter Five in this volume.)

Writing-to-Learn From Multiple Texts

Writing in response to multiple texts has been called *discourse synthesis*. As defined by Spivey and her colleagues (Spivey, 1990; Spivey & King, 1989), discourse synthesis is a type of reading-to-write that involves composing a new text by selecting, organizing, and connecting content from multiple sources. Discourse synthesis is an important "real world" writing task—for example, students are expected to write reports from multiple texts in school and employees frequently compose memos, reports, and other documents from diverse sources. Unfortunately, only two studies of discourse synthesis that are related to its effect on learning were identified.

In a study by Greene (1993), college students who enrolled in a course on European history were asked to write either an informational report or a problem-based essay using six sources in addition to their prior knowledge. Think-aloud protocols were collected on three occasions: (1) when the writing task was initially assigned; (2) when students were ready to begin a draft; and (3) immediately after they finished the writing task. In addition, pretests and immediate and delayed posttests of content knowledge were administered. Among the results of the study was the finding that both writing tasks resulted in improved learning about the given historical event. However, this study, unlike previously reviewed studies, did not show that differences between the two writing tasks differentially affected student learning. In a finding similar to Penrose's (1992) finding, though, students did interpret the tasks differently. Those asked to write reports tended to interpret the task as one requiring greater reliance on provided sources, while those writing problem-based essays believed they should integrate more prior knowledge with source information.

The second study did not directly examine student learning, but the data suggest that learning occurred. In order to investigate how various reading and writing activities interact over time in discourse synthesis, McGinley (1992) conducted a case study of seven college students as they composed a persuasive essay from two articles on the topic of mandatory drug testing in the workplace. Composing from sources was found to be a recursive process of reading, writing, and thinking. Students assumed various roles as readers and writers, including a reader of source material, a note writer and reader, and a writer and a reader of the essay. In debriefing interviews, students reported using reading and writing in various ways. For example, students reported reading source texts primarily to acquire new information, while they claimed that taking and reviewing notes helped them plan and organize their ideas. Overall, students reported that all the reading and writing activities they used helped them to transform the information in the source texts and to formulate the arguments to use in their persuasive essays. This result hints that students may have experienced knowledge restructuring as they composed a persuasive essay from multiple texts.

The research reviewed in this section has investigated the role that writing has on learning as accretion. This research has highlighted the very complex role that writing has on acquiring knowledge from informative prose. Writing-to-learn involves a complicated interaction among the writing task, the text or texts read, and learner variables such as prior topic knowledge and interpretation of task. As Schumacher and Nash (1991) have observed of research on writing-to-learn, "the recent research which has been done has resulted in a complex and somewhat confusing pattern of findings" (p. 68). More research is certainly needed, as will be pursued further in the final section of this chapter.

What Methods Have Been Developed to Teach Students to Write in Response to Informative Prose?

This section explores research on instructional methods designed to teach students to write in response to informative prose—both single texts and multiple texts. Instructional interventions regarding responding to single texts have focused almost exclusively on summarization.

As mentioned in the previous section, few studies support summarization as an effective studying strategy *unless* students received instruction in how to write summaries. In the research on summarization, several researchers had documented developmental differences in summarizing, in that older and more expert readers wrote more effective summaries than younger and less-skilled readers (see Brown & Day, 1983; Taylor, 1986;

Winograd, 1984). Therefore, following the tradition of expert-novice research, researchers began to teach the strategies used by older, more expert readers to younger and less skilled readers in an attempt to make novice summarizers more like expert summarizers.

A notable example is the work of Day (1980) and colleagues (Brown & Day, 1983; Brown, Day, & Jones, 1983), who have generated five summarization rules based on an earlier model (Kintsch & van Dijk, 1978): (1) delete redundant information; (2) delete unimportant information; (3) provide a general term to replace lists of specific items; (4) select a topic sentence if one is available in the text; and (5) invent a topic sentence if none is available. Brown and Day (1983) evaluated the summary writing of fifth, seventh, and tenth graders, as well as college students, on the basis of the five summarization rules and found developmental differences in the use of these rules. Day (1980) investigated the effect of teaching the rules to low-achieving community college students and found that the training dramatically improved the summary writing ability of these students. Then, Brown, Day, and Jones (1983) taught the rules to fifth-grade students. With the instruction, fifth graders equaled older students in ability to select the most important ideas for their summaries.

Many other attempts to teach students to summarize informative prose using Day's or similar rules followed, for example McNeil and Donant (1982), Bean and Steenwyk (1984), Hare and Borchardt (1984), and Rinehart, Stahl, and Erickson (1986). All studies found that careful instruction in summarization rules and strategies improved students' ability to write effective summaries.

Other methods of teaching students to compose summaries have been tested. For instance, Taylor and her colleagues (Taylor, 1982; Taylor & Beach, 1984; Taylor & Berkowitz, 1980) taught middle grade students to create hierarchical summaries of textbook prose. The hierarchical summarization task consists of first preparing a skeletal outline based on headings, subheadings, and paragraphs, and then writing a main idea statement for every point on the outline. In all studies, subjects who were trained to compose hierarchical summaries outperformed control groups on recall measures of textbook learning.

Another approach to teaching summarization was to make use of a visual representation of the structure of the text to be summarized.

Armbruster, Anderson, and Ostertag (1987) used such a visual representation to teach a problem-solution text structure to fifth graders who would encounter this structure often in reading their U.S. history textbooks. Students were taught to identify the text structure in existing text and to write summaries of the text that captured the text structure. The text structure/summarization instruction was effective in improving reading comprehension and summary writing. With regard to summary writing, structure-trained students included a significantly higher proportion of ideas rated as most important and fewer ideas rated as least important in their summaries of problem-solution passages than did untrained students. Structure-trained students also wrote summaries that were rated significantly higher on quality of writing, including organization, focus, and integration.

In sum, several studies have shown that well-designed instruction that helps students learn how to summarize informative prose has a positive effect not only on their ability to write effective summaries, but also on their comprehension and recall of text content.

Although there have been several studies conducted on summary composition for a single informative text, much less research has been done on methods to teach students to respond in writing to the reading of multiple texts, i.e., discourse synthesis. However, one notable example of such instruction is Raphael and Englert's Cognitive Strategy Instruction in Writing (CSIW) (Raphael & Englert, 1990; Raphael & Hiebert, 1996). The CSIW project grew out of the researchers' work in attempting to improve elementary students' reading and writing of informative prose, including content area textbooks and informational trade books. One purpose of CSIW is to provide instruction about expository text structures because "instruction in expository text structures might help students synthesize information from multiple sources, integrate their ideas in meaningful ways, avoid simply copying from published documents, and, in the end, produce a meaningful synthesis of information" (Raphael & Hiebert, 1996, p. 174). Instruction in text structure is accomplished through the use of "think sheets," which provide concrete reminders to students of strategies for effective reading and writing in the form of questions, statements, and graphic organizers. Among the think sheets developed over the years in CSIW are separate sheets for the various text structures of informative prose, such as explanation or compare-contrast. The think sheets are used to help students identify how authors use categories of information corresponding to text structures in their writing and therefore how the students might include categories of information and text structures in their own writing.

CSIW has been implemented in classrooms where students work collaboratively to frame questions about topics; collect information from various sources, including various forms of informative prose; organize the information; and write reports. The researchers claim that students learn principles of organizing information and the value of shared knowledge (Raphael & Hiebert, 1996), as well as many other attributes of good writers (Raphael & Englert, 1990).

Another notable attempt to teach discourse synthesis is found within the Concept-Oriented Reading Instruction (CORI) program at the University of Maryland (Guthrie et al., 1996; Guthrie, Van Meter, McCann, Anderson, & Alao, 1998). CORI is much broader in scope and intent than simply teaching students to write from multiple sources, but discourse synthesis is part of the program. CORI is a year-long instructional intervention designed to increase students' engagement in reading, writing, and science. The four phases of the program include

1. observe and personalize—students observe the environment and generate questions of personal interest to investigate;
2. search and retrieve—students are taught to use the library, find informational science trade books, and search these books for answers to their questions;
3. comprehend and integrate—students are taught to read, summarize, take notes, and reflect critically on the information they find in informational books;
4. communicate to others—students are taught to present the answers to the questions they are researching in many forms, including journals, written reports, class-authored books, and "informational stories."

CORI has been implemented and studied in 2 third- and 2 fifth-grade classrooms. Peformance measures of the effect of the intervention reveal that CORI students gained in the following strategies: searching multiple texts, representing knowledge, transferring concepts, comprehending informative prose, and interpreting narrative. The increased use of strategies was highly positively correlated with intrinsic motivations for literacy (Guthrie et al., 1996). In addition, CORI students exhibited greater conceptual learning (as measured by drawing and writing tasks) and higher literacy engagement (as measured by a task involving learning from multiple texts) (Guthrie et al., 1998).

Because CORI has so far been studied as a complete composite program, it is impossible at this point to determine whether individual components of the program, or the program as a whole, account for its effectiveness. Furthermore, the literature reveals little about the specifics of the instruction students received, other than that it involved "explicit instruction" (Guthrie et al., 1996, p. 313) and "direct strategy instruction" (Guthrie et al., 1998). Nonetheless, CORI is an example of a successful attempt to teach students how, among other things, to compose from multiple informative texts.

Future Directions

Based on this overview of research on responding to informative prose, at least the following recommendations seem warranted. Essentially, more research is needed on each of the areas reviewed in this chapter: (a) research on what writing students actually do in response to informative prose; (b) research on writing-to-learn, especially learning as knowledge restructuring; and (c) research on instruction designed to help students write in response to informative prose.

There is surprisingly little research on classroom practices regarding writing in response to informative prose. Applebee's (1984) exemplary study of writing in secondary classrooms is well over a decade old, and there has never been a comparable large-scale study of writing in elementary classrooms. Other large-scale research on writing in the classroom is done in conjunction with the NAEP, but this research has so far been limited to grades 8 and 12, and it does not specifically investigate writing in response to informative prose. Much research on classroom writing practices needs to be done—large- and small-scale, longitudinal and cross-sectional, and across all educational levels. (See also Applebee, Chapter Four in this volume.)

A second area of needed research is research on writing-to-learn. Albeit complex and confusing, research has revealed something about the role of writing in knowledge accretion. Obviously, much more research is needed to disentangle the effects of the multiple interacting variables (texts, tasks, and learner) and eliminate some of the confusion. For example, with regard to writing tasks, one area of possible research is to investigate writing other than the rather mundane expository writing that is usually done in response to informative prose. In publications directed at language arts and English teachers, interesting and creative ideas for writing activities are offered as suggestions for fostering writing in the classroom. For example, two of the suggestions I found in a recent article (Mitchell, 1996) that might be assigned after students read one or more pieces of informative prose include "Write a conversation between Booker T. Washington and W.E.B. DuBois" (p. 94), and "I am Joe's stomach. Here's what I experience" (p. 96). Responding to informative prose by composing narratives or poetry are other possibilities offered. It does not appear that research on the effect of these types of writing tasks on learning has been conducted to date.

Although more research is needed to clarify the role of writing in knowledge accretion, an even more pressing need, in my opinion, is research on the role of writing in restructuring knowledge. Schumacher and Nash (1991) offer many insightful suggestions about how researchers might approach the study of the effect of writing on restructuring knowledge—both the kinds of writing tasks that might engender knowledge restructuring as well as ways to measure knowledge restructuring. One writing task that might promote knowledge restructuring (and is consistent with Schumacher and Nash's suggestions) is discourse synthesis. Because writers engaged in discourse synthesis select, organize, and connect information from several source texts, they perform the kinds of cognitive operations and transformations that are presumed to underlie knowledge restructuring. However, very little research has been conducted on the role of discourse synthesis in creating new knowledge structures.

More research on how to teach writing-to-learn also is needed. Instructional studies are relatively sparse, yet U.S. national test data (e.g., Applebee et al., 1990, 1994) suggest that the need for instruction is great. Instructional research on writing-to-learn by accretion in ways other than summarizing would be useful, and again, given the importance of discourse synthesis and its possible role in knowledge restructuring, instruction on how to compose from multiple sources also would be welcome. Both research and practitioner communities would benefit from further research on existing programs such as CSIW and CORI, as well as research and development of other instructional programs that teach students how to write from several pieces of informative prose.

Without a doubt, writing in response to informative prose will continue to receive the attention of researchers and practitioners for some time to come.

References

Ackerman, J.M. (1993). The promise of writing to learn. *Written Communication, 10*, 334–370.

Alvermann, D.E., & Moore, D.W. (1991). Secondary school reading. In R. Barr, M.L. Kamil, P. Mosenthal, & P.D. Pearson (Eds.), *Handbook of reading research* (Vol. 2, pp. 951–983). White Plains, NY: Longman.

Anderson, R.C., & Biddle, W.B. (1975). On asking people questions about what they are reading. In G.H. Bower (Ed.), *Psychology of learning and motivation* (Vol. 9, pp. 89–132). New York: Academic Press.

Anderson, T.H., & Armbruster, B.B. (1984). Studying. In P.D. Pearson, R. Barr, M.L. Kamil, & P. Mosenthal (Eds.), *Handbook of reading research* (pp. 657–679). New York: Longman.

Applebee, A.N. (1984a). *Contexts for learning to write: Studies of secondary school instruction.* Norwood, NJ: Ablex.

Applebee, A.N. (1984b). Writing and reasoning. *Review of Educational Research, 54*, 577–596.

Applebee, A.N., Langer, J.A., Jenkins, L.B., Mullis, I.V.S., & Foertsch, M.A. (1990). *Learning to write in our nation's schools: Instruction and achievement in 1988 at grades 4, 8, and 12.* Princeton, NJ: Educational Testing Service.

Applebee, A.N., Langer, J.A., Mullis, I.V.S., Latham, A.S., & Gentile, C.A. (1994). *NAEP 1992 writing report card.* Princeton, NJ: Educational Testing Service.

Armbruster, B.B., Anderson, T.H., & Ostertag, J. (1987). Does text structure/summarization instruction facilitate learning from expository text? *Reading Research Quarterly, 22*, 331–346.

Baumann, J.F. (1984). The effectiveness of a direct instruction paradigm for teaching main idea comprehension. *Reading Research Quarterly, 20*, 92–115.

Bean, T.W., & Steenwyk, F.L. (1984). The effect of three forms of summarization instruction on sixth graders' summary writing and comprehension. *Journal of Reading Behavior, 16*, 297–306.

Berkowitz, S.J. (1986). Effects of instruction in text organization on sixth-grade students' memory for expository reading. *Reading Research Quarterly, 21*, 161–178.

Brown, A.L., & Day, J.D. (1983). Macrorules for summarizing texts: The development of expertise. *Journal of Verbal Learning and Verbal Behavior, 22*, 1–14.

Brown, A.L., Day, J.D., & Jones, R.S. (1983). The development of plans for summarizing texts. *Child Development, 54* , 968–979.

Cook, L.K., & Mayer, R.E. (1983). Reading strategies training for meaningful learning from prose. In M. Pressley & J. Levin (Eds.), *Cognitive strategy research: Educational applications* (pp. 87–131). New York: Springer-Verlag.

Day, J.D. (1980). *Training summarization skills: A comparison of teaching methods.* Unpublished doctoral dissertation, University of Illinois, Urbana-Champaign.

Durst, R.K. (1989). Monitoring processes in analytic and summary writing. *Written Communication, 6*, 340–363.

Emig, J. (1977, May). Writing as a mode of learning. *College Composition and Communication,* 122–127.

Faw, H.W., & Waller, T.G. (1976). Mathemagenic behaviors and efficiency in learning from prose. *Review of Educational Research, 46*, 691–720.

Gage, J.T. (1986) Why write? In A.R. Petrosky & D. Bartholomae, *The teaching of writing* (85th yearbook of the National Society for the Study of Education, pp. 8–29). Chicago: University of Chicago Press.

Greene, S. (1993). The role of task in the development of academic thinking through reading and writing in a college history course. *Research in the Teaching of English, 27*, 46–75.

Guthrie, J.T., Van Meter, P., McCann, A., Anderson, E., & Alao, S. (1998). Does Concept-Oriented Reading Instruction increase motivations, strategies, and conceptual learning from text? *Journal of Educational Psychology, 90*(2), 261–278.

Guthrie, J.T., Van Meter, P., McCann, A.D., Wigfield, A., Bennett, L., Poundstone, C.C., Rice, M.E., Faibisch, F.M., Hunt, B., & Mitchell, A.M. (1996). Growth of literacy engagement: Changes in motivations and strategies during Concept-Oriented Reading Instruction. *Reading Research Quarterly, 31*, 306–332.

Hare, V.C., & Borchardt, K.M. (1984). Direct instruction of summarization skills. *Reading Research Quarterly, 20*, 62–78.

Hayes, D.A. (1987). The potential for directing study in combined reading and writing activity. *Journal of Reading Behavior, 19*, 333–352.

Kintsch, W., & van Dijk, T.A. (1978). Toward a model of text comprehension and production. *Psychological Review, 85*, 363–394.

Langer, J.A. (1986). Learning through writing: Study skills in the content areas. *Journal of Reading, 29*, 400–406.

Langer, J.A., & Applebee, A.N. (1987). *How writing shapes thinking: A study of teaching and learning.* Urbana, IL: National Council of Teachers of English.

McNeil, J., & Donant, L. (1982). Summarization strategy for improving reading comprehension. In J.A. Niles & L.A. Harris (Eds.), *New inquiring in reading research and instruction* (pp. 215–219). Rochester, NY: National Reading Conference.

McGinley, W. (1992) The role of reading and writing while composing from sources. *Reading Research Quarterly, 27*, 226–247.

Mitchell, D. (1996). Writing to learn across the curriculum and the English teacher. *English Journal, 85*, 93–97.

Newell, G.E. (1984). Learning from writing in two content areas: A case study/protocol analysis. *Research in the Teaching of English, 18*, 265–287.

Newell, G.E., & Winograd, P. (1989). The effects of writing on learning from expository text. *Written Communication, 6*, 196–217.

Penrose, A.M. (1992). To write or not to write: Effects of task and task interpretation on learning through writing. *Written Communication, 9*, 465–500.

Pressley, M., Johnson, C.J., Symons, S., McGoldrick, J.A., & Kurita, J.A. (1989). Strategies that improve children's memory and comprehension of text. *The Elementary School Journal, 90*, 3–32.

Raphael, T.E., & Englert, C.S. (1990). Reading and writing: Partners in constructing meaning. *The Reading Teacher, 43*, 388–400.

Raphael, T.E., & Hiebert, E.H. (1996). *Creating an integrated approach to literacy instruction*. Fort Worth, TX: Harcourt Brace College Publishers.

Rinehart, S.D., Stahl, S.A., & Erickson, K.G. (1986). Some effects of summarization training on reading and studying. *Reading Research Quarterly, 21*, 422–438.

Rosaen, C.L. (1990). Improving writing opportunities in elementary classrooms. *The Elementary School Journal, 90*, 419–424.

Rumelhart, D.E., & Norman, D.A. (1981). Analogical processes in learning. In J.R. Anderson (Ed.), *Cognitive skills and their acquisition* (pp. 335–359). Hillsdale, NJ: Erlbaum.

Schumacher, G.M., & Nash, J.G. (1991). Conceptualizing and measuring knowledge change due to writing. *Research in the Teaching of English, 25*, 67–96.

Smith, C.B. (1990). Trends in reading/literacy instruction. *The Reading Teacher, 44*, 680.

Spivey, N.N. (1990). Transforming texts: Constructive processes in reading and writing. *Written Communication, 7*, 256–287.

Spivey, N.N., & King, J.R. (1989). Readers as writers composing from sources. *Reading Research Quarterly, 24*, 7–26.

Taylor, B.M. (1982). Text structure and children's comprehension and memory for expository material. *Journal of Educational Psychology, 74*, 323–340.

Taylor, B.M., & Beach, R.W. (1984). The effects of text structure instruction on middle-grade students' comprehension and production of expository text. *Reading Research Quarterly, 19*, 134–146.

Taylor, B.M., & Berkowitz, S. (1980). Facilitating children's comprehension of content area material. In M. Kamil & A. Moe (Eds.), *Perspectives on reading research and instruction* (pp. 64–68). Washington, DC: National Reading Conference.

Taylor, K. (1986). Summary writing by young children. *Reading Research Quarterly, 21*, 193–208.

Tierney, R.J., & Shanahan, T. (1991). Research on the reading-writing relationship: Interactions, transactions, and outcomes. In R. Barr, M.L. Kamil, P. Mosenthal, & P.D. Pearson (Eds.), *Handbook of reading research* (Vol. 2, pp. 246–280). White Plains, NY: Longman

Tierney, R.J., Soter, A., O'Flahavan, J.F., & McGinley, W. (1989). The effects of reading and writing upon thinking critically. *Reading Research Quarterly, 24*, 134–169.

Winograd, P. (1984). Strategic difficulties in summarizing texts. *Reading Research Quarterly, 19,* 404–425.

Wittrock, M.C. (1990). Generative processes of comprehension. *Educational Psychologist, 24,* 345–376.

Wittrock, M.C., & Alesandrini, K. (1990). Generation of summaries and analogies and analytic and holistic abilities. *American Educational Research Journal, 27,* 489–502.

PART THREE

DEVELOPMENT OF COMPETENCE

Dale D. Johnson
Louisiana Tech University

CHAPTER SEVEN

Just the Right Word: Vocabulary and Writing

The difference between the right word and the almost right word is really a large matter. It's the difference between lightning and the lightning bug. (Mark Twain, 1888)

Words serve different purposes when we read and when we write. A reader needs to recognize words and assign meanings to them; a writer must choose words to convey ideas. The reader decodes words into meanings, but the writer encodes ideas into words. Readers often get the sense of a word from the narrow or broad context in which it is found. The writer has the obligation to be more precise than a reader and must use the right word that will best transmit the intended meaning. The communication process is successful to the degree that the reader can approximate the same ideas the writer had in mind. It is not the words themselves that are so critical. Rather it is the rich reservoir of meaning underlying the words that counts. Words are simply summary symbols for concepts, labels that facilitate the communication of meanings.

The purpose of this chapter is to shed light on what we know about vocabulary, especially its importance to writing. Five sections are included. The first examines the notion of word by considering descriptions and examples of lexemes and other synonymous terms. The second section highlights vocabulary research conducted during the past century and features the classic Rinsland study (1945) of words used in children's writing. In the third section, the focus is on more recent vocabulary reports and compilations published during the past two decades. The next section discusses issues of vocabulary and writing and describes vocabulary resources available to writers. The final section gives classroom recommendations for educators who want to help budding writers expand their vocabularies and access the words they need.

Words

Vocabulary is the Everest of a language. There is no larger task than to look for order among the hundreds of thousands of words which comprise the lexicon. (Crystal, 1995, p. 117)

What is a word? The most recent edition of *The New Shorter Oxford English Dictionary* (Brown, 1993, pp. 3716–3717) requires four tightly packed, small-font columns to define *word*. *Webster's Elementary Dictionary* (1982), on the other hand, defines *word* simply as "a sound or combination of sounds that has meaning and is spoken by a human being" (p. 569). The first major computer analysis of a large corpus of English words found in natural printed language text used this definition of *word*: "a continuous string of letters, numerals, punctuation marks and other symbols uninterrupted by space…" (Kucera & Francis, 1967, p. xxi). Drum and Konopak (1987) state, "A word, an acoustic configuration of speech sounds and a written rendition (more or less) of these sounds, comes or is assigned to refer to things, events, and ideas arbitrarily" (p. 73). McArthur and McArthur (1996) posit eight kinds of words: orthographic, phonological, morphological, lexical, grammatical, onomastic, lexicographical, and statistical (pp. 1026–1027).

The lexicon of a language includes all the meaningful units of the language. Crystal (1995) has introduced the word *lexeme* (an abbreviation for *lexical item*) to handle all units of lexical meaning, and has identified three types of lexemes:

1. Base words or roots and their morphological inflections and derivations (for instance, *help, helps, helping, helpful, unhelpful*). The meaning of each derived word is dependent on the meaning of the base word.

2. Individual words, idioms, and slang terms (such as *vegetable, varnish, vacuum, a chip off the old block, the big house*). The individual words have meanings unpredictable by rules of English morphology. The intended meanings of the idiomatic and slang expressions are not the same as the combined meanings of the individual words. The entire expression has a unique meaning of its own in the same way as an individual word.

3. Multiword verbs (for example, *drink up, sit down, put up with*). Sometimes called *phrasal verbs*, each is a unique unit of meaning larger than a single word.

Pinker (1994) asserts that confusion about what a word is arises because the word *word* is not scientifically precise and refers to two types:

1. "Syntactic atoms" (p. 147) are words built out of parts using the rules of morphology, and they behave as the smallest, indivisible units of syntax. Included are noun forms (*guitarist, guitarists*), verb forms (*strum, strums, strummed, strumming*), derivational suffixes (*strummable*), compounds (*shoeshine, playpen, strum-pick*), prefixes (*understrumming, unacceptable*), and irregulars (*mouse-mice; child-children; sing, sang, sung*). Pinker's "syntactic atoms" are the same as Crystal's first type of lexeme, the morphologically derived words.

2. *Listemes* (a term coined by Di Sciullo & Williams, reported in Pinker, p. 142) are units of meaning to be rote-memorized. These are words that cannot be generated by morphological rules (*fudge, fancy*). Listemes cannot be produced mechanically from rules. Idioms also are considered listemes. Pinker says, "There is no way to predict the meaning of *kick the bucket, buy the farm, spill the beans, bite the bullet, …give up the ghost, hit the fan,* or *go bananas* from the meanings of their components…" (p. 148). Pinker observes that idioms must be memorized to be learned just as all other single-word listemes must be. Pinker's listemes parallel Crystal's second category of lexemes.

Crystal and Pinker both identify two types of lexemes or words: (1) morphological products created by application of various layers of morphological rules, and (2) listemes, which are pure symbols for meanings (words, idiomatic expressions, slang phrases) that, because they are morphologically unpredictable, must be memorized to be learned.

To these two types of lexical items, Crystal adds multiword verbs. It is this three-part definition of *lexeme* that underlies this chapter. Although *lexeme* is a more complete and embodying term for this three-part definition, *word*, of course, is the common term. Both will be used interchangeably in this chapter.

How Many Words Are There in English?

Estimates of the size of the English language lexicon vary widely depending on the word corpus analyzed. In an early examination of elementary school books, Thorndike (1936–1937) found more than 38,000 different words in use. Rinsland's (1945) study of children's writing samples revealed 25,632 different words used by children in grades 1–8. In Kucera and Francis's (1967) analysis of more than 1 million words of printed text across 15 adult genres, the researchers found 50,406 different words used. Carroll, Davies, and Richman (1971) identified 86,741 different words in their computer analysis of published school materials for grades 3–9. Both the Webster and the Oxford dictionaries now claim about 500,000 words, and because they include somewhat different listings, their combined lexicon might be closer to 750,000 words. A *Guide to the Oxford English Dictionary* (Berg, 1993) states that the dictionary has 290,500 different entries and with variant spellings, combinations, and derivations includes 616,500 word forms; it is acknowledged that "given that the research of English vocabulary extends to rapidly expanding technical and scientific fields, as well as to slang, jargon, and dialect, not even OED can hope to achieve total inclusiveness" (p. 4). The English language lexicon is far larger than that of other languages. Denning and Leben (1995) report that German has fewer than 200,000 words, French about 150,000, and Russian about 130,000.

Crystal (1995, p. 119) estimates that there also are a half-million abbreviations in English, many with clear lexical meanings. Add to the lexicon the scientific terms; idioms; established slang expressions; words used uniquely in such English-speaking nations as Nigeria, Singapore, and Kenya; and all the neologisms and slang expressions used but not yet recorded. Crystal speculates that a million different lexemes would be a conservative estimate and double that number might be more accurate. The English language, then, comprises a fluid lexicon of between 1 and 2 million lexemes—quite a resource from which a writer can choose just the right word!

How Did English Get So Many Words?

Many English lexemes have been in the language for more than 1,000 years, since the language's Anglo-Saxon beginnings. Included among these old words are some of today's most frequently occurring words (*in, love, drink, hand*). Numerous words have been "borrowed" from other languages, a practice that has gone on since the arrival of Christian missionaries in Saxony. Borrowing from foreign languages continues today. The words *mumps, slogan, ski, brat, mosquito, toboggan, tycoon, chocolate, caravan,* and *kindergarten* came to the English language from Iceland, Scotland, Norway, Ireland, Spain, Canada, China, France, Persia, and Germany, respectively. They are representative of the thousands of words that have been absorbed into the English lexicon from diverse lands and cultures.

Crystal (1995) states, "Most English vocabulary arises by making new lexemes out of old ones, either by adding an affix to previously existing forms, altering their word class, or combining them to produce compounds" (p. 128). An example of affixation includes *wise/unwise*, and an example of altering word class is *child/childlike*. *Flowerpot* and *boxcar* are examples of compound words. New words also are formed through blending (*channel/tunnel, chunnel*) and clipping (*influenza, flu*) existing words. Finally, new lexemes are being created continuously, especially in the sciences, technical fields, and professions such as teaching or law. It has been estimated, for example, that more than 1 million different insects inhabit our planet, each eventually needing at least one word. Everyday language usage continues to generate new words. Language buffs even use morphological rules to create new, bogus words:

accordionated: adj. being able to drive and refold a map at the same time.

elecelleration: n. the mistaken notion that the more one presses an elevator button the faster the elevator will arrive.

phonesia: n. the affliction of dialing a telephone number and forgetting whom you were calling just as someone answers.

How Many Words Do People Know?

No one knows for certain how many words people know. It all depends on what is counted as a word, the methodology used in counting or estimating word knowledge, and varying underlying assumptions about what "knowing a word" means.

Vocabulary researchers have ranged in their estimates of first-grade children's oral vocabulary size from 2,500 words (Dolch, 1936) to 25,000 words (Smith, 1941). Most recently, and perhaps most accurately, Clark (1993) estimated that "from the age of two on, children on average master around 10 new words a day to arrive at a vocabulary of about 14,000 words by age six" (p. 13). Chall (1987) estimates that first-grade children probably know about 6,000 words, and she differentiates between two kinds of vocabulary knowledge: words children know the meanings of and might use orally, and words recognized in print. She points out that it is not until about fourth grade that children can recognize in print 3,000 of the words they knew the meaning of in first grade.

Johnson and Johnson (1992) describe the four separate but overlapping components (production and reception; oral and written) of an individual's vocabulary, as shown in Figure 1. We produce or receive language that is oral or written.

Experience tells us that the oral vocabularies of preschool and early primary-grade children are much larger than their reading and writing vocabularies. A greater match between the oral and written vocabularies develops over time. Both Clark (1993) and Aitchison (1994) refer to the words that we know in the mind, but may not necessarily use, as our *mental lexicon*. For most adults it is likely true that the receptive word stores, oral and written, are larger than the pool of words actually produced in

Figure 1. Categories of Vocabulary
(see Johnson & Johnson, 1992, p. 213)

	Processes	
Capacity	Oral	Written
Receptive	Listening	Reading
Productive	Speaking	Writing

speaking and writing; we can understand more words when we hear or read them than we show an understanding of in our speaking and writing. In other words, at any stage of development, most of us know more words than we use. It probably also is true that most of us use more words in our writing than in our speaking (unless giving a prepared speech), because speaking is spontaneous, whereas most writing is not. When we write, we can take our time, think, and revise. Writers are more free to be risk-takers and use more uncommon words than speakers.

Crystal (1995) reports on a small study undertaken to estimate the relative size of adults' receptive and productive (he uses the terms *passive* and *active*) vocabularies. In discussing the discrepancies in the estimations of the size of an English speaker's vocabulary, he writes, "Apart from anything else, there must always be two totals when presenting the size of a person's vocabulary: one reflecting active vocabulary (lexemes actively used in speech or writing) and the other reflecting passive vocabulary (lexemes known but not used)" (p. 123). Crystal selected a sample of 1% of dictionary entry words. He asked three subjects to indicate for each word whether it was known well, known vaguely, or not known (passive vocabulary) and whether it was used often, occasionally, or never (active vocabulary). The subjects were an office secretary, a businesswoman who was an avid reader, and a university lecturer. Crystal's findings, which reveal that the subjects reported knowing the meanings of about 25% more words than they used in their speaking or writing, are shown in Figure 2.

Graves (1986) reviewed studies of vocabulary size conducted between 1891 and 1960 and found a range of estimates for university graduate students of 19,000 to 200,000 words. Nagy and Anderson (1984) estimated that high school graduates know 45,000 words; Pinker (1994) observed that 45,000 words are almost three times as many words as the 18,000 different words that Shakespeare used in writing all his works (p. 150).

Determining the size of the average English speaker's vocabulary never will be precise. There are too many variables and idiosyncrasies: What counts as a word? How do we know what is in someone's mental lexicon? What are our research methodologies? How accurate are our estimations? On top of these problems, thousands of common English words have more than one meaning. Johnson, Moe, and Baumann (1983) found 6,530 multiple-meaning words in their corpus of 9,000 words for elementary schools,

Figure 2. Active and Passive Vocabulary Size
(see Crystal, 1995, p. 123)

	Secretary	Businesswoman	Lecturer
Active (Productive)	31,500	63,000	56,250
Passive (Receptive)	38,300	73,350	76,250

72% of the entire corpus. Some polysemous words have only two or three meanings, but others have many. The word *set*, for example, in the *Oxford English Dictionary*, has 464 meanings, *run* has 396 meanings, and *go* has 368 meanings (Ash, 1995, p. 87). More than 50 years ago Rinsland (1945) acknowledged this problem for researchers who count words, when he decided to first complete the count of 6 million words and then start the count of meanings.

Vocabulary study is enormously complicated because words themselves are complicated. We do not know the precise number of lexemes in the language, but we do know that the number increases daily. We know that languages have more meanings than words, hence the abundance of words with multiple meanings. We do not know how many words the average English speaker knows, but we are certain that most individuals know many more words than they use in speaking or writing. We know that many words are very old; many have been borrowed from foreign languages; and most are generated as needed and are created morphologically. We know that large numbers of words are available to writers, either within a writer's inner language or between the covers of a rich array of vocabulary reference works.

Early Vocabulary Research

A word is not a crystal, transparent and unchanging, it is the skin of a living thought and may vary greatly in color and content according to the circumstance and time in which it is used. (Oliver Wendell Holmes, Jr., 1918)

Poets, songwriters, novelists, and journalists have been fascinated with words for centuries. Since the late 1800s, teachers, education researchers, textbook publishers, and psychologists also have displayed an interest in vocabulary study. Some of the greatest names in language research, such as Edward Thorndike, Ernest Horn, Henry Rinsland, and Edgar Dale, have undertaken large-scale studies designed to generate word lists.

Numerous vocabulary research investigations have been conducted during the past century. The fifth edition of *Bibliography of Vocabulary Studies* (Dale, Razik, & Petty, 1973) cites nearly 3,000 studies conducted between 1874 and 1972, and vocabulary study continued to hold strong interest throughout the 1970s and 1980s. Most early vocabulary research was of four types: the study of word knowledge as an indication of intelligence; the development of word lists; the improvement or enlargement of vocabulary; and the determination of textbook readability. Vocabulary-related research was a popular choice by established researchers and among many writers of masters theses and doctoral dissertations. Publication titles showed extensive research interest in the compilation of specialized word lists. Dissertations, theses, and articles reported the development of word lists from such topics as children's themes, health education, kindergarten speech, classroom films, musical words, radio vocabulary, comic strips, war words, and safety vocabulary. The famous list by Dolch, "The Combined Word List," was developed in 1927 and continues to be used by many teachers today.

Thorndike analyzed words found in general reading materials and ranked them on frequency of occurrence. This work led to the publication of the acclaimed *The Teacher's Word Book of 20,000 Words* (1931); a later study with Lorge was published as *The Teacher's Word Book of 30,000 Words* (1944). Thorndike's work was the standard vocabulary corpus until the publication of Kucera and Francis's computer analysis in 1967. An oft-cited study of the speaking vocabulary of primary-grade children was published by Murphy in 1957. It continued to be a benchmark of oral vocabulary until the publication of the computer analysis of 200,000 words of oral language used by first graders conducted by Moe, Hopkins, and Rush in 1982.

Of greater pertinence to this volume are three studies that created word lists from the written language of children and adults. Horn (1926) completed an analysis of the words adults use in their writing and published *A Basic Writing Vocabulary: 10,000 Words Most Commonly Used in Writing*. Rinsland's (1945) *A Basic Vocabulary of Elementary School Children* made a lasting contribution; Hillerich's *A Writing Vocabulary of Elementary Children* (1978) analyzed a smaller collection of words than

Rinsland examined but presented more current data. In the studies cited earlier, Thorndike and Lorge's corpus was 4½ million words, Horn's total was 5 million, and Rinsland's was 6 million; Hillerich's count was about 400,000 words.

Rinsland was the first researcher to broadly sample the writings of children in all elementary grades from across the United States. His study began in 1936 under a grant from the Works Projects Administration of Oklahoma. The study was designed to do what no other vocabulary research had done previously:

1. broadly sample children's writing;
2. gather continuous data for all eight grades;
3. provide raw frequencies for each word in each grade;
4. provide a ranked listing based on frequency; and
5. provide a comparable measure of frequencies across grades.

Rinsland's ultimate goal was to generate a scientifically determined basic vocabulary list that would be useful to the writers of school books. He contacted the administrators of 1,500 schools within all the geographic, economic, and social strata of the United States, requesting original and genuine materials written by children. He described the project and its value and asked that the writings include personal notes, stories, poems, compositions, exam papers, reports, and observations. A total of 708 schools (47%) responded, and "each paper was read by a number of experienced teachers familiar with children's work in the respective grades to determine authenticity or naturalness of the children's compositions" (1945, p. 7). To assure uniformity of treatment, nine rules for tabulation were established. Rinsland followed the Horn model wherein plurals, contractions, and other inflections, derivations, and abbreviations were each treated as a separate word because "children experience some difficulty in learning derivatives" (p. 8) and because "this list is to be used for teaching children" (p. 8). This practice by Rinsland tended to enlarge the total count. Another of Rinsland's tabulation rules, however, must have greatly reduced the size of the count: "Delete slang, provincialisms, colloquial expressions, as determined by the dictionary, as well as trade names and proper names of persons and places, except very well known terms" (p. 8). Tabulators also were instructed to delete "baby talk." All 6,012,359 words in the corpus were hand tabulated, recorded on large sheets of paper, entered in ledgers, and checked. (The reader is reminded that studies such as the Rinsland, Horn, and Thorndike works were undertaken before computers were available to facilitate data reduction. Recall, also, that Rinsland's study was begun in 1936 and the final report was published in 1945.)

The Rinsland team found 25,632 different words from the total sample of 6,012,359 words. Different words ranged from 5,099 in Grade 1 to 17,930 in Grade 8. Total words written ranged from 353,874 in Grade 1 to 1,088,343 in Grade 8. Older students obviously wrote more and used a greater quantity of different words than younger students, as would be expected. (As mentioned earlier, Rinsland discovered early in the tabulation process that a serious problem existed because English has so many multiple-meaning words. This problem exists with nearly all word-count studies. Each of the following uses of *back* has a completely different meaning: to *back a candidate*, to *back down the driveway*, to *back off*, or to *take something back*, yet word-count studies would list *back* as only one word. Textbook writers, teachers, and others who were interested in using words found in the productive vocabularies of school children, however, have realized the value of the compilation of words prepared by Rinsland.)

More recent computational analyses have become the standard sources of frequency-ranked words for researchers and others. Kucera and Francis (1967) analyzed a sample only one-sixth the size of the Rinsland sample. Theirs was a body of 1,014,232 words drawn from random samples of continuous discourse within 15 genres of written materials all published in a single calendar year. The researchers cautioned that multiple-meaning words were grouped together as the same word type. Kucera and Francis pointed out, "In the present state of the art a semantic count, even if desirable, is beyond the reach of computer technology. We can only advise the user of the word lists in this book to be aware of how homographs, variant spellings, and morphological variation may influence his conclusions" (p. xxi). The investigators found 50,406 different words in their corpus. Their report included both a ranked list based on frequency with the number of occurrences (for example, the word *the* is most frequent with 69,971 occurrences and many words occurred only once, such as *accordion, imprint, worsened*), and an alphabetical list of the 50,406 words.

Carroll, Davies, and Richman (1971) analyzed more than 5 million words of text taken from 1,045 publications intended for students in grades 3–9. The computer analysis identified 86,741 different words. Their report presented an alphabetical list of the words that included each word's frequency of occurrence within the grade level and subject matter of the materials sampled. For example, *tadpole* occurs most frequently in science materials and *take* is distributed across grades and subject matters. A ranked list of the words, with their frequency of occurrence, is included in their report. The researchers state that their list "does adequately represent a very important and distinctive section of our culture, namely, the printed language of the American elementary educational system" (p. xii). These researchers also cautioned that their study tabulated graphic words, so differences in meanings and functions were not discerned. Their purpose in compiling this "American school lexicon" was to produce a citation base for *The American Heritage School Dictionary*. Nonetheless, numerous writers and researchers have found their work a valued resource.

More Recent Interest in Vocabulary

Vigorous writing is concise. A sentence should contain no unnecessary words, a paragraph no unnecessary sentences, for the same reason that a drawing should have no unnecessary lines and a machine no unnecessary parts. This requires not that the writer make all his sentences short, or that he avoid all detail and treat his subjects only in outline, but that every word tell. (William Strunk, Jr., 1918)

The decade between 1978 and 1988 was one of intensified interest in vocabulary by education researchers and education writers. The principal focus of the work published during this period was the development of vocabulary as a way to improve reading comprehension. Four books, a themed journal issue, and numerous articles dealt with research procedures or instructional methodologies designed to examine or enhance vocabulary and comprehension. The first of these, *Teaching Reading Vocabulary* (Johnson & Pearson, 1978, 1984), began the vocabulary revival that came to characterize the decade. The presentation, exemplification, and advocacy of semantic mapping (webbing) and semantic feature analysis—two schema-based, concept-associational (instructional) strategies—is the major legacy of the 1984 work.

In 1986 the International Reading Association commissioned its first themed issues of two of its journals. The special issue of the *Journal of Reading* had vocabulary as its theme in recognition of the continuing vocabulary renaissance. Invited articles were contributed by such noted researchers as Patricia Anders, Camille Blachowicz, Michael Graves, Bonnie von Hoff Johnson, Joan Nelson-Herber, William Powell, Robert Ruddell, and Steven Stahl, among others. In the issue's introduction, the guest editor wrote:

> The decade of the 1980s could be characterized as the period of rediscovery of the importance of vocabulary instruction to reading comprehension. No longer satisfied with tabulations of word frequencies, reading researchers, theoreticians, and instructional designers have focused their attention on the acquisition and instruction of vocabulary. Convention presentations, journal articles, and book chapters which address the many considerations of vocabulary development are at an all time high. It is appropriate that the *Journal of Reading* devote an entire issue to this essential component of reading development. (Johnson, 1986, p. 580)

Topics in the vocabulary issue included instructional strategies, costs and benefits of various strategies, contributions of vocabulary to inferential comprehension, evaluation of vocabulary, principles of effective instruction, and eight others.

Marzano and Marzano (1988) in *A Cluster Approach to Elementary Vocabulary Instruction* and Nagy (1988) in *Teaching Vocabulary to Improve Reading Comprehension* presented somewhat opposing views about vocabulary acquisition. Nagy's work convincingly demonstrated the power of context and the benefits of wide reading for vocabulary development. Marzano and Marzano, acknowledging the contribution of wide reading to vocabulary growth, pointed out that direct instruction often is necessary for subject matter comprehension, or whenever context is insufficiently rich, to enable appropriate inferences about word meanings. (See also Hayes, Chapter One in this volume, and Applebee, Chapter Four in this volume.) A major contribution of the Marzano and Marzano volume is their use of semantic clusters, described later in this chapter.

McKeown and Curtis's (1987) "state-of-the-art" volume *The Nature of Vocabulary Acquisition* included chapters by such established vocabulary researchers as Isabel Beck, Jeanne Chall, Priscilla Drum, Patricia Herman, Joel Levin, William Nagy, and others. The editors asked contributors to address several questions in their chapters:

1. What does it mean to know the meaning of a word? How do individuals differ in what they know about word meanings?

2. How does knowledge of word meanings develop? How many word meanings are typically known by individuals at various ages?

3. What is the relationship between vocabulary knowledge and comprehension? What implications does this relationship have for the ways that growth in word knowledge can be promoted? (p. 2)

Unfortunately McKeown and Curtis did not prepare a concluding chapter that summarized, compared, and contrasted what their contributors said. The reader is left wondering about the editors' opinions and whether they thought their volume had brought readers any closer to the "powerful framework" for vocabulary study that they set out to find. Despite this omission, the book became the seminal vocabulary volume of the decade.

Four major vocabulary research compilations were published in the early 1990s. Two appeared as chapters in the *Handbook of Reading Research: Volume II* (Barr, Kamil, Mosenthal, & Pearson, 1991). The first of these was "Word Meanings" written by Anderson and Nagy (pp. 690–724), who challenged the standard theory of word meanings that held that words are made up of semantic features. They took the position that word meanings are inevitably context sensitive, and they faulted practices that encouraged reliance on dictionaries and glossaries as sources of word meanings. Anderson and Nagy decried the outdated practice of teaching lists of isolated, unrelated words. Their theoretical analysis gave solid scholarly support for their conclusion: "The most obvious implication of our analysis is as follows: For enhancement of children's vocabulary growth and development, there can be no substitute for voluminous experience with rich, natural language" (p. 722).

In the same volume, Beck and McKeown contributed a chapter titled "Conditions of Vocabulary Acquisition" (pp. 789–814). The chapter summarizes research on what it means to know a word (it usually is not all or nothing), the size and growth of vocabulary (estimates vary widely), vocabulary assessment (different types of measures yield different results), learning vocabulary through context (words are learned from context, but how?), and learning vocabulary through direct instruction (some strategies work, and some words must be taught directly). The authors concluded, "The body of research discussed here seems to indicate that the best way to reach this goal (i.e., vocabulary development) is to help students add to their repertoires both specific words and skills that promote independent learning of words, and also to provide opportunities for which words can be learned" (p. 810).

The Handbook of Research on Teaching the English Language Arts (Flood, Jensen, Lapp, & Squire) also published in 1991, included the chapter, "Research on Vocabulary Instruction: Ode to Voltaire" by Baumann and Kameenui (pp. 604–632). The authors directed the chapter toward reading-vocabulary instruction and its relationship to text comprehension. The summary listed what is known and not known about vocabulary. They recommended both teaching words directly and teaching strategies that enable individuals to acquire words on their own. They concluded their chapter with three suggested instructional objectives and the means to achieve them, but the authors acknowledged that their objectives and means were based as much on their intuitions as on hard data.

Martha Rapp Ruddell contributed the chapter "Vocabulary Knowledge and Comprehension: A Comprehension-Process View of Complex Literacy Relationships" to the fourth edition of Theoretical Models and Processes of Reading (Ruddell, Ruddell, & Singer, 1994, pp. 414–447). The author set out to develop a comprehension-process analysis of the vocabulary-comprehension relationship. She stated,

> I define comprehension, then, as a process in which the reader constructs meaning while, or after, interacting with text through the combination of prior knowledge and previous experience, information in text, the stance he or she takes in relationship to the text, and immediate, remembered, or anticipated social interactions and communication. (p. 415)

After reviewing vocabulary/comprehension research through this prism, Ruddell concluded that four factors influence how words are learned: prior knowledge of the reader, information available in text, reader stance, and social interactions (such as discussion or cooperative learning).

The 15-year period from the late 1970s until the early 1990s was one of strong interest in vocabulary. During this time educators became convinced that most words probably are learned from oral and written contexts—that is, through listening and reading. We learned that direct instruction can be effective in teaching specific words for specific purposes. We learned that direct instruction works best when learners have multiple exposures—concept-associational, contextual, and definitional—to the words to be learned. During this period, as during the earlier period of intense vocabulary activity reviewed previously, the emphasis was predominantly on reading vocabulary and learning words as a way to improve comprehension. Little work has been located pertaining to vocabulary and writing, the topic of the next section.

Vocabulary and Writing

Writers love words. And while some writers get excited over a particular pen or a more powerful word processing program, words remain the most important tool the writer has to work with.... A rich vocabulary allows a writer to get a richness of thought onto the paper. However, the writer's real pleasure comes not from using an exotic word but from using the right word. (Ralph Fletcher, 1993)

Writers with a purpose recognize the importance of words. In an article titled, "Dear Mrs. Roosevelt: Cries for Help from Depression Youth," Robert Cohen (1996, pp. 271–276) included letters written to First Lady Eleanor Roosevelt during the depths of the Great Depression. The following excerpt was the opening of a letter written by a 13-year-old Arkansas girl in the winter of 1936:

I am writing you for some of your old soiled dresses if you have any. I am a poor girl who has to stay out of school on account of dresses, and slips, and a coat. I am in the seventh grade in school but I have to stay out of school because I have not books or clothes to ware. I am in need of dresses and slips and a coat very bad. (p. 272)

An eleventh grader in Georgia wrote,

I wish to have my teeth attended to. I'm having a terrible time with two of my teeth.... My mouth gets sore and it hurts all the time. All my teeth are decayed except my front teeth and they are starting to decay. I can't have them fixed because my daddy hasn't the money to fix them and he only says teeth are supposed to come out sometime but this is all the teeth I'll ever have. I've shedded all the teeth I'm supposed to. (p. 272)

These letters are powerful not because their writers used exotic words, but rather because they used just the right words to describe the poignancy of their existences and the hope that Mrs. Roosevelt would help them.

In his contribution "The History of the Profession," Squire (1991, pp. 3–17), notes that textbooks dealing with writing instruction did not appear in U.S. schools until the early 19th century. He observes, "As recently as 25 years ago, half of the nation's high school teachers of English had not studied composition beyond freshman composition, and almost no elementary school teacher had formally studied language development or the teaching of writing" (p. 6). By 1992 all but 16% of eighth-grade teachers reported that they had received special training in teaching writing (Applebee, Langer, Mullis, Latham, & Gentile, 1994). Proponents of the recent emphasis on total writing process have urged that spelling, grammar, usage, and other skill instruction be embedded in the process. What seemed to be missing in the earlier grammar/usage approaches to writing and in the more recent writing process methodologies is any serious attention to word selection within writing development. The NAEP 1998 Writing Report Card for the Nation and States (Greenwald, Persky, Campbell, & Mazzeo, 1999) makes no specific mention of the role of vocabulary or word selection anywhere within its 213 pages.

Flower and Hayes (1994) have articulated a cognitive process theory of writing. In their model, they refer to three writing processes: planning, which includes goal setting and organizing; translating; and reviewing. Word selection comes into play during any of the three writing processes, and each word chosen is important. "As composing proceeds, a new element enters the task environment which places even more constraints upon what the writer can say. Just as a title constrains the content of a paper and a topic sentence shapes the options of a paragraph, each word in the growing text determines and limits the choices of what comes next" (p. 934) (see also Hayes, Chapter One in this volume). The New York Public Library Writer's Guide to Style and Usage (1994) puts it simply: "Good usage means using the right words at the right time for the right reasons" (p. 6).

Vocabulary is critical to writing; therefore, educators and researchers need to consider the following questions:

1. Because numerous words are learned through rich oral language interactions and through wide reading, should we be concerned about how writers select words from their receptive vocabularies to use in their writing?

2. How can we help students access their inner storehouses of words?

3. Should we teach words directly in an attempt to improve writing?

4. What roles can or should reference sources, including a thesaurus and specialized word books, play in writing development?

Duin and Graves (1986, 1987, 1988) conducted a series of studies designed to investigate the effect of teaching vocabulary during prewriting on students' use of the words in their writing and on the quality of that writing. In a *Reading Research Quarterly* article (1987), Duin and Graves reported teaching 13 carefully selected words related to the theme "Space" to seventh graders. In Treatment 1, the 13 words were given varied and deep instruction, which included questioning, discussing, recording, reading passages, using words in memos, noting words, keeping log books, and more for 6 days. Activities included both vocabulary and writing tasks. Treatment 2 was identical to Treatment 1, but omitted writing activities. Treatment 3 incorporated vocabulary instruction using worksheets. Results showed that Treatment 1 subjects did best, followed by Treatment 2. Treatment 3 did least well on posttests of vocabulary, judgments of writing quality, and measures of attitude toward the unit. The researchers concluded, "The central implication is that teaching a related set of words to students before they write an essay in which the words might be used can improve the quality of their essays" (p. 311). Given the small number of words (13), the one-grade sample (Grade 7) used in the study, and the labor-intensive experimental treatments (6 days), one might want to weigh the practicality and benefits of such instruction. The studies by Duin and Graves and two earlier researchers' reports that are too flawed and confounded to be included here, were the only reports of empirical research conducted on the effect of vocabulary instruction on writing located for this chapter.

Unless one is engaged in stream-of-consciousness writing, one writes for a purpose and with a particular audience in mind, both of which influence word selection. For example, scholarly writing involves appropriate technical jargon; fiction writing and songwriting sometimes have an affinity for slang; and descriptive writing dictates the use of colorful words. Menu writers occasionally use overblown descriptions such as "Fresh fruit salad—transported in a pineapple boat for the highest vibration and your transmutation, with yogurt on the side for accent or dressing sprinkled with coconut...$6.35" (reported by Dickson, 1990, pp. 137–138). People who write for comedians have other challenges. Even an ordinary grocery list requires careful word selection if someone other than the writer or an immediate family member is doing the shopping.

The name Roget has become synonymous with thesaurus, but Roget originally did not set out to create a thesaurus of words and their synonyms to aid speakers and writers. He was a medical doctor who engaged in a lifetime hobby of trying to organize and classify all human knowledge. Roget developed six main categories of such knowledge: abstract relations, space, the material world, the intellect, volition, and sentient and moral powers. He subclassified these six into 1,000 semantic subcategories that became sections of Roget's well-known thesaurus (1852). The work was revised and the index greatly enlarged in 1854, and since then many revisions, new editions, and adaptations have been published. Although a brilliant accomplishment, Roget's thesaurus never was found to be the easiest reference to use: "Many a frustrated writer, seeking help in Roget, has found himself wandering in a maze where each turn of thought promises to produce the desired synonym, although none of them does" (Laird & Lutz, p. v). The major problem was one of access because Roget's thesaurus was organized thematically, not alphabetically.

A second problem, and this might be true of all thesauri, has to do with the notion of synonymity. Strictly speaking, there are no synonyms with identical meanings. Words may mean nearly the same thing, but may differ either in frequency (compare *tie* with *tether*) distribution (synonymous technical jargon, *file* or *portfolio*, for example), and connotation (consider *lectern*, *rostrum*, *pulpit*) (Rodale, Urdang, & LaRoche, 1986).

Most modern thesauri are organized alphabetically, and for each entry word, the meanings, synonyms, related words, contrasting words, and antonyms often are included. Writers use thesauri to help them choose words of similar meaning, words stronger or weaker in force, words that are more formal or more folksy than the one in mind, idiomatic expressions that convey the same idea, or words that contrast or are opposite in meanings. A writer uses a thesaurus to avoid using the same word repetitively. A thesaurus is used when one is trying to find the exact word or one is trying to recall a word buried frustratingly in the back of one's mind. The thesaurus is an essential tool and constant companion of professional writers, and perhaps it ought to be essential for writers at all stages of development.

Thesauri are available for children and youth of all ages. *Words to Use* (Drysdale, 1974) is a children's thesaurus organized thematically in the same manner as Roget's original work. All the included words are clustered within six broad, color-coded categories: The World We Live In, Living Things, Being Alive, How We View the World, Living Together, and Words for Sentence Building. The subcategories (e.g., The Senses) and sub-subcategories (e.g., Hearing) are cleverly organized, illustrated, and displayed. The thesaurus includes an index and instruction on the use of a thesaurus. *Roget's Children's Thesaurus* (1994), intended for ages 8–12, and *Roget's Student Thesaurus* (1994), written for students ages 10–14, represent alphabetized thesauri. Included with entry words are the parts of speech, definitions, example sentences, synonyms, antonyms, and idioms. Some children's thesauri include other features such as word play, etymology, and writing tips, as well.

Another vocabulary resource organized in a way similar to Roget's thesaurus is found in *A Cluster Approach to Elementary Vocabulary Instruction* (Marzano & Marzano, 1988). Based on an analysis of more than 70,000 words commonly used in elementary school texts, the researchers organized words into semantic categories. They identified 61 "super clusters" (e.g., Occupations); 430 "clusters" (e.g., Outdoor Professions, Artists, Public Servants); and 1,500 "miniclusters" (e.g., Painters, Musicians). Within the miniclusters are the words with the closest semantic ties (e.g., *drummer, singer, violinist, composer*), although the words within a minicluster typically are not synonyms. An index is included in the volume's appendix. This work has the potential to be useful to student writers, particularly at the prewriting and composing stages of the writing process. Although these are just a few examples, there is no shortage of materials available for writers to use to find "just the right word" to express what they want to say.

Recommendations for the Classroom

How very commonly we hear it remarked that such and such thoughts are beyond the compass of words. I do not believe that any thought, properly so called, is out of the reach of language.... I have never had a thought which I could not set down in words. (Edgar Allan Poe, 1943)

The information in this chapter can be summarized simply: The English language has an enormous stock of lexemes, more than 2 million when we include lexical abbreviations and technical words. Lexemes include three types: words created through morphological rules, listemes and idioms, and multiword verbs. We have no definite idea of the size of anyone's vocabulary. Probably most children entering school have at least 14,000 words in their mental lexicons, and their vocabularies may have grown to 45,000 words or more by the time they leave high school. They have learned on average 10 words a day for 12 years. We realize that most individuals know more words than they use in their oral or written production. Very little research has been done relating vocabulary to writing.

From this review, the following guidelines are offered to those interested in helping young writers expand their vocabularies and use just the right words in their writing:

1. Involve students in rich oral language activities including conversations, discussions, debates, participating in and attending plays, listening to speeches, watching quality films and television programs.

2. Promote and enable wide reading, daily, of many genres of print, and have students engage in discussions of their current and previous readings.

3. Provide direct instruction with important words that might otherwise become stumbling blocks to students' writing. Strategies that include a combination of concept-associational, contextual, and definitional attention to the words hold the most promise.

4. When students engage in the writing process, encourage them to be active seekers of just the right words, especially during prewriting, composing, and revising. Encourage students to search their own mental lexicons and to use words they do not ordinarily use in their speaking or writing.

5. Teach students why, when, and how to use a thesaurus. Ideally each writer should have his or her own thesaurus. Familiarize students with larger thesauri and the variety of other word-finder books and resources available in the library, on CD-ROMs, and at pertinent Web sites. Encourage the regular use of the thesaurus when writing.

Words are both the windows through which we see the world, and the symbols that enable us to be understood by others. All humans are judged by the words they use. "To the imaginative writer, and especially to the poet, language is a medium for self-expression. Hard and unyielding up to a point, words can nonetheless be so manipulated as to bear the impress of a particular mind" (Bernard Groom, 1934).

References

Aitchison, J. (1994). *Words in the mind: An introduction to the mental lexicon* (2nd ed.). Oxford, UK: Blackwell.

Anderson, R.C., & Nagy, W.E. (1991). Word meanings. In R. Barr, M.L. Kamil, P. Mosenthal, & P.D. Pearson (Eds.), *Handbook of reading research: Volume II* (pp. 690–724). White Plains, NY: Longman.

Applebee, A.N., Langer, J.A., Mullis, I.V.S., Latham, A.S., & Gentile, C.A. (1994). *NAEP 1992 writing report card*. Washington, DC: U.S. Department of Education.

Ash, R. (1995). *The top 10 of everything*. London: Dorling Kindersley.

Barr, R., Kamil, M.L., Mosenthal, P., & Pearson, P.D. (Eds.). (1991). *Handbook of reading research (Volume II)*. New York: Longman.

Baumann, J.F., & Kameenui, E.J. (1991). Research on vocabulary instruction: Ode to Voltaire. In J. Flood, J.M. Jensen, D. Lapp, & J.R. Squire (Eds.), *Handbook of research on teaching the English language arts* (pp. 604–632). New York: Macmillan.

Beck, I., & McKeown, M. (1991). Conditions of vocabulary acquisition. In R. Barr, M.L. Kamil, P. Mosenthal, & P.D. Pearson (Eds.), *Handbook of reading research: Volume II* (pp. 789–814). White Plains, NY: Longman.

Berg, D.L. (1993). *A guide to the Oxford English dictionary*. Oxford, UK: Oxford University Press.

Brown, L. (Ed.). (1993). *The new shorter Oxford English dictionary* (Vols. 1–2). Oxford, UK: Clarendon Press.

Carroll, J.B., Davies, P., & Richman, B. (1971). *The American heritage word frequency book*. Boston: Houghton Mifflin.

Chall, J.S. (1987). Two vocabularies for reading: Recognition and meaning. In M.G. McKeown & M.E. Curtis (Eds.), *The nature of vocabulary acquisition* (pp. 7–17). Hillsdale, NJ: Erlbaum.

Clark, E. (1993). *The lexicon in acquisition.* Cambridge, UK: Cambridge University Press.

Cohen, R. (1996). Dear Mrs. Roosevelt: Cries for help from Depression youth. *Social Education, 60*(5), 271–276.

Crystal, D. (1995). *The Cambridge encyclopedia of the English language.* Cambridge, UK: Cambridge University Press.

Dale, E., Razik, T., & Petty, W. (1973). *Bibliography of vocabulary studies* (3rd ed.). Columbus, OH: The Ohio State University.

Denning, K., & Leben, W.R. (1995). *English vocabulary elements.* New York: Oxford University Press.

Dickson, P. (1990). *Slang! Topic-by-topic dictionary of American lingoes.* New York: Pocket Books.

Dolch, E.W. (1936). How much word knowledge do children bring to grade 1? *Elementary English Review, 13*, 177–183.

Drum, P.A., & Konopak, B.C. (1987). Learning word meanings from written context. In M.G. McKeown, & M.E. Curtis (Eds.), *The nature of vocabulary acquisition* (pp. 73–87). Hillsdale, NJ: Erlbaum.

Drysdale, P. (1974). *Words to use: A junior thesaurus.* New York: William H. Sadlier.

Duin, A.H., & Graves, M.F. (1986). Effects of vocabulary instruction used as prewriting technique. *Journal of Research and Development in Education, 20*, 7–13.

Duin, A.H., & Graves, M.F. (1987). Intensive vocabulary instruction as a prewriting technique. *Reading Research Quarterly, 22*(3), 311–330.

Duin, A.H., & Graves, M.F. (1988). Teaching vocabulary as a writing prompt. *Journal of Reading, 32*, 204–212.

Fletcher, R. (1993). *What a writer needs.* Portsmouth, NH: Heinemann.

Flood, J., Jensen, J.M., Lapp, D., & Squire, J.R. (Eds.). (1991). *Handbook of research on teaching the English language arts.* New York: Macmillan.

Flower, L., & Hayes, J.R. (1994). A cognitive process theory of writing. In R.B. Ruddell, M.R. Ruddell, & H. Singer (Eds.), *Theoretical models and processes of reading* (4th ed., pp. 928–950). Newark, DE: International Reading Association.

Gordon, C.J., Labercane, G.D., & McEachern, W.R. (Eds.). (1992). *Elementary reading: Process and practice.* Needham Heights, MA: Ginn Press.

Graves, M.F. (1986). Vocabulary learning and instruction. In E. Rothkopf (Ed.), *Review of research in education* (pp. 49–89). Washington, DC: American Educational Research Association.

Greenwald, E.A., Persky, H.R., Campbell, J.R., & Mazzeo, J. (1999). *The NAEP 1998 writing report card for the nation and the states.* Washington, DC: U.S. Department of Education, Office of Educational Research and Improvement.

Harris, T.L., & Hodges, R.E. (Eds.). (1995). *The literacy dictionary: The vocabulary of reading and writing.* Newark, DE: International Reading Association.

Hillerich, R.L. (1978). *A writing vocabulary of elementary children.* Springfield, IL: Charles C. Thomas.

Horn, E. (1926). A basic writing vocabulary: 10,000 words most commonly used in writing. *University of Iowa Monographs in Education* (First Series, No. 4).

Johnson, D.D. (Ed.). (1986). Vocabulary [Special issue]. *Journal of Reading, 29*(7).

Johnson, D.D., & Johnson, B.V. (1992). Vocabulary development. In C.J. Gordon, G.D. Labercane, & W.R. McEachern (Eds.), *Elementary reading: Process and practice* (pp. 212–226). Needham Heights, MA: Ginn Press.

Johnson, D.D., Moe, A.J., & Baumann, J.F. (1983). *The Ginn word book for teachers: A basic lexicon.* Lexington, MA: Ginn and Company.

Johnson, D.D., & Pearson, P.D. (1978). *Teaching reading vocabulary.* New York: Holt, Rinehart and Winston.

Johnson, D.D., & Pearson, P.D. (1984). *Teaching reading vocabulary* (2nd ed.). Fort Worth, TX: Holt, Rinehart and Winston.

Kucera, H., & Francis, W.N. (1967). *Computational analysis of present-day American English.* Providence, RI: Brown University Press.

Laird, C., & Lutz, W.D. (1985). *Webster's new world thesaurus.* New York: Simon & Schuster.

Marzano, R.J., & Marzano, J.S. (1988). *A cluster approach to elementary vocabulary instruction.* Newark, DE: International Reading Association.

McArthur, T., & McArthur, R. (Eds.). (1996). *The concise Oxford companion to the English language.* Oxford, UK: Oxford University Press.

McKeown, M.G., & Curtis, M.E. (Eds.). (1987). *The nature of vocabulary acquisition.* Hillsdale, NJ: Erlbaum.

Moe, A.J., Hopkins, C.J., & Rush, R.T. (1982). *The vocabulary of first-grade children.* Springfield, IL: Charles C. Thomas.

Murphy, H.A. (1957). Spontaneous speaking vocabulary of children in primary grades. *Journal of Education, 140,* 1–104.

Nagy, W.E. (1988). *Teaching vocabulary to improve reading comprehension.* Newark, DE: International Reading Association.

Nagy, W.E., & Anderson, R.C. (1984). How many words are there in printed school English? *Reading Research Quarterly, 19,* 304–330.

New York Public Library writer's guide to style and usage. (1994). New York: HarperCollins.

Pinker, S. (1994). *The language instinct: How the mind creates language.* New York: HarperPerennial.

Rinsland, H.D. (1945). *A basic vocabulary of elementary school children.* New York: Macmillan.

Rodale, J.I., Urdang, L., & LaRoche, N. (1986). *The synonym finder.* New York: Warner Books.

Roget, P.M. (1852). *Thesaurus of English words and phrases classified and arranged so as to facilitate the expression of ideas and assist in literary composition.* New York: Thomas Y. Crowell.

Roget's children's thesaurus (Rev. ed.). (1994). New York: HarperCollins.

Roget's student thesaurus (Rev. ed.). (1994). New York: HarperCollins.

Ruddell, M.R. (1994). Vocabulary knowledge and comprehension: A comprehension-process view of complex literacy relationships. In R.B. Ruddell, M.R. Ruddell, &

H. Singer (Eds.), *Theoretical models and processes of reading* (4th ed., pp. 414–447). Newark, DE: International Reading Association.

Ruddell, R.B., Ruddell, M.R., & Singer, H. (Eds.). (1994). *Theoretical models and processes of reading* (4th ed.). Newark, DE: International Reading Association.

Smith, M.K. (1941). Measurement of the size of general English vocabulary through the elementary grades and high school. *Genetic Psychological Monographs, 24,* 311–345.

Squire, J.R. (1991). The history of the profession. In J. Flood, J.M. Jensen, D. Lapp, & J.R. Squire (Eds.), *Handbook of research on teaching the English language arts* (pp. 3–17). New York: Macmillan.

Thorndike, E.L. (1931). *The teacher's word book of 20,000 words.* New York: Teachers College, Columbia University.

Thorndike, E.L. (1936–1937). The vocabulary of books for children in grades 3–8. *Teachers College Record, 38,* 196–205, 316–323, 416–429.

Thorndike, E.L., & Lorge, I. (1944). *The teacher's word book of 30,000 words.* New York: Teachers College, Columbia University.

Webster's elementary dictionary. (1982). Lexington, MA: Ginn and Company.

Richard E. Hodges

Professor Emeritus, University of Puget Sound

CHAPTER EIGHT

Mental Processes and the Conventions of Writing: Spelling, Punctuation, Handwriting

The process of writing most likely comes readily to those for whom this chapter is intended. As professionals and students, we have probably used untold reams of paper to engage in personal and public writing. With writing instrument in hand (or fingers on a computer keyboard), we have become accustomed to transposing thoughts into written language with little conscious reflection on the mental processes that spell our chosen words or that punctuate the text, including spaces between words, paragraph indentations, and needed capital letters. Nor do we customarily recall the neuromuscular processes that produce their written or typed forms; yet all the while we are mindful of the "slips of the pen" which occasionally occur. As well-educated, experienced adults we are, in short, informed written language users.

But, what about the novice writer for whom the challenge of learning the uses of written conventions is only beginning? What paths of understanding are traveled en route from novice to expert writer? And how do these pathways influence the acquisition of written conventions?

Margaret Snowling (1994) offers the following description of the process:

When young children first begin to write, the motor demands of the task are themselves challenging and a great deal of effort goes into the production of the first recognizable words. As well as coordinating their motor movements, children draw on the visual experience of printed words, they work out how to translate spoken words into written form and they learn about the convention that words are written from the left to the right with spaces in between. Considering the complexities of these various processes, it is not unreasonable to expect that it will take 4 to 5 years to master the basics of the [English] spelling system, and the task of learning exceptional spellings inevitably continues into adulthood. (p. 111)

Cast in this way, learning to spell and write in conformity with written English conventions are indeed challenging undertakings, even formidable for some young learners. Yet, most novice writers do become proficient users of these conventions. But what mental processes lead to success or account for failure? In search of an answer, scholars in some related disciplines devise theories and create models they believe will explain how these processes are learned and applied in the production of written language.

This chapter will examine, from the perspectives of four theoretical frameworks, how writers become conversant with and use the conventions of written English. First, it will briefly recount the historical development of English writing conventions in order to establish the prior conditions that have led to contemporary written usage. It will then examine how the various written convention processes are conceptualized in selected theoretical approaches, and, in doing so, we will find that orthographic conventions have garnered the most theoretical attention. Next, this chapter will propose that a common conceptual thread connects these respective models, which poses important implications for educational practice. Finally, it will venture that current rapid technological advances in written communication predict significant reformulations of writing conventions and their processes.

What are the conventions of written English? *Conventions* refers to the socially accepted graphical practices, arrived at by usage and agreement, that are used in the production of standard written English. These conventions include the prescriptive orthographic practices that constitute standard English spelling; punctuation, the standardized graphic symbols that mark the syntactic and semantic structures of sentences; and hand-writing and print conventions that distinguish English script. These three writing conventions—spelling, punctuation, handwriting and print—are, in Britain's National Curriculum, the "presentational skills" (http://easy web.easynet.co.uk/~fireflies/national-curriculum/engenner.html) that characterize standard written English.

Historical Context

The historical development of English written conventions informs contemporary usage by explaining why some components pose distinctive problems for writers—difficulties that interest scholars and other authorities who have raised important theoretical and practical questions about the processes of learning to write conventionally.

English Orthography

The modern English writing system began in the British Isles near the end of the 6th century A.D., with efforts by Roman and Irish missionaries to convert the Anglo-Saxons to Christianity. In order to spread written Scripture, the missionaries accommodated Irish forms of the Latin alphabet to spoken Anglo-Saxon, or Old English, adding four graphic symbols—ash **æ**, thorn **Þ**, eth **ð**, wynn **Ƿ**—to represent Anglo-Saxon speech sounds not provided for in the Latin alphabet. By the end of the 10th century, a reasonably stable system for writing Old English was in use (see Crystal, 1995; Scragg, 1974).

Several pivotal events had impact on the transformation of Old English orthography into its present Modern English form. One of these events took place in 1066 when the Norman French, led by William, Duke of Normandy, defeated Harold II at the Battle of Hastings. For nearly three centuries, French dominated as the language of the ruling class, markedly influencing spoken and written English, especially the lexicon, because of its uses in royal court, parliament, and law (Scragg, 1974). In addition, toward the end of this Middle English period, the vowel system of the spoken language began a transformation in which the pronunciations of thousands of words shifted away from their written forms, the so-called Great Vowel Shift.

The years 1500 to 1700, the Early Modern English period, were turbulent times for English orthography, presaged in 1476 by the establishment of the first printing press in Westminster by William Caxton. Books now could be disseminated from a single setting of type, bringing a level of stability to written English that handwritten manuscripts were unable to provide. With their presses, printers replaced scribes as artisans, arbiters, and caretakers of English spelling. In addition, the earlier part of this period marked a rebirth of classical studies in which Latin and Greek became the languages of scholarship. The result was a massive infusion of Latin and Greek words and their spellings into written English.

With the proliferation of printed materials and the imposition of prescriptive language standards, most present-day spelling conventions were secured by the close of the 17th century, only to become even more firmly entrenched in written usage with the publication of Samuel Johnson's *A Dictionary of the English Language* in 1755. Seventy-three years later, Noah Webster's *New American Dictionary of the English Language* established distinctions between British and American spelling conventions (for example, *labour-labor, theatre-theater*) that became permanent features of contemporary American English orthography. (For more on the historic development of English orthography, see Johnson, Chapter Seven in this volume.)

Punctuation

Punctuation is usually the last part of a writing system to become standardized and its conventions can vary widely within and among languages (see Bateson, 1983; Coulmas, 1996; Crystal, 1995; Parkes, 1993; Partridge, 1953). Present-day English punctuation evolved from early written Greek, in which words were not spatially separated, nor were punctuation marks used to indicate prosodic and grammatical features of a text. In those times, writing was meant to be read aloud. Gradually, graphic marks were added to text for purposes of rhetorical clarity in oral reading; for example, vertical lines to indicate when and how long to pause for breath.

With the inclusion of rhetorical markers, written texts became more "reader friendly" and the idea was bolstered that writing might also serve as silent speech. Isadore of Seville, a 7th-century theologian, observed, for instance, that written text made possible "conversation across time and space [for] letters have the power to convey to us silently the sayings of those who are absent" (cited by Manguel, 1996, p. 49). More graphic markers and print devices were devised by scribes to aid readers in gaining meaning from text—spaces between words, indentation, capitalization, and the use of "points," or punctuation marks, although not in any systematic way.

As with spelling, the invention of movable print provided a powerful catalyst for printers to codify punctuation usage, most notably in marking the grammatical and semantic senses of written text. As one 17th-century author advised, "Great care ought to bee [sic] had in writing, for the due observing of points: for, the neglect thereof wil [sic] pervert the sence [sic]" (Hodges, 1644). By the end of the 17th century, the graphic forms of punctuation marks were largely stabilized, although their respective uses continued to evolve, as, for example, apostrophes (Little, 1986) and commas.

Handwriting

Handwriting, "the tongue of the hand," (Abu Hayyan at-Tawhidi, 2 A.D., cited by Coulmas, 1996, p. 193) is a fairly recent occurrence for the general population (see Crystal, 1995; Gaur, 1992; Thornton, 1996). Up to the time of the invention of movable print in the 15th century, scribes, or copyists, were the principal transmitters of written language. For much of the literate world, readers read; they did not write. Those who did write were, for the most part, scholars, schoolmasters, and other professionals for whom writing was a practical art, as well as those for whom writing was a privilege of the upper class.

Because writing was not a school subject in 17th-century England nor in the American colonies, students (mostly boys) who learned to write did so under the tutelage of a private writing master (Monaghan, 1988). The growing demands of 18th-century commerce, however, hastened needs for writing. By the 19th century, being able to write was valued both as an indicator of literacy and for its aesthetic qualities in Spencerian and other elaborate forms of script (Thornton, 1996).

Established handwriting practices changed significantly around the beginning of the 20th century, influenced by the new science of behaviorism and its approach to scientific inquiry. Scholarly focus now turned to more practical ends—maximizing efficiency in producing written script stemming from the acquisition of the most efficient neuromuscular movements underlying its production. To the extent that handwriting instruction remains a formal part of school programs, it continues to reflect principles and practices developed early in the 20th century.

Models and Processes of Written English Conventions

As the foregoing summary suggests, the historical roots of orthography, handwriting, and punctuation collectively contribute to the complex relationships that form the conventions of written English. Of these conventions, the orthographic system has attracted the most scholarly attention generally because a basic command of the system is necessary in order to read and write. Unhappily for learners, however, accomplishing this goal is compounded by an apparent "quasi-regularity" of English orthography (Plaut, McClelland, Seidenberg, & Patterson, 1996).

Of the two processes—reading and writing—"spelling English is a considerably more troublesome task than reading it" (Barry, 1994, p. 30), primarily because of differences between the word processing demands each task requires. Simon and Simon (1973) point out that *reading* written English requires recognition strategies that will obtain enough information about a word to distinguish it from other words possible in a given context. Sometimes, context alone is sufficient, as in *Four score and seven* _____ *ago.* On the other hand, *spelling* written English requires recall strategies that elicit complete information about a word if it is to be produced correctly according to standard orthographic conventions.

Precisely because spelling English is both structurally complex and demanding of its users, researchers in a number of related fields of inquiry (such as cognitive science, neuropsychology, neurophysiology, educational psychology, and education) regard spelling processes as rich sources to probe for understanding how more general mental processes function. One of the principal objects of interest guiding these explorations is the spelling errors that writers make, because correctly spelled words do not illuminate whether rote memorization or the application of word knowledge produced them. Spelling errors, on the other hand, provide a means for probing underlying mental processes because the types of errors reveal clues about the sources and kinds of information writers use to spell words. As John Dryden (1678) stated, "Errors like straws upon the surface flow; he who would search for pearls must dive below" (cited by Hodges, 1991, p. 779).

Four contemporary theoretical models have been selected that differently formulate the mental processing involved in learning and using the conventions of writing, particularly spelling: *serial* models; *connectionist* models; *dual route* models; and *developmental stage* models. Following are brief descriptions of the origins and theoretical foundations of each model and some illustrations of supportive research for each.

Serial Models

Through much of the first half of the twentieth century, behaviorism prevailed as a theory and scientific movement that heavily impacted educational theory and practice. Objective, quantifiable observations became the tools of scientific inquiries into human behavior, behaviors that were perceived as the consequences of learned responses to environmental stimuli, as, for instance, spelling behavior.

In an ideal alphabetic orthography, Brander Matthews (1913) observes, "there shall be a single symbol for every sound and a single sound for every symbol, so that anyone seeing a word for the first time could not help knowing how to pronounce it and that anyone hearing it for the first time would know instantly how to spell it" (p. 292). For users of English orthography, however, the alphabetic principle seems a distant reality. Ernest Horn (1929), one of the twentieth century's prominent spelling researchers, addresses this orthographic dilemma by contending that each word to be learned is an individual spelling problem, some words more problematic than others. To illustrate, Horn claims that the word *circumference* can be spelled 396,900,000 ways by using the spellings of identical or similar sounds of words likely to be known by sixth-grade children. Learning to spell, he concludes, involves committing to memory the series of letters forming words, one word at a time. Thus, spelling behavior is, in effect, an outcome of serial learning.

In serial models of spelling behavior, letter frequencies, word frequencies, and word length are important factors that can affect both learning rate and accurate recall of the letter sequences of words committed to memory. Because they are observable, quantifiable evidence of the types of disruptions affecting the sequential spelling process, spelling errors provide useful data in accounting for breakdowns in serial processing due to these factors. In serial processing, spelling error types include letter *substitutions*, letter *omissions*, letter *distortions* (or reversals), and letter *additions*—the acronymic SODA errors (Spache, 1940).

A representative serial processing study is A.R. Jensen's 1962 investigation of the extent to which spelling errors are distributed in accordance with predictions based on the "serial position effect." That is, given words of equal length, letters are better remembered at the beginning (primacy effect) and at the end (recency effect) of words. Jensen collected the spelling errors made by college students in an experimental setting and plotted the errors on the basis of letter position in words. The graphs reflected a bow-shaped curve indicative of a serial position effect found in general serial learning tasks, thus supporting the idea that spelling is a serial learning process. Jensen's study was later replicated, producing essentially the same results. The investigators noted, however, that the shape of the curve is extremely sensitive to the scoring procedures used (Kooi, Schutz, & Baker, 1965).

The application of serial learning to spelling performance has waned in subsequent years as explanations have turned inward toward cognitive processing. Some serial learning proponents continue to raise theoretical challenges, however. Houghton, Glasspool, and Shallice (1994), for instance, contend that serial recall is central in all forms of spelling production—written, typed, and oral—because letters of words have to be recalled and produced in their proper order, regardless of medium. They describe two types of spelling errors: "competence" errors that result from attempting to spell inadequately learned words for which a writer has incomplete or inaccurate representations of written forms; and "performance" errors, resulting from breakdowns in the production process, errors that writers can detect and correct. Houghton et al. conclude that spelling processes are "parasitic" on more basic serial mechanisms.

In Wing and Baddeley's (1980) study of spelling errors in handwriting, serial processes perform key functions in writing words whose spellings are already known. They posit a "short-term memory buffer" in which words from memory are temporarily stored in anticipation of letter-by-letter writing. They describe two error types: "convention" errors, which are uncorrectable misspellings because the words' conventional spellings are unknown to the writer; and "slips," which are correctable misspellings attributed to carelessness or inattention.

Connectionist Models

Although behaviorist views of spelling had generally wide acceptance through the mid-twentieth century, they also had dissenters. F.P. Robinson (1940), for example, reviewed a small body of research in which children's misspellings pointed to elements of reasoning in their spelling production. With the upsurge of cognitive psychology in the 1960s, higher mental processes took center stage away from rote memory in spelling theories (Treiman, 1993), as exemplified by the 1980 publication, *Cognitive Processes in Spelling* (Frith, 1980).

The mid-twentieth century also witnessed the emergence of the field of cognitive science, in which researchers are interested in how knowledge is represented and processed in the mind. A primary research approach is the development of cognitive processing models that can be simulated with computers. Connectionist models serve this purpose.

Connectionist models presume that learning consists of building relationships among familiar elements of sensory and motor experiences, then linking these relationships with further experiences to form concepts—a "bottom-up" process (Adams, 1990, p. 196). In connectionist vernacular, connectionist models of cognition utilize neuron-like units, or nodes (Olson & Caramazza, 1994), in which information is stored and which, when activated, connect and interact to carry out mental operations, such as recognizing and pronouncing words or spelling them. Connectionist models also are called parallel distributed processing, or "PDP," models because sets of interactions can be activated at the same time.

In computer simulations, connections among nodes are assigned adjustable "weights" to reflect their relative statistical strengths in contributing to learning some cognitive activity (Plaut, McClelland, Seidenberg, & Patterson, 1996). In spelling, for example, word frequencies, ordinal relationships of letters in graphemes (e.g., *t* is the "stronger" letter in *th*), and regularity of phoneme-grapheme correspondences, among others, are factors that make relative contributions to learning the conventional spellings of words (Treiman, 1993). The quasi-regularity of English orthography makes the complexities of spelling processes particularly useful in testing connectionist models.

Connectionist models of spelling begin with an assumption that word spellings do not have local representations. Instead, information (such as

phonological, morphological, and orthographic information) that is needed to spell given words is stored as patterns of activation in sets of nodes
(Kreiner, 1992; Kreiner & Gough, 1990). No distinctions are made for
words whose spellings conform to orthographic rules and those that do not.
All words are processed in the same way within a single processing system
that takes into account the relative degrees of orthographic consistency
in the conventional spellings of words (Plaut et al., 1996).

A recent example of a connectionist spelling model is Olson and
Caramazzo's (1994) computer program, NETspell, which tests the power of
connectionist models to spell from dictation; that is, from phonological
representations to written ones. The program incorporates information
about the statistical distributions of phonemes in words in relation to
their graphemic correspondences. Weightings are manipulated to produce "phonologically plausible" spellings—words that a reader can correctly pronounce even though misspelled, as *zar* for *tsar*, but not *coshle* for
social, which violates spelling convention.

A test of NETspell produced an 80–83% success rate in generating
plausible spellings, but only after extensive manipulation. What the computer program lacked, the researchers concluded, was lexical content—
graphemic information, such as positional constraints, placed on
graphemic representations of the words being spelled. NETspell was also
unable to distinguish homophones because it lacked needed semantic and
grammatical information. Nor could it handle exceptional words such as
aisle whose conventional spellings cannot be achieved from phonological
information alone. The researchers, in effect, demonstrated that spelling
rules in the absence of word knowledge will not account for successful conventional spelling behavior.

Dual-Route Models

Connectionist models are designed to demonstrate the rule of
Occam's Razor—that the simpler of competing theories, such as a single-
process model of spelling production, is preferable to models that require
multiple processes to achieve the same end. Dual-route models, as their
name describes, refute this contention.

Dual-route models are especially prominent in studies of word recognition in reading. The question that these models try to answer is, How are

readers able to pronounce words they have not seen or whose spellings do not reflect phonology? When dual-route modeling is applied to spelling, however, an obverse question is asked, namely, How are spellers able to spell words correctly when they do not already know the spellings, or when conventional spellings do not reflect phonology? The theoretical assumption underlying both questions is that the mind stores lexical information in two separate locations: one a sublexical memory store of orthographic tactics (Cummings, 1988, p. 9) that associates phonemes with graphemes, and the other a rote visual memory store of the spellings of known words. Accordingly, spellers and readers have two routes available to them to retrieve stored information with which to spell words or to pronounce their graphic forms—one lexical and word-specific, the other sublexical and generative. In dual-route models, then, proficient spelling consists of the ability either to retrieve the spellings of known words or to assemble their conventionally spelled forms (see Barry, 1994; Plaut et al., 1996).

Dual-route models of spelling gain support from evidence gathered by cognitive neuropsychologists who delve into the nature of cognitive disorders that result from brain damage. Of special interest to dual-route proponents are insights gleaned from the spelling difficulties of patients with forms of acquired central dysgraphia—impairments of abilities to write. These patients display inabilities to process spellings through one of the dual routes, either lexical or generative. Patients for whom the lexical route seems impaired are generally unable to spell correctly from dictation known words of varying frequency and orthographic regularity. Patients for whom the generative, or phonological, route seems impaired, however, are unable to spell dictated nonwords with orthographically regular spellings (Seymour & Evans, 1994).

The spelling behaviors of dysgraphic subjects underscore a basic premise of dual-route theory, that learning and using English orthography involves the activation of parallel neural routes; one visual and word-specific, the other phonological, sublexical, and generative in spelling words. For dysgraphic persons, however, the spelling process is limited to the activation of a single neural route, resulting in severely limited spelling production.

How, then, does a dual-route model apply to normal spellers? To what extent is conventional spelling produced by actuating one or the other routes, one leading to orthographic word memory, the other to sublexical orthographic knowledge? What factors invoke the selection of one route over the other in spelling production? Or, do the two routes interact during the course of spelling? Such questions underlie much of the research aimed at testing the adequacy of dual-route modeling to account for spelling performance.

Kreiner (1992, 1996) proposes that two factors trigger the choice of routes experienced spellers follow—word familiarity (lexical memory) and polygraphy (multiple spellings of a phoneme). In his two-strategy model, both routes are invoked simultaneously, with one of the routes compensating for the other's weaknesses; word familiarity compensating for high polygraphy, and low polygraphy compensating for low word familiarity. In Kreiner's model, the extent of polygraphy of a word activates the choice of routes to follow. Other researchers (Kreiner & Gough, 1990; Perfetti, 1992; Sloboda, 1980) also highlight the importance of a lexical memory route in spelling, because orthographic rules alone will not provide conventional spellings of many words (see Hanna, Hanna, Hodges, & Rudorf, 1966). Perfetti (1992) suggests that, because of polygraphy, spelling presents a good test of the quality of word representations in memory.

A shortcoming of some dual-route models stems from narrow descriptions of the kinds of sublexical information the generative route is said to lead to, often learned phoneme-grapheme correspondences alone. As several studies indicate, however, additional sublexical units provide vital information for effective spelling performance.

Treiman (1992) has called attention to the neglect of dual-route models to link groups of phonemes with comparable groups of graphemes in the intrasyllabic structure of syllables—their onsets and rimes (such as *sl-* [onset] and *-ip* [rime] of *slip*). She also observes that, for beginning spellers, the phonetic complexity of some onset consonant clusters, such as *sl-*, can intensify learning the spelling of words containing them. Treiman, however, also points out that rimes are the sublexical structures that give rise to the familiar phonograms and word families of reading instruction. Goswami (1988) and Goswami and Bryant (1992) show that the alliterative properties of onsets (such as *pl-* in *place, please, plan, plop*) and rimes that produce rhyming words (such as *-ay* in *pay, day, say, away*) make it possible for children to categorize words in terms of phonological similarities that contribute to the development of analogical spelling strategies.

Ehri's foundational research into the role that word knowledge plays in spelling and reading also delineates the intimate relationship that exists between phonology and print—that printed words are, as she describes, "visual phonology" (Ehri, 1994, p. 349). She extends the repertoire of sublexical word knowledge to include familiarity with spelling patterns across words, orthographic tactical rules, and root and affix spellings, all of which provide orthographic information spellers can use to form analogies to the spellings of known words when attempting to spell unfamiliar ones (Ehri, 1992b).

Studies of English orthographic structure also have established that, when phoneme-grapheme relationships are analyzed in larger sublexical environments, increasingly stable orthographic patterns are found (see Albrow, 1972; Carney, 1994; Cummings, 1988; Hanna et al., 1966; Venezky, 1970, 1981, for various interpretations). Thus, learning how sublexical units affect orthographic patterning is a fundamental process in the development of orthographic word knowledge (Ehri, 1991, 1992b; Goswami, 1988; Goswami & Bryant, 1990; Kreiner, 1996; Treiman, 1992, 1994).

Snowling (1994) is one of a small number of scholars who addresses the complex challenges that confront novice writers as they cope with the various conventions of writing. She delineates why it takes many years for most spellers to become proficient users of English orthography. And she faults dual-route models that neglect the interdependent relationships between lexical and phonological processes in learning to spell. Treiman (1993), in turn, maintains that the ultimate test of dual-route models that attempt to explain how spelling is learned depends on the models' application to real-life settings, not experimental conditions, and which developmental stage the models address.

Developmental Stage Models

Unlike connectionist models and some dual-route models, in which no distinction is made between the cognitive processing of adults and children, developmental stage theory holds that knowledge construction is a differential, hierarchical process, growing out of cultural experience and distinguished in terms of invariant, qualitatively different stages of cognitive maturation. Inquiries into how knowledge is constructed concerning the conventions of writing fall naturally into the realm of developmental stage theory.

One of the pioneering studies of the developmental roots of written language acquisition was conducted by Ferreiro and Teberosky (1982) who, within a Piagetian framework, drew a vibrant picture of a few 4- to 6-year-old Argentinean children coming to grips with the conventions of written language in the initial stages of learning to read and write. Although they focused mostly on learning to read and to spell, this study is one of the few investigations that encompasses handwriting and punctuation in a broader context of writing conventions. Ferreiro and Teberosky emphasize the importance of adult models for novice writers because "individuals cannot discover on their own certain conventions of the written language system. This kind of knowledge is transmitted socially by those who value it" (p. 269). They counsel against the theoretical pitfalls of "developing a one-sided view of written language development by overemphasizing reading [comprehension] and minimizing the importance of the production of written text" (pp. 276–277).

Charles Read's research into preschoolers' creative unconventional spellings is arguably the pioneering early investigation of learning to spell from a developmental perspective. From his studies, Read ascertained that young children from the outset bring to bear emerging knowledge of relationships between phonology and print in their spelling efforts (see Read, 1971, 1975, 1986). Other researchers have since extended and refined the qualitative changes that take place in children's construction of orthographic knowledge as a consequence of maturation and experience. Among productive contributors have been Edmund Henderson and his students at the University of Virginia (see, for example, Gentry, 1978, 1982; Henderson & Beers, 1980; Morris, 1980; Templeton & Bear, 1992; Zutell, 1979). The core concept of the Virginia group's developmental spelling model is that spelling proficiency is a function of word knowledge that grows incrementally through a series of stages that the study defines according to levels of spelling ability (see Templeton & Bear, 1992). (For more on children's development of orthographic knowledge, see Johnson, Chapter Seven in this volume.)

Although many scholars now generally accept the idea of a sequential development of orthographic knowledge, some reject the notion of unrelenting movement through rigid spelling stages that build incrementally toward conventional spelling. They view spelling ability in its genesis, arising from interactions among children's budding concepts of phonology, orthography, and words (see Ehri, 1991; Goswami & Bryant, 1990; Snowling, 1994; Treiman, 1993, 1994; and Schickedanz, Chapter Three in this volume).

Children's spelling errors are regarded as especially rich indicators of the kinds of mental processing novice writers use at various developmental stages. The interpretation of spelling errors from a developmental perspective also points to fundamental theoretical differences with other spelling models. The misspelling *gril* for *girl*, for instance, would be construed in a serial model as a reversal error. In a developmental stage framework, however, *gril* is regarded as a plausible misspelling of the phonological form /gərl/ commonly made by novice writers in an early stage of the growth of orthographic knowledge.

Treiman (1993, 1994) describes spelling development as phase-like rather than stage-like, with emergent phonological, orthographic, and lexical knowledge variously emphasized by novice writers who are en route to spelling proficiency. For Ehri (1991), reading and spelling are dynamically interactive. Using dual-route theory as a framework, she shows how memories of discrete word spellings develop alongside and in conjunction with growing orthographic knowledge. She regards children's misspellings as representations of assembled, or generated, spellings of words not yet stored in memory.

Goswami and Bryant (1990) find fault with developmental stage models that do not account for novices' early uses of analogy as a spelling-reading strategy. In addition, they maintain that developmental models not only need to describe the characteristic forms of developmental changes, but also the conditions causing the changes. Goswami and Bryant's model specifies three causal factors that can explain individual and qualitative differences in children's progress in learning to read and spell: (1) phonological skills that are necessary for preschoolers to identify rhyme and alliteration patterns (and which make possible the use of analogy among words as a spelling strategy); (2) instruction in identifying phonemes; and (3) the reciprocal influences of reading and spelling.

Snowling (1994) takes issue with standard developmental stage models that neglect the range of difficulties children face in moving toward proficient spelling. She argues that spelling development needs to be cast in terms of the processing demands made on young learners rather than in terms of stage-like developmental changes, which, she argues, oversimplify phonological spelling processes. In her model, children's imperfect phonetic renderings of standard spellings establish a phonological framework in which orthographic information about words, word fragments, and spelling patterns can be organized. This framework directs children's attention when reading to the diversity of ways in which phonemes, rimes, and other sublexical units are represented orthographically. Snowling contends that children's reading skills place an upper limit on individual spelling ability, because only rarely is reading ability exceeded by spelling proficiency.

A basic insight emerges from developmental spelling research: that spelling and reading share a common component—orthographic word knowledge—that develops from children's experiences in putting words into print and reading them. The interactions between these processes foster further development of tacit understandings of orthographic conventions and their roles in reading and writing.

Punctuation in Models of Writing Conventions

Punctuation also is a system of graphic conventions, one that shapes the prosodic, syntactic, and semantic flow of written text. For experienced readers, punctuation usually resides quietly in print, implicitly drawn from in rendering meaning from text. For writers, however, the punctuation system can be both complex and troublesome to master. As described earlier, one reason for difficulties in learning the system stems from the unstable usage practices of some punctuation elements, such as commas and apostrophes (Little, 1986). A second reason is due to the multiple functions of certain punctuation marks, such as periods (or full stops) that close sentences and abbreviations, capital letters that start sentences and proper nouns, and question marks and exclamation marks that signal both prosody and syntax (Crystal, 1987, 1995; Nunberg, 1990). The unconventional punctuation of writers of any age provides informative insights into their perceptions of the boundaries, syntax, and meanings of sentences (Shaughnessy, 1977, p. 18).

With few exceptions, studies of how novice writers learn about the punctuation system and its uses are conducted within a developmental stage framework. Relative to the numerous investigations of spelling development, however, research has been sparse concerning punctuation development. Representative of earlier developmental research into children's growing understandings of punctuation conventions is the aforementioned work of Ferreiro and Teberosky (1983), and that of Edelsky (1983), and Cordiero, Giacobbes, and Cazden (1983). These studies portray the gradual, often erratic, struggles that novice writers encounter in their pursuits toward understanding how conventional punctuation works in print. In a later study, Wilde (1987, 1992) followed the spelling and punctuation development of 6 third- and fourth-grade Native American children over a 2-year period. Her observations of these young writers led her to conclude that learning conventional punctuation is appreciably more difficult than learning conventional spelling.

One movement toward redressing of research into punctuation development has been the formation in 1993 of The Punctuation Project housed at Manchester Metropolitan University in England. A topical publication under the project directors' editorship brings together several papers that examine how children and adults develop conceptual understandings of the nature and uses of punctuation (Hall & Robinson, 1996).

Handwriting in Models of Writing Conventions

Models of spelling and punctuation emerge with shifting theoretical conceptions of cognition and learning. Contemporary models of handwriting development, however, remain largely reminiscent of late nineteenth- and early twentieth-century behaviorist views in which automatic handwriting resulted from neuromuscular connections, motor learning, and habit formation (Thornton, 1996).

Several prominent scholars of the early 1900s studied handwriting, among them Charles Judd and Edward Thorndike. The University of Chicago's Frank Freeman, however, was especially influential in charting new directions for handwriting instruction in schools. Using a stopwatch, movie camera, and a device strapped to a writer's hand that recorded movements, he calculated what he considered were the best "rhythmic" movements needed to produce legible handwriting, legibility being gauged by uniformity of slant, alignment, quality of line or stroke, letter formation, and spacing. Freeman reported his findings and their instructional implications in his eventful book, *The Teaching of Handwriting* (1914). Freeman's handwriting model became a mainstay of handwriting curricula in schools, especially because it allowed for the accommodation in handwriting instruction for individual physiological variation and maturational development (Thornton, 1996).

Maturation and neurophysiology have continued to be regarded as critical components of learning to write legibly, although now set within a developmental framework and closely related to spelling development. In this context, learning to write begins as a kind of global representation of meaning, in imitation of environmental examples such as adult writing (Ferreiro & Teberosky, 1982; Heald-Taylor, 1984). Writing imposes severe motor demands on young learners (Snowling, 1994) and appears to follow a common developmental path for children learning to write with an alphabetic orthography. The writing sequence flows from initial scribbling into drawing, and moves on through production of rudimentary letter shapes, conventional letters, letter strings, invented spellings, and culminates in the production of conventional spellings written with conventional script (Sulzby, 1991).

Once basic literacy is established, writing increasingly becomes an automatic, habituated part of word knowledge (Henderson, 1992). To this extent, then, handwriting, and also typing, are products of both neuromotor habits and conceptual knowledge because writers must know the conventional uses of letter forms such as upper case, lower case, cursive, and print that are dictated by the demands of text.

Neuromotor processes involved in writing that gained the attention of early twentieth-century psychologists remain of interest today to some researchers. In serial processing models, for example, both spelling and handwriting are described as serial processes because spelling is how letters are ordered in words, and handwriting is how word spellings are produced (see Wing & Baddeley, 1980).

In serial models, writing errors are caused by breakdowns in the serial process. Houghton et al. (1994) examined spelling errors in typing, concluding that typed spelling errors, such as letter repetitions and omissions, are results of serial processing failures that either misload spelling information into a short-term "buffer" or fail to select the right letter to type in a spelling sequence. Ellis, Young, and Flude (1987) attribute typing errors, such as letter doubling, perseveration, and reversals, to the rapid pace of typing in comparison to the much slower pace of handwriting; such typing errors are, in effect, "slips of the fingers" rather than "slips of the pen." Ellis et al. also report that the same types of errors show up in the handwriting of some patients with acquired dysgraphic impairments.

A Recapitulation and a Glimpse Into the Future

The intent of this chapter has been to survey some theoretical models that are thought to represent ways in which the conventions of writing are learned, processed, and produced. This survey led to four scholarly approaches from which most theoretical models concerning the production of written language have been developed to date. Within these fields of study, comprehensive models were sought that might encompass the respective components of written conventions—orthography, handwriting (including typing), and punctuation. No comprehensive model was found, however, although a few developmental researchers, such as Ferreiro and Teberosky (1982), have provided insightful glimpses of the holistic approaches taken by young novices toward the acquisition of the conventions of writing.

For a variety of historical, cultural, and scholarly reasons, the orthographic conventions of English writing have gained most of the attention of researchers, which the relative sparseness of coverage given to punctuation and handwriting in this chapter visibly reflects. One reason for the greater attention given to spelling as an object of scientific inquiry grows out of the close relationship of spelling with reading. A second reason originates in the quasi-regularity of English orthography that provides substantial opportunities to explore complex mental processes from the vantage points of various theoretical perspectives.

Each of the theoretical models of spelling production reviewed here exhibits distinctive features that their respective advocates regard as fundamental—for example, frequencies of letter sequences, neuronal connections, visual memory, sublexical and word knowledge, and knowledge construction. Yet the respective frameworks appear to share a common characteristic: orthographic patterning. Writing systems, after all, are conventionalized graphic patterns that, depending on their orthographic structures, represent morphemes, syllables, and phonemes of a language, or their various combinations. Learning and producing the orthographic patterns of a writing system are synonymous with spelling ability.

Patterning is also a basic component of the other writing conventions—of the punctuation system whose graphic markers shape the construction and meaning of written language; and of the neuromuscular movements that guide the hand in forming letter shapes to produce words and punctuation in conventional written English. Comprehensive theoretical models of the conventions of writing—spelling, writing, punctuation—will not only need to account for how the patterns of the respective components are learned, processed, and produced, but also how they are collectively transposed into conventional written text by conversant writers.

The theoretical models reviewed in this chapter also have served as foundational sources to support various instructional methods. Some methods come readily to mind—a focus on memorization and practice in serial processing; building primary associations among the orthographic elements of words in connectionist processing; recognizing and building on the complementary relationship between spelling and reading word knowledge in dual-route processing; and, in the context of developmental stage theory, providing learning experiences in literacy instruction that foster a progressive understanding of the structure and functions of the conventions of writing. You are invited to consider other ramifications that these theoretical models suggest for instructional practice.

In a recent news item, the playwright Arthur Miller deplored the imminent replacement of "hard copy" manuscripts with electronic counterparts that fail to document an author's corrections of "slips" of the pen or fingers, of word changes and syntactic manipulation to sharpen meaning, and of blocks of text "cut and pasted" the old-fashioned way, which all reveal to the discerning viewer a writer's thought processes at work. Miller's lamentation brought back memories of viewing at New York City's Pierpont Morgan Library a page from John Steinbeck's handwritten draft of *Travels With Charley* (1962), which vividly revealed the construction and polishing of a word master at work. And I recalled viewing at the

British Museum manuscript pages of Charlotte and Emily Brontë, each in a tiny handwriting style that suggested meticulously crafted rows of crocheted script. So, I agree with another recent writer's judgment that, "matrix dots and laser sprays and pixels of L.C.D. (can never convey) the cursive flow of thought" (Morris, 1995, cited in Thornton, 1996, p. 191).

What does the future hold for current theoretical and practical conceptions of the conventions of writing? Will scholars one day theorize how the conventions of electronic script are processed and learned and educators ponder their instructional implications? Time, cultural change, and paradigm shifts will tell.

References

Adams, M.J. (1990). *Beginning to read: Thinking and learning about print.* Cambridge, MA: MIT Press.

Albrow, K.H. (1972). *The English writing system: Notes toward a description.* London: Longman for the Schools Council.

Barron, R.W. (1980). Visual and phonological strategies in reading and spelling. In U. Frith (Ed.), *Cognitive processes in spelling* (pp. 195–213). London: Academic Press.

Barry, C. (1994). Spelling routes (or roots or rutes). In G.D.A. Brown & N.C. Ellis (Eds.), *Handbook of spelling: Theory, process and intervention* (pp. 27–49). Chichester, UK: John Wiley & Sons.

Bateson, J. (1983). A short history of punctuation. *Verbatim, 9,* 6–7.

Bissex, G.L. (1980). *GNYS AT WRK: A child learns to read and write.* Cambridge, MA: Harvard University Press.

Bradley, L., & Huxford, L. (1994). Organizing sound and letter patterns for spelling. In G.D.A. Brown & N.C. Ellis (Eds.), *Handbook of spelling: Theory, process and intervention* (pp. 425–439). Chichester, UK: John Wiley & Sons.

Britain's National Curriculum. (1996). General requirements for English: Key stages 1–4. [Online]. Available: http://easyweb.easynet.co.uk/~fireflies/national-curriculum/enggener.html [1996, August 20]

Brown, G.D.A., & Ellis, N.C. (Eds.). (1994). *Handbook of spelling: Theory, process, and intervention.* Chichester, UK: John Wiley & Sons.

Carney, E. (1994). *A survey of English spelling.* London & New York: Routledge.

Cassidy, S. (1990). When is a developmental model not a developmental model? *Cognitive Systems, 2,* 329–344.

Cordeiro, P., Giacobbe, M.E., & Cazden, C. (1983). Apostrophes, quotation marks, and periods: Learning punctuation in the first grade. *Language Arts, 60,* 323–332.

Coulmas, F. (1996). *The Blackwell encyclopedia of writing systems.* Cambridge, MA: Blackwell Publishers.

Crystal, D. (1987). *The Cambridge encyclopedia of language.* Cambridge, UK: Cambridge University Press.

Crystal, D. (1995). *The Cambridge encyclopedia of the English language.* Cambridge, UK: Cambridge University Press.

Cummings, D.W. (1988). *American English spelling: An informal description.* Baltimore: The Johns Hopkins University Press.

Dryden, J. (1972). *All for love.* D.M. Veith (Ed.). Lincoln, NE: University of Nebraska Press. (Original work published 1678)

Edelsky, C., (1983). Segmentation and punctuation: Developmental data from young writers in a bilingual program. *Research in the Teaching of English, 17,* 135–156.

Ehri, L.C. (1991). Development of the ability to read words. In R. Barr, M.L. Kamil, P. Mosenthal, & P.D. Pearson (Eds.), *Handbook of Reading Research: Volume 2* (pp. 383–417). White Plains, NY: Longman.

Ehri, L.C. (1992a). Reconceptualizing the development of sight word reading and its relationship to reading. In P.B. Gough, L.C. Ehri, & R. Treiman (Eds.), *Reading acquisition* (pp. 107–143). Hillsdale, NJ: Erlbaum.

Ehri, L.C. (1992b). Review and commentary: Stages of spelling development. In S. Templeton & D.R. Bear (Eds.), *Development of orthographic knowledge and the foundations of literacy: A memorial festschrift for Edmund H. Henderson* (pp. 307–332). Hillsdale, NJ: Erlbaum.

Ehri, L.C. (1994). Development of the ability to read words: Update. In R.B. Ruddell, M.R. Ruddell, & H. Singer (Eds.) *Theoretical models and processes of reading* (4th ed.) (pp. 323–349). Newark, DE: International Reading Association.

Ellis, A.W. (1993). *Reading, writing and dyslexia: A cognitive analysis* (2nd ed.). Hillsdale, NJ: Erlbaum.

Ellis, A.W., Young, A.W., & Flude, B.M. (1987). "Afferent dysgraphia" and the role of feedback in the motor control of handwriting. *Cognitive Neuropsychology, 4,* 465–486.

Ferreiro, E., & Teberosky, A. (1982). *Literacy before schooling.* Exeter, NH: Heinemann.

Freeman, F. (1914). *The teaching of handwriting.* Boston: Houghton Mifflin.

Frith, U. (Ed.). (1980). *Cognitive processes in spelling.* London: Academic Press.

Frith, U. (1985). Beneath the surface of developmental dyslexia. In K.E. Patterson, J.C. Marshall, & M. Coltheart (Eds.), *Surface dyslexia.* London: Routledge & Kegan Paul.

Gaur, A. (1992). *A history of writing* (Rev. ed.). New York: Cross River Press.

Gentry, J.R. (1978). Early spelling strategies. *The Elementary School Journal, 79,* 88–92.

Gentry, J.R. (1982). Developmental Spelling: Assessment. *Diagnostique, 8,* 52–61.

Goswami, U. (1988). Children's use of analogy in learning to spell. *British Journal of Experimental Psychology, 6,* 21–33.

Goswami, U., & Bryant, P. (1990). *Phonological skills and learning to read.* Hillsdale, NJ: Erlbaum.

Goswami, U., & Bryant, P. (1992). Rhyme, analogy, and children's reading. In P.B. Gough, L.C. Ehri, & R. Treiman (Eds.) *Reading acquisition* (pp. 49–63). Hillsdale, NJ: Erlbaum.

Gough, P.B., Ehri, L.C., & Treiman, R. (Eds.), (1992). *Reading acquisition.* Hillsdale, NJ: Erlbaum.

Goulandris, N.K. (1994). Teaching spelling: Bridging theory and practice. In G.D.A. Brown & N.C. Ellis (Eds.), *Handbook of spelling: Theory, process and intervention* (pp. 407–423). Chichester, UK: John Wiley & Sons.

Hall, N., & Robinson, A. (Eds.). (1996). *Learning about punctuation* (The Language and Education Library, 9). Portsmouth, NH: Heinemann.

Hanna, P.R., Hanna, J.S., Hodges, R.E., & Rudorf, E.H., Jr. (1966). *Phoneme-grapheme correspondences as cues to spelling improvement.* Washington, DC: U.S. Government Printing Office.

Heald-Taylor, B.G. (1984). Scribble in first grade writing. *The Reading Teacher, 38,* 4–8.

Henderson, E.H. (1992). The interface of lexical competence and knowledge of written words. In S. Templeton & D.R. Bear (Eds.), *Development of orthographic knowledge and the foundations of literacy: A memorial festschrift for Edmund H. Henderson* (pp. 1–30). Hillsdale, NJ: Erlbaum.

Henderson, E.H., & Beers, J.W. (Eds.). (1980). *Developmental and cognitive aspects of learning to spell: A reflection of word knowledge.* Newark, DE: International Reading Association.

Hodges, R. (1644). *The English primrose.* London: Richard Cotes. (Scolar Press Facsimile edition. Menston, UK: The Scolar Press, 1969).

Hodges, R.E. (1991). The conventions of writing. In J. Flood, J.M. Jensen, D. Lapp, & J.R. Squire (Eds.), *Handbook of research on teaching the language arts* (pp. 775–786). New York: Macmillan.

Hodges, R.E. (1972). Theoretical frameworks of English orthography. *Elementary English, 49,* 1089–1097, 1105.

Horn, E. (1929). A source of confusion in spelling. *Journal of Educational Research, 19,* 47–55.

Hotof, N. (1980). Slips of the pen. In U. Frith (Ed.), *Cognitive processes in spelling* (pp. 287–307). London: Academic Press.

Houghton, G., Glasspool, D.W., & Shallice, T. (1994). Spelling and serial recall: Insights from a competitive queuing model. In G.D.A. Brown & N.C. Ellis (Eds.), *Handbook of spelling: Theory, process and intervention* (pp. 365–404). Chichester, UK: John Wiley & Sons.

Jensen, A.R. (1962). Spelling errors and the serial-position effect. *Journal of Educational Psychology, 53,* 105–109.

Kooi, B.Y., Schutz, R.E., & Baker, R.L. (1965). Spelling errors and the serial-position effect. *Journal of Educational Psychology, 56,* 334–336.

Kreiner, D.S. (1992). Reaction time measures of spelling: Testing a two-strategy model of skilled spelling. *Journal of experimental psychology: Learning, memory, and cognition, 18,* 765–776.

Kreiner, D.S. (1996). Effects of word familiarity and phoneme-grapheme polygraphy on oral spelling time and accuracy. *The Psychological Record, 46,* 49–65.

Kreiner, D.S., & Gough, P.B. (1990). Two ideas about spelling: Rules and word-specific memory. *Journal of memory and language, 29,* 103–118.

Lennox, C., & Siegel, L.S. (1994). The role of phonological and orthographic processes in learning to spell. In G.D.A. Brown & N.C. Ellis (Eds.), *Handbook of spelling: Theory, process and intervention* (pp. 93–109). Chichester, UK: John Wiley & Sons.

Little, G.D. (1986). The ambivalent apostrophe. *English Today, 8*, 15–17.

Manguel, A. (1996). *A history of reading*. New York: Viking.

Matthews, B. (1913). Spelling and spelling reform. In P. Monroe (Ed.), *A cyclopedia of education* (Vol. 4, p. 392). New York: Macmillan.

Monaghan, E.J. (1988). Literacy instruction and gender in colonial New England. *American Quarterly, 40*, 18–41.

Morris, D. (1980). Beginning reader's concept of word. In E.H. Henderson, & J.W. Beers (Eds.) *Developmental and cognitive aspects of learning to spell* (pp. 97–111). Newark, DE: International Reading Association.

Morris, E. (1995, January 16). Life and letters: This living hand. *The New Yorker*, 66–67.

Nunberg, G. (1990). *The linguistics of punctuation*. Stanford, CA: Center for the Study of Language and Information, Stanford University.

Olson, A., & Caramazza, A. (1994). Representation and connectionist models: The NETspell experience. In G.D.A. Brown & N.C. Ellis (Eds.), *Handbook of spelling: Theory, process and intervention* (pp. 337–363). Chichester, UK: John Wiley & Sons.

Parkes, M.B. (1993). *Pause and effect: An introduction to the history of punctuation in the West*. Los Angeles: University of California Press.

Partridge, E. (1953). *You have a point there: A guide to punctuation and its allies*. London: Hamish Hamilton.

Perfetti, C.A. (1992). The representation problem in reading acquisition. In P.B. Gough, L.C. Ehri, & R. Treiman (Eds.), *Reading acquisition* (pp. 145–174). Hillsdale, NJ: Erlbaum.

Plaut, D.C., McClelland, J.L., Seidenberg, M.D., & Patterson, K. (1996). Understanding normal and impaired word reading: Computational principles in quasi-regular domains. *Psychological Review, 103*, 56–115.

Read, C. (1971). Preschool children's knowledge of English phonology. *Harvard Educational Review, 41*, 1–34.

Read, C. (1975). *Children's categorizations of speech sounds in English*. Urbana, IL: National Council of Teachers of English.

Read, C. (1986). *Children's creative spelling*. London: Routledge & Kegan Paul.

Robinson, F.P. (1940). Misspellings are intelligent. *Educational Research Bulletin, 19*, 436–442.

Scragg, D.G. (1974). *A history of English spelling*. Manchester, UK: Manchester University Press.

Seymour, P.H.K., & Evans, H.M. (1994). Sources of constraint and individual variations in normal and impaired spelling. In G.D.A. Brown & N.C. Ellis (Eds.), *Handbook of spelling: Theory, process and intervention* (pp. 129–153). Chichester, UK: John Wiley & Sons.

Shaughnessy, M.P. (1977). *Errors and expectations: A guide for the teacher of basic writing*. New York: Oxford University Press.

Simon, D.P., & Simon, H.A. (1973). Alternative uses of phonemic information in spelling. *Review of Educational Research, 43*, 115–137.

Sloboda, J.A. (1980). Visual imagery and individual differences in spelling. In U. Frith (Ed.), *Cognitive processes in spelling* (pp. 231–248). London: Academic Press.

Snowling, M. (1994). Towards a model of spelling acquisition: The development of some component skills. In G.D.A. Brown & N.C. Ellis (Eds.), *Handbook of spelling: Theory, process and intervention* (pp. 111–128). Chichester, UK: John Wiley & Sons.

Spache, G. (1940a). A critical analysis of various methods of classifying spelling errors. *Journal of Educational Research, 31,* 111–134.

Spache, G. (1940b). Validity and reliability of the proposed classification of spelling errors. *Journal of Educational Research, 31,* 204–214.

Steinbeck, J. (1962). *Travels with Charley.* New York: Viking Press.

Sulzby, E. (1991). The development of the young child and the emergence of literacy. In J. Flood, J.M. Jensen, D. Lapp, & J.R. Squire (Eds.), *Handbook of research on teaching the English language arts* (pp. 273–285). New York: Macmillan.

Templeton, S., & Bear, D.R. (Eds.). (1992). *Development of orthographic knowledge and the foundations of literacy: A memorial festschrift for Edmund H. Henderson.* Hillsdale, NJ: Erlbaum.

Thornton, T.P. (1996). *Handwriting in America.* New Haven, CT: Yale University Press.

Treiman, R. (1985). Phonemic awareness and spelling: Children's judgments do not always agree with adults'. *Journal of Experimental Child Psychology, 39,* 182–201.

Treiman, R. (1992). The role of intrasyllabic units in learning to read and spell. In P.B. Gough, L.C. Ehri, & R. Treiman (Eds.), *Reading acquisition* (pp. 65–106). Hillsdale, NJ: Erlbaum.

Treiman, R. (1993). *Beginning to spell: A study of first-grade children.* Oxford, UK: Oxford University Press.

Treiman, R. (1994). Sources of information used by beginning spellers. In G.D.A. Brown & N.C. Ellis (Eds.), *Handbook of spelling: Theory, process, and intervention* (pp. 75–91). Chichester, UK: John Wiley & Sons.

Venezky, R.L. (1970). *The structure of English orthography.* The Hague: Mouton.

Venezky, R.L. (1981). Letter-sound regularities and orthographic structure. In M.L. Kamil (Ed.), *Directions in reading: Research and instruction* (30th Yearbook of the National Reading Conference, pp. 57–83). Washington, DC: National Reading Conference.

Waters, G.S., Bruck, M., & Seidenberg, M. (1985). Do children use similar processes to read and spell words? *Journal of Experimental Child Psychology, 39,* 511–530.

Wilde, S. (1987). *Spelling and punctuation development in selected third and fourth grade children* (Research Report No. 17; Occasional Papers, Program in Language and Literacy). Tuscon, AZ: Arizona Center for Research and Development, University of Arizona.

Wilde, S. (1992). *You kan red this!: Spelling and punctuation for whole language classrooms, K–6.* Portsmouth, NH: Heinemann.

Wing, A.M., & Baddeley, A.D. (1980). Spelling errors in handwriting: A corpus and a distributional analysis. In U. Frith (Ed.), *Cognitive processes in spelling* (pp. 251–285). London: Academic Press.

Zutell, J. (1979). Spelling strategies of primary school children and their relationships to Piaget's concept of decentration. *Research in the Teaching of English, 13,* 69–80.

PART FOUR

CLASSROOM PRACTICE

Richard T. Vacca and Jo Anne L. Vacca

Kent State University

CHAPTER NINE

Writing Across the Curriculum

Students and their teachers are finding that writing can be a powerful means of making sense of experience and constructing meaning. Whether first graders or engineering majors in college, students can be shown how to use writing to think, understand, and learn. In this chapter, we first illustrate how writing functions as an instrument of discovery, speculation, and learning in the lives of two learners in classrooms quite different from each other. Then, we explain how two types of writing, *expressive* and *transactional*, can be incorporated into classroom learning situations depending on the purposes of the writing assignments given to students. While explaining some of the differences between expressive and transactional writing, we also make distinctions between low-stakes and high-stakes writing assignments and review several key research studies that clarify the influences of different types of writing on students' learning, and the kinds of decisions teachers make related to writing in their classes. In the concluding section of the chapter, we explore several instructional principles and activities to support writing across the curriculum.

Writing in the Lives of Two Learners

James, a first grader, listens to his teacher read Jean Marzollo's *Happy Birthday, Martin Luther King* (1993). This wonderfully written and illustrated book highlights the important events of King's life and gives young children a picture of U.S. society in his time. In James's classroom, it is expected that students use language to learn; as part of their development as a community of learners, James and his classmates talk and write about what they read or have heard read to them. *Happy Birthday, Martin Luther King* provides an occasion to use writing to think about and reflect on King's life. The teacher asks, "What if Martin Luther King, Jr., were alive today? What would he have been disappointed about?" Some may wonder whether first graders have the ability to think and respond to a question that requires them to be analytic and speculative. Yet examine James's writing as he grapples with the question and speculates that Martin Luther King would be angry if he were alive today:

> If Martin L. king wher a liv he wood be age. dcos tenagrs are doing vials and. they bring guns to. Schoohl and they kill poepel. But he wats Feetm! to. Reing he dos not wut poeple seprt he wats. Feetm! (quoted in Vacca, Vacca, & Gove, 2000, p. 314)

James does not let the conventions of punctuation and spelling get in his way as he thinks on paper. Nor does he shy away from the use of "big" words like *angry, violence, freedom,* and *separate* to express his feelings and thoughts. He knows that at this stage of the writing process, his teacher is more concerned about what is on his mind than on the surface features of his writing. This is not to say that she does not want James and his classmates to excel in all aspects of writing, including its mechanics, but she recognizes that making sense of experiences and thinking analytically are important functions of writing. Her asking a "What if...?" question prompts James to think about the text. He uses this occasion to express in writing his dismay at the violence that is all too real in his world. James reasons that Martin Luther King would not want teenagers to bring guns to school or to kill people. James also uses his understanding of the life and times of King to interact personally with the concept of integration, as he asserts that "he [King] dos not wut [want] poeple seprt [separate]." Throughout the piece, James is speculative and analytic, and even uses a refrain from one of King's speeches, "Let freedom ring," to support his speculation that King would be angry if he were alive today.

In Michael's sophomore level mechanical engineering course, his professor at Clemson University uses writing assignments on a regular basis to engage students in classroom conversation, speculation, synthesis, question generation, and problem solving (Young, 1997). One of the writing strategies within the professor's instructional repertoire, the 5-minute essay, typically occurs toward the end of a class period. This strategy simply involves asking students to use their notes to summarize in their own words: (1) what they have learned in class, and (2) what questions and concerns they still have. The 5-minute essay, sometimes called a quickwrite or a freewrite, allows the professor to collect the responses, read them before the next class, and respond individually to students.

At the end of a class session on statics, the equilibrium mechanics of stationary bodies, Michael writes a 5-minute essay that includes the following:

1. The method of joints is a way of analyzing structures (trusses) by observing the forces at each joint in the structure. For every structure a system of equations can be developed to solve for the forces at these joints. If the structure is partially constrained, the structure has more equations than unknowns and will collapse under force. A statically indeterminate structure is likely to be rigid but the forces of the joints cannot be found because there are more unknowns than equations. Only a statically determinate structure will be rigid and have the minimum # of elements, thus producing the same # of equations as unknowns.

2. Is a statically indeterminate structure always rigid? (quoted in Young, 1997, p. 28)

The 5-minute essay benefits both the instructor and the students. The engineering professor incorporates the strategy into his teaching because it is a good technique to discover what students think and understand in relation to the course material. His quick reading of the 5-minute essays before the next class informs him what students like Michael are learning and the concepts with which they are having difficulty. He writes responses to Michael's and other students' questions and then uses several of their questions to begin the next class period. Michael and other members of the class benefit by demonstrating their learning; that is, they have the opportunity to summarize their understandings of the class lecture, and in the process, raise questions about the ideas that remain troublesome. As a result, Michael and his classmates are more likely to be *metacognitively* aware of what they know and do not know about the material. The 5-minute essay also encourages the class to put technical terms and new concepts into their own words.

An analysis of James's and Michael's writing reveals, also, that their use of language is considerably different. In James's piece, the writing is *expressive*. His voice is full of concern and consternation as he interacts personally with events surrounding Martin Luther King's life. Michael, on the other hand, is more didactic and "textbookish" as he reviews his class notes and summarizes what he has learned in the 5-minute essay. Michael's use of language is more *transactional*. (See Applebee, Chapter Four in this volume, for further discussion of expressive and transactional writing.)

Expressive and Transactional Functions of Language

Writing across the curriculum is grounded in writing theory that evolved in the 1970s in England as part of a 5-year longitudinal study of the writing abilities of adolescents ages 11 to 18 (Britton, Burgess, Martin, McLeod, & Rosen, 1975). James Britton's research team developed a theoretical model of writing to better understand and study the types of writing used by early adolescents and teenagers in school situations. The researchers' model included a description of the writing process and classifications of the writer's sense of audience and the functions of written language in academic learning. The research team sought to describe and explain how sense of audience and language functions contribute to students' understanding and learning in school writing situations.

As one of the consequences of the research, Britton et al. hypothesized that writing to learn centered around the distinction between expressive and transactional functions of language. A transactional writing function is closely associated with the language of schooling. It is academic and formal in nature and intended to inform, persuade, and instruct. Transactional discourse is not the discourse of students' everyday use of language, which is expressive and informal. Rather, transactional writing sounds "academic." Britton and his team discovered that transactional functions of writing dominated all school subjects and that the audience for transactional writing consisted primarily of the teacher. As students moved through the secondary grades, transactional writing was overwhelmingly reduced to informative tasks in which students were required to report and record information being studied. Despite the minimal uses of expressive writing in the research sample, Britton's research team hypothesized that expressive functions of writing are best suited for exploration and discovery. When school-related writing encourages informal, everyday language to express thoughts, feelings, and opinions, students are more likely to think about and explore new ideas encountered in learning situations. Vacca and Linek (1992), however, noted in a research review of writing across the curriculum that the expressive function is often missing in students' writing in content area classrooms, especially in situations in which teachers have not been exposed to the theory and practice of writing as an instrument of learning, reflection, and discovery. As a result, students are expected to produce transactional types of writing without experiencing the kind of "internal talk" or "thinking aloud on paper" that allows them to make connections between what they know already and what they are studying or writing about. Opportunity to think on paper using expressive language affords students a greater reservoir of ideas than would be available if this step were omitted or if topics were discussed orally.

Low-Stakes Writing Assignments as Learning Opportunities

Distinctions between expressive and transactional functions of writing can be considered in the context of *low-stakes* and *high-stakes* writing in school situations. The difference between low-stakes and high-stakes writing is best exemplified in the Writing Across the Curriculum (WAC) movement that took hold in higher education in the 1970s. The WAC movement in colleges and universities has an underlying purpose: "to improve student learning and writing by encouraging faculty in all disciplines to use writing more often and more thoughtfully in their classroom" (Young & Fulwiler, 1986, p. 1). Students write more and think more when they engage in low-stakes writing assignments.

Peter Elbow (1997) advocates low-stakes writing so students can use writing to interact personally with ideas and information without the pressure of producing polished, finished products. Teachers often assign writing, not to provide opportunities for students to produce excellent pieces of writing, but to help students to explore ways of making sense of course material. According to Elbow (1997), high-stakes writing assignments "also produce learning but they are more loaded because we judge the writing carefully for soundness of content and clarity of presentation" (p. 5). A research paper or a persuasive essay, for example, often represents high-stakes writing in which students work through steps and stages to compose a finished product.

Low-stakes writing, on the other hand, is often predraft or first-draft writing. It usually is messy, tentative, and unfinished in the sense that the writing "evinces thought but does not merit the careful scrutiny which a finished piece of writing deserves" (Gere, 1985, p. 4). Low-stakes writing is more concerned with students' exploration of ideas than with clarity of presentation. More often than not, it prompts students to tap into their storehouse of memories—their prior knowledge—in order to connect what they know to what they are studying. Low-stakes writing assignments, interestingly, allow teachers to increase the volume of writing that occurs in a class. Therein lies one of the practical benefits of low-stakes writing: because so much of what students write about is tied to what they are reading, writing that is low-stakes is more likely to result in students reading course material on a regular basis, rather than delaying reading until it is time to take a test on the material. Although low-stakes writing activities connect writing and reading in academic subjects, students are not limited to learning from texts. Low-stakes assignments also may be tied to class lectures, discussions, demonstrations, experiments, field trips, video, and film for various purposes: to observe, record, infer, generalize, predict, apply, annotate, summarize, question, and critique. How these thinking operations occur, and under what circumstances, are questions that research and classroom inquiry have attempted to answer.

Research Support for Writing Across the Curriculum

Several decades of writing process research have contributed much to teachers' understanding of how, and under what conditions, young children, adolescents, and adults learn to write. In comparison, there are fewer experimental and descriptive studies related to students' use of writing in learning situations. Although writing across the curriculum is well grounded in theories of writing and language use, there remains a "slender empirical base" associated with writing in academic subjects (Newell & Winograd, 1989). Nevertheless, several pivotal research studies support the utility of writing to learn in academic disciplines. These studies show that regardless of the purpose of the writing—whether the task prompts informative uses of writing or analytical thinking and exploration—students who use writing to learn have a considerable advantage over students who do not engage in writing for this purpose. Writing, arguably, is an effective instrument for exploring and understanding an academic subject. The challenge for researchers has been to determine "what works and under what conditions" as they attempt to identify the effects of different types of writing and academic abilities on student learning.

Teachers also have engaged in classroom inquiry and research to explore and understand what works in their classrooms, although these inquiries are quite different from those of the disciplined researcher. Teachers who have disseminated their findings through publication often have done so in descriptive, sometimes narrative, discourse in which they "come to know" by painting a portrait of students and their classrooms. Such research is perhaps best exemplified in the collection of studies *Coming to Know: Writing to Learn in the Intermediate Grades*, edited by Nancie Atwell (1990). For the most part, however, teacher research goes unpublished and therefore unnoticed by the larger educational community. Teachers engage in classroom inquiry to understand and improve practice and to grow professionally, not necessarily to disseminate findings through publication or conference presentations.

Early studies of writing in various disciplines (Applebee, 1981; Martin, D'Arcy, Newton, & Parker, 1976) describe content area teachers' uses of writing in their classrooms. Martin and her colleagues situated their observational research in England as a follow-up to Britton's work, while Applebee reported on the writing activities that occurred in classrooms throughout the United States. Despite being conducted an ocean apart, the findings and conclusions drawn from each study are remarkably similar. Both research studies reveal that writing tasks in content area classrooms are limited to assignments that focus on reproducing information rather than using information to think more deeply about subject matter. Both studies report little evidence of writing that requires students to elaborate on what they are learning, to make discoveries, or to think analytically about course material. Informational writing tasks mainly direct students to take notes and answer questions. Such tasks serve a "report back" function as students record and review information covered in text readings or class presentations.

Several key research studies have been conducted to better understand the influences of different types of writing on students' learning. Two influential studies reported in 1987 support the hypothesis that writing can influence learning in important but different ways. Marshall (1987) studied the effects of writing on students' understanding of literary texts. He discovered that when students write essays, they develop better literary understanding over time than when writing answers to study questions. Study questions restrict the extent of learning, but essays tend to encourage extended thinking. Langer and Applebee (1987) also examined the effects of different types of writing on students' learning. They found that different types of writing prompted different ways of thinking about course material. Informational writing activities resulted in narrow thinking in which students focused on textual information to support their written responses to questions. Essay writing, however, had an effect similar to those identified in Marshall's research. Essays require students to reconceptualize content and focus on larger, interpretive issues rather than merely reviewing and reproducing information.

Several studies (Newell, 1984; Newell & Winograd, 1989, 1995) support and extend the findings of earlier research. When students write about what they have read, both the writing task and the difficulty of the text material contribute to the kind of learning that takes place. Analytical writing assignments in which students connect personal experiences, thoughts, and opinions produce better results than notetaking or study questions on various measures of student performance such as time on task and the recall of information from text.

In their 1995 study, Newell and Winograd tapped into the implicit beliefs of a high school teacher of U.S. history to better understand the kinds of decisions she made related to writing in her classes. They observed the teaching practices of the teacher, whom they called "Jane Adams," as she adapted writing assignments in her "general level" and "academic level" classes based on her implicit knowledge of the abilities of students of varying academic abilities can and cannot do. The researchers interviewed Adams regularly in order to better understand her beliefs about the uses of writing in her general and academic classes. They found that her plans, her curricular decisions, and her uses of writing differed dramatically in the two classes.

Adams, like most thoughtful teachers, had developed an implicit theory of writing across the curriculum that informed her understanding of what works, what does not work, and what works best with a particular student. In one of the interview sessions, she explained,

> When [academic students] begin the school year I can usually assume that they are prepared. One thing that really does distinguish the better student is their memory for information. And if [information] is lacking, they seem to learn it fast and then remember it as we go along. My job then becomes trying to get them to make sense of all of that as they are learning it. Writing and talking help with this. The general students are another issue for me—typically they don't know as much, and so I start worrying about coverage with them. You know, they have different experiences by the time they get to the eleventh grade. (quoted in Newell &Winograd, 1995, p. 141)

Although Adams did not assign many analytic writing assignments to the general level students, Newell and Winograd followed up their observational study of her classes with experimentally designed research. They were interested in determining what students of varying academic abilities learned, and how much they learned, when assigned different types of writing activities. The researchers found that academic level students benefited from analytical writing activities—but so did general level students. Although the general students' performances on posttest measures of recall were not as strong as academic students' performances, they benefited more from analytic writing than from answering study questions about the passages they read. Newell and Winograd concluded that both analytical writing and study questions can serve useful functions in students' learning. (Study questions might best be used in learning situations that require students to review large amounts of information in preparation for more demanding intellectual activities.) (See also Armbruster, Chapter Six in this volume.)

As noted earlier, teacher research and inquiry related to writing across the curriculum helps teachers to better understand what happens in their classrooms when they scaffold writing activities and assignments to support students' interaction with ideas and information (Atwell, 1990; Donoahue, Van Tassell, & Patterson, 1996; Patterson, Santa, Short, & Smith, 1993) Teachers who engage in research initiate classroom inquiry to answer practical questions. Many of these research studies are descriptive—utilizing portfolio assessment techniques and qualitative methods such as observation, interviews, and document analysis (examining students' writing).

One of the important influences on classroom inquiry in the U.S. has been teachers' participation in national writing projects. Beginning in 1973, the Bay Area Writing Project (and the scores of sites today that evolved from the Bay Area model under the umbrella of the National Writing Project) has been overwhelmingly successful in tapping the expertise of teachers who have developed and inquired into best practices in the writing process and in writing in academic subjects (Camp, 1982; see also Applebee, Chapter Four in this volume). The Bay Area model, based on the notion of "teachers teaching teachers," has resulted in collaborative professional development programs and a sustained interest in inquiry related to writing across the curriculum.

Implications for Classroom Practice

The implicit models of writing-to-learn that teachers construct in their minds are played out daily in actual classroom practice. These implicit models of instruction are characterized by the beliefs that teachers hold about students, learning and teaching, literacy, curriculum, and assessment. Jane Adams, the subject of Newell and Winograd's 1995 study, is a prime example of how a teacher's beliefs about learners, academic ability levels, and content coverage within the curriculum influence instructional decisions, planning, and the use of various writing activities. If writing is to become an integral part of classroom practice, teachers need to reflect on what they believe about writing to learn and why. To what extent does a teacher's professional knowledge—based on understandings of language in use, research, and authoritative opinion on writing—influence his or her beliefs about writing as an instrument of learning? To what extent have personal and professional experiences with writing in academic disciplines shaped beliefs and principles underlying classroom practice? In what ways does one's understanding of teaching and learning in a discipline influence practice?

Art Young (1997) expresses several statements of belief about writing in academic subjects that he proposes as general principles for classroom practice. First and foremost, a teacher must believe that the purpose of writing in an academic subject is to create a classroom environment that supports active learning and interactive teaching. Writing is a catalyst for student engagement and interaction with ideas, and a medium for honest communication between teacher and student. In addition, a teacher must integrate writing into the daily life of the class. As Young puts it, writing in a content subject "will not work for most students and teachers if it is assigned, written, and then not discussed in class, not used to further class goals" (pp. 30–31). Moreover, writing cannot be perceived as busy work by students; they must understand the "why" of writing assignments. Writing-to-learn helps to build community within the classroom—"a community of scholars learning about the subject being studied" (p. 31). Finally, teachers must believe that they enter into relationships with students when they assign writing. Writing must be read. When teachers are not eager to read what students write, they not only send mixed messages to students, but they work against creating an active learning environment.

Because writing promotes different types of learning, students need many occasions to write in content area classrooms. Planning instructional activities to include a variety of writing tasks is one of the hallmarks of effective classroom practice. Depending on the content objectives of the teacher, students can engage in various functions of language that take into consideration informational, personal, and imaginative uses of writing to think about and interact with the ideas and information being studied.

Use Informational Writing to Move Beyond Simple Recall. Informational writing plays an important role in students' learning when teachers scaffold writing tasks to support thinking and learning. Too often, however, students are expected to use informational writing merely to recall information. When writing focuses only on information recall, it plays a restricted and narrow role in students' thinking about course material.

There is an impressive body of research that supports the value of writing summaries and taking notes, two of the more valuable types of informational writing tasks (Alvermann & Phelps, 1998; Brozo & Simpson, 1995; Vacca & Vacca, 1999). An effectively written summary, for example, requires students to reduce a text to its main points. The 5-minute essay written by Michael, the engineering major, that was presented earlier in this chapter, is an effective technique for summarizing information. Many students, however, will need additional instructional support to effectively reduce a text to its main points. If assignments require students to summarize what they read, they most likely will need to be shown how to discern and analyze text structure, and to distinguish important information from less important information. Simply requiring students to write a summary without explicit explanations and modeling often results in their reproducing textual information without an analysis or synthesis of the important points in a text.

Based on their studies of people who summarize effectively, Kintsch and van Dijk (1978) formulated a set of rules on how to write summaries. They determined that there are four essential steps in writing a summary that require students to do more than regurgitate information from a text:

1. *Include no unnecessary details.* Students must learn how to distinguish important from trivial and repetitive information. Brainstorming and listing bits of information and ideas encountered in a text is one way to begin this process.

2. *Collapse lists.* In this step, students categorize bits of information into larger categories. Developing a graphic representation or organizer is an excellent tool for chunking information around more inclusive concepts (Vacca & Vacca, 1999).

3. *Identify and develop topic sentences.* Students should search the text for explicit topic sentences and create their own topic sentences where none exist in a text. Using graphic organizers will help support students in this phase of summary development.

4. *Integrate information.* Drafting requires students to use key concept words, phrases, and topic sentences to compose the summary. Whereas the first three steps prepare students to write the summary, this step requires students to put words on paper into a coherent piece of writing.

Using a process for summary writing avoids the reproduction of information without analysis and synthesis. Likewise, notetaking should extend beyond verbatim text reproductions. Instead, students should be encouraged to both take and "make" notes that help them to paraphrase, react critically, question, or respond personally to what they read. Eanet and Manzo (1976) studied the importance of writing notes in which students act on what they are learning through various types of text annotations. For example, teachers need to show students how to construct thesis notes to highlight implicit main ideas; question notes to raise significant issues or unresolved conceptual conflicts by writing questions; critical notes to capture reaction and response to the main ideas of the text presentation; or summary notes to condense main ideas into a concise statement.

Use Journal Writing to Support Personal Interactions With Course Material. Text annotations can be recorded in academic journals or, as they are sometimes called, learning logs. Entries in academic journals represent low-stakes writing assignments that allow students to use expressive language to interact personally with ideas and information encountered in course material and class lectures and discussions. Journals should be used regularly to create a visible, permanent record of what students are thinking and learning throughout the school year. Students can use journals at the beginning of class periods to generate ideas, write predictions, and arouse curiosity about topics to be studied, and use them later to record thoughts and feelings in response to what they have read. Journals can also be used to explore concerns as students respond to questions such as, What did I like or dislike about class today? What did I understand about today's class work? What is not clear or confusing about the ideas presented in today's class? (Vacca & Vacca, 1999)

Journals also may be used to help students solve problems and interpret or analyze course content. A high school biology teacher, for example, asked students to use their journals to compare and contrast Lamarck's and Darwin's theories of evolution. Each student was given a picture of an animal with at least one obvious adaptive trait. The pictures, which the teacher had collected from colorful photographic wildlife magazines, immediately caught students' interest and enthusiasm. The students were assigned to write two scenarios in their journals: one that described how

Lamarck might have explained the development of the trait and another that described how Darwin might have explained it. One student's journal entry recorded these explanations:

> Lamarck would have said that a long time ago elephants had really small ears. The ears weren't used for anything. As time went by, many flies began to eat away at the elephant's skin. To swat the flies, the elephants grew their ears longer. Each time the elephants had babies, the ears grew progressively larger until now when you see the huge elephant ears.

> Darwin would have said there used to be few elephants with large ears, but many with small ears. The small eared (sic) elephants had survived more often than the large eared ones because the ears were not needed. The fly population began to increase. The flies ate the elephants (sic) skin. The elephants with the small ears got eaten. The elephants with the big ears swatted the flies away. The short eared ones reproduced and passed on the large ears to their children. After many generations the elephants all have large ears.

The biology teacher does not grade for content when she assigns journal writing. Rather she gives students "participation points." She reads the entries to see how well students are grasping concepts. Having read the Lamarck and Darwin scenarios, she realized that many of the students were unclear about the differences between the two theories of evolution. She used the students' journal entries as a means of performance assessment, which allowed her to help clarify the two theories during follow-up class discussion.

Sometimes teachers use a double-entry journal format to help students respond personally to course material. This format allows students to record dual entries that are conceptually related according to prompts given by the teacher. Often, a teacher will ask students to provide a description or explanation in one column and their reactions or responses in the other column. To create the double-entry format, students divide sheets of notebook paper in half lengthwise; younger children can use the entire left page of a notebook as one column and the right page as another column. Examine this third grader's journal entry as she describes and reacts to the clothes worn by pilgrim girls in response to her teacher's read-aloud of Alice Dalgliech's *The Thanksgiving Story* (1954):

Clothes

Pilgrim girls wear three petticoats, a pair of stockings, garters, a waistcoat, one coif, a apron, and shoes. Petticoats are long dresses under the real dress, and they are brownish. A garter is a thin string to keep stockings up. Coifs are tight fitting caps, and they are white.

Feelings

If I wore a waistcoat, I would feel important [sic]. Oh, and if I had to put on that many petticoats, I would SCREAM! The garters would slow down the blood in my leg. In the summer, I would be hot and itchy. I guess I wouldn't want to wear them!

Use Imaginative Writing to Encourage Students to Play With Ideas and Think Creatively About Subjects Being Studied. Students need opportunities to interact with ideas and information by engaging in imaginative types of writing, including poems, scenarios, dialogues, unsent letters, and fictitious interviews (Vacca & Linek, 1992). Poems, in particular, provide a creative form for showing what has been learned. Young (1997), for example, maintains that writing poems allows students to generate new and fresh perspectives on the subject under study. He notes that college-level instructors in biology, mathematics, business, and women's studies have been assigning ungraded poems to encourage students to play with language and ideas and to increase the quantity and quality of student-teacher interactions.

In elementary, middle, and high school classrooms content area teachers have been experimenting with the use of biopoems as a writing-to-learn tool. Biopoems allow students to put large amounts of material into precise language within the context of a poetic form (Gere, 1985). In a middle school language arts class, for example, the teacher invited students to write a biopoem on one of the characters from Natalie Babbitt's *Tuck Everlasting* (1975). To scaffold the activity, the teacher encouraged students to follow a biopoem pattern, or a line-by-line structure for composing the biopoem, as a means of thinking about their choice of character. One of the students chose to develop his biopoem around the character of Miles Tuck:

Miles

Young-strong-smart-hardworking
Relitive (sic) to Jesse, his brother
Lover of fishing, his children, and working
Who feels heartbroken, hates living forever
Who needs kinship, family, and love
Who fears never seeing his children, living forever,
and never being loved again
Who gives love-fun
Who would like to see his family
outside world
Resident of Treegap
Tuck

Other poetic patterns such as a diamante (a poem in the shape of a diamond) can be used to allow students to play with ideas they are studying. The following is a diamante written by a second grader to "show" learning about birds—a topic she researched as part of a unit on wildlife. After much modeling and demonstration by the teacher on how to write a diamante, the student, Erin, wrote this poem:

Birds

small, pretty
flying, eating, chasing
nests, worms, eggs, beaks
singing, talking, calling
furry, beautiful
feathers

In addition to writing poems with preset patterns, teachers often encourage students to use poetic forms of writing without imposing a structure for them to follow, as is the case in this example from a middle school unit on the Holocaust:

My Fate

Hello, my name is David,
By the name you may know,
That I'm a Jew, I'm not safe…
There's no place I can go.

If I don't try to hide
Deathcamp will be my fate,
I simply can't imagine…
How Hitler can have so much hate.

Use Essay Writing to Encourage Analytical Thinking. When students combine reading, especially from multiple sources of information, with writing essays, they are likely to think more deeply about the subject they are studying (Spivey, 1984). Essays create opportunities for students to develop reasoned explanations as they discover, analyze, and synthesize ideas through the process of writing. Whereas informational, journal, and imaginative writing tasks are relatively low-stakes writing, essays demand more finished pieces of writing. As a result, essays are considered within the domain of high-stakes writing assignments, along with research papers and reports. However, because the stakes are higher with essay writing, the expectations for students to engage in the writing process are greater.

Concluding Comment

To increase the volume of writing in academic subjects, teachers incorporate a variety of writing tasks into their instructional plans. When teachers assign low-stakes writing, the emphasis is on exploring ideas and interacting personally with information. Low-stakes writing assignments need to be read but not necessarily graded by teachers for content, organization, or mechanics, because low-stakes writing is informal, unfinished writing. Teachers should not expend energy on students' errors but should focus more on using writing to help students become more knowledgeable and conversant with the academic content. Content exploration is at the heart of writing across the curriculum because it invites discovery, speculation, and reflection.

Although errors in the mechanics of writing are to be expected in low-stakes writing situations, students need to be aware of their responsibilities as writers. Therefore, they must recognize that they will be held accountable for spelling, punctuation, and grammatical usage in high-stakes writing situations. High-stakes writing, such as essays and research papers, demands a different, more complex, level of response and evaluation of students' finished products. Whether students engage in high-stakes or low-stakes writing, however, the act of writing can be a powerful instrument of learning in every content area.

References

Alvermann, D., & Phelps, S. (1998). *Content area reading and literacy: Succeeding in today's diverse classrooms* (2nd ed.). Boston: Allyn & Bacon.

Applebee, A. (1981). *Writing in the secondary school: English and the content areas.* Urbana, IL: National Council of Teachers of English.

Atwell, N. (Ed.). (1990). *Coming to know: Writing to learn in the intermediate grades.* Portsmouth, NH: Heinemann.

Britton, J., Burgess, T., Martin, N., McLeod, A., & Rosen, H. (1975). *The development of writing abilities.* London: Macmillan.

Brozo, W., & Simpson, M. (1995). *Readers, teachers, learners: Expanding literacy in secondary schools* (2nd ed.). New York: Merrill.

Camp, G. (1982). *A success curriculum for remedial writers.* Berkeley, CA: The National Writing Project, University of California, Berkeley.

Donoahue, Z., Van Tassell, M.A., & Patterson, L. (Eds.). (1996). *Research in the classroom: Talk, texts, and inquiry.* Newark, DE: International Reading Association.

Eanet, M., & Manzo, A. (1976). REAP—a strategy for improving reading/writing/study skills. *Journal of Reading, 19,* 647–652.

Elbow, P. (1997). High stakes and low stakes in assigning and responding to writing. In M. Sorcinelli & P. Elbow (Eds.), *Writing to learn: Strategies for assigning and responding to writing across the disciplines* (pp. 5–13). San Francisco: Jossey-Bass.

Gere, A. (Ed.). (1985). *Roots in sawdust: Writing to learn across the curriculum.* Urbana, IL: National Council of Teachers of English.

Kintsch, W., & van Dijk, T. (1978). Toward a model of text comprehension and production. *Psychological Review, 85,* 363–394.

Langer, J., & Applebee, A. (1987). *How writing shapes thinking: A study of teaching and learning* (Research Report No. 22). Urbana, IL: National Council of Teachers of English.

Marshall, J. (1987). The effects of writing on students' understanding of literary texts. *Research in the Teaching of English, 21,* 30–63.

Martin, N., D'Arcy, P., Newton, B., & Parker, R. (1976). *Writing and learning across the curriculum.* Montclair, NJ: Boynton/Cook.

Newell, G. (1984). Learning from writing in two content areas: A case study/protocol analysis. *Research in the Teaching of English, 18,* 265–287.

Newell, G., & Winograd, P. (1989). The effects of writing on learning from expository text. *Written Communication, 6,* 196–217.

Newell, G., & Winograd, P. (1995). Writing about and learning from history texts: The effects of task and academic ability. *Research in the Teaching of English, 29,* 133–163.

Patterson, L., Santa, C.M., Short, K.G., & Smith, K. (Eds.). (1993). *Teachers are researchers: Reflection and action.* Newark, DE: International Reading Association.

Spivey, N. (1984). *Discourse synthesis: Constructing texts in reading and writing.* Newark, DE: International Reading Association.

Vacca, R.T., & Linek, W.M. (1992). Writing to learn. In J.W. Irwin & M.A. Doyle (Eds.), *Reading/writing connections: Learning from research* (pp. 145–159). Newark, DE: International Reading Association.

Vacca, R.T., & Vacca, J.L. (1999). *Content area reading: Literacy and learning across the curriculum* (6th ed.). New York: Addison Wesley Longman.

Vacca, J.L., Vacca, R.T., & Gove, M. (2000). *Reading and learning to read* (4th ed.). New York: Addison Wesley Longman.

Young, A. (1997). Mentoring, modeling, monitoring, motivating: Response to students' ungraded writing as academic conversation. In M. Sorcinelli & P. Elbow (Eds.), *Writing to learn: Strategies for assigning and responding to writing across the disciplines* (pp. 5–13). San Francisco: Jossey-Bass.

Young, A., & Fulwiler, T. (1986). Introduction. In A. Young & T. Fulwiler (Eds.), *Writing across the disciplines: Research into practice* (pp. 1–3). Montclair, NJ: Boynton/Cook.

Children's Books

Babbitt, N. (1986). *Tuck everlasting*. New York: Farrar, Strauss & Giroux.

Dalgliesh, A. (1954). *The Thanksgiving story*. (Ill. by H. Sewell). New York: Scribner.

Marzollo, J. (1993). *Happy birthday, Martin Luther King*. (Ill. by B. Pinckney). New York: Scholastic.

James Flood and Diane Lapp
San Diego State University

CHAPTER TEN

Teaching Writing in Urban Schools: Cognitive Processes, Curriculum Resources, and the Missing Links— Management and Grouping

In recent years several writing researchers have demonstrated that children develop writing abilities by being active members of an effectively organized writing classroom in which they are offered opportunities to write frequently, where they receive supportive writing instruction from their teachers, and where they are assessed continuously by themselves, their teachers, and their peers (Dahl & Farnan, 1998; Dyson & Freedman, 1997). Although effective environments for developing writing competence exist in many classrooms, this chapter focuses on the successful writing development of children in urban classrooms. Urban classrooms have become more diverse than ever in the history of U.S. education and in classrooms throughout the world (Greaney, 1996; Krashen & Terrell, 1983; Tinajero & Flor Ada, 1993). The changing demographics of urban classrooms in the United States reflect a significant shift from a plurality of native English speakers to a minority of native English speakers who come to school with various levels of proficiency in English (Krashen & Terrell, 1983). In many U.S. urban classrooms, students range from the speech emergence stage of English in which they can express themselves haltingly in a few words or phrases to the highest stages of bilingual functioning. Still other children speak English language variants as their primary language (Moore, 1998). This range of English language skill makes the teaching of writing to children in urban classrooms an extremely formidable task.

In an effort to meet the needs of children who come to school from a variety of language backgrounds and a wide range of proficiencies in English writing, several researchers have studied the effects of various types of instruction on the writing development of children in urban schools (Dahl & Farnan, 1998; Dyson & Freedman, 1991). These researchers have investigated the best approaches to teaching writing in urban classrooms to children from language backgrounds other than English, as well as to children from English variant backgrounds, and they have concluded that a process approach to writing is the most appropriate mode of instruction (Dahl & Farnan, 1998; Dyson 1993; Graves, 1981). These researchers argue that a process writing approach, which is based on constructivist notions that writers develop their skills by constructing and revising texts in an orderly if not always predictable manner, is most appropriate for children from a wide variety of language backgrounds because it enables children to write frequently, continually revising the content as well as the form. They also argue that teaching children to write is an act of construction in which students interact with their teachers to construct effective texts. Tway (1991) maintains that "teaching is a linguistic process in which individuals in a classroom interact with language and each other as they move toward collaborative constructions of meaning" (p. 426).

In analyzing effective writing instruction, researchers have discovered two sets of factors—cognitive processes and curriculum resources—that are related to effective writing instruction and learning (see Figure 1). In the first set of factors, cognitive processes, we know that the child's psychological disposition toward learning to write, including issues of motivation, and his or her cognitive and linguistic abilities are critical factors for writing development. Two other closely related areas exist within the set of cognitive processes: the writing activities that learners are engaged in as they progress through their writing program, and the self-assessment they involve themselves in as well as the assessment they receive from others.

Flood & Lapp

Figure 1. Critical Factors Affecting Writing Process Instruction

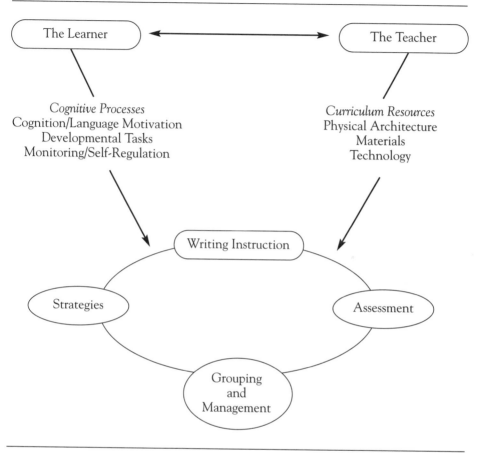

The second set of factors, curriculum resources, deals with the classroom environment in which children are expected to write.

Although each of these factors is an essential part of an effective process approach to writing instruction, most of the existing writing research has focused on the cognitive processes of writing, the psychological aspects of the instructional process, the assessment of writing development, the writing activities in which children participate, the classroom environment, and technology. Little attention, however, has been given to researching the effectiveness of the management and grouping of students in writing programs. These issues will be addressed later in this chapter.

Cognitive Processes: Psychological Factors, Writing Activities, and Assessment of Children's Writing in the Primary Grades

There is an abundance of research on the cognitive processes involved in learning to write. The research includes studies of children's psychological disposition to writing, their writing activities, and assessment of their attempts to write. Each of these elements is involved in every act of writing. Because these three variables are closely intertwined and interact with one another during the writing process, all three factors will be addressed as a single interactive unit.

In Donald Graves's landmark 1975 study, he found that primary-grade children's actions showed that their composing, which involved cognitive processes, writing activities, and assessment, began during the process of drawing or working with crayons. He found that a story often emerged within children's explorations. Graves's 1981 study, which he undertook with colleagues in New Hampshire, spanned two years and involved two groups of children. One group of eight children was observed from the beginning of first grade to the end of second grade, and a second group of eight children was observed from the beginning of third grade through the end of fourth grade. The research included analyses of written products, direct observations of students as they wrote, and interviews with the children before, during, and after writing. As the children composed, the researchers took notes, and the children were asked questions about discussions with their peers and their teachers.

After analyzing his data, Graves defined the children's writing process as "a series of operations leading to the solution of a problem" (1981, p. 4). He argued that the process begins when the writer consciously or unconsciously starts considering a topic and ends when the written piece is published. Graves emphasized the idea that composing actually commences before the physical process of writing begins. He identified a series of subprocesses associated with writing, such as topic selection, rehearsing, assessing information, attending to spelling and handwriting, reading, organizing, editing, and revising; the same process elements were evident whether the children were 6 or 10 years old.

Other researchers working in urban schools with children whose first language is English or whose second language is English found the same array of psychological subprocesses used by the children who participated in their studies (Tinajero & Flor Ada, 1993). Dyson and her colleagues (1989, 1991, 1993, 1995) found that the decision to write was often spontaneous for the youngest writers in urban schools, who often began with the desire to write a caption for their own pictures.

Bereiter and Scardamalia (1987) noted that young children use the "what next" strategy, moving from one piece of information to another, writing from one idea to the next, confident that they are clearly expressing their meaning. Many researchers (see, for example, Dahl & Farnan, 1998; Graves, 1981) have found that planning is not an important element in young children's writing because the process is both visible and overt for them. Children talk about what they are going to write about and often talk their way through a writing episode. This serves the purpose of hearing the sounds within a word so they can decide which letters to select to represent these sounds. Young children reread aloud what they have written, almost as though they are cycling back to check meaning that will help them figure out what will come next.

During the primary grades the emphasis subtly changes from talking out ideas and focusing on handwriting and spelling to focusing on content. Children become increasingly able to select information for their writing without having to overtly rehearse it. For example, Cioffi (1984), who studied two children for 2 years, discovered that over the course of the study one of the children decreased the time he spent composing orally, saying each word aloud as he wrote it and drawing pictures to illustrate it, from a median of about 77% of his composing time to a median of 22%. Silent writing, on the other hand, increased from 0% to 57% of his composing time. Cioffi also found a similar trend with the other student in his study, although the changes were not so dramatic in her writing. Tinajero and Flor Ada (1993), in their studies of bilingual Mexican American children in urban schools in El Paso, Texas, found the same pattern of development regardless of the language in which the children were writing.

MacGillivray's (1994) qualitative research, which described a year with first graders, showed that children write in three broad categories: here and now, the past, and fantasy. She found that the children held some writing values in common, such as keeping the audience's interest and being able to read their own writing regardless of spelling. She also found that some children used writing as an act of unity to resolve peer issues, while others used writing as a way of joining others in collaboration.

Dyson's (1993, 1995) research suggests that children across the primary grades learn the social and personal power of print. They create a personal system for generating and encoding written text by learning about their own purposes for writing and the expectations and needs of others. Dahl and Farnan (1998) note that these push/pull relationships between symbolic form and social function and between the self and others are the tensions that children deal with in their writing development in their early years. (See also Dyson, Chapter Two in this volume.)

Previous research on writing development has demonstrated children's growing control of spelling and of print conventions such as capital letters, punctuation, and paragraphing over the course of the school years. (See also Chaper Eight in this volume for more discussion of the conventions of writing.) While this informative body of research has helped teachers interpret aspects of children's knowledge, it has not dealt with the notions that Dyson (1993, 1995) explores. In her theory of writing development, children construct rules of written language for themselves as they engage in making meaning. She maintains that their central focus in writing is the development of comprehensive systems for writing across symbol systems, such as written language and art. This view has challenged teachers to think broadly about writing, considering the causal and communicative factors that affect writing development.

Dyson's (1989, 1991, 1993, 1995) research addresses the social and cultural contexts that influence what and how children write. She found the following:

1. Children use the cultural information they know from movies, cartoons, videos, nursery rhymes, jump-rope rhymes, and neighborhood raps in their writing.

2. Writing purposes from a child's perspective differ widely from more traditional school-centered notions. Its topics, language choices, and forms are often shaped by what is valued in the child's world.

Cognitive Processes: Psychological Aspects, Writing Activities, and Assessment of Children's Writing in the Intermediate Grades

We know a great deal about primary grade children's writing but less about children in the intermediate grades as writers. Calkins (1994) describes intermediate grade writers in all settings—urban, suburban, and rural—as children who attempt to write significant and important pieces as they gain self-awareness of their writing. As children shift in self-consciousness and expand the kinds of writing they attempt in the intermediate grades, it is particularly important to understand the roles that writing plays for individual learners. McGinley and Kamberelis (1996), in their research with third and fourth graders, describe the functions that writing and reading serve in a classroom. The researchers found that as children expanded their writing repertoires, they wrote most frequently about personal experiences, using writing to create new selves, to hone their interests, and to become characters in imaginary worlds. McGinley and Kamberelis found that intermediate grade children used writing for personal exploration as they thought about social problems, social action, and their own identities.

Dahl and Farnan (1998) maintain that the writing strategies of children in the intermediate grades indicate four broad categories of activities:

1. generating ideas by becoming aware of relevant ideas and the ability to organize them.

2. formulating meaning by developing the message itself with consideration of audience and by constructing the language and linking the concepts.

3. evaluating by reviewing the constructed message and monitoring its development.

4. revising by restructuring so that the author's meaning is clear.

Dahl and Farnan further argue that these strategies do not proceed in linear order and the generation and revision of written ideas occur at any time during composing.

Curriculum Resources: The Role of Classroom Environment in Writing Development

In several decades of studies, researchers have thoroughly examined the physical aspects of classroom environments from architectural issues to issues of interaction between students and classroom architecture. These studies overwhelmingly conclude that architecture plays a critical role in learning. The arrangement of furniture, materials, centers, and artwork influences the behaviors of students and teachers that encourages or discourages writing attempts (Loughlin & Martin, 1987).

Taking into account the effects of context within a classroom, Cazden (1986) maintains that children learn best in environments that provide for language-rich experiences—she describes these as "environmentally assisted" classrooms. Loughlin and Martin (1987) state: "The arranged environment functions as an instructional tool, complementing and reinforcing other strategies that the teacher uses to support children's learning" (p. 6). Loughlin and Suina (1982) have shown that the arrangement of trade books determines whether or not they are used in classroom writing instruction. Other studies have shown that when writing materials and writing tools are accessible to students, the writing development of children in these classrooms is affected greatly (Dahl & Farnan, 1998). Materials that are attractive to the children and supported by the teacher in her efforts to teach children to write are used spontaneously and frequently by children.

Studies of interactive environments also have demonstrated the importance of the relation between environment and writing development. Johnson and Johnson (1975), in their studies of interdisciplinary approaches to understanding classroom climates, maintain that learning is heavily dependent on children's interactions with one another, their teachers, and physical environment. In classrooms in which this interaction is positive, children grow in their understanding of collaborative construction (Cazden, 1986).

The social aspects of classroom environments also have been studied and have been reported to greatly affect students' learning. From Amidon and Flanders's interactional studies in the 1960s to Dahl and Farnan's summary of writing studies that included investigations in urban classrooms in 1998, researchers have provided strong evidence that classrooms are social organizations that are created by teachers and students. These social organizations directly and indirectly affect the ways that children learn to write.

Curriculum Resources: Using Technology to Teach Writing to Primary Grade Children

Technology is a critical part of the resources that are available for classroom teachers and their students. Dickinson's (1986) research in a first/second-grade classroom investigated the ways in which technology affected writing and classroom social organization. He found that when computers were integrated into the classroom, the teacher expected them to be used for writing and social studies curriculum projects. The teacher and researcher discovered that children began increasingly to ask to work together at the computer because their ideas were more accessible to one another when they both viewed the screen. As students became more collaborative on the computer, their talk began to include discussions of planning what to write, self-monitoring, discussions of spelling, and responses to one another's ideas. This was in marked contrast to the writing experiences they had when they used pencil and paper for writing activities at their desks.

In Jones and Pelligrini's (1996) study examining the effect of word processing on the writing of first graders, the researchers found that word processing, when compared to paper-and-pencil writing, helped students to write narratives. They speculated that the technology took emphasis away from the mechanical aspects of writing, giving students opportunities to focus on words and ideas.

Cochran-Smith, Kahn, and Paris's (1990) study of a 5-year-old writer found that word processing was a qualitatively different experience for this child as compared to paper-and-pencil writing. The computer provided a tool that supported the child's developing writing skills. As in Jones and Pelligrini's study, word processing de-emphasized the mechanical concerns about handwriting, letter formation, and alignment of words that the child had with paper-and-pencil activities. Instead, the technology supported the notion that writing is about words and ideas. The child shifted her attention to letter-sound correspondence, content, and organization, and away from the purely physical and mechanical aspects of writing. In addition, word processing provided an environment in which a teacher's aide could work productively with this child; the aide was able to intervene during the writing rather than after its completion. Word processing created opportunities and a social context in which this young writer could approach the writing differently than she did when she used pencil and paper.

Curriculum Resources: Using Technology to Teach Writing to Intermediate Grade Students

Bangert-Drowns (1993) examined the effects of technology use on four writing measures of intermediate grade students' writing performance: writing quality, amount of writing (number of words), frequency of revision, and effective use of conventions. His analysis showed that a majority of studies reported increased writing quality when word processing was used in classroom writing assignments. He found that less-skilled writers benefited more from word processing than did their higher skilled peers. He argued that less-skilled writers, who had been disengaged from writing tasks, experienced increased motivation for writing when word processing was implemented.

The Missing Links: Arrangement and Grouping in Writing Instruction

Although there are many studies about the effectiveness of management and grouping for instruction in general (see Indrisano & Paratore, 1991, and Doyle, 1996, for an overview), few studies exist that specifically deal with grouping for writing instruction. This lack of research may be the result of the recent emergence of writing as a field of inquiry that is researched widely (Dahl & Farnan, 1998; Tway, 1991), or it may be that past research has ignored the role that grouping plays in writing instruction. Barr and Dreeban (1983) believe it is the latter: "While only the most exceptional of teacher effectiveness studies treat relations among the elements of instruction, virtually none identifies a connection between the activities of teachers and the characteristics of the setting in which teaching takes place—the classroom" (p. 34). In our review of the literature, we did not find any studies that examined students, teachers, classrooms, and grouping. Therefore, grouping appears to be the missing link in understanding how a process approach to writing instruction can be under-taken successfully in a classroom

To learn more about the role of grouping in process writing instruc-tion, we conducted a series of research studies during the past 3 years at Oak Park School, an urban elementary school in San Diego with a multi-linguistic population. After interviewing the entire staff of this 1,000-student elementary school, we found that grouping children for instruction was the single greatest barrier to implementing a process approach to writ-ing instruction (Flood & Lapp, 1997; Lapp & Flood, 1997; Lapp, Flood, Moore, Goss, & LeTourneau, 1997). Teachers noted that they needed a comprehensive management system, which would include specific sug-gestions for grouping, to ensure that all of their students were receiving ap-propriate instruction in flexible grouping patterns that would help them progress as writers. We isolated the variable "Grouping students for writing instruction" as the most problematic part of their instructional program. In their interviews, teachers reported that they were comfortable with their ability to manage their instruction and with their knowledge of materials, but that they were not comfortable with their knowledge and practices in grouping for writing instruction. They found grouping for writing ex-tremely difficult because their children's performances revealed so many extremes. Some children were capable of and willing to write effective pieces of prose all day, whereas others could only write very limited texts for very limited periods of time.

The teachers also noted that some children needed direct instruc-tion in specific elements of the craft of writing while others had mastered all the developmentally appropriate elements of the craft. They were con-cerned because homogeneous grouping appeared to be the solution, which was not an acceptable route for them because they believed strongly in the negative effects of homogeneous grouping on children as explained by Barr and Dreeban (1989). They had been successfully using a model of flexible grouping designed by Lapp and Flood (1997) and Flood, Lapp, Flood, and Nagel (1992), in which children are grouped in heterogeneous groups for the majority of their instruction, with smaller portions of time given to homogeneous grouping. They found this model to be a successful way to meet the needs of all their children and wanted to use it in their instructional writing program. The teachers explained that they did not want to return to homogeneous grouping as the sole grouping pattern for writing. They also explained that they wanted children to be engaged in writing, to be on task, to receive necessary supports through frequent assessment, and conferencing. In an effort to meet these needs, we developed and tested a model for grouping students flexibly so that they were engaged, on task, assessed, and involved in conferencing. We call this model C.A.R.S. (Center-Activity Rotation System). The fundamental tenet of C.A.R.S. is the belief that students and teachers will provide sufficient time, motivation, and involvement in order for students to become proficient writers.

The C.A.R.S. Model

In the C.A.R.S. model, students rotate among several center activities. In most cases, these are not permanent, physical centers; rather, they are activity-based centers that can be removed easily and quickly when they are completed. These centers can be stored in bags or folders for easy access. (See Figure 2 for a C.A.R.S. model rotation system.)

C.A.R.S. begins with assigning children to heterogeneous groups for their center activity, as illustrated in Figure 2, which depicts a classroom of 30 children. Children are given a weekly rotation plan that helps them move among the five center activities included in the illustration. From Monday through Thursday, they rotate among these center activities; Friday is a "catch-up" day for any work that they have missed while they were working in the teacher-sharing center.

As Figure 2 demonstrates, the teacher uses homogeneous grouping for her teacher-sharing time. As the children begin working at their first center activity, the teacher calls a homogeneous group of children who need work on the same element of writing to the teacher-sharing station. While they are there, the children receive direct instruction in several aspects of writing. When they are finished, the children return to the heterogeneous groups, and the teacher then calls another homogeneous group of children to her station. She aligns her instruction to the center-activities rotations so that children will not miss their work in the centers.

In order to make this activity work in a classroom, several writing centers need to be created: a writing center where children compose; a

Figure 2. C.A.R.S. Center-Activities Rotation System in the Classroom

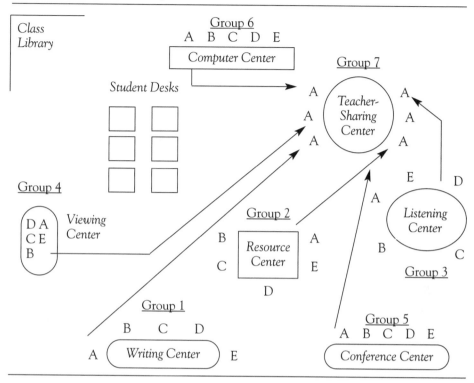

resource center where reference books are housed; a listening center, where children listen to information about their writing topics; a viewing center where children watch informational films and videos; a conference center where children confer about a specific piece of writing; a computer center where children have access to the Internet; and a teacher-sharing center where the children come individually or in small groups to work with the teacher on their writing. These centers are designed by teachers who are working in specific environments, and, therefore, can be modified to specific situations. For example, if Internet access is not yet available, children may spend additional time in the Resource Center.

Center 1: Writing Center

Five children can write separately on a variety of topics in different formats in an array of notebooks and journals. While the children in the group are engaged in their own writing, there is a social element to their work, as they ask for correct spellings, vocabulary words, and stylistic elements from one another, and share their written words.

Center 2: Resource Center

Five children can work in this center which is adjacent to the Writing Center to make the two centers easily accessible to one another. A few children can work together with a set of encyclopedias while others can work independently on the newspaper, an atlas, a magazine, or a book of facts. Children can use these materials freely and take notes on the information that they will want to use in their writing. While they are at this center, students can go to the school resource center or library in search of more material for their writing.

Center 3: Listening Center

Children can work in this center listening to information, stories, and poems on tapes that are related to topics in their writing. The purpose of this center is to ensure that students begin to grasp the relationship between oral and written language. At this center children often read their works to each other. They also have the opportunity in this center to record their writing pieces, then listen to them in order to self-assess their overall message as well as the components of their message.

Center 4: Viewing Center

In this center, children can view videos, films, and DVDs that contain information that will further enhance their writing.

Center 5: Conference Center

Children can conference in pairs about their work. They rotate with one another so that all the children have the opportunity to give and receive feedback with their peers.

Center 6: Computer Center

Children can work on individual computers, searching the Internet for materials that they can use as they write their stories, essays, poems, and reports. They can bookmark Web sites that have information that they want to read again. As they search the Internet, they can take notes that will help them as they write.

Center 7: Teacher-Sharing Center

The number of children who work directly with the teacher in this center varies according to the needs of the children. In this center the teacher works with individuals as well as small groups of homogeneously grouped children who need explicit instruction in specific aspects of writing.

Putting It All Together

A great deal of research has been conducted about the processes that are used by children in urban schools as they write. Many researchers have studied the process approach to writing in which children actively construct texts by experimenting with them is the best instructional format for multilingual populations within a single classroom. But little research has been conducted about the roles and functions of effective classroom management and grouping for writing instruction. In a series of studies we conducted at an urban, multiethnic, multiracial, multilingual elementary school, we discovered that teachers believed that management and grouping were the "missing links" that prevented them from providing effective instruction in writing for the children in their classrooms.

A teaching model called C.A.R.S. was developed and evaluated in their school. The model is situated within a center approach to teaching, which ensures that every child has the opportunity to write at each of the centers that are created for writing instruction. Each child works with the teacher receiving direct, personal instruction in writing; each child also receives feedback from his or her peers. The model allows for a balance between student choice and teacher-directed activities.

As researchers become more informed about the teaching of writing, changes in classroom practices will occur that will offer children many opportunities to write, to confer, to share, and to publish. Writing instruction is a highly complex phenomenon; it requires us to integrate what we know about cognitive processes and curriculum resources into classroom programs that are well managed and well structured.

Future Directions for Research

More research is needed to learn the effect of classroom environments on writing instruction and writing development. This chapter has presented a model for grouping children in urban classrooms for writing instruction that maximizes student writing time. Other research that addresses the question of classroom environment, especially in the area of grouping, might include the following:

1. the generation and evaluation of alternate models of grouping for writing instruction.

2. the effect of the number of adults (teachers, aides, parent volunteers) who are involved in the classroom on the patterns of grouping that are used for writing instruction, and the effect of these new patterns on students' writing growth.

3. the effect of cross-age tutors on the grouping patterns that are used in the classroom and the effect of these new patterns on students' writing growth.

4. the effect of speakers of the child's first language on the child's writing growth in first and second languages—that is, do adults who are working in classrooms with children whose first language is the same as theirs enable them to develop as writers?

5. the effect of time allotted to individual aspects of the C.A.R.S. model on children's writing development.

References

Amidon, E.J., & Flanders, N.A. (1963). *The role of the teacher in the classroom: A manual for understanding and improving teachers' classroom behavior.* Minneapolis, MN: Paul S. Amidon & Associates.

Bangert-Drowns, R.L. (1993). The word processor as an instruction tool: A meta-analysis of word processing in writing instruction. *Review of Educational Research, 63,* 69–93.

Barr, R. (1989). *The social organization of literacy instruction* (38th Yearbook of the National Reading Conference). Chicago: National Reading Conference.

Barr, R., & Dreeban, R. (1983). *How schools work.* Chicago: University of Chicago Press.

Bereiter, C., & Scardamalia, M. (1987). *The psychology of written composition.* Hillsdale, NJ: Erlbaum.

Calkins, L.M. (1994). *The art of teaching writing* (Rev. ed.). Portsmouth, NH: Heinemann.

Cazden, C.B. (1986). Classroom discourse. In M.C. Wittrock (Ed.), *Handbook of research on teaching* (3rd ed., pp. 432–463). New York: Macmillan.

Cioffi, G. (1984). Observing composing behaviors of primary-aged children: The interaction of oral and written language. In R. Beach & L.S. Bridwell (Eds.), *New directions in composition research* (pp. 171–190). New York: The Guilford Press.

Cochran-Smith, M., Kahn, J., & Paris, C.L. (1990). Writing with a felicitous tool. *Theory into Practice, 29,* 235–247.

Dahl, K., & Farnan, N. (1998). *Children's writing: Perspectives from research.* Newark, DE: International Reading Association; Chicago: National Reading Conference.

Dickinson, D.K. (1986). Cooperation, collaboration and a computer: Integrating a computer into a first-second grade writing program. *Research in the Teaching of English, 20,* 357–378.

Doyle, W. (1996). Academic work. *Review of Educational Research, 53*(2), 159–199.

Dyson, A.H. (1989). *Multiple worlds of child writers: Friends learning to write.* New York: Teachers College Press.

Dyson, A.H. (1991). Viewpoints: The word and the world—reconceptualizing written language development, or do rainbows mean a lot to little girls? *Research in the Teaching of English, 25,* 97–123.

Dyson, A.H. (1993). *The social worlds of children learning to write in an urban primary school.* New York: Teachers College Press.

Dyson, A.H. (1995). Writing children: Reinventing the development of childhood literacy. *Written Communication, 12,* 4–46.

Dyson, A.H., & Freedman, S. (1991). Writing. In J. Flood, J.M. Jensen, D. Lapp, & J.R. Squire (Eds.), *Handbook of research on teaching the English language arts* (pp. 754–777). New York: Macmillan.

Edelsky, C. (1982). Writing in a bilingual program: The relation of L1 and L2 texts. *TESOL Quarterly, 16,* 211–228.

Flood, J., Jensen, J.M., Lapp, D., & Squire, J.R. (Eds.). (1991). *Handbook of research on teaching the English language arts.* New York: Macmillan.

Flood, J., & Lapp, D. (1997, December). *Grouping: The unending story.* Paper presented at the annual meeting of the National Reading Conference, Scottsdale, AZ.

Flood, J., Lapp, D., Flood, S., & Nagel, G. (1992, April). Am I allowed to group? Using flexible patterns for effective instruction. *The Reading Teacher, 45*(8), 608–616.

Graves, D. (1975). The writing processes of seven-year-old children. *Research in the Teaching of English, 9,* 227–241.

Graves, D. (Ed.). (1981). *A case study observing the development of primary children's composing, spelling and motor behaviors during the writing process.* (Final report, NIE Grant No. G-78-0174. ED 2180653). Durham, NH: University of New Hampshire.

Greaney, V. (Ed.). (1996). *Promoting reading in developing countries.* Newark, DE: International Reading Association.

Hornberger, N.H. (1994). Continua of literacy. In B.M. Ferdman, R. Weber, & A.G. Ramírez (Eds.), *Literacy across languages and cultures* (pp. 103–139). Albany, NY: State University of New York Press.

Hudelson, S., & Serna, I.A. (1994). Beginning literacy in a whole language bilingual program. In A.D. Flurkey & R.J. Meyer (Eds.), *Under the whole language umbrella* (pp. 278–294). Urbana, IL: National Council of Teachers of English.

Indrisano, R., & Paratore, J.R. (1991). Classroom contexts for literacy learning. In J. Flood, J.M. Jensen, D. Lapp, & J.R. Squire (Eds.), *Handbook of research on teaching the English language arts* (pp. 477–488). New York: Macmillan.

Johnson, D.W., & Johnson, R.T. (1975). *Learning together and alone: Cooperation, competition, and individualization.* Englewood Cliffs, NJ: Prentice Hall.

Jones, I., & Pelligrini, A.D. (1996). The effects of social relationships, writing media, and microgenetic development of first-grade students' written narratives. *American Educational Research Journal, 33*, 691–718.

Koda, K. (1997). Orthographic knowledge in L2 lexical processing: A cross-linguistic perspective. In J. Coady & T. Huckin (Eds.), *Second language vocabulary acquisition* (pp. 35–52). New York: Cambridge University Press.

Krashen, S.D., & Terrell, T.D. (1983). *The natural approach: Language acquisition in the classroom.* Hayward, CA: Alemany Press.

Lapp, D., & Flood, J. (1997, November). *Flexible grouping in action.* Paper presented at the annual meeting of the California Reading Association, San Diego, CA.

Lapp, D., Flood, J., Moore, J., Goss, K., & LeTourneau, M. (1997, November). *Grouping students for instruction.* Paper presented at the annual meeting of the California Reading Association, San Diego, CA.

Loughlin, C.E., & Martin, M.D. (1987). Supporting literacy: Developing effective learning environments. New York: Teachers College Press.

Loughlin, C.E., & Suina, J.H. (1982). *The learning environment: An instructional strategy.* New York: Teachers College Press.

MacGillivray, L. (1994). Tacit shared understandings of a first-grade writing community. *Journal of Reading Behavior, 26*(3), 245–266.

McGinley, W., & Kamberelis, G. (1996). *Maniac Magee* and *Ragtime Tumpie*: Children negotiating self and world through reading and writing. *Research in the Teaching of English, 30*, 75–113.

Moore, J. (1998) *Black English speakers: An examination of language registers of high and low achieving elementary school children.* Unpublished doctoral dissertation, San Diego State University and Claremont Graduate School.

Odlin, T. (1989). *Language transfer: Cross-linguistic influence in language learning.* New York: Cambridge University Press.

Richards, J.C. (1973). Error analysis and second language strategies. In J.W. Oller & J.C. Richards (Eds.), *Focus on the learner: Pragmatic perspectives for the language teacher.* Rowley, MA: Newbury House.

Selinker, L. (1992). *Rediscovering interlanguage.* New York: Longman.

Tinajero, J., & Flor Ada, A. (1993). *The power of two languages.* New York: Macmillan/McGraw-Hill.

Tway, E. (1991). The elementary school classroom. In J. Flood, J.M. Jensen, D. Lapp, & J.R. Squire (Eds.), *Handbook of research on teaching the English language arts* (pp. 425–437). New York: Macmillan.

Colette Daiute

City University of New York

CHAPTER ELEVEN

Writing and Communication Technologies

Using computers for writing development is complicated. Computers can be tools for enhancing written language, yet using the computer requires literacy. Also, computer use is embedded in communication—in classrooms, on the Internet, and in other contexts—which can enhance motivation for learning to write. Nevertheless, children communicating via computers face social and ethical challenges, requiring that they understand and control the contexts, purposes, and processes of written language. For these reasons, children using complex computer systems are involved in critical literacy as they continue to master the mechanics of writing. The following statements by high school students express a range of such possibilities and issues related to using communication technologies, which play an increasingly important role in writing development.

> Technology helps me in school when it comes to down to doing reports, research projects, and...just doing things like that make life easier, make school a lot easier. (Ryman, age 17)

> That's when I really know computers could do a lot of stuff—we was [sic] talking to kids overseas. We had kin—like a penpal thing—and met different kids from different boroughs and made us like family. It, was, it was good. (Marcel, age 17)

Basically being, you know, computer literate, that's the most helpful thing for me 'cause, you know, computers in basically the year 2000 is going to take over this world. (Tina, age 17)

It's going to be hard for low-income students to go against somebody who's, well, more financially stable. (Marcel, age 17)

These quotes are from interviews with New York City high school seniors who participated in a project that supplied computers, tutoring, and other kinds of support to more than 100 students from the time they were in the sixth grade. As part of the project, these students from schools serving low-income neighborhoods had access to a range of computer tools at home as well as in school for 7 formative years of their education (Daiute, Ausch & Chen, 1997). When asked about how the computer enhances written language, Ryman, Tina, Marcel, and others echoed views that have been debated by scholars and educators for many years in relation to the role of computer technology in writing. These students identify computers as tools that can be helpful in a variety of ways, especially in the writing process. At the same time, these comments imply a range of social issues concerning technology. This chapter addresses these issues by reviewing theoretical perspectives that help make sense of how computers relate to writing instruction. Based on this analysis, I suggest that critical literacy must become an aspect of writing instruction by the upper elementary years.

In *Writing and Computers* (1985), I argued that the computer—like any writing instrument—is one of many tools used in the composing process and in the process of developing expertise as a writer. Consistent with this argument, other scholars also have explained that writing with computers is different—not better or worse in any absolute sense—from writing with instruments like pencil or pen on paper. Computer writing practices also must be considered in the social contexts where they occur— like classrooms and cyberspace. Thus, it is important to understand *how* computers function among the many tools of written communication.

Communication Technologies

Scholars and educators have conceptualized writing in relation to the increasingly widespread use of "communication technologies"—a range of electronic technologies that provide tools for creating written texts (Selfe & Selfe, 1994). Communication technologies include networking capacities on the Internet, such as chatrooms, electronic mail, electronic bulletin boards, online information database searches, multi-user simulations, and game environments; these technologies are typically referred to as "cyberspace." Software such as word processing programs, spelling checkers, grammar checkers, outlining programs, and multimedia composing tools are also communication technologies. The use of these technologies has been discussed in the midst of persistent debates that have shaped theory and practice with computers.

Debates about correspondences between face-to-face communication and virtual communication in contexts like e-mail and chatrooms have been intense, in particular as these contexts support and complicate the development of identity and knowledge, which occur in cyberspace almost exclusively in writing. Debates about issues of cognitive and social control have framed theory, research, and practice of computer-based writing. Some scholars have argued, for example, that technology controls human cognition and social interaction (Kerr, 1999; Selfe, & Selfe, 1994), while others view technology as a means to enhance cognition (Jones, 1994; Pea & Kurland, 1984). Debates about control have addressed the issue of whether technologically mediated communication limits expression and creativity as it requires the transformation of ideas and language into numerical patterns (Selfe, & Selfe, 1994). Issues of social control occur because expensive communication technologies are not readily available to all children and because the hidden workings of such complex systems reproduce many social problems like discrimination (Kerr, 1999; Selfe & Selfe, 1994).

There have also been debates about computer cognition—whether computers can think and how they might be tools for thinking. When applied to writing processes, this ambiguous notion of computer cognition reflects, on the one hand, the idea that computer programs can carry out functions of writing when they are programmed with processes that imitate human writers' problem solving, and on the other hand, that computers can be programmed to support writers' activities. For instance, word processors that automatically check spelling and grammar as a writer composes are designed to mimic human cognition. In contrast, writers who turn off these automatic options and apply them selectively when they have questions about specific spelling and grammatical constructions are using a program to support their own cognition. Other examples of computer supports include using word processing capacities for collaborative writing and using the Internet to do research.

As increasing numbers of young people spend time communicating on the Internet, scholars and educators debate whether communication in chatrooms is so aimless and cryptic that it barely counts as literacy. Marcel, who was quoted earlier, did not have strong literacy skills, but he conveyed the excitement of using computers to communicate with people from all over the world, as if writing on the computer were as effortless as talking. Thus, while scholars debate the value of the Internet, young people who might not otherwise write at all outside of school spend hours engaging with print, which is essential to fluent and purposeful literacy (McCutcheon, 1995).

Theories of Writing

The prevailing theories of writing during the past 20 years have yielded diverse interpretations and evaluations of communication technologies, so I present a brief summary of the major theoretical perspectives as they relate to writing. (See also Applebee, Chapter Four in this volume.) Cognitively focused theories, emphasizing composing processes and expert strategies such as planning, apply most readily to applications of computer processing and artificial intelligence capacities, including word processing programs and spelling checkers. In contrast, sociocultural theories emphasizing the contexts, purposes, and practices of writing have been applied mostly to interpret children's uses of networking capacities, such as chatrooms and e-mail (Daiute, 1985). Sociopolitical analyses of literacy add insights about how technologies reflect inequities and the impact of such inequities on the development and use of written language. For example, Marcel's comment about the difficulties of low-income students competing with students from more financially stable families hints at issues of access to electronic communication tools in education, the workplace, and public forums; this comment about such inequities reflects a developing critical awareness that is an essential part of literacy development.

Writing as a Cognitive Process

When microcomputers first offered word processing tools for children, theories of writing and writing instruction focused on composing processes, including planning, revising, and editing (Flower & Hayes, 1981; Graves, 1982). Cognitive science research provided the basis for two approaches to describing the composing process—cognitive strategy theory and writing process theory. These approaches identified a universal set of composing processes emphasizing discovery in prewriting phases and reflection in revising phases. Cognitive strategy research on writing identified, for example, the importance of background knowledge in generating text plans, and writing process theorists emphasized that writers must work from their own personal narratives as the foundation for some types of writing. Although links between writing and memory have not been made as explicitly in writing process theory as in cognitive strategy theory, the importance of children's recalled experiences has been a tenet of composing process research and practice. Major differences also exist between these theories, most notably that the cognitive strategy approach characterizes writing as primarily problem solving, while process theory characterizes writing as primarily creative discovery. These theories have led to different applications of computers as writing tools.

Conceptualizing writing as problem solving has led to research and development of interactive composing programs (Daiute & Kruidenier, 1985; Pea & Kurland, 1984). Research comparing the practices of relatively expert and novice writers has offered findings about the importance of planning among expert writers, in particular guiding writing with a clear sense of goals and plans for achieving these goals in texts (Flower & Hayes, 1981). Computer programs that prompt writers to think about their goals and methods of achieving goals appear to help beginning writers slow down, read their writing, and become more strategic about the composing process (Cochran-Smith, 1991; Daiute & Kruidenier, 1985; Schwartz, 1982; Woodruff, Bereiter, & Scardamalia, 1981–1982). In contrast, theory and practice emphasizing creative aspects of writing have tended to minimize the role of technology, except as a publishing tool.

Writing as Sociocultural Context

As a desire to account for cultural differences in writing development has increased, teachers and researchers have sought theories to explain how context influences writing (Dyson, 1993; Heath, 1983; Vygotsky, 1934/1978). According to sociocultural theories of writing, learning to write means being socialized into a set of values, practices, and symbol systems; texts are cultural artifacts, and the activities involved in creating texts are group-specific rather than universal practices. With their focus on context and text, sociocultural theories emphasize communication and thus involve linking writing closely with speech, reading, and practical activities. Although some researchers focus mostly on literacy practices, sociocultural theory has spawned the notion of "genres" as text forms that carry cultural norms (Cope & Kalantzis, 1993).

Sociocultural explanations apply most readily to communication technologies like cyberspace. Writing in the context of communication technologies, where audiences are part of dynamic textual interactions, might help writers generate salient topics and learn strategies for getting readers' attention. Such contexts also raise issues of interpersonal and intergroup relations around specific texts. At the same time, acknowledging that writing evolves in communication contexts highlights the need for explicit instruction in the forms of writing required in unfamiliar contexts (Delpit, 1988). (For further discussion of sociocultural theories of writing, see also Dyson, Chapter Two in this volume, and Schickedanz, Chapter Three in this volume.)

Perspectives on Literacy as a Political Tool

Sociopolitical explanations of literacy are consistent with sociocultural theories in their emphasis on context as defining the meanings and forms of written language (Freire & Macedo, 1987). Sociopolitical theory differs, however, in its analysis of literacy as a means of power. Sociopolitical theorists explain literacy failure among children and youth from minority and low-income backgrounds as an obvious consequence of inequities they suffer in mainstream contexts like school. An extension of this perspective is the argument that writers must learn the discourses of mainstream contexts almost as if these discourses were foreign languages, and they must learn to use multiple discourses in purposeful ways, in particular to extend their capacities for knowledge and participation in society. Sociopolitical perspectives have, in particular, directed attention to cyberspace as a context where social inequities are played out in the writing process and influence writing development (Daiute, 1985; Selfe & Selfe, 1994). Cyberspace and tools are two useful metaphors in explaining relationships between communication technologies and writing. The following sections discuss research from these theoretical perspectives to explore how communication technologies play a role in writing development and instruction.

Cyberspace: Community, Communication, and Writing

In cyberspace, communication interactions occur through writing—sometimes in codes and often in written dialogue or extended prose. Cyberspace, which is sometimes called virtual reality, also refers to storage capacity, providing large databases (libraries) of information accessible via the Internet. With a modem, telephone line, and a subscription to an Internet service provider, computer users can communicate in writing with people far away or in the next room and can connect to information databases stored on computers at network locations. Echoing debates about human/machine relationships, discussions about cyberspace and literacy have, on the one hand, led to the conclusion that cyberspace is an optimum context for the development of writing skills, and, on the other hand, that cyberspace limits written communication because of injustices similar to those in face-to-face society.

Cyberwriting Mirrors Communication in Life

Since the 1970s when they were first used in the workplace, computer networks have been described as democratic environments that enable people to interact more equitably than they would in face-to-face situations in which skin color, gender, physical strength, and other physical characteristics may lead to discrimination (Hiltz & Turoff, 1978). One argument is that people who meet in cyberspace can create their own identities through written discourse, whereas in person, physical characteristics lead to a range of discriminations. Also in this vein is the argument that communicating in cyberspace chatrooms and e-mail involves children in writing for reasons other than communicating with a teacher or writing for its own sake. Because cyberspace audiences can respond immediately, writers there often envision more authentic reasons to write (Cohen & Reil, 1990; Cummins & Sayers, 1995). Some classroom teachers have always involved children in writing for specific purposes and audiences (other than as exercises) by providing opportunities such as writing workshops and writing to members of the community for information, but these practices are still not the norm. In addition to the opportunity to communicate with distant and unknown audiences, children may be attracted to writing in cyberspace because they perceive it to be unmonitored and thus an adventure.

Written interactions in cyberspace occur among any number of people who enter a chatroom when they log in to the Internet. Organizations and individuals who create chatrooms establish rules, as did the New York City Board of Education, which monitors written interactions on NYCenet for profanity and other forms deemed inappropriate. In many cases, frequent participants in chatrooms establish their own communication mores, which sometimes include ways around rules. The problem with some chatrooms is that there is very little monitoring to protect children from offensive or dangerous interactions. The gradual evolution of such communication practices suggests that cyberspace is like face-to-face communities in some ways, but there are also important differences between face-to-face and Internet interactions, in particular differences of ethics and accountability. For example, even though people appear to establish relationships in cyberspace chatrooms, they can simply turn off the computer and avoid the consequences of their interactions. Another problem is that word processing functions like cutting and pasting can be applied to copy others' cyber conversations and transform them. These and other features of cyberspace make it collaborative and conversational—phenomena that have been shown to support writing development. But arguments in favor of cyberspace as a context for writing development may not apply if the nature of interaction does not support purposeful, communicative, socially conscious writing. In order to understand how writing develops in cyberspace, we must study cyberspaces as cultures where people create values and practices.

In spite of considerable uncertainty about the nature of cyberspace, one of the main observations has been that students of all ages find writing on computers and communicating in cyberspace to be highly motivating—an attitude that has not been reported regarding traditional writing instruction environments (Cochran-Smith, 1991; Daiute, 1985; Hoot & Silvern, 1988). One formal study (Cohen & Reil, 1990) indicated, moreover, that texts written by students for Internet acquaintances received higher quality ratings by teachers than similar writing samples created for the teacher in the classroom. Cohen and Reil (1990) conducted a study of 44 seventh-grade students in Israel who wrote two sets of essays—one in traditional form for an exam and one sent to peers in another country via e-mail. Analyses showed that the e-mail essays were better in several ways than the essays written for the exam. Writing in cyberspace seems more purposeful and meaningful to students because it involves reaching "real" audiences.

It is important to note, however, that when there are no structured activities or specific common interests or purposes, online chat tends to cease or degenerate into meaningless chatter. Thus, while cyberspace may be a motivating and interactive context for writing, an important area for curriculum development is the creation of purposeful activities that can provide explicit links between writing in cyberspace and writing required in academic contexts. For example, curricula guiding children to do reports on whales could contain references to topic-specific chatrooms and instructions to search the Internet for information about whales.

From a sociopolitical perspective, scholars have argued that explanations about the democratic nature of communication in cyberspace are "overoptimistic" and incorrect (Selfe & Selfe, 1994). According to this view, technologies including literacy are instruments of power (Freire & Macedo, 1987). Because technology is expensive and the means of technological production remain in the hands of an elite few, the problems and inequities caused by economic status in society recur with technology (Menser & Aronowitz, 1996; Selfe & Selfe, 1994). These abstractions become real with reports that middle-class suburban public schools have begun to provide their students with Internet connections while public schools in neighboring urban areas do not (Menser & Aronowitz, 1996). Of course, the difference between having computers with Internet connections and not having them may be offset by more substantive class discussion in technologically poor city schools, but access to Internet databases for research reports seems likely to offer benefits. Ryman, like other students quoted at the beginning of this chapter, explains:

The library had like two books, and I was the one that had the computer at home and could get access to the Internet, and I went online and got all the information that they [students in my groups at school] needed, and also I typed everybody's papers for them, cause not a lot of kids have computers.

Economic issues can make a difference in writing development in several ways. Because literacy development depends in large part on having extensive, engaging exposure to print and involvement with communication technologies is print intensive, students who do not have access to these technologies may be at a disadvantage. If children from poor and low-income families and schools continue to have limited access to technologies, like online information databases and e-mail, their writing skills may continue to fall behind those of their middle-class peers. In terms of producing writing, children who have access to word processing tools have supports for the writing process and means of producing print in the form of newsletters or flyers. Such tools may be especially important to children in poor and low-income neighborhoods because they provide ways of connecting with children from similar neighborhoods in other cities as well as with children from suburban and rural communities. Of course, if communication technologies limit writing development, pen and paper are sufficient, provided that writing and reading instruction are enriching and effective.

In addition to issues of access and equality of opportunity, the ways students use communication technologies also are related to power. Some scholars have argued that when computers are available for students from poor and low-income backgrounds, children learn to use them in "deskilled" ways (Menser & Aronowitz, 1996), such as learning word processing skills, more than learning to use the computer for research and publishing. This trend toward emphasizing computer skills for entry into low-level employment rather than for research and critical thinking requires continuing research and educators' attention. In addition, students who have limited access may have less control over technologies, in particular because they may not be aware of the limits or the possibilities of technology. Students who have had experience using word processing and spelling checkers, for example, learn quickly that programs can not identify words that are spelled incorrectly for the context in which they occur

(Daiute, 1986), but students are not spontaneously aware of the broader contexts in which they work.

Scholars have argued that writing in cyberspace is limited by a machine that operates according to mathematical principles, with textual interactions often being reduced to cryptic, coded language or manipulated by machine features such as the size of the screen (Selfe & Selfe, 1994). Results of a study with 57 seventh and ninth graders in a city junior high school showed that students produced longer texts when they used the computer than when they used pencil or pen on paper (Daiute, 1986). The structure of the longer texts indicated, however, that regardless of where in the text additions made most sense, these 10- to 13-year-olds tended to put additions at the end of the text, perhaps because this required fewer word processing commands. Because writing has always been affected by the tools used to produce it, these results are no surprise. The dramatic increase in the length of texts written on word processors underscores the need to consider the writing instrument as part of the writing process. With such knowledge, teachers can guide students in how to use computer tools to achieve substantive discursive purposes. For example, teaching students how to revise paragraphs to conform to certain organizational patterns, such as beginning paragraphs with topic sentences, can occur with practice using cut-and-paste word processing capacities.

The *Orillas* project has developed structured activities in cyberspace to benefit those who do not have much power (Cummins & Sayers, 1995). This project involves establishing connections between sister schools in countries with different dominant languages that have interest in bilingual communication. For example, schools in Puerto Rico have been paired with schools in the United States to exchange information about each others' countries, schools, and students. In addition to exchanging such "cultural packages," sister schools can engage in collaborative projects such as making a database of proverbs and discussing the proverbs as illustrations of their cultures. The project was designed to privilege minority languages like Spanish by establishing communication in that language most of the time. In this way, students in the U.S. have the chance to write in Spanish, which they may be studying, while native Spanish speakers in U.S. and Puerto Rican classrooms are the language experts, in contrast to the more typical low-status roles that they are often implicitly given (Cummins & Sayers, 1995).

Much more research is essential for examining the nature of young people's written communication in cyberspace. Useful research agendas would focus on exploring how children transfer classroom writing instruction to spontaneous Internet contexts, including chatrooms, e-mail, and database searching, and how the communication potential of cyberspace can be used to augment children's social influence, learning, and skills.

Cyberplay Is a Developmental Process

Writing in cyberspace often involves playing with knowledge, identity, and language itself, which can serve both developmental and social purposes. Writing in cyberspace seems somewhere between speaking and writing, which may explain why many people who do not like to write in other contexts spend their precious free time writing in cyberspace. This speech-like quality makes a range of communication in cyberspace appealing, expansive, and problematic.

While simulating real-life communication, cyberspace is also a place for fantasy. Theories and observations that cyberspace serves as a mask have noted that young people interacting in cyberspace often play out ideal or feared identities that they keep hidden during face-to-face interactions. Cyberspace is a place where people can create identities for themselves and see how others react. Although identity has not been a major focus of composition research in the past, the issue of context has gradually expanded to consider how identities are created in social context through oral and written language (Daiute, 1998; Lightfoot, 1997). One researcher who has spent many years interacting in cyberspace explained that adolescents and adults in multi-user simulated games write about themselves to invent, expand, and hide aspects of their identities (Turkle, 1995). Multi-user games are interactive fictions in which participants write themselves into stories and create discourse identities, and this use of cyberspace is like a diary that writes back. Diaries have served the function of identity development for a long time, and writing in cyber-communities makes this identity function highly salient. By providing such a setting where written identities can interact, cyberspace may help people understand and improve themselves, but certain fictional identities may be harmful, unethical exaggerations.

In cyberspace, children can engage in functional interactions that sometimes defy limits and conventions of physical reality, as when they write to professional scientists who are available online to answer scientific questions and to engage children in helping with scientific inquiries, such as gathering and measuring rainfall in their neighborhoods (Kerr, 1999). While children may be quite serious in their interactions with professional scientists, they are "playing" scientist as they use scientific language to perform the professional scientific activities (Reddy, 1996). Not being able to see the adult science writers with whom they interact may allow children to work uninhibitedly and playfully in an "as-if" mode that supports cognitive development. When writing about science in cyberspace, children are writing to learn, which is difficult to create meaningfully in traditional classroom settings (Scardamalia, Bereiter, McLean, Swallow, & Woodruff, 1989).

Arguments that anonymity minimizes discrimination are countered with troubling observations that creating cyber-identities also can be dishonest and exploitive. Just as children can write themselves new identities as amateur scientists, they can engage in role-playing in cyberspace with consequences that may be dangerous. Because of the anonymity of the context, participants can craft writing to present false identities—using written language to pretend they are younger, older, or in other ways different from what they are in face-to-face interactions. Cyberspace is, for example, a context where adults have pretended to be children in chatrooms. Cyberspace can be a context where people play out fantasies that allow them to shed old fears or envision new possibilities, but cyberspace also can be a context where their worst problems flourish unchecked (Turkle, 1995). For these as well as pedagogical reasons, promoting cyberspace requires ongoing research and curriculum development efforts. Children should also be encouraged to talk about their cyberspace interactions with adults and peers as a way to build bridges between virtual and physical worlds and to reveal personal and interpersonal consequences.

In summary, communication technologies, including cyberspace and computer writing tools, are useful because they make explicit some of the social and cognitive aspects of writing. Children can use communication technologies to connect with people from different parts of the world as soon as they can write, but access to these tools requires critical thinking, including strategies for managing technical aspects of the computer and strategies for reading the messages that convey meanings in the absence of facial expressions, gestures, or other contextual cues. Thus, as communication technologies provide supports for writing, the nature of these technologies makes it increasingly obvious that writing skill involves reflection and analysis of the social milieu.

Using Technological Tools for Thinking and Composing

In much of the discussion about technology and writing throughout the last 20 years, the computer has been described as a tool, and this metaphor has evolved in relation to theories of writing as a cognitive process. Computer tools have been described as scaffolds that extend writers' composing processes and transform writers' knowledge and discourse. After explaining the concept of *distributed cognition*, this section offers two ideas about how various computer tools can be used to enhance cognitive aspects of composing—*distributed composing* and *transformational composing*.

Distributed Cognition

One way of conceptualizing communication technologies for writing is as tools for *distributed cognition* (Salomon, 1993), which refers to thinking as it occurs in context—thinking that embodies the range of physical and interpersonal supports both leading up to and during the thinking process. According to this theory, other people and environmental factors—including writing tools—extend an individual's knowledge and cognitive processes. The processing and networking capacities of computer tools make them especially interesting and sometimes problematic as extensions of human thought.

Another aspect of the distributed cognition theory is that social interactions involved in problem solving around meaningful activities are what eventually guide effective cognitive processes like writing and reading. For writers, distributed cognition means imagining and anticipating readers' responses, and one of the difficulties of learning to write is to engage in composing processes with imagined audiences (Bereiter & Scardamalia, 1987; Daiute, 1985; see also Applebee, Chapter Four in this volume). The more explicit the social interaction context, the more support there is for beginning writers to choose appropriate composing strategies, rhetorical forms, and specific words. Writers with such social awareness also might decide to suspend their thinking about an audience in favor of a freewriting mode or attention to aesthetic aspects of texts (Elbow, 1976).

Distributed Composing

Distributed composing is interactive composing that sets the writer's thought and action in broader social and physical contexts. For example, a writer reflects on his or her audience as the basis for deciding on a text revision and then carries out a revision using the word processor. The word processor presents the text in a form the reader can view immediately on the computer monitor or later on a printout. Computers can extend writing processes in a variety of other ways as well. For example, word processors reduce short-term memory burdens, especially for younger writers who find it easier to type and correct mistakes than to form letters, words, and sentences, and easier to give commands than to recopy entire texts (Hoot & Silvern, 1988). Similarly, spelling checkers extend writers' capacities by identifying words that are not included in the program's online dictionary, leaving authors to decide if or how they have mistyped or misspelled an identified word and to select an appropriate alternative if necessary. Such information processing explanations are the basis for arguing that if children know, for example, that an electronic spell-checking phase will help them focus on individual words, it may be easier for them to suspend editing as they compose, leaving more attention for generating ideas, revising, and editing independently—a strategy that scholars have suggested for some time (see Elbow, 1976; Graves, 1982).

Several studies have examined students' composing processes with and without computers, and in doing so have made discoveries about the nature of the composing process (see Cochran-Smith, 1991; Daiute, 1986). Other studies have shown that students who used word processors were more willing and prolific when they used these tools than when they used pencils and paper (see Daiute, 1986; Jones, 1994). Instruction in how to use word processing features, however, was not enough to result in revision if children did not know how to accomplish this important part of the writing process (Bridwell-Bowles, Johnson, & Brehe, 1987; Daiute &

Kruidenier, 1985). These studies have suggested that revising involves social and practical motivation as well as expertise.

In addition, studies of word processing also have offered information about how interventions in composing processes might work. For example, studies of online prompting to remind, organize, and suggest planning and revising strategies have indicated that interactive composing can address information processing difficulties. In one instance, students who had the prompting program available on the computers in their urban middle school did more quality revising than their classmates who either used word processors without such tools or used pens and paper (Daiute & Kruidenier, 1985). The prompting program that was accessible from the word processor offered students a selection of prompts to check a text for completeness, clarity, and correctness. After selecting one of these options, students saw a list of features that the program would prompt further. Some of the prompting options identified filler words such as *kind of* and *sort of*, while most of the options suggested strategies for students to apply independently to help them re-read and revise their own texts. Students who used this program from October through June did more revising than a group of peers who used only a word processor. Another group of students who used pens and thus had to recopy entire texts when revising made more revisions of ideas than students who used word processors alone. With word processing alone, students did more editing than revising. In summary, students who made the most appropriate revisions (as determined by a group of teachers) were those who used online prompting and word processing. If beginning writers can benefit from simple computerized reminders to re-read and evaluate their texts, they can benefit much more from interactions with teachers and peers who respond to the form, content, and rhetorical force of their writing.

In another study, 4- to 6-year-old writers who composed with talking word processors became more sensitive to phoneme/grapheme correspondences, as measured on independent assessments, than children who did not hear what they wrote read aloud as they composed (Hoot & Silvern, 1988). This study indicates that benefits from a writing tool can be most dramatic for writers struggling with form and fine motor coordination. No one can make revisions without having at least some idea of the conventions that constitute good writing, clear thinking, and effective communication in a particular context, but young writers may or may not act on such knowledge as a function of the tools at their disposal.

Transformative Composing

According to sociocultural theory, speech and other coded interactions constitute thinking. When symbolic tools are used in purposeful ways, "as speech and the use of signs are incorporated into any action, the action becomes transformed and organized along entirely new lines," (Vygotsky, 1934/1978, p. 24). Just as writing is a symbol system that transforms speech, writing with symbolic tools like word processors and e-mail engages young people in yet another set of cultural symbols. Building on Vygotsky's explanation that symbolic acts transform thinking, *transformative composing* is the deliberate use of composing interactions, contexts, and tools to enhance learning. As discussed earlier, teachers and researchers have found that critical analysis of one's own writing is extremely difficult, which is why approaches to writing that transforms knowledge are rare (Bereiter & Scardamalia, 1987). Activities from recopying to outlining can engage writers in closer reading of their texts, which may help them to identify areas for improvement, but purposeful interaction with one's audience around specific texts seems to be necessary to engage the social and material symbolism identified by Vygotsky as transformative thinking. Research has offered several examples to show that curricula for using communication technologies in effortful ways are needed to foster transformational composing (see Daiute, 1985; Woodruff, Bereiter, & Scardamalia, 1981–1982).

Collaborative writing is a socially embedded use of word processors. As tools that allow writers to merge and revise ideas in text, word processors can be integral to creative and critical composing. Collaborative writing with a partner involves children in composing processes that make explicit the social nature of writing. When composing with a partner, student writers have the benefit of experiencing the role of writer and reader as they respond to a partner's suggestion of specific text sequences and listen to a partner's reactions (Daiute, Campbell, Griffin, Reddy, & Tivnan, 1993; Dale, 1997). The word processor is not absolutely necessary for collaborative writing, but it makes creating a coauthored text more feasible because individual contributions can be merged into one via typing, merging, and editing capacities. The collaboration is, thus, embodied in the word processed text.

Children engage in a range of playful and metacognitive strategies when composing with peers. Research that compares interactions between peers composing at the computer and the same peers composing with their teacher indicates, moreover, that children's peer collaborative composing is varied and productive (Daiute et al., 1993). In this study, the teacher engaged her 18 third-grade students in a range of composing processes, such as thinking about the purpose of the text, readers' possible reactions to the text, and the requirements of the genre they were using, so collaborating with the teacher was useful. When working with their teacher, physical aspects of the children's writing were not so obviously different from hers, which may have made them eager to take over the keyboard to introduce sentences—a method of controlling the writing process. With that kind of physical control, the children could act on the teacher's substantive suggestions for text content and process. In this context, an experienced writer (the teacher) can engage students in making the kinds of extensive revisions via the sophisticated revising and editing functions of word processors—like cutting and pasting—which they as inexperienced writers tend not to use (Bridwell-Bowles et al. 1987). Nevertheless, with peers, children tended to engage in transformative thinking via their intensely playful experimentation with knowledge, identity, and language; free exchange of ideas; and sharing of personal, affective experiences. Interestingly, this playful orientation in peer collaborative writing on the computer has been associated with more improvement than has writing with only the teacher (Daiute et al., 1993).

Because they provide image and sound processing with word processing, children can use multimedia composing tools to transform their writing skills. Using graphics engages children who would not otherwise be attentive to textual features that provide support for their writing. Images include details and nuances that are more difficult for beginning readers to glean from text. In addition, integrating verbal and nonverbal messages is purposeful and enriching. Visual images also serve as a focal point for shared discussion, because children can coordinate picture viewing via gestures and description, discuss what they see, and develop ideas in the socially mediated context. Daiute and Morse (1993) studied a group of eight underachieving fourth graders for several months as they used a multimedia composing tool to create a book about their cultures and communities. The students worked as a group and individually, gathering visual images, sounds, artifacts, and texts that they thought represented their cultures. As a group, these fourth graders digitized their collections into a shared database, and then each student selected images from the database to use in individual reports. Students selected images and sounds from popular culture—pictures of favorite rap singers, candy bar wrappers, baseball cards, images from youth magazines, and curriculum-related images pertaining to minority cultures. The written texts students created about these images tended to be more expanded than writing they had done before this activity. In addition, the composing processes in this context were most revealing, because children used the activity and multimedia tools provided to compensate for their disabilities in productive ways. For example, one boy who was reported to have great difficulty with written language in part because he was hyperactive, shifted quickly across the image, sound, and text tools represented on the multimedia screen, but wrote an extended text because the media provided several productive composing channels rather than only the sequential stream of written words. Thus, the boy used the range of tools to transform his disability into an ability. Similarly, research that compared results of various storytelling modes, including text and two kinds of video—one that prompted comprehension and another that did not—also showed that multimedia tools support literacy (Sharp, Rowe, & Kinser, 1995).

Some of the most dramatic transformational functions of computers occur when they provide a means of communication that would otherwise be impossible, as, for example, those with physical disabilities. Talking word processors provide flexible writing tools for the blind. Electronic networks provide speech-like communication channels for the deaf, and software activated by single strokes, breath, and other limited physical inputs provide means of communication for the seriously disabled (Brooks, 1994).

Teachers also can use communication technologies to transform and restructure their classroom practice (Bruce, Michaels, & Watson-Gegeo, 1985). Researchers have described how children often have more expertise with computers than their teachers do and thus can take on positions of leadership in the classroom, which may be especially important for children who are underachieving in literacy and other abilities. Using technology such as word processing and the Internet can engage children in communication activities that support written language, in particular by engaging them in using text to display and extend their expertise. Similarly, teachers can combine the lecture and workshop methods of instruction in on-line classrooms where students can write, share, critique, and revise essays via e-mail during part of the class and listen to explicit instruction during another part of the class (Barrett & Paradis, 1988). Although technology can be a catalyst to such pedagogical transformation, the technology is typically only one aspect of a much larger educational reform.

Using Communication Technologies Requires Critical Literacy

Analyses of cyberspace and computer writing tools indicate the need for teachers and students to be reflective, critical users of literacy and communication technologies. Critical literacy is an awareness of issues of equity and power in the forms, functions, and contexts of literacy (Freire & Macedo, 1987). Critical literacy work involves children in thinking and talking about how, for example, they might have created brief, vague texts in contexts in which they did not have a strong sense of purpose or in which they felt that other people were simply not interested in what they had to say. As people engage in learning the mechanics of encoding and decoding written language, they can benefit from being able to assess what supports or inhibits their use of those skills. Basic writing becomes fluent writing as students engage with audiences for specific purposes. Written communication provides students with invaluable experience on how their writing has been problematic, providing the basis for developing critical perspectives—perspectives on self in society. Critical theory has traditionally been considered for adult students, but teachers and scholars have begun to demonstrate that students can use literacy to manipulate power for their own ends (Heath & Mangiola, 1991). This theory must be extended to critical uses of communication technologies.

Critical literacy involves teachers, children, and parents in reflecting on how communication is embedded in values, practices, and relationships. For example, in many classrooms children are granted use of computer word processors as a reward for good behavior for completing their work. Such application is inconsistent with research suggesting that word processing can be most helpful to the weakest writers, who are also likely to be the last ones to finish drills and the ones with the most problematic behavior (Daiute, 1985). With awareness of computer tools as means of production, teachers can help children think through what will help them to broaden their literacy experiences and to develop specific skills.

Literacy classes are also appropriate contexts for addressing the use of communication technologies, such as relationships between community and identity, publishing and plagiarizing. The public and malleable quality of online text makes multiple authorship and copying increasingly possible. For this reason, issues of what counts as authorship, including the dialogic quality of text and the possibility of plagiarism, should become more central in writing instruction. Writing that is immediately public, as it is in cyberspace and collaborative composing, illustrates the need for discussion about issues related to participating in communities. These issues include ethical presentation of self and assuming responsibility for safety in response to deceitful presentation. To the extent that online writing involves community and the need for shared values and practices, children need guidance in thinking about these issues and their responsibilities to communities.

Students who maintain unreflective and uncritical views of technology may not realize that although learning word processing skills can ultimately be useful for getting a job, using word processing to express their own views and to connect with other like-minded youth in an organized manner is a way to become active members of society.

One way to prepare children for critical literacy practice is to involve them in analyses of written language communities. Children can, for example, be guided to analyze cyberchats. They can note how different people write, and how they use words to present themselves, to share their expertise, and to make friends. Pairs of classes can alternate anonymous classroom and online chats, later comparing how people interacted in writing and in face-to-face interactions. Class groups can have discussions beginning with questions such as, What do we know about the people writing in the chat? How do we know this from their writing? What don't we know? How does what they say and how they say it compare to who they say they are? The answers to these questions can then evolve into a discussion of how children prefer to interact and what makes them feel uncomfortable. After sharing experiences with Internet chats in which the students do not know their interlocutors, discussion about in-person classroom conversations can address questions such as, Are there interactions in writing technologies that put certain people down? How do these relate to put-downs in face-to-face interactions? How would we like online interaction to be, and what would we like it to be about? If class members keep printouts of their online written interactions, they can point to specific aspects of text and implied messages as bases for their discussion, and teachers can help guide them to create a list of strategies for writing on computers.

Research on the development of metacognitive strategies indicates that by the upper elementary grades, children can engage in the goal setting, monitoring, and reflective processes required for critical literacy if they are working in meaningful, supportive contexts (Bereiter & Scardamalia, 1987). In addition, research has begun to examine uses of technology for critical literacy development in older beginning writers (Mahiri, 1998), but more research should be devoted to the nature and development of critical communication technology use among children.

Issues-oriented online conversations, debates, and collaborative writing of newsletters can provide meaningful structure for organizing written interactions in cyberspace, but these must be extended with curriculum activities, because teaching and guided practice leads to skill development (Bereiter & Scardamalia, 1987; Daiute et al., 1993; Delpit, 1986; Vygotsky, 1978). Written conversation online can lead to instruction on persuasive writing-based community-building outside of school. A book about how children can participate in the law, for example, could be the basis for a youth chatroom on children's rights (Nunez & Marx, 1997). As children interact online about legal issues that affect them, they also could write to lawyers in order to be exposed to legal language and ways of thinking. The plethora of perspectives among children from diverse sociocultural backgrounds working on the Internet from their classrooms also supports the development of critical literacy, because children respond with greater interest to points of view expressed by their peers than to the same views expressed by teachers (Daiute et al., 1993).

In conclusion, a critical literacy perspective is one that argues for children's need to participate in discussions about their views of the world and the role that writing plays in this world. Writing is a medium that can engage children in many aspects of identity and community-building, but these children need more support with communication technologies than they have been receiving. Communication technologies make context and knowledge explicit, but children need to be socialized to critical literacy—to evaluate their literacy actions and to determine how these actions affect society and support their own development. Emphasis should be on teaching children to use technological writing tools, like other resources, to increase their own capacities and skills as learners, thinkers, and communicators. For example, children can learn to use a range of computer software when writing reports, such as large research databases, online encyclopedias, and online chatrooms where they can interview people in interest groups relevant to their research. Children need to develop skills to organize their ideas and written conventions in ways that are appropriate for diverse, relevant communication contexts. While using computer communication to participate in a range of established institutions (such as professional chatrooms and research databases), children can also think about the technology in terms of equitable access to the tools of power. Children can be guided to use cyberspace and computer writing tools to write about their ideas and hopes to children in other parts of the world. However, it is clear that in order to model and support meaningful, safe interactions in cyberspace for our students and children, we adults have substantial learning to do.

The development and use of communication technologies has far outpaced research on computer-mediated writing. Qualitative research that examines how teachers and children integrate communication technologies into writing instruction can offer invaluable information about interactions of social, cognitive, and physical aspects of writing. From the perspective of critical literacy theory, the most important questions address social, cognitive, and physical aspects of writing from students' points of view. Process questions like, How do teachers integrate communication technologies into writing instruction? and How do students from various writing backgrounds and expertise use communication technologies in their writing? are important questions that can be addressed by teacher research, or by teams of teachers and researchers, observing and analyzing processes and effects of communication technologies in the classroom. Similarly, questions like What do children learn about writing? can offer insights about students' reflection about writing. Asking young people to express their knowledge about the writing process and writing context invites reflection that can develop into untapped research on critical literacy. Discussions about the purpose and audiences of writing as they relate to social issues like those addressed above can begin with discussion of writing technologies.

References

Barrett, E. & Paradis, J. (1988). Teaching writing in an online classroom. *Harvard Educational Review, 58*, 154–171.

Bereiter, C., & Scardamalia, M. (1987). *The psychology of written composition.* Hillsdale, NJ: Erlbaum.

Bridwell-Bowles, L., Johnson, P., & Brehe, S. (1987). Composing and computers: Experienced writers. In A. Matsuhashi (Ed.), *Real time modeling production processes* (pp. 8–107). Norwood, NJ: Ablex.

Brooks, H. (1984). *A child's access to technology as access to society.* Unpublished dissertation, Harvard Graduate School of Education, Cambridge, MA.

Bruce, B.C., Michaels, S., & Watson-Gegeo, K. (1985). How computers can change the writing process. *Language Arts, 62*, 143–149.

Cochran-Smith, M. (1991). Word processing and writing in elementary classrooms: A critical review of related literature. *Review of Educational Research, 61*, 107–155.

Cohen, M., & Reil, M. (1990). The effect of distant audiences on students' writing. *American Educational Research Journal, 26*, 143–159.

Cope, B., & Kalantzis, M. (1993). *The powers of literacy: A genre approach to teaching writing.* Pittsburgh, PA: University of Pittsburgh Press.

Cummins, J., & Sayers, D. (1995). *Brave new schools: Challenging cultural illiteracy through global learning networks.* New York: St. Martin's Press.

Daiute, C. (1985). *Writing and computers.* Reading, MA: Addison-Wesley.

Daiute, C. (1986). Physical and cognitive factors in the revising process: Insights from studies with computers. *Research in the Teaching of English, 20*, 140–159.

Daiute, C. (1998). Points of view in children's writing. *Language Arts, 75*, 138–149.

Daiute, C., Ausch, R., & Chen, P-Y. (1997). *Contradicting a program for "at risk" urban youth.* Final report to the Stanton Heiskell Center, Project Tell, New York.

Daiute, C., Campbell, C., Griffin, T.M., Reddy, M., & Tivnan, T. (1993). Young authors' interactions with peers and a teacher: Toward a developmentally sensitive sociocultural literacy theory. In C. Daiute (Ed.), *The development of literacy through social interaction* (pp. 41–63). San Francisco: Jossey-Bass.

Daiute, C., & Kruidenier, J. (1985). A self-questioning strategy to increase young writers' revising processes. *Applied Psycholinguistics, 6*, 308–318.

Daiute, C., & Morse, F. (1993). Access to knowledge and expression: Multimedia writing tools for children with diverse needs and strengths. *Journal of Special Education Technology, 12*, 1–35.

Dale, H. (1997). *Co-authoring in the classroom: Creating an environment for effective collaboration*. Urbana, IL: National Council of Teachers of English.

Delpit, L. (1988). The silenced dialogue: Power and pedagogy in educating other people's children. *Harvard Educational Review, 58*, 280–298.

Dyson, A.H. (1993). Sociocultural perspective on symbolic development in primary grade classrooms. In C. Daiute (Ed.), *The development of literacy through social interaction*. (pp. 25–40) San Francisco: Jossey-Bass.

Elbow, P. (1976). *Writing without teachers*. New York: Oxford University Press.

Flower, L., & Hayes, J. (1981). A cognitive process theory of writing. *College Composition and Communication, 28* (2), 122–128.

Freire, P., & Macedo, D. (1987). *Literacy: Reading the word and the world*. Cambridge, MA: Begin & Garvey.

Graves, D. (1982). *Teachers and children at work*. Exeter, NH: Heinemann.

Heath, S.B. (1983). *Ways with words*. New York: Oxford University Press.

Heath, S.B., & Mangiola, L. (1991). *Children of promise: Literate activity in linguistically and culturally diverse classrooms*. Washington, DC: National Education Association.

Hiltz, S.R., & Turoff, M. (1978). *The network nation: Human communication via computer*. Reading, MA: Addison-Wesley.

Hoot, J., & Silvern, S. (Eds.). (1988). *Writing with computers in the early grades*. New York: Teachers College Press.

Jones, I. (1994). The effect of a word processor on the written composition of second grade pupils. *Computers in the Schools, 11*, 43–54.

Keifer, K., & Smith, C. (1983). Textual analysis with computers: Tests of Bell Laboratories' computer software. *Research in the Teaching of English, 17*, 201–215.

Kerr, S. (1999). Visions of sugarplums: The future of technology, education, and schools. In M.J. Early & K.H. Rehage (Eds.), *Issues in curriculum: Ninety-eighth yearbook of The National Society for the Study of Education* (pp. 169–198). Chicago, IL: The University of Chicago Press.

Lightfoot, C. (1997). *The culture of adolescent risk-taking*. New York: Guilford Press.

Mahiri, J. (1998). *Shooting for excellence: African-American and youth culture's role in new century schools*. Urbana, IL: National Council of Teachers of English.

McCutcheon, D. (1995).Cognitive processes in children's writing: Developmental and individual differences. *Issues in Education, 1*, 185–191.

Menser, M., & Aronowitz, S. (1996). On cultural studies, science, and technology. In S. Aronowitz, B. Martinsons, M. Menser, & J. Rich (Eds.), *Technoscience and cyberculture* (pp. 7–28). New York: Routledge.

Nunez, S.J., & Marx, T. (1997). *And justice for all*. Brookfield, CT: Milbrook Press.

Pea, R.D., & Kurland, M.D. (1984). *Toward cognitive technologies for writing*. Technical Report No. 30, Bank Street College of Education. New York: Center for Children and Technology.

Reddy, M. (1996). *Doing science in a second grade classroom*. Unpublished doctoral dissertation. Cambridge, MA: Harvard Graduate School of Education.

Salomon, G. (Ed.). (1993). *Distributed cognition: Psychological and educational considerations*. New York: Cambridge University Press.

Scardamalia, M., Bereiter, C., McLean, R., Swallow, J., & Woodruff, E. (1989). Computer supported intentional learning environments. *Journal of Educational Computing Research, 5*, 51–68.

Schwartz, H.J. (1982). Monsters or mentors: Computer applications for humanistic education. *College English, 44*, 141–152.

Selfe, C.L., & Selfe, R.J., Jr. (1994). The politics of the interface: Power and its exercise in electronic contact zones. *College Composition and Communication, 45*, 480–504.

Sharp, D.L.M., Rowe, D., & Kinzer, C. (1995). Dynamic visual support for story comprehension and mental model building by young, at-risk children. *Educational Technology Research and Development, 43*, 25–42.

Turkle, S. (1995). *Life on the screen: Identity in the age of the Internet*. New York: Simon & Schuster.

Vygotsky, L.S. (1978). *Mind in society*. Cambridge, MA: Harvard University Press. (Original work published 1934)

Woodruff, E., Bereiter, C., & Scardamalia, M. (1981–1982). On the road to computer assisted compositions. *Journal of Educational Technology Systems, 10*, 133–148.

PART FIVE

ASSESSMENT OF WRITING

Robert C. Calfee
University of California, Riverside

CHAPTER TWELVE

Writing Portfolios: Activity, Assessment, Authenticity

Writing assessment has been on the leading edge of educational practice for the past quarter century. This is an immodest claim, and perhaps un-expected coming from a person associated with the reading domain, but one that I advance with certainty and enthusiasm. In the 19th century, secondary teachers emphasized the expression of ideas through the prepa-ration of essays. They assumed that high school graduates planning to at-tend college (a favored elite) required this talent, whether their career goals were literature or law, medicine or math. The advent of multiple-choice tests during the post–World War II era, the demonstration of high correlations between such tests and actual writing performance, and in-creasingly intense mandates for accountability and efficiency all led states to dispense with composition examinations for external evaluation of stu-dents' literacy achievement. The decision ignored a common-sense prin-ciple: students and teachers, for better or worse, both ask "Will it be on the test?" A fundamental principle in contemporary schooling is that what is tested is what will be taught if what is tested really matters, and the stakes are high. The evidence is pervasive that reliance on externally mandated high-stakes testing undermines curriculum goals and thwarts teachers' professional judgments (see Association for Supervision and Curriculum Development, 1999; Kane & Mitchell, 1996; Office of Tech-nology Assessment, 1992).

In the 1980s, a few states (most notably South Carolina in 1983) countered the multiple-choice trend by initiating statewide writing assessments, in large part to redirect the attention of classroom teachers to the critical importance of instructing students not just to recognize proper grammar (easily incorporated in the multiple-choice format), but to *construct* a composition. The Commission of the College Entrance Examination Board had so recommended during the academic reform movements of the 1960s. The Bay Area Writing Project, emerging in the 1960s and continuing into the 1970s, reconnected English teachers to the fundamental ideas of the writing process: purpose, voice, audience, and coherence; develop, draft, reflect, revise, polish, publish. (See also Vacca & Vacca, Chapter Nine in this volume.)

The synergy between pressures for statewide writing assessment and efforts to support authentic writing within the classroom was arguably genuine at the outset of these movements. With this turn of events, new conceptions of the proper classroom assessment of writing emerged (or perhaps re-emerged) in clearly articulated fashion. Before the second World War, the teacher's assignment of a grade generally went unquestioned. The student's task was to present a product, the composition, which was reviewed subjectively. One hoped that the criteria focused primarily on development of ideas and coherence of the argument, although some teachers probably relied more on surface features such as length, spelling, punctuation, and syntax.

With the emergence in the 1960s of external mandates, the assessment task became more public and demanding. One pressure came from the articulation of explicit standards for judging writing quality, often in the form of analytic rubrics. The teacher's review of the final product had to go beneath the surface, examining difficult issues such as organization, coherence, style, and voice. Moreover, the teacher was expected to appraise process as well as product—a variation on the old-fashioned idea of "showing your work." To be sure, districts and states were slow to address these issues; cost-efficiency considerations were paramount, ruling out any approach that was complex or costly. Holistic criteria ruled the day, often taking shape as "good, better, best," with standards set more by what the average student could do than by any notion of an ideal essay. The bottom line is that most states now currently employ writing assessments as part of their accountability systems.

Pressure also came from psychometricians, whose flags bore daunting labels like reliability and validity, generalizability and standard error of measurement, and whose arguments took the form of complex formulas and acronymic computer programs. Opponents of writing assessment argued that teacher judgments were subjective, biased, and unreliable. It was one thing for parents to confront the classroom teacher about their child's grade, but quite different when a state legislature assembled experts to challenge data from an entire state (Hambleton, Jaeger, Koretz, Linn, Millman, & Phillips, 1995; Koretz, Stecher, Klein, & McCaffrey, 1994; LeMahieu, Gitomer, & Eresh, 1995; Linn, 1994; Linn & Baker, 1996). Writing professionals (and psychometricians) have responded to the task in a variety of ways, and today we know how to design assessment systems that yield trustworthy and generalizable measures (Herman, Gearhart, & Baker, 1993; Kane & Mitchell, 1996; Supovitz, MacGowan, & Slattery, 1997). To be sure, obtaining quality results is expensive, variations in the writing tasks and contexts makes a difference (Nystrand, Cohen, & Dowling, 1993; Valencia & Au, 1997), and some educators worry that practical accommodations may undercut the validity of the assessments (e.g., Mabry, 1999; Wolf & Davinroy, 1998).

From these upheavals have emerged a variety of ideas and labels—authenticity, rubrics, alternatives, and portfolios (Baron & Wolf, 1998; Darling-Hammond, Ancess, & Falk, 1995; Wiggins, 1993). Although this chapter focuses on portfolios, these entries, along with others that might be added, have emerged as a collage of intertwined concepts. The most significant themes include the concepts of validity and teacher professionalism, a conviction that a construct like writing must not be operationalized by what is easy to instruct and assess, and that the classroom teacher is the essential true witness in making decisions about what is valid and what is not (Freedman, 1993; Seidel & Walters, 1997).

My goal is to lay out three ways in which writing portfolios have come to operate in classrooms to support instruction and assessment—ways that often reflect the impact of external mandates and procedures. Some of these influences are positive (efforts to clearly articulate the standards for judging a work), and others are detrimental (a simplistic shopping list of genres—five-paragraph essay, persuasive argument, personal narrative). The following section provides a brief survey of the portfolio concept. I assume that the reader is generally familiar with the topic, but additional background readings can be found in several contemporary sources (e.g., Baker, O'Neil, & Linn, 1993; Black, Daiker, Sommers, & Stygall, 1994; Calfee & Perfumo, 1996; Farr & Tone, 1998; Harp, 1991; Herman, Aschbacher, & Winters, 1992; Hewitt, 1995; O'Malley & Pierce, 1996; Phye, 1997; Tierney, Carter, & Desai, 1991; Yancey & Weiser, 1997). Next comes a discussion of the three manifestations to which the title alludes: the portfolio as "something to do," as a test, and as a reflection of genuine performance. The chapter concludes with a proposal for building on the positive aspects of the present state of affairs, and for using current policies and practices to enhance curriculum, instruction, and assessment.

Perspectives on Portfolios

What should a writing portfolio "be"? As Bird (1990) points out, the educational use of the portfolio concept relies on metaphorical associations—we imagine the architect marching into an important meeting with a large folder that she lays out on the boardroom table, displaying project sketches for clients' review and critique: a professional exchange, explanations of the design concept, and pointed comments about unique features of the plan.

How well does the portfolio metaphor transfer to the classroom? Metaphors can support understanding, but they also have limits and can mislead. The basic purpose of a metaphor is to use a familiar concept to illuminate an unfamiliar or novel entity. How does a young writer's portfolio compare to the architectural image? Three contrasts seem pertinent. First is the level of expertise (Chi, Glaser, & Farr, 1988; Geisler, 1994). Schoolchildren are novices with much to learn. They are not high-powered professionals who must demonstrate their virtuosity, but learners who must show their learning. The expert emphasizes the polished product; the learner brings in rough drafts and successive approximations. Experts focus on uniqueness; learners show that they can replicate models. The ideal classroom portfolio, therefore, (a) displays a sequence of works-in-progress that reflect progress, (b) mirrors the work of experts while attempting some degree of imagination, and (c) includes reflections by teacher and learner on the evidence of growth and understanding.

Although laid out as contrasts, these dimensions are inherently developmental, and the meaning changes from kindergarten through high school. (See Tierney, Carter, & Desai, 1991, and Belanoff & Dickson, 1991, for discussion of the continuum from early elementary to college years.)

The second contrast between professional and student portfolios deals with purpose and audience. Experts construct portfolios to convince other experts of their expertise; they are generally seeking recognition and employment. Novices—whether kindergartner or high school graduate—construct portfolios in quite different contexts. What motivates students to create portfolios? Completing assignments to avoid hassles. Getting good grades. Satisfying parents' concerns. Motivation also can be intrinsic, as when executing a substantial project of personal interest. The audiences for which they write are most often teachers, sometimes parents, and occasionally someone outside the school context. What should be the purpose and audience of writing portfolios for students at various levels of development? As long as classrooms are isolated communities, answering this question poses a challenge. But imagine situations in which more genuine efforts are made to connect families with schoolwork; a concrete example might be the parent-teacher-student conference described later, in which the student uses a portfolio to present his or her accomplishments across a span of time. The purpose becomes clear-cut, as does the audience.

The third contrast has to do with scope. Experts handle large projects, significant activities, real jobs. Students work in 15- to 50-minute blocks; any project that spans a weekend is unusual. Worksheets appear at one end of the spectrum; students spend a few minutes on a task that the teacher marks in a few seconds. A composition—book report or research paper—falls at the other end of the continuum, and might take the better part of a week. In the middle are assignments that may take an entire class period in the later grades, or homework assignments that require an hour or more. To be sure, one can find situations in which students engage in tasks that last for 2 or 3 weeks, such as the annual science fair. Imagine a writing fair: a yearly event in which students present their works—not just the final product, but the sweat and tears from initial conception to the published version. The notion of a composition could be broadened to include drama and poetry, debate and declamation—perhaps even a Web site or two. Such events have surely emerged here and there, most often as literary yearbooks, as a demonstration of learning as well as accomplishment.

Writing Portfolios in Contemporary Practice: Three Images

What do writing portfolios look like in today's classrooms? My aim here is to feature empirical more than normative answers—an emphasis on what appears as current practice rather than an ideal of what should be. Building on available research and reviews as well as personal experience, this section explores the three perspectives in the title: activity, assessment, and authenticity. For each perspective, I will consider in turn the relevance of the contexts discussed in the previous section: novice-expert, purpose-audience, and scope.

The Portfolio as Classroom Activity

Classroom management is a major challenge for teachers. In the elementary grades, the teacher needs to keep part of the class occupied while he or she works with an instructional group. Students in noninstructional groups receive tasks to keep them occupied; the criteria for these tasks are that they are infinite, they are diverse, reflecting variations in student achievement levels, and they can be assigned with little or no instruction. Worksheets fill this bill nicely, as do free writing exercises. Portfolios—collections of student work—likewise provide a variety of tasks that can occupy otherwise empty time slots. Because portfolios are open-ended receptacles, they can absorb a virtually infinite amount of energy. Some are little more than collections of worksheets, writing journals, and other documents. Indeed, portfolio systems may incorporate worksheets as part of the portfolio process: The instructions may say, "Fill out this page—tell what you did, why you did it, what you liked most, and how you could make it better." The answers can be scripted like any other worksheet template.

In middle school and high school classes, whole-class activity structures are more commonplace; the teacher conducts the daily lecture, after which students complete a writing task. Before the second World War, such assignments were done as homework, but increasingly classroom time is allocated to the task. Whatever the details of the situation, the products can fit into manila folders, allowing the teacher to "do portfolios" with little change in his or her management practices.

To be sure, portfolios can provide an impetus for substantial changes in activity structures. Klimenkoff and LaPick (1996) present a dramatic example of portfolio impact in a primary-grade classroom. These authors explored the potential for individual students to assume greater responsibility in setting learning goals and documenting reflective evidence about their accomplishments across the school year. The culminating event was the quarterly teacher-parent-student conference. The portfolio played a purposeful role in this essential activity, one that moved beyond hours and days within classroom walls to encompass months of effort and the parental audience.

For the portfolio to have a positive impact on classroom activities, including the teacher's management, design is of central importance. "Anything goes (into it)" does not constitute a design, but what design might work? Calfee and Perfumo (1996) suggest several design questions: What should go into the portfolio (and why)? How should portfolio evidence be entered and annotated (and why)? What provisions for critique and commentary are given to the student and reviewers (and why)?

The "whys" are critically important. Students need to grasp the concept of the *learning portfolio*, a collection of works that demonstrates not just accomplishment but growth, not "things I have done" but "things I have learned," not "what I have had to do" but "what you should know about my work" (Calfee, 1997; Diederich, 1974; Hill, Ruptic, & Norwick, 1998). Personal views must align with external standards; at some point, students must demonstrate that they have learned something by establishing that they have attained a performance level adequate to meet a predetermined standard. Activities, in summary, must be driven by authentic purpose rather than by the need to fill time.

The Portfolio as Classroom Assessment and External Evaluation

The connection between a document collection and evaluation of an individual does not emerge from dictionary definitions of the portfolio concept, but must be constructed from other sources. The metaphor given earlier does offer some insights. Experts create their collections for a purpose—to submit their work for critical judgment by potential clients. In schooling, a critical tension has emerged in recent decades between internal versus external mandates for assessment of students, schools, and other entities (Black et al., 1994; Freedman, 1993; Resnick & Resnick, 1996; Stecher & Herman, 1997; Winograd, Martinez, & Noll, 1999). Who should determine student achievement, classroom teachers or state and district authorities? Adequate discussion of this tension is clearly beyond the scope of this chapter, but a few reflections may enlighten the place of portfolios for local tasks (grading) and large-scale accountability (ranking schools within a state).

Let us first discuss the internal setting. What can portfolios contribute to classroom assessment that improves on existing procedures? Why not rely on quizzes, textbook end-of-unit tests, homework assignments, and final exams? For one thing, portfolios have the potential to do a better job in handling practical day-to-day assessment tasks. Students, especially in the upper years of schooling, must be graded. Portfolios in the best models allow teachers to evaluate not just the final writing product, but also the record of progress from a student's starting point through drafts and revisions, through to the final version. A portfolio can incorporate reflections and reactions from others, including fellow students. Summarizing a database of such rich proportions in a single indicator—a grade—strikes some observers as absurd, leading to calls for narrative summaries and profiles (Brookhart, 1999; Cross & Frary, 1999; Freedman, 1982).

Some portfolio advocates resist the idea that student portfolios be graded, and reject altogether the idea of submitting such documents to external judgment (e.g., Tierney & Clark, 1998). They see portfolios as personal creations, understandable only by the student, and therefore not proper objects for evaluation. Advocates of this position view "portfolio assessment" as an oxymoron. Pragmatically, however, grades do matter, for feedback to students and parents and for college applications, among other purposes (Brookhart, 1994). What is a sound basis for constructing grades? Should teacher judgments of student achievement be given serious consideration for this purpose? The answer, it seems to me, is clearly an unqualified "yes." Education entails more than recognizing the correct answer to a factual question; Resnick (1987; Resnick & Hall, 1998) describes higher order thinking as nonalgorithmic, complex and uncertain, calling for multiple solutions and criteria, requiring self-regulation and effort, and dependent on strategy and structure. The challenge is to enhance the validity and reliability of teacher assessments to assure today's demanding audiences of the trustworthiness of professional judgments. (Heller, Sheingold, and Myford, 1998, offer a rare glimpse into what happens in the minds of portfolio raters.)

How can portfolio techniques assure this trustworthiness? Informally designed portfolios are unlikely to assure local audiences. Parents, school board members, and community members will trust portfolio information (and similar artifacts such as exhibitions and "fairs") only when they can connect student performances with familiar achievement models, and when they can see evidence linking performance with students' success in admission to higher education, in gaining a job, and in becoming an effective worker and citizen. For better or worse, many citizens believe that standardized tests tell the tale. Because the Scholastic Assessment Test stands as the primary hurdle for college admission, this belief is understandable.

Face validity re-emerges as a critical consideration in this discussion. Downplayed by psychometricians, the idea that a test should resemble what nonexperts view as significant learning goals has returned under the label of "construct validity" (Haertel, 1999; Messick, 1995; Nichols & Smith, 1998; Stecher & Herman, 1997; Wiley & Haertel, 1996). It is not enough to show that one test correlates with another; rather, the assessor must merge a variety of sources of evidence into a persuasive argument for a student's competence in a given domain. Because validity now takes shape as an argument (Kane, 1992), educators confront a new challenge. In recent decades, the job was to explain "normal curve equivalents" and "item-response theory" to principals and school board members. Most in these audiences gave up on the technical details and relied on simple comparisons: "What you are saying is that my kid/our school/this district is better than other kids/schools/districts." For portfolios to realize their potential, the challenge is to discover methods and reporting formats that allow audiences to understand the profiles that characterize complex performances: "What you are saying is that my kid/our school/this district is doing a good job here, but needs to improve there."

A complementary set of issues focuses on consequential validity, the uses of test results to inform various audiences, to identify students for various rewards and punishments, and to evaluate programs and educational institutions. A key word is *accountability*, the notion that students, teachers, schools, and other players in the educational enterprise should be publicly responsible for their actions and results. How should various outcomes be assessed so that the decisions made maximize the benefits and minimize the costs? And the costs are not simply dollars and cents, but include the loss of talented students whose creative energies fall through the testing cracks, or a young person's decision to drop out of school when he or she is retained in the same grade. What are the relative merits of standardized tests and complex performance-based assessments when gauged against this criterion? Numerous scholars have addressed this question, but the issues are technically demanding and politically complex, leading to little resolution (e.g., Murphy, 1994; Underwood, 1998; Yen, 1998).

Second, the external environment comes into play. Rather amazingly, several states and numerous districts have turned to portfolios as a basis for large-scale assessment (Baron & Wolf, 1996; Kane & Mitchell, 1996; Koretz, 1998; Valencia & Au, 1997). Unlike the South Carolina project mentioned earlier, these programs went beyond on-demand writing samples and asked classroom teachers to turn in extensive collections of student work, incorporating process as well as the final product. These programs seemed amazing because of the inherent cost, lack of control, and revelation of low performance levels. Educators typically received guidelines for conducting the assessments, but standardization went by the wayside in many instances. In one situation, for instance, teachers received extensive instructions for compilation of student writing portfolios. Each portfolio was to encompass three genres, each including a draft and polished version along with a student self-reflection, compiled from late fall to early spring. On the surface, this appeared to be a reasonable design, but the actual folders revealed wide variation in the "reading" of these guidelines by teachers, schools, and districts. Some portfolios stretched over six months, with evidence of extensive (and impressive) teacher support and feedback, and student process-product records of extraordinary quality. Other folders spanned only a week or two, evidencing little instructional support, the initial draft separated by a day or two with little in the way of teacher response. The devil can appear in the details—many of the portfolios lacked dating, and so the evaluator was often unable to judge how the process played out in time.

Why have policymakers employed complex performance-based assessments that fly in the face of psychometric traditions and ignore cost considerations? One argument is that portfolio-performance programs emphasize external construct validity over internal test reliability. The argument is a twist on the typical advice in test theory courses: validity becomes more critical than reliability. Reliability in the service of invalidity, however, is not a virtue. A second argument rests on face validity. As noted earlier, what is tested ought to mirror what has been taught. In an earlier behavioral-objective era, multiple-choice tests provided a close match to curricular practices. Today's instructional goals often stress more substantial accomplishments; for example, from the California Reading/Language Arts sixth-grade standards, "Analyze how the qualities of character affect the plot and resolution of the conflict" (California State Department of Education, 1998). As the instructional emphasis shifts from breadth to depth, assessment should follow this lead. To be sure, the volatility of the educational policy environment confounds such principles; in California, for instance, the Reading/Language Arts standards were immediately undercut by the governor's decision to institute a high-stakes multiple-choice test for the state's schools. Understandably, construct validity was ignored.

Such are the vagaries of externally mandated assessment policies. For advocates of performance-based assessments, the bottom line is quite simple. In order to receive official sanction, evidence from complex student activities must meet standards of trustworthiness and believability that are even higher today than those established for standardized multiple-choice tests. Teachers can do whatever they wish, but in order to "count," measures must meet reasonable standards of reliability and consistency. Policy makers demand simplistic, holistic, and individual scores—"On a scale of 1–10, George gets a grade of 7.14."

The internal-external tension will remain with us as long as policy makers insist on simple and inexpensive procedures for capturing complex and expensive phenomena. Other fields—medicine and engineering, for instance—counter this tension by reliance on prestige. No one expects the work of a doctor or engineer to be gauged simply and cheaply. Nor is the work of educators in other developed countries subjected to these criteria. On the other hand, in the United States we expect all children to achieve high standards of achievement, despite daunting challenges reflecting socioeconomic diversities for families and communities. Standardized tests do an excellent job of mirroring these socioeconomic patterns; more complex assessment methods have yet to demonstrate that they operate any differently (Baker & O'Neil, 1996; Garcia & Pearson, 1994; Murphy, 1994; Supovitz & Brennan, 1997; Wiley & Haertel, 1996).

The Portfolio as a Scaffold for Authentic Writing

The aim of all these policy efforts is to improve students' writing achievements. The assumption is that "real" writing tests will lead teachers to include writing assignments in daily work and provide instruction in composition skills. Early evidence suggested support for the first assumption, but less movement in the second direction. Advocates of process writing, most notably the Bay Area Writing teams, moved to fill this lacuna by laying out concrete stages through which a novice writer could move from an initial idea or assignment toward the finished product (Tobin & Newkirk, 1994). The writing portfolio emerged as a natural companion to authentic writing, a professional task worth compiling in a folder.

Thematic projects, an outgrowth of the whole language movement (Goodman, Goodman, & Hood, 1989; Smith, 1990), also played a supportive role in portfolio assessment. Projects—lengthy and complex tasks that combined reading, research, production, and writing from a variety of subject matters—required a place to store intermediary elements along the way. In practice, the assignments assumed a variety of shapes, sometimes leading to little that was worth keeping, but in the most laudatory instances producing outcomes well described as "exhibitions." Here the model of architect or fashion designer presenting a collection of polished works matches the classroom activity, incorporating a sense of purpose, audience, and professionalism.

But authentic writing entails more than implementation of the stages of process writing, the assignment of thematic projects, or the use of portfolios. It demands a shift in the underlying conception of teachers' goals and students' understandings. Who are "real writers," and what marks their activities? In preparing this chapter, I consider myself a "real writer"; likewise, I was a real writer when I recently wrote a four-page letter of protest to a local business. I assembled a folder for the chapter—the initial letter asking for a chapter, notes from background readings, a preliminary sketch, a couple of rough drafts. Besides the "paper" collection, my computer contains several files with annotated readings and papers. In contrast, the protest letter emerged during a single intense half-hour effort with no backup materials or notes—nothing like a portfolio. Both were authentic tasks, but differences in purpose, audience, and scope determined my approach to each, including the background effort and supporting material required.

What are the most appropriate models for the young "real writer"? When does a writing task require background materials? What in the two previous examples render them authentic? The earlier discussion of the portfolio concept provides some insights. The student's level of previous accomplishment matters in answering such questions. I have, over the decades, acquired rhetorical structures and strategies that allow me to organize a composition in my mind, where I can hold it while my fingers worry about details like sentences, spelling, and punctuation. The young learner, on the other hand, has not automated many parts of the writing process. Memory overload becomes a real threat, and the novice needs to employ support systems even for relatively short pieces. Several years ago while visiting a third-grade class, I asked the students, "How do you start writing something?" Several hands flew into the air, and all agreed, "Indent and capitalize!" In fact, the real starting points are ideas, words, and relations. The typical "story starter" supplies a lead line, but for the novice the real job is to think about the ending. Process writing models suggest that the teacher employ webbing strategies ("Think of as many foods as you can") as a way to generate ideas that can be shaped into a draft. A good idea, but my familiarity with research and experience in classrooms suggests that young students often have to rely on other resources to reach alternatives to indent-and-capitalize. In particular, elementary classrooms seldom rely on reading-to-write, models, or explicit instruction about generic structures, such as how to craft a story around a thematic point or construct an argument around point-counterpoint (Calfee, 1998). Once the student has constructed an initial draft, then the writing process comes into play. Unfortunately, the most daunting challenge for the novice is getting started, creating an "image" of a work. *If students are not provided an opportunity to learn the skills and strategies required for authentic writing assignments, then the authenticity of the assessment task makes little difference.*

The size and character of the task also matter. A work that relies on personal experience and knowledge can sometimes be generated from within. For the protest letter, I relied on my own complaint, which was fresh, vivid, and compelling. Preparing this chapter was another matter, and required the assembly of a substantial amount of background material, including review and analysis of other sources, and the crafting of a complex expository structure aimed toward a coherent, comprehensible, and persuasive argument.

What is the proper scope and grain for writing tasks as a student moves from kindergarten through the high school years? Answers to this question would seem to have significant implications for instruction and assessment. One might think that the massive collection of state standards would provide a clue, but a great deal must be read between the lines. The previous example from the California standards (see page 288) illustrates the difficulty; consider the ways in which one could assess the relation of character and plot. Here is another sixth-grade test sample from California: "Use a variety of effective and coherent organizational patterns, including comparison and contrast; organization by categories; and arrangement by spatial order, order of importance, or climactic order." Although more detailed than the earlier example, the macro-objectives typical of contemporary standards (for which we should be grateful) are not easily standardized. Current practice seems to range from copying to composing sentences (sometimes filling in the blanks) in the primary years to the five-paragraph essay by the middle grades—some distance from the standards as I would interpret them. The underlying principle seems remarkably parallel to the stage model of reading: begin with letters, move to words, then sentences and paragraphs, and finally the completed assignment. Whole language advocates, who assume that both reading and writing emerge as naturally as spoken language, argue for "real" reading and writing, and encourage the novice to jump in with psycholinguistic guessing and invented spelling. Many novices will cheerfully follow such advice, but lacking any sense of goals and methods, they are unlikely to move toward expertise.

For the classroom teacher or the state director of testing programs, this range of possibilities poses both opportunities and problems. The research base that might inform decisions is, to the best of my knowledge, slim to none. And so I will call on a reasonably broad range of experiences in classroom settings to make a suggestion. An authentic writing task, although it may begin with collections of ideas and words, must end with a message, which means a scope adequate to communicate something of substance. Copying a sentence from the board may provide opportunities for practice at handwriting skills, but it is not "writing," nor do the results warrant inclusion in a writing portfolio. Is a sentence or a paragraph of adequate scope? One can imagine occasional instances, but the communicative intent is undermined when an assignment begins with such constraints: "Write a sentence about your favorite food," or "Write a paragraph describing the circus." To be sure, asking kindergartners to compose lengthy works requires substantial scaffolding, and works better for the youngest students when they join together in cooperative groups. The "how to" literature is full of examples demonstrating the feasibility of this strategy (e.g., Muschla, 1991). Coherence rather than length is the primary aim, but communication-driven compositions tend to be more fully developed, and tend to receive higher teacher ratings (Calfee & Perfumo, 1996).

The final consideration regarding what background materials are necessary for a writing task centers around purpose and audience. Writing is hard work, and the quality of the final product is likely to be higher when the author has an engaging purpose for writing and an audience in mind. The greater the motivation and the more significant the audience, the more likely the writer will invest the time, energy, and effort needed to compose a work of high caliber. Writing to the teacher in response to a prescribed assignment is the typical paradigm, but it wears thin over the years. Opportunities to move beyond the classroom are boundless. For primary-grade students, parents and relatives are readily at hand, and if relatives have limited literacy skills, peers can read the students' works. The principal is an untapped audience; consider a letter about the school lunch menu written to the person who is in charge. Freedman's (1997) account of the messages between inner-city high school students in San Francisco and London demonstrates the results when purpose and audience are genuine, and the benefits when the classroom situation does (London) and does not (San Francisco) support the effort. To repeat an earlier point, for portfolio assessment to realize its goal, student work must warrant compilation, and the instructional conditions must provide support for all students to realize their potential. The challenge for valid assessment is to answer the questions of

"Whose work?" (Gearheart & Herman, 1998; Schuster, 1996), and "Under what conditions?" Portfolios, to serve as valid indicators of student progress and accomplishment, must incorporate information about the opportunity to learn as well as the opportunity to perform (Calfee & Pearson, in press), including students' self-assessment of their efforts and their "stories" about the writing process (such as what happened in the classroom, who helped at home, and whether they reached original goals).

A Merging of Perspectives—and More

Each of the preceding images carries values and limitations in its own right, but they need to be blended into an overall image. As Calfee and Perfumo (1996) observed, the portfolio concept is under threat.

> The portfolio movement will eventually fall of its own weight. Selected teachers will rely on their professional judgment for deciding what to teach and how to teach it, and for rendering assessments to interested audiences. External audiences may entertain the idea of portfolios, performances, and exhibitions, but cost-effectiveness will eventually carry the day. (p. 80)

This doleful prediction is coming to pass; several states have retreated from their commitment to authentic assessment, and the "one right answer" mentality now dominates assessment policy in an increasing number of states that previously relied on portfolios. These policy shifts reflect cost considerations, questions about scoring reliability, and the difficulty of assuring standardized arrangements for collecting student work (Koretz, 1998). They also fly in the face of evidence that performance-based assessment, including portfolios, positively influence curriculum and instruction at the classroom level (Stecher, 1998). These effects are uneven, to be sure, reflecting district and school support for professional development and monitoring of compliance with mandated procedures. Less is known about the impact on teacher preparation programs, but writing still lacks the policy attention that reading receives, and preservice courses in classroom assessment remain few and far between (Stiggins, 1994).

The previous sections show that the portfolio concept presently appears as many things to different people. Some educators see such diffuseness as a virtue, but in this "age of accountability," fuzziness is unlikely to prevail. Nor should it. Portfolios offer many advantages over multiple-choice tests and other restricted assessment methods, such as "fill in the blank" or "write to the prompt." But to position portfolios within classroom assessment and to link them to large-scale accountability, advocates must create a convergence of design, a plan that provides the classroom teacher with a road map—when to call on the portfolio concept, how to implement the procedures, how to evaluate student performance, and how to report the results to various audiences. This summons aims not to limit the concept, nor to impose draconian constraints, but rather to suggest how a fundamentally innovative strategy for the assessment of student achievement can be adapted to the realities of today's classrooms.

Pessimism serves little purpose for educators. The portfolio concept offers promise. The task, then, is to build on promising ideas and experience to help teachers improve instructional practice and policy makers to garner trustworthy evidence for decision making. In this final section, I present a proposal for portfolio design that incorporates the three previous perspectives: (1) it provides a task framework that keeps students occupied; (2) it generates performance data that can serve for both local and large-scale assessment; and (3) it constitutes a genuine writing activity in which the notion of a "collection" is inherent to the task. But this proposed portfolio design goes beyond these perspectives toward a practical strategy for adapting the portfolio concept to classroom practice. It describes the concrete first level of a ramp that leads from current activity structures and reading-writing projects of limited scope, assuming teachers whose professional background in writing curriculum and instructional practices may be limited, toward tasks of greater magnitude and complexity, with portfolios serving to document developmental progress during the school year and across grades for students and for teachers. The starting point recommended below may appear modest. And if the proposal stops at the end of this section, that concern is appropriate. Nonetheless, the experiences of states and districts that have plunged into portfolios without a clear developmental progression suggests that we need to try different strategies.

The design springs from the California Learning Assessment System (CLAS) (Gearhart & Wolf, 1997; Underwood, 1998), a state-mandated program that lasted only 2 years before it was torpedoed, partly because of concerns about its reliability as an indicator of individual student achievement (Mislevy, 1995), partly because some of the reading materials inflamed various citizen groups (Underwood, 1998). The California Department of Education encountered difficulties in the development and implementation of CLAS. Pilot testing was inadequate, many teachers received information about the test at the last minute, and scoring and reporting of the results were haphazard. Moreover, these events took place at a time when the department was in disarray, the superintendent under fire from conflict of interest charges and engaged in political battles with the governor. Unfortunately, this turmoil obscured the strengths of the CLAS design, and even today the effort is viewed by many state policy makers as a failed experiment. On the other hand, California districts, more than a few classrooms throughout the state, and numerous schools elsewhere in the United States are reported to have adopted the CLAS model in one form or another.

The CLAS design builds on an integrated reading-writing assignment. Students receive a reading assignment, typically a page or two, with a broad, blank, right-hand margin where students are encouraged to jot reading notes. After finishing the text, students complete a variety of questions—some short-answer items of a more or less factual sort (the text remains available for re-reading), along with longer and more reflective queries. Students next assemble in small groups to discuss the reading and to draft notes in preparation for a writing assignment that is thematically related to the original text. The third task is the writing assignment: students respond individually to an on-demand prompt, using their previous notes as the starting point.

CLAS incorporates several important features. First, students begin from a common resource base, because real writers seldom begin cold turkey; we read something, contact colleagues, and assemble ideas and words. Second, students are given an opportunity to reflect both individually and with peers. The latter is especially important from a Vygotskian perspective, which shows that critical thinking develops through social interactions (Vygotsky, 1978). Third, the writing assignment is scaffolded; students know from the outset that they will eventually write a paper, and the activity structure supports the preparation of writing notes. Finally, the task generates a rich database for assessing literacy—reading notes, responses to reading questions, group notes, discussion, and the final writing assignment.

The CLAS model offers promise as the first part of the ramp, as long as its original function is not as a mandated statewide test, but as an instructional activity with potential to support more effective classroom assessment, and as a link to external accountability for a school, a district, or a state. The model has several strengths: it connects standardized situations to free-form projects, links reading and writing, provides a developmental template, and cuts across a broad range of curriculum areas.

In its original formulation, the CLAS model was not designed as a classroom activity, and it had several inherent shortcomings. I have experimented with a variation, CLAS-Plus, that is designed to enhance the basic model for classroom practice (and for research purposes), but that also blurs the distinction between assessment and instruction. In CLAS-Plus, standardization is relaxed to provide greater opportunity to explore students' potential under optimal conditions. Although this strategy may trouble some readers, the ultimate criterion is the generalizability of the indicators. If student rank is consistent over a collection of tasks, even though the task details vary from student to student, then one can trust the procedures. Tension is prevalent in almost all portfolio assessments; by their very nature, portfolio assessments thwart efforts to achieve complete standardization. Nonetheless, building on a solid conceptual framework opens the way for variations on an established theme. The framework needs to specify the task dimensions, criteria for selecting passage materials and writing prompts, and the instructional context (what support is allowed and what is not).

The enhancements fall into three basic categories: (1) ensuring that the instructions are clear, (2) engaging students in active participation in the task, and (3) establishing purpose and audience. Within the first category, procedures call for the classroom teacher to begin the assessment with a webbing exercise that connects students to the theme of the reading passage. The participants in our pilot study were low-achieving middle school students and teachers. One passage dealt with same-sex schools: "Imagine what it would be like to be in a school with only boys or only girls." Responses were recorded on the board and discussed, setting the stage for reading the passage.

As an example of an enhancement in the second category (engaging students), rather than a blank margin, prompt questions were sprinkled throughout the margins to encourage students to jot reactions. Active engagement also was fostered by arranging workable groups and providing explicit guidance about group process (such as explaining the balance between collective and individual contributions, keeping the final composition in mind).

In the third category, the writing prompt included an external reference for the task: "Take the information you have read and discussed with your classmates, and write a letter to the principal giving him your opinion of single-sex schools and whether our school should have single-sex classes. Lay out the pluses and minuses of this approach, and express your position on the matter." In our exploration of CLAS-Plus, we focused on evaluation of the final writing task, assessing performance through three rubrics: length, coherence, and mechanics (spelling, punctuation, and grammar). Students did far better than we had predicted. Papers were on average a bit more than half a page in length, and the organization permitted the message to come through. Mechanical correctness left something to be desired, but did not stand in the way of comprehension of the message.

CLAS-Plus, like the original CLAS model, has many features of an on-demand assessment. In particular, topic and time are constrained, as are resources and assistance. Nonetheless, the model connects with the writing portfolio concept. For the novice writer, the aim is to show growth, to demonstrate changes in performance from beginning to end of the school year. CLAS-Plus permits the documentation of "minigrowth," the progression from initial thoughts to rough draft and on to polished product within a couple of days. A collection of CLAS-Plus exercises from the beginning to the end of the year provides a picture of long-term growth. In addition, the collection offers students the opportunity for self-assessment. For all these reasons, these abbreviated tasks merit inclusion in a folder, even if each entry is of limited scope.

In addition, the CLAS-Plus design incorporates several essential ingredients found in large-scale portfolios, and hence provides a framework for more extensive writing assignments. For instance, despite the pervasive separation of reading and writing instruction throughout schooling (Nelson & Calfee, 1998), most genuine writing tasks call for integration of these two domains; the individual thinks, reads, makes notes, thinks some more, reads some more, prepares a draft, reads the draft and makes changes, and gradually converges on the final composition. Process-writing concepts capture portions of this interweaving, but proponents seldom emphasize the critical importance of assembling readings and notes during this process. Assembling and reviewing, annotating copies of background texts, making notes on notes, scribbling on a rough draft—for those of us who are professional writers, these activities fill our manila folders (or our computer files), our writing portfolios. The purpose of the collection is obvious—the need to keep the elements of the project together in an organized conglomeration until the job is finished.

CLAS constituted a miniature portfolio exercise, unrecognizable as such because California did not pass out manila folders. The design led students through elements from reading, notetaking, thinking, and writing, all in the service of the preparation of a final product. In the absence of an appropriate design, students may place their work in a manila folder, but the result quickly becomes a chaotic collection of papers, little more than activities. CLAS-Plus points the way to expansion of the miniature design toward larger, more authentic projects. Introducing novices to the topic remains a critical task in any event, but may cover two or three class sessions, with students taking notes along the way. Rather than providing an abbreviated text, the teacher may direct students to original sources in the library or on the Internet. Marginal notes now begin to fill the student's journal. Cooperative work is not a 15-minute exchange, but multiple discussions over days. Drafting, revision, review of the overall paper—the task moves from the linear stages of CLAS to the iterative procedures typical of genuine writing. And the transformation comes about incrementally, rather than as the sudden assignment of a portfolio, hence the notion of a ramp.

At all stages, the CLAS model provides a rich source of data for evaluation of student skills and knowledge. California used CLAS for on-demand assessment, but examined only the final products with little attention to process elements. If notetaking during reading supports comprehension, then assessing students' marginal notes (a form of writing) should yield insights into comprehension responses (another form of writing). California did not assess the marginal notes. If preparation prior to the final composition is a key element in the final product, then students' scribbles during the group sessions (and additions to these notes during the "real writing") should yield information about the quality of the final product. Finally, if self-critique plays an essential part in the improvement of a composition, then the assignment should include a final self-assessment by the student, summarizing the strengths and weaknesses of his or her draft.

Imagine a portfolio design built around this full range of design elements—relatively standardized on-demand micro-assignments that quickly display the student's capacity and willingness to handle various reading-writing tasks, collected across the months of the school year, intertwined with larger project-assignments that offer students greater choice in how to approach the task, driven by individual interests and persistence.

The model can be viewed as an instructional strategy, but it also moves into place a substantial assessment machinery. The assessment parallels that of expert portfolios in important respects. The quality of the final product, the capacity to articulate and explain the work, the ability to compare and contrast with other pieces—experts are expected to handle themselves well in these arenas. For the novice, however, the model offers other possibilities: appraisal of long-term growth, now aimed toward specific components of the reading-writing process; judgments about students' capacities to move through the stages of a reading-writing exercise; and consideration of students' insights into their strengths and limitations in handling the task.

All performance assessments, but especially portfolios, have encountered generalizability problems; student rankings depend greatly on the choice of task and somewhat less on raters. Despite the enthusiasm in many quarters for performance assessment, and despite a substantial amount of descriptive research demonstrating the impact of task-rater factors, remarkably little conceptual or experimental work has aimed toward solving these problems. The additional contextualization provided by a common text (and hence more control over students' starting points for writing) and common scaffoldings (efforts to make the instructions explicit) offer promise for resolving task and rater inconsistencies. The approach outlined in this chapter presumes that the value of portfolios and other performance-based assessments for large-scale accountability may emerge not from more determined efforts by centralized authorities to standardize conditions, but by the development of conceptual designs directed toward enhancing classroom practice. The CLAS-Plus example suggests that such designs can start small and then grow to substantial proportions, moving teachers and students in succession through comfortable activities to assessment outcomes and on to authentic writing and reading tasks.

References

Association for Supervision and Curriculum Development. (1999). Using standards and assessments. *Educational Leadership, 56*(6). Special Issue.

Baker, E.L., & O'Neil H.F., Jr. (1996). Performance assessment and equity. In M.B. Kane & R. Mitchell (Eds.), *Implementing performance assessment: Promises, problems, and challenges* (pp. 183–199). Mahwah, NJ: Erlbaum.

Baker, E.L., O'Neil, H.F. Jr., & Linn, R.L. (1993). Policy and validity prospects for performance-based assessment. *American Psychologist, 48,* 1210–1218.

Baron, J.B., & Wolf, D.P. (Eds.). (1996). *Performance-based student assessment: Challenges and possibilities. Ninety-fifth yearbook of the National Society for the Study of Education, Part I.* Chicago, IL: NSSE. National Society for the Study of Education.

Belanoff, P., & Dickson, M. (Eds.). (1991). *Portfolios: Process and product.* Portsmouth, NH: Boynton/Cook.

Bird, T. (1990). The schoolteacher's portfolio: An essay on possibilities. In J. Millman & L. Darling-Hammond (Eds.), *The new handbook of teacher evaluation.* (pp. 241–256). Newbury Park, CA: Sage.

Black, L., Daiker, D.A., Sommers, J., & Stygall, G. (Eds.). (1994). *New directions in portfolio assessment: Reflective practice, critical theory, and large-scale scoring.* Portsmouth, NH: Heinemann.

Brookhart, S.M. (1994). Teachers' grading: Practice and theory. *Applied Measurement in Education, 7,* 279–301.

Brookhart, S.M. (1999). Teaching about communicating assessment results and grading. *Educational Measurement: Issues and Practice, 18,* 5–13.

Calfee, R.C. (1997). Assessing development and learning over time. In J. Flood, S.B. Heath, & D. Lapp (Eds.), *Handbook for literacy educators: Research on teaching the communicative and visual arts* (pp. 144–166). New York: Macmillan.

Calfee, R.C. (1998). Leading middle-grade students from reading to writing: Conceptual and practical aspects. In R.C. Calfee & N.N. Nelson (Eds.), *The reading-writing connection: The ninety-seventh yearbook of the National Society for the Study of Education.* Chicago: University of Chicago Press.

Calfee, R.C., & Pearson, P.D. (in press). *The role of performance-based assessments for large-scale accountability.* Washington, DC: Council of Chief State School Officers.

Calfee, R.C., & Perfumo, P. (Eds.). (1996). *Writing portfolios: Policy and practice.* Hillsdale, NJ: Erlbaum.

California State Department of Education. (1998). *English-language arts content standards for California public schools kindergarten through grade twelve.* Sacramento, CA: Author.

Chi, M.T., Glaser, R., & Farr, M.J. (Eds.). (1988). *The nature of expertise*. Hillsdale, NJ: Erlbaum.

Cole, M., Engestrom, Y., & Vasquez, O. (Eds.). (1997). *Mind, culture and activity : Seminal papers from the laboratory of comparative human cognition*. New York: Cambridge University Press.

Cross, L.H., & Frary, R.B. (1999). Hodgepodge grading: Endorsed by students and teachers alike. *Applied Measurement in Education, 12*, 53–72.

Darling-Hammond, L., Ancess, J., & Falk, B. (1995). *Authentic assessment in action*. New York: Teachers College Press.

Diederich, P.B. (1974). *Measuring growth in English*. Urbana, IL: National Council of Teachers of English.

Farr, R., & Tone, B. (1998). *Portfolio and performance assessment: Helping students evaluate their progress as readers and writers*. (2nd ed.). New York: Harcourt Brace.

Freedman, S.W. (1982). Some reasons for the grades we give compositions. *English Journal, 71*, 86–89.

Freedman, S.W. (1983). Student characteristics and essay test writing performance. *Research in the teaching of English, 17*, 313–324.

Freedman, S.W. (1993). Linking large-scale testing and classroom portfolio assessments of student writing. *Educational Assessment, 1*, 27–52.

Freedman, S.W. (1997). *Exchanging writing, exchanging cultures: Lessons in school reform from the United States and Great Britain*. Cambridge, MA: Harvard University Press.

Garcia, G.E., & Pearson, P.D. (1994). Assessment and diversity. In L. Darling-Hammond (Ed.), *Review of research in education*, (Vol. 20, pp. 337–391). Washington, DC: American Educational Research Association.

Gearhart, M., & Herman, J.L. (1998). Portfolio assessment: Whose work is it? Issues in the use of classroom assignments for accountability. *Educational Assessment, 5*, 41–56.

Gearhart, M., & Wolf, S.A. (1997). Assessing writing processes from their products. *Educational Assessment, 4*, 265–296.

Geisler, C. (1994). *Academic literacy and the nature of expertise: Reading, writing, and knowing in academic philosophy*. Hillsdale, NJ: Erlbaum.

Goodman, K.S., Goodman, Y.M., & Hood, W.J. (1989). *The whole language evaluation book*. Portsmouth, NH: Heineman.

Haertel, E.H. (1999). Performance assessment and education reform. *Phi Delta Kappan, 80*, 662–667.

Hambleton, R.K., Jaeger, R.M., Koretz, D., Linn, R.L., Millman, J., & Phillips, S.E. (1995). *Review of the measurement quality of the Kentucky instructional results information system* (KIRIS). Frankfort, KY: Kentucky Office of Education.

Harp, B. (1991). *Assessment and evaluation in whole language programs*. Norwood, MA: Christopher-Gordon.

Heller, J.I., Sheingold, K., & Myford, C.M. (1998). Reasoning about evidence in portfolios: Cognitive foundations for valid and reliable assessment. *Educational Assessment, 5*, 5–40.

Herman, J.L., Aschbacher, P.R., & Winters, L. (1992). *A practical guide to alternative assessment*. Alexandria, VA: Association for Supervision and Curriculum Development.

Herman, J.L., Gearhart, M., & Baker, E.L. (1993). Assessing writing portfolios: Issues in the validity and meaning of scores. *Educational Assessment, 1*, 201–224.

Hewitt, G. (1995). *A portfolio primer: Teaching, collecting, and assessing student writing.* Portsmouth, NH: Heinemann.

Hill, B.C., Ruptic, C., & Norwick, L. (1998). *Classroom-based assessment.* Norwood, MA: Christopher-Gordon.

Kane, M.B., & Mitchell, R. (Eds.). (1996). *Implementing performance assessment: Promises, problems, and challenges.* Mahwah, NJ: Erlbaum.

Kane, M.S. (1992). An argument-based approach to validity. *Psychological Bulletin, 112*, 527–535.

Klimenkoff, M., & LaPick, N. (1996). Promoting student self-assessment through portfolios, student-facilitated conferences, and cross-age interaction. In R.C. Calfee & P. Perfumo (Eds.), *Writing portfolios: Policy and practice* (pp. 239–260). Mahwah, NJ: Erlbaum.

Koretz, D. (1998). Large-scale portfolio assessments in the U.S.: Evidence pertaining to the quality of measurement. *Assessment in Education, 5*, 309–334.

Koretz, D., Stecher, B., Klein, S., & McCaffrey, D. (1994). The Vermont portfolio assessment program: Findings and implications. *Educational Measurement: Issues and Practice, 13*(2), 3–16.

LeMahieu, P.G., Gitomer, D.H., & Eresh, J.T. (1995). Portfolios in large-scale assessment: Difficult but not impossible. *Educational Measurement: Issues and Practice, 14*(3), 11–16, 25–28.

Linn, R.L. (1994). Performance assessment: Policy promises and technical measurement standards. *Educational Researcher, 23*, 4–14.

Linn, R.L., & Baker, E.L. (1996). Can performance-based student assessments be psychometrically sound? In J.B. Baron & D.P. Wolf (Eds.), *Performance-based student assessment: Toward access, capacity, and coherence* (pp. 84–103). Chicago: National Society for the Study of Education.

Mabry, L. (1999). Writing to the rubric: Lingering effects of traditional standardized testing on direct writing assessment. *Phi Delta Kappan, 80*, 673–679.

Messick, S. (1995). Validity of psychological assessment: Validation of inferences from persons' responses and performances as scientific inquiry into score meaning. *American Psychologist, 50*, 741–749.

Mislevy, R.J. (1995). *On inferential issues arising in the California Learning Assessment System* (Technical Report). Princeton, NJ: Educational Testing Service.

Murphy, S. (1994). Writing portfolios in K–12 schools: Implications for linguistically diverse students. In L. Black, D.A. Daiker, & G. Stygall (Eds.), *New directions in portfolio assessment: Reflective practice, critical theory, and large-scale scoring* (pp. 140–156). Portsmouth, NH: Heinemann.

Muschla, G.R. (1991). *The writing teacher's book of lists.* Englewood Cliffs, NJ: Prentice Hall.

Nelson, N.N., & Calfee, R.C. (Eds.), (1998). *The reading-writing connection: The yearbook of the National Society for the Study of Education.* Chicago, IL: University of Chicago Press.

Nichols, P.D., & Smith, P.L. (1998). Conceptualizing the interpretation of reliability data. *Educational Measurement: Issues and Practice, 17*(3), 24–36.

Nystrand, M., Cohen, A.S., & Dowling, N.M. (1993). Addressing reliability problems in the portfolio assessment of college writing. *Educational Assessment, 1*, 53–70.

Office of Technology Assessment. (1992). *Testing in American schools: Asking the right questions.* (OTA-SET-519). Washington, DC: U.S. Government Printing Office.

O'Malley, M.J., & Pierce, L.V. (1996). *Authentic assessment for English language learners: Practical approaches for teachers.* Reading, PA: Addison-Wesley.

Phye, G.D. (Ed.). (1997). *Handbook of classroom assessment.* San Diego, CA: Academic Press.

Resnick, D.P., & Resnick, L.B. (1996). Performance assessment and the multiple functions of educational measurement. In M.B. Kane & R. Mitchell (Eds.), *Implementing performance assessment: Promises, problems, and challenges* (pp. 23–38). Mahwah, NJ: Erlbaum.

Resnick, L.B. (1987). *Education and learning to think.* Washington, DC: National Academy Press.

Resnick, L.B., & Hall, M.W. (1998). Learning organizations for sustainable education reform. *Daedalus, 38*, 214–256.

Schuster, C.I. (1996). Climbing the slippery slope of assessment: The programmatic use of writing portfolios. In L. Black, D.A. Daiker, & G. Stygall (Eds.), *New directions in portfolio assessment: Reflective practice, critical theory, and large-scale scoring* (pp. 314–324). Portsmouth, NH: Heinemann.

Seidel, S., & Walters, J. (1997). *Portfolio practices: Thinking through the assessment of children's work.* Washington, DC: National Educational Association.

Smith, C.B. (1990). (Ed.). *Alternative assessment of performance in the language arts.* Bloomington, IN: ERIC Clearinghouse on Reading and Communication Skills.

Stecher, B. (1998). The local benefits and burdens of large-scale portfolio assessment. *Assessment in Education, 5*, 335–351.

Stecher, B.M., & Herman, J.L. (1997). Using portfolios for large-scale assessment. In G.D. Phye (Ed.), *Handbook of classroom assessment* (pp. 491–516). San Diego, CA: Academic Press.

Stiggins, R.J. (1994). *Student-centered classroom assessment.* New York: Merrill.

Supovitz, J.A., & Brennan, R.T. (1997). Mirror, mirror on the wall, which is the fairest test of all? An examination of the equitability of portfolio assessment relative to standardized tests. *Harvard Educational Review, 67*, 472–502.

Supovitz, J.A., MacGowan, A. III, & Slattery, J. (1997) An examination of the interrater reliability of portfolio assessment in Rochester, New York. *Educational Assessment, 4*, 237–259.

Tierney R.J., Carter, M.A., & Desai, L.E. (1991). *Portfolio assessment in the reading-writing classroom.* Norwood, MA: Christopher-Gordon.

Tierney, R.J., & Clark, C. (1998). Portfolios: Assumptions, tensions, and possibilities (Theory and research into practice). *Reading Research Quarterly, 33*, 474–486.

Tobin, L., & Newkirk, T. (Eds.). (1994). *Taking stock: The writing process movement in the 1990's.* Portsmouth, NH: Boynton/Cook.

Underwood, T. (1998). The consequences of portfolio assessment: A case study. *Educational Assessment, 5,* 147–194.

Valencia, S.W., & Au, K.H. (1997). Portfolios across educational contexts: Issues of evaluation, teacher development, and system validity. *Educational Assessment, 4,* 1–35.

Vygotsky, L.S. (1978). *Mind in society: The development of higher psychological processes.* Cambridge, MA: Harvard University Press.

Wiggins, G.P. (1993). *Assessing student performance.* San Francisco: Jossey-Bass.

Wiley, D.E., & Haertel, E.H. (1996). Extended assessment tasks: Purposes, definitions, scoring, and accuracy. In M.B. Kane & R. Mitchell (Eds.), *Implementing performance assessment: Promises, problems, and challenges* (pp. 61–89). Mahwah, NJ: Erlbaum.

Winograd, P., Martinez, R.B., & Noll, E. (1999). Alternative assessments of learning and literacy: A U.S. perspective. In D.A. Wagner, R.L. Venezky, & B. Street (Eds.), *Literacy: An international handbook,* (pp. 203–209). Boulder, CO: Westview Press.

Wolf, S.A., & Davinroy, K.A.H. (1998). "The clay that makes the pot"—the loss of language in writing assessment. *Written Communication, 15,* 419–464.

Yancey, K.B., & Weiser, I. (Eds.). (1997). *Situating portfolios: Four perspectives.* Logan, UT: Utah State University Press.

Yen, W.M. (1998). Investigating the consequential aspects of validity: Who is responsible and what should they do? *Educational Measurement: Issues and Practice, 17,* 5.

Roselmina Indrisano and James R. Squire

Afterword

During the past 25 years, research and scholarship in writing have passed through several stages. At one time an almost exclusive concern with product—with *what* students write—was viewed particularly in high school in relation to Aristotelian rhetoric: unity, coherence, emphasis. In the intervening years, these worthy views have been expanded to include attention to writing at all educational levels, including preschool.

Researchers who study emergent literacy have informed the educational practice of those who initiate the young. Further, awareness of the interrelationships of reading and writing has grown, as attention has shifted from exclusive concern with the product to the processes of writing. More recently, understanding of the ways in which the surrounding environment, intellectual as well as physical and social, has commanded attention and has yielded critical insights into classroom practice.

The growing complexity of our views of writing stresses not only the diversity of the genres of writing, but also the diversity of the writers themselves. Some constants remain, however—the importance of talk in shaping writing, the importance of reading on the writer, the function of writing in the learning of all the academic disciplines, the limited experiences most young people have with writing, and the need to create writing curricula that teachers can implement.

Given this diversity, the needs for additional research in writing are manifest. Clearly, the extensive advances in recent decades are only a prelude to developments in the years to come.

COMMENTARY

Classroom teachers repeatedly emphasize that improvement in teaching writing is necessarily dependent on the improvement of teaching conditions to permit greater teacher-student interaction. To teachers, the size of classes and the number of classes that meet each day dictate what they can do. Hence, a consideration of class size is an important dimension of writing research, theory, and practice, and must be included here.

Roselmina Indrisano and James R. Squire

Edmund J. Farrell and Julie M. Jensen
The University of Texas at Austin

Appendix A

Rhetoric and Research on Class Size

One could easily make the case that the most influential document on the need to establish a reasonable class load for secondary teachers of English was published nearly 50 years ago. Within 6 months after "Determining an Efficient Teaching Load in English" by William J. Dusel appeared in the October 1955 issue of the *Illinois English Bulletin*, the Michigan Council of Teachers of English had ordered 1,000 copies of the article to distribute to teachers and administrators, while councils in Virginia, Kentucky, New York, and California had requested permission to reprint the document in their journals.

As part of his doctoral study "to determine the best means of improving the effectiveness of classroom teaching in [secondary] English, the reasonableness of the present teaching load, and the adequacy of teacher-education programs," Dusel (1955, p. 3) requested 430 experienced teachers in 150 communities in California to score a one-page typed essay titled "One Hectic Day," written by a student named "Fred" (pp. 3–5). After finding four archetypal methods of evaluation—the teacher who skims the paper, the teacher who marks every error with no comment, the teacher who rewrites the paper for the student, and the teacher who carries on a written dialogue with the student to discuss the student's purpose and plan—Dusel concluded that only the fourth method of evaluation was effective in stimulating the student to write more effectively. Unfortunately, the method was time consuming:

> The average amount of time required to mark papers so as to show concern for ideas and to teach writing and thinking was 8.6 minutes per 250 words. The total time required to mark a week's supply of 250-word compositions in this way would be at least 21.5 hours. (p. 13)

Dusel estimated that the time required both to meet classes and to mark compositions effectively would total 50.8 hours, exclusive of the time required for lesson planning and preparation for teaching other required skills and knowledge (1955, p. 15). This estimation led him to recommend that "full-time [secondary] English teachers...be assigned a teaching load of four daily one-hour classes of 25 pupils each" (p. 16). Since 1955 the National Council of Teachers of English (NCTE), through resolutions passed at national conventions and statements issued by the Secondary Section Committee, has repeatedly echoed Dusel's recommendation that secondary teachers of English have no more than 100 students and four classes a day (NCTE, 1991).

In 1959 the following recommendation appeared in *The American High School Today*, James Bryant Conant's well-publicized report on the conditions of the nation's high schools:

> The time devoted to English composition during the four years should occupy about half the total time devoted to the study of English. Each student should be required to write an average of one theme a week. Themes should be corrected by the teacher. In order that teachers of English have adequate time for handling these themes, no English teacher should be responsible for more than one hundred pupils. (pp. 50–51)

In 1965 the prestigious Commission on English of the College Entrance Examination Board recommended in its report *Freedom and Discipline in English* "that the English teacher be assigned no more than four classes a day" and "that the average class size be no more than 25 pupils" (p. 12).

Although one might not be able to maintain that the Dusel report directly influenced the recommendations of either Conant or the Commission on English, one could safely say that important individuals and groups had reached the same conclusion as did Dusel—that secondary teachers

Farrell & Jensen

of English were overburdened and should not have more than 100 students a day. One could further say that all such recommendations, including those of Dusel, were important pieces of rhetoric rather than of research, their persuasion founded in logic rather than in hard evidence.

For historians of the profession, Dusel's work exists in the prehistory of writing theory and instruction. It was published 8 years before Braddock, Lloyd-Jones, and Schoer (1963) would declare writing research to be in a stage of alchemy, and nearly 2 decades before writing pedagogy would begin its steady progression from assigning and grading to guiding students throughout a multistage writing process. Given, then, the hindsight of approximately 45 years of theoretical work and research in composition since the publication of "Determining an Efficient Teaching Load in English," a contemporary reader might find the document wanting in a variety of ways:

1. Dusel's emphasis upon making English teachers and their curriculum more "efficient" places greater emphasis on teachers' use of time than on the quality of students' performance. The report appears to equate the number of minutes a teacher spends reading a draft Socratically with the ultimate merit of a student's writing. Not mentioned are common means teachers now use to reduce time spent on evaluating papers, such as sampling techniques, peer or group evaluation, and checklists for self-evaluation.

More fundamentally, the value of teachers' commentaries on student papers remains open to question. During the 1980s, several composition scholars analyzed accumulated evidence on the relationship between teachers' commentaries and students' writing performance, analyses that create a useful lens through which to view Dusel's assumptions. In 1982 Sommers noted

> Although commenting on student writing is the most widely used method for responding to student writing, it is the least understood. We do not know in any definitive way what constitutes thoughtful commentary or what effect, if any, our comments have in helping our students become more effective writers. (p. 148)

In 1984, Knoblauch and Brannon came to a more forceful conclusion: "We have scarcely a shred of empirical evidence to show that students typically even comprehend our responses to their writing, let alone use them purposefully to modify their practice" (p. 1).

Finally, in his exhaustive meta-analysis of research in written composition, Hillocks (1986) left room for further research while finding unsustainable the belief that teachers' comments on students' papers perforce led to improved writing:

> The results of all these studies strongly suggest that teacher comment has little impact on student writing. None of the studies of teacher comment show statistically significant differences in the quality of the writing between experimental and control groups. Indeed, several show no pre-to-post gains for any groups, regardless of the type of comment.... However, a comparison of the studies suggests that in most of them the comments by teachers are diffuse; they range over substance, development, organization, style, mechanics, and so forth.... It may be...that when comments are focused and tied to some aspect of instruction, either prewriting or revision, they do increase the quality of writing. (pp. 165, 168)

Since the assessments of Sommers, Knoblauch and Brannon, and Hillocks, studies of teacher response to student writing have been plentiful. A review by Straub (1997) credits recent researchers with developing theories about which kinds of comments are most helpful, analyzing how teachers read and respond to student writing, studying ways students process comments and use them in their own writing, and surveying students' perceptions of the value of various types of teacher comments: "A theory of response is emerging, and research in composition is beginning to show what teachers have long suspected, hoped, or assumed: that students read and make use of teacher comments and that well-designed teacher comments can help students develop as writers" (p. 92). (See also Vacca and Vacca, Chapter Nine in this volume.)

2. "Determining an Efficient Teaching Load in English" presents a student's paper solely as product, leaving unknown the context and process that brought it into being. What prompted the student, Fred, to write "One Hectic Day" is not specified, nor is the audience for his paper clear, beyond the teacher in the role of examiner. One might reasonably infer that the composition was assigned: Fred's opening sentence, "To start this out, I guess I had better back up a little" does not read like the initial sentence of one who has created his own topic and thereby "owns" it.

In 1955 little attention was being given to the importance of "invention," to prewriting activities that might have helped Fred generate ideas to enrich his theme—brainstorming, notetaking, webbing, free writing, or using heuristics, such as Aristotle's topics; Richard Young, Alton Becker, and Kenneth Pike's particle, wave, and field; Kenneth Burke's pentad; or the "who? what? when? where? why? and how?" familiar to journalists. (For a fuller discussion of prewriting techniques, see Lindemann, 1995, pp. 105–125; see also Applebee, Chapter Four in this volume.)

While conceding that "the preparation and motivation of a class for a writing experience are equally as important as the opportunity to write," Dusel goes on to say, "these are complex matters of technique...and cannot be discussed here" (1955, p. 14). While one might maintain that Dusel's focus was appropriately on the time it takes to evaluate a composition effectively (*effective*, like *efficient*, is an oft-repeated word in the study) and not on the process of writing, another could justifiably argue that Fred's paper should not have been decontextualized: if his teacher had intelligently assisted with and intervened in the stages of Fred's writing, the teacher might have saved time given to evaluating a weak draft, thereby making his or her own teaching more effective and Fred's academic life more rewarding. When Freedman (1987) conducted a survey of the response practices of 560 teachers judged among the most successful in their communities by directors of sites of the National Writing Project, she found that teachers reported "in-process response" to be most helpful, stating, "It occurs not only to drafts of student writing, but also to ideas and plans" (p. 157).

3. In trying to establish "averages," "Determining an Efficient Teaching Load in English" ignores the great variability in types of writing, in students' performance in writing, and in the time needed to evaluate that performance. In the report, Dusel (1955) comments on variability in work load among teachers in various fields:

> [C]onventional surveys of teachers' work-weeks mean no more than would time scores on a cross country race in which individual runners had been assigned separate courses of various distances over different terrains. No matter how accurately measured, these time scores would show only how long each man took to arrive at the finish line. They would not indicate how far he had run, or how fast, or what obstacles he had surmounted—or avoided. (p. 2)

Yet, by seeking to establish the average amount of time taken to evaluate one 250-word sample of writing and, through extrapolation, to make an argument for reducing the load of all secondary teachers of English, Dusel fails to take into account differences in the amount of time it might take to evaluate a 250-word draft of transactional writing as compared to a 250-word draft of expressive or literary writing. Ignored also are differences in the time a competent (and presumably efficient) teacher might spend in reading a 250-word draft by a student in a basic English class and one written by a student in an Advanced Placement class.

Through averaging, Dusel (1955) concluded that full-time secondary teachers of English should be "assigned a teaching load of four daily one-hour classes of 25 pupils each." However, he overlooked the inequity in the composition load he recommended for the different grade levels: "Seventh, eighth, and ninth graders would write approximately 100 words each week; tenth graders approximately 200 words; eleventh and twelfth graders approximately 350 words a week" (p. 7). One might justifiably infer that, were the recommendation fulfilled, the twelfth-grade teacher would spend far more hours evaluating papers than would the seventh-grade teacher.

4. Though somewhat of a minor matter, Dusel probably underestimated the time that it would have taken a teacher in 1955 to evaluate a student's 250-word draft. "One Hectic Day," Fred's account of an episodic excursion to the snow, was typed; most papers submitted by students at that time were handwritten, many of them almost illegibly scrawled, as the 430 California teachers participating in the study might have testified readily. (Whether computers are beginning to relieve teachers of the drudgery of trying to decipher students' longhand and whether they are affecting the time given to evaluating papers are matters worthy of a contemporary study.)

5. Although "Determining an Efficient Teaching Load in English" makes the case for reducing the instructional load of secondary teachers of English, it unfortunately leaves to a separate document, one not so widely circulated, the matter of inservice education. Dusel's report (1955) recommends the following:

> In-Service Education: The full report of this aspect of the California Council study has appeared in a separate article, "In-Service Education for the Language Arts," *Educational Administration and Supervision*, 1955. The re-

port lists the kinds of in-service training most frequently requested by English teachers, and outlines ways of setting up an in-service program organized around a language arts committee drawn from the entire faculty. (pp. 17–18)

By separating the means of inservice education from the argument for reducing teaching load, "Determining an Efficient Teaching Load in English" leads most of its readers to assume fallaciously that a reduction in class size would automatically result in improved instruction in composition, which is an insupportable assumption. For example, Dusel's first three prototypal teachers—those who mark to assign a grade, to indicate faults, or to correct for the student—would not necessarily alter their behaviors when provided fewer students. On this matter, Glatthorn (1991) comments,

> Surprisingly, perhaps, teachers do not seem to vary their teaching methods when they teach smaller classes. Although there are some conflicting findings here, two major studies found that giving teachers smaller classes did not result in different teaching practices. In a two-year study in Ontario, Shapson and his colleagues (1978) determined that smaller classes did not result in greater individualization of instruction, even though the teachers involved were sure that greater individualization would occur. Field studies conducted by the Far West Regional Laboratory of two urban schools and two rural schools reached the same conclusion. As Filby (1980) noted in reviewing the results of these studies, the teachers were not likely to try dramatically different methods of instruction even though they had smaller classes, perhaps because they were not trained in such approaches. (p. 444)

What that training should be and how to determine its efficacy through carefully controlled studies are issues central to improving instruction in composition.

6. Like most documents urging a reduction in the teaching load of secondary teachers of English, Dusel's report presumes that most secondary teachers of English are conscientious professionals who carefully structure composition assignments and spend inordinately large amounts of time evaluating students' resultant work. However, one might question such a presumption after reading Applebee's (1981) *Writing in the Secondary School*. The data Applebee reports from both an observational study in two high schools and a stratified national survey of secondary teachers' in-

structional practices indicate that at the time of the book's publication, wide discrepancies existed between what the profession advocates for writing and what teachers reportedly do.

For example, in the classrooms observed, only 3 minutes elapsed between the teacher's introduction of a writing topic and the time students were expected to begin writing; only 47% of the English teachers surveyed reported assigning up to two pages of writing for a typical assignment; only 10% of all teachers surveyed reported that student writing was read regularly by other students; only 59% of English teachers "regularly" asked students to write more than one draft (of students surveyed, only 23% claimed to make changes that went beyond spelling, mechanics, usage, or word choice on successive drafts); for student writing in all subject areas, the teacher in the role of examiner was the principal audience (Applebee, 1981, pp. 93–97; see also Applebee, Chapter Four in this volume).

7. "Determining an Efficient Teaching Load in English" fails to present convincing empirical data that reducing the load of secondary teachers of English will improve instruction and students' performance. As Glatthorn (1991) points out, relatively few studies have examined the effects of class size on the teaching of English. Consequently the 1986 report of the NCTE Task Force on Class Size and Workload in Secondary English Instruction "seemed to be able to make only weak claims about the advantages of smaller classes" (p. 244). Existing studies do not always support advocates of smaller English classes. For example, after examining achievement gains made by 7,500 seventh- and eighth-grade students in 265 English classes, Johnson and Scriven (1967) concluded that class size had no consistent effect on the gains, even between classes of 24 students or fewer and classes of 34 students or more. Warburton (1961) compared groups of 100 or more students with groups of 30 to 35 students in twelfth-grade English and found the achievement of students in the large groups to be superior in composition, reading, and listening.

General Research on Class Size

Despite few studies on how class size affects the secondary teaching of English, general studies of class size and its effects are bountiful, with hundreds of such studies spanning the twentieth century. About the plenitude of this research, the authors of *Class Size and Teacher Load* (New England School Development Council, 1975) comment,

> Research and discussion of the issues of class size, pupil-teacher ratios, and teacher load have appeared in educational literature since the turn of the century. Over 300 such reports and discussions can be found, but well over 200 were dismissed by Blake (1954), either because the article in question represented the private judgment of the writer or because the reported research was poorly designed. An estimate of the number of acceptable studies on class size and related issues, including the 22 accepted by Blake, would not exceed 60, covering the educational range from kindergarten through college. Of those 60, not more than a handful meet contemporary requirements with respect to research design and statistical and practical validity. (p. 3)

Although the extant literature uniformly emphasizes the impact of class size on school budgets, it fails to consistently agree on the effect of class size on educational quality, most often determined by student achievement on one or more standardized tests. Overlooked in most studies is the effect of class size on students' personal and social maturation—that is, on their development in the affective rather than the cognitive domain.

Oft quoted and criticized in the literature on class size is a meta-analysis undertaken by Glass and Smith (1978) of 77 class-size studies dating from 1900. After creating 725 comparisons of student achievement in larger and smaller classes, these researchers concluded that class sizes of 20 to 40 make little difference in students' achievement, with the greatest gains reserved for classrooms containing 15 or fewer pupils. Ten months later, Smith and Glass (1979) conducted a second meta-analysis of affective and instructional effects of larger and smaller classes, in which they developed 371 comparisons from 59 studies. From this analysis they concluded that smaller classes, by a factor of nearly 9 to 1, would show superior outcomes in student, teacher, and instructional effects, including students' behavior and self concepts, and teachers' morale and professional growth. (See also the International Reading Association's resolution on class size, Appendix B in this volume.)

A common criticism of Smith and Glass's two analyses was their focus on general class reduction when, in fact, class size may have diverse effects on students with different abilities, in different grades, and in different subject-matter areas. The Educational Research Service (ERS) (1980), which concluded that findings on the instructional effects of class size were inconclusive, faulted Glass and Smith's work on three grounds: (1) that by failing to distinguish subtle relationships between variables, it had led to oversimplified results; (2) that it had produced generalizations based on too small a number of comparisons; and (3) that it had often come to contradictory interpretations of improved student achievement (Porwell, 1978). However, when Hedges and Stock (1983), using refined statistical techniques for meta-analysis, re-analyzed Glass and Smith's data, they essentially confirmed their predecessors' findings.

Disputes notwithstanding, ERS and Glass and Smith do agree on three major points: (1) class size affects the educational environment (e.g., smaller classes positively influence students' behavior); (2) the relationship between class size and students' achievement is indirect (e.g., smaller classes lead to better communication of expectations, to more individual attention to students' interests and needs, and to more student-teacher interactions); and (3) students will achieve more in classes of 15 or fewer (Mier, 1984).

In response to calls for more focused analyses, Robinson and Wittebols (1987) examined 100 studies of class size conducted between 1950 and 1985. Finding no optimum class size that applies to all types of students at all grade levels and in all subject areas, they advocated tailoring decisions on class size to specific instructional goals. Among their more specific conclusions were these:

a) reductions in class size were most effective in grades K–3;

b) reading achievement was higher in small classes in half of the K–3 studies;

c) ethnic minority and economically disadvantaged students achieved more in smaller classes; and

d) because many teachers did not change their teaching methods to take advantage of smaller class size, support for inservice education is necessary.

Reducing Class Size in the Elementary School

Though "Determining an Efficient Teaching Load in English" makes no mention of the instructional burden of elementary teachers, much of the research on class size focuses exclusively on the elementary classroom; moreover, elementary teachers of the language arts share with their secondary colleagues a history of attempts to reduce teaching loads through advocacy.

Among the most vocal advocates of small elementary school classes are national professional associations. The International Reading Association, for example, in a 1999 resolution, affirmed its belief that "excellence in classroom reading instruction can be achieved by a combination of reduced class size and high quality teacher preparation and ongoing professional development" (see Appendix B, page 326 in this volume). Though some set no optimum number of students, others have class-size recommendations that are officially endorsed by the association. The National Association of Elementary School Principals (1996–1997) advocates a class size ratio of 15:1, "especially for at risk children" (p. 45). The National Association for the Education of Young Children (1991) varies its recommendations according to the age of the children, suggesting a maximum of 1:10 for 5-year-olds, 1:12 for 6- to 8-year-olds; and 1:14 for 9- to 12-year-olds (p. 41). Finally, English associations, most commonly the National Council of Teachers of English, have shown a longstanding interest in elementary class size:

> "Statement of Workload of Elementary Language Arts Teachers," approved by the NCTE Board of Directors in 1977, recommends that "the elementary classroom teacher should not be responsible for more than 25 pupils per class."
>
> An NCTE brochure titled "Incentives for Excellence: What School Board Members Can Do to Encourage Excellence in Their Language Arts Programs" (1984) cites five ways to promote quality instruction, among them to reduce the size of classes in which composition is taught. Noting the demands on teachers' time presented by students who "learn to write by writing," the brochure recommends no more than 25 students per elementary classroom, "where the most fundamental work of all occurs in the teaching of writing."
>
> "Teaching Composition: A Position Statement" (1985), prepared by the NCTE Commission on Composition, advocates frequent writing assignments and frequent individual attention from elementary teachers who have no more than 20 students each. Like other contemporary professional resources on writing instruction, the position statement casts the teacher

as one who provides guidance and support throughout the composing process, not as one who comments merely on the writing product. Discounting much of the research on class size, the statement stresses that standardized tests and other formal measures alone are inadequate gauges of writing ability.

In 1995 the NCTE Board of Directors passed its most recent of many resolutions on class size, one declaring that "In all the clamor for school improvement, little attention is paid to class size and teacher-student ratios as factors affecting the learning of all students. English and language arts teachers' class size and student load have been continuing concerns of NCTE through much of its history (p. 3). In response to the resolution, the Elementary Section Committee of NCTE recommended that the elementary teacher should be responsible for not more than 25 pupils per class, and for not more than 20 pupils per class in kindergarten and first grade.

In *What Is English?*, a personal reflection on a conference sponsored by the Coalition of English Associations, Peter Elbow (1990) comments on the class load of elementary teachers of the language arts:

> We can't ask teachers to provide the kind of one-to-one help that all students need occasionally—to have conferences and get to know students and think about them as individuals—unless we cut back that load. Because very young children need so much more individual attention, early elementary teachers need to cut back their loads of twenty-five and thirty students to twenty. (p. 220)

The official report of the conference, *The English Coalition Conference: Democracy Through Language* (Lloyd-Jones & Lunsford, 1989), includes resolutions approved by participants on the "Rights and Responsibilities of Students and Teachers." Among the recommendations is the following: "Because of intensive student-teacher interaction, a necessary condition for effective learning and teaching is "no more than 20 students for elementary teachers" (p. 48).

State Initiatives to Reduce Numbers in Elementary Classes

Those who control purse strings usually defend the status quo by pointing to conflicting evidence from research on class size; nevertheless, in recent years legislators in a number of states have mandated reductions in the size of elementary classrooms. In the belief that small classes can have the greatest effect on young learners, these legislators have funded ambitious and costly plans involving the earliest grades of the elementary school.

Indiana's PRIME TIME was launched in 1984 when sufficient money was appropriated to support a pupil:teacher ratio of 18:1 in first-grade classes across the state. In successive appropriations through 1989, kindergarten and first grade classes were reduced to 18 students, and second- and third-grade classes were limited to 20 students. A 1987 evaluation concluded that PRIME TIME had been most effective in improving teachers' attitudes and morale, that it was moderately effective in improving children's self-concepts, but that its effects on academic achievement were small (Hazard, 1989).

A cornerstone of the class reduction effort in Nevada is the importance it places on inservice education. The full 1989–1990 school year was used for planning and for preparing teachers for a reduction in kindergarten and first-grade classes to 15 students in 1990–1991, Grade 2 classes to 15 students in 1991–1992, Grade 3 classes to 15 students in 1992–1993, continuing in phases until Grades 4 through 6 had 21 students and Grades 7 through 12 had 25 students in core subjects (Hazard, 1989).

Tennessee's class reduction effort, its first phase labeled the Student/Teacher Achievement Ratio project (Project STAR) and its second phase named Lasting Benefits, has been the largest and longest-lasting experimental study of the effects of small class size on learning and development. Beginning in 1984 researchers tracked students from 25 urban schools, 16 suburban schools, and 39 rural schools from across the state to determine if reducing class size results in improved achievement. Included in the research were three kinds of classes: small classes with 13 to 17 students, regular classes with 21 to 25 students and a full-time aide, and regular classes (21 to 25 students) without an instructional aide (Viadero, 1995). Drawing on STAR data involving 7,000 students, researchers concluded that, compared to large classes, small classes (a) result in fewer students being held back a grade, (b) benefit minority students the most, (c) give students more individual attention, (d) are friendlier and more intimate, (e) have fewer discipline problems, and (f) show higher student participation in school activities.

Using a body of data on 7,000 students, phase two of the study, Lasting Benefits, pursued the question of whether the gains persisted. Students were tracked in normal-sized fourth- through seventh-grade classrooms, where it was found that "in 8th grade, students who had small classes in grades K–3 remained significantly ahead of those who were in regular classes" (Achilles, 1996, p. 77). Stressing the "substantial positive benefits of early, small-class experiences for student achievement and development" (p. 76), principal investigator Achilles (1996) noted that "leaders in 11 states have agreed with STAR findings and have enacted class-size initiatives" (p. 77).

Driven by poor performance on reading and mathematics tests, California passed legislation in the summer of 1996 to implement a program for the 1996–1997 school year that offered school districts a financial incentive to voluntarily reduce class sizes from an average of 29:1 to 20:1. Founded on the assumption that basic-skills problems identified early will reduce academic problems later, the program first restricts enrollment in Grade 1, then Grade 2, then finally kindergarten or Grade 3. Though many Californians, including teachers, touted the merits of small classes—the time allowed for individual attention to students, the reduction in distractions, the smaller number of referrals for special education and for disciplinary reasons, and the potential for raising early reading levels—hasty implementation brought problems. Of 895 eligible districts, 853 signed on to the program, and then scrambled for space, searched for qualified teachers, and struggled to make the most of their piece of a nearly billion-dollar appropriation (NCTE, 1997a).

Two hundred million dollars allocated for facilities is expected to cover the cost of less than 60% of an estimated 18,400 classrooms (Johnston, 1997)—sometimes portable buildings, sometimes space converted from other purposes, sometimes rearranged space within existing classrooms to accommodate two teachers and 40 students. Of the additional teachers, hired at a cost of $750,000,000, more than half were inexperienced, nearly half were uncredentialed, and one in four was a former substitute (Johnston, 1997). At the time of this writing, it is too soon to predict whether California can raise its children's achievement in reading and mathematics through a program criticized as having too little money, too few teachers, too few classrooms, and a teaching force inexperienced in ways of best capitalizing on small classes.

Continuance of the Class-Size Debate

One can assume that the matter of optimum class size for both elementary and secondary schools will continue to be an issue in the decades ahead. One can further assume that the issue will be joined not only by the usual groups—professional associations or unions representing teachers, and school boards and taxpayer associations representing the public—but by new constituencies, those hoping to introduce electronic technologies into the educational mainstream and those wishing to privatize public education. Undergirding competitive views, as always, will be questions of efficiency and finance: For example, can computerized classrooms make education less burdensome for teachers and more productive for students? In all subjects? For all students? For all instructional purposes? At what cost? Can private companies run public schools and produce better academic results with fewer tax dollars? At what expense to teachers and to traditional educational goals?

Clearly, proponents of smaller classes cannot ignore the financial implications of their advocacy. As Templeton (1972) notes, "The impact of class size on school finance is obvious: as class size decreases, more teachers must be hired and more classrooms built. Because instructional costs usually constitute about 80 percent of a school district's expenditures, the added costs can be enormous" (p. 1). For instance, reduction from 30 to 29 students per class in a school system enrolling 15,000 students would require hiring 17 additional teachers; reducing class load from 30 to 25 in a large metropolitan district would require adding hundreds of teachers at a cost of millions of dollars. Yet, in *The Manufactured Crisis: Myths, Fraud, and the Attack on America's Public Schools* (1995), Berliner and Biddle argue that such expenditures are warranted:

> It is time to put to rest the foolish notions that it would make no difference if Americans provided extra funds for their schools.... Extra funds for schools in a typical district would require more tax dollars, but if one goes by the evidence, that extra expenditure would enable those schools to hire and hold more talented teachers, decrease average class size, upgrade

programs, and improve facilities—and these steps would pay off in higher average levels of student achievement, subsequent earnings, and contributions to the nation. (p. 78)

While legitimately concerning themselves with expenditures for education, the cost-conscious must beware of committing the fallacy of composition. Though a single student does not compose an overload for a teacher, the addition of enough single students can eventually constitute an unbearable burden. Teachers can, and do, reach a point of feeling oppressively fatigued by their "loads," though this fatigue point may vary according to numerous variables—subject matter, instructional goals, students' abilities, teachers' competencies, time of day. Whatever the point of felt oppression may be, no one can gainsay the heavy pedagogical responsibility of teachers who conscientiously respond to stacks of students' papers each week. Those primarily concerned with educational finance must ultimately take into account the high cost of teacher burnout, including the cost of annually educating newcomers to replace skilled and experienced teachers who have prematurely left the profession because of stress.

Conclusion

The mixed results of research on class size, allowing interested parties to support any argument, led Maeroff (1991) to propose that optimum class size rests on teachers' perceptions. Teachers who perceive their classes as being too large are prone, among other problems, to suffer poor morale; to have less enthusiasm, lower job satisfaction, lower professional self-esteem, and less time to grow professionally; and, finally, to leave the profession prematurely. Maeroff concludes, "Debating the impact of class size on student learning will not change existing situations. The perceptions of teachers are the reality with which they live every day in the nation's classrooms, and they must learn how to coexist, in reasonable comfort, with that reality" (p. 56).

Though Maeroff may be correct, elementary and secondary teachers of composition will nevertheless continue to agitate for more humane classroom conditions, ones that will allow them to put into fruitful practice all that has been learned about the teaching of composition since Dusel's "Determining an Efficient Teaching Load in English" first appeared in

1955. Until their classroom conditions have been ameliorated substantially, Dusel's work, whatever its limitations, will continue to remind these teachers of the wide discrepancy between what is and what might be.

References

Achilles, C.M. (1996). Students achieve more in smaller classes. *Educational Leadership*, 53, 76–77.

Applebee, A.N. (1981). *Writing in the secondary school*. Urbana, IL: National Council of Teachers of English.

Berliner, D.C., & Biddle, B.J. (1995). *The manufactured crisis: Myths, fraud, and the attack on America's public schools*. Reading, MA: Addison-Wesley.

Blake, H.V. (1954). *Class size: A summary of selected studies in elementary and secondary schools*. Doctoral dissertation. New York: Teachers College, Columbia University.

Braddock, R., Lloyd-Jones, R., & Schoer, L. (1963). *Research in written composition*. Urbana, IL: National Council of Teachers of English.

Commission on English. (1965). *Freedom and discipline in English*. New York: College Entrance Examination Board.

Conant, J.B. (1959). *The American high school today*. New York: McGraw-Hill.

Dusel, W.J. (1955). Determining an efficient teaching load in English. *Illinois English Bulletin*, 43, 1–19.

Educational Research Service. (1980). Class-size research. A critique of recent meta-analysis. *Phi Delta Kappan*, 62, 139–141.

Elbow, P. (1990). *What is English?* New York: Modern Language Association.

Filby, N.A. (1980). *Evidence of class-size effects*. Paper presented at the annual conference of the American Educational Research Association, Anaheim, CA.

Freedman, S.W. (1987). *Response to student writing*. Urbana, IL: National Council of Teachers of English.

Glass, G.V., & Smith, M.L. (1978). *Meta-analysis of research on the relationship of class-size and achievement*. San Francisco, CA: Far West Laboratory for Educational Research and Development.

Glatthorn, A.A. (1991). Secondary English classroom environments. In J. Flood, J.M. Jensen, D. Lapp, & J.R. Squire (Eds.), *Handbook of research on teaching the English language arts*. New York: Macmillan.

Hazard, J. (1989). Reducing class size—Affordable? Efficient? *Education Week*, 9, 21.

Hedges, L.V., & Stock, W. (1983). The effects of class size: An examination of rival hypotheses. *American Educational Research Journal*, 12, 63–85.

Hillocks, Jr., G. (1986). *Research on written composition*. Urbana, IL: ERIC Clearinghouse on Reading and Communication Skills and the National Conference on Research in English.

International Reading Association. (1999). *International Reading Association resolution on class size reduction*. Newark, DE: Author.

Johnson, M., & Scriven, E. (1967). Class size and achievement gains in seventh- and eighth-grade English and mathematics. *School Review*, 75, 300–310.

Johnston, R.C. (1997). Class-size cuts in California bring growing pains. *Education Week, 16*(1), 38–39.

Knoblauch, C.H., & Brannon, L. (1984). *Rhetorical traditions and the teaching of writing.* Upper Montclair, NJ: Boynton/Cook.

Lindemann, E. (1995). *A rhetoric for writing teachers.* New York: Oxford University Press.

Lloyd-Jones, R., & Lunsford, A.A. (Eds.). (1989). *The English coalition conference: Democracy through language.* Urbana, IL: National of Teachers of English.

Maeroff, G.I. (1991). Class size as an empowerment issue. *Education Week, 10,* 56.

Mier, M. (1984). *Class size and writing instruction.* Urbana, IL: ERIC Clearinghouse on Reading and Communication Skills.

National Association for the Education of Young Children. (1991). *Accreditation criteria and procedures.* Washington, DC: Author.

National Association of Elementary School Principals. (1996–1997). *NAESP platform.* Alexandria, VA: Author.

National Council of Teachers of English. (1984). *Incentives for excellence: What school board members can do to encourage excellence in their English language arts programs.* Urbana, IL: Author.

National Council of Teachers of English. (1991). *Lost in the Crowd: A handbook on class size and teacher workload.* Urbana, IL: Author.

National Council of Teachers of English. (1995). *Convention news: NCTE Resolutions.* Urbana, IL: Author.

National Council of Teachers of English. (1997a). California scrutinizes class size program. *The Council Chronicle, 6,* 1, 3–4.

National Council of Teachers of English. (1997b). *Council-grams, 40,* 1–16.

National Council of Teachers of English Board of Directors. (1977). *Statement on workload of elementary language arts teachers.* Urbana, IL: Author.

National Council of Teachers of English Commission on Composition. (1985). *Teaching composition: A position statement.* Urbana, IL: Author.

New England School Development Council. (1975). *Class size and teacher load.* Newton, MA: Author.

Porwell, P.J. (1978). *Class size: A summary of research.* Arlington, VA: Educational Research Service. (ED 153 372)

Robinson, G., & Wittebols, J. (1987). *Class size research: A related cluster analysis for decision making.* Arlington, VA: Educational Research Service.

Shapson, S.M., Wright, E.N., Eason, G., & Fitzgerald, J. (1978). *Results of an experimental study of the effects of class size.* Paper presented at the annual meeting of the American Educational Research Association, Toronto. (ED 151 985)

Smith, M.L., & Glass, G.V. (1979). *Relationship of class-size to classroom processes—teacher satisfaction and pupil affect: A meta-analysis.* Washington, DC: National Institute of Education. (ED 190 698)

Sommers, N. (1982). Responding to student writing. *College Composition and Communication, 33,* 148–156.

Straub, R. (1997). Students' reactions to teacher comments: An exploratory study. *Research in the Teaching of English, 31,* 91–119.

Templeton, I. (1972). *Class size. Educational management review series, Number 8.* Eugene, OR: ERIC Clearinghouse on Educational Management.

Viadero, D. (1995). Less is more. *Education Week, 14,* 33–35.

Warburton, J.T. (1961). An experiment in large-group instruction. *Journal of Secondary Education, 36,* 430–432.

Appendix B

International Reading Association Resolution on Class-Size Reduction

The International Reading Association supports the idea of reduced class size, but expects the full benefits of this reform to be realized only with well-educated teachers and reading specialists. Smaller is better, according to new research on reducing class size, and smaller classes in the early grades can lead to higher reading achievement if teachers are adequately prepared to take advantage of the change through high quality professional development.

Reductions in class size can change the dynamics of a classroom. Smaller classes can allow teachers to better assess student needs and to more appropriately individualize instruction. In smaller classes each student receives a larger portion of the educational resources represented by the teacher's instructional time and, consequently, has an opportunity for greater learning. Each of these benefits can best be realized with well-prepared teachers who provide exemplary reading instruction.

The members of the International Reading Association recognize that every child should get more personal attention, that discipline should be maintained in classrooms, and that optimal reading achievement occurs when we give our young people a solid foundation in the early grades. A smaller class size by itself is not sufficient to improve reading achievement; however, class-size reductions can increase opportunities for well-trained teachers to meet these critical needs.

Be it therefore resolved that the International Reading Association believes excellence in classroom reading instruction can be achieved by a combination of reduced class size and high quality teacher preparation and ongoing professional development.

Be it further resolved, the International Reading Association acknowledges that research shows that if class size is reduced from current averages (which are substantially more than 20 students per class) to below 20 students, the increase in reading achievement can be substantial. For disadvantaged and minority students the effects can be even greater. Class reductions of this magnitude can allow knowledgeable teachers to make the adjustments necessary to provide the best reading instruction.

Be it further resolved that the International Reading Association recognizes that research has found that students, teachers, and parents report positive effects from the impact of class-size reductions on the quality of classroom reading activity.

Be it further resolved, the International Reading Association supports reduced class size, which demands a concurrent commitment to increased and improved professional development so the benefits of this policy can be fully realized.

—*Adopted by the Delegates Assembly, May 1999*

Board of Directors at Time of Adoption
Kathryn A. Ransom, President
Carol M. Santa, President-Elect
Carmelita K. Williams, Vice President
Alan E. Farstrup, Executive Director
James V. Hoffman
John W. Logan
Lesley Mandel Morrow
Betsy M. Baker
Adria F. Klein
Diane L. Larson
Kathryn H. Au
Patricia A. Edwards
Timothy Shanahan

Annotations by Sarah E. Dietrich and Margaret Harrington

Boston University

Appendix C

Recommended Reading

Bereiter, C., & Scardamalia, M. (1987). *The psychology of written composition*. Hillsdale, NJ: Erlbaum.

> The authors present a theory of writing based on their analysis of the cognitive functions required for writing. They propose two models of composing: the knowledge-telling model (common to immature writers) and the knowledge-transforming model (common to more expert writers). Numerous examples from studies conducted by the authors provide support for their theory.

Britton, B.K. (1970). *Language and learning*. Harmondsworth, Middlesex, UK: Penguin.

> Britton proposes that language is the principal means that humans use to organize and classify representations in their lives. These representations include both participant and spectator events. This book presents an elaboration of this theory.

Brown, A., & Day, J. (1983). Macrorules for summarizing texts: The development of expertise. *Journal of Verbal Learning and Verbal Behavior, 22*, 1–14.

> Three studies are presented of writers of varying ages and expertise and their use of macrorules (deleting, generalizing, and integrating) in summarizing expository text. The researchers identify six basic rules of summarization. Findings of the studies show that there is a developmental pattern in summarizing and using macrorules.

Calfee, R., & Perfumo, P. (1996). *Writing portfolios in the classroom.* Mahwah, NJ: Erlbaum.

> The assessment of student writing through the use of portfolios is the major theme of this work. Various aspects of writing portfolios have been studied and are explained here by researchers, practitioners, and others concerned with students' writing. Exemplary projects that included the use of writing portfolios are also reported.

Calkins, L. (1994). *The art of teaching writing* (New edition). Portsmouth, NH: Heinemann.

> In this new edition of her classic work on teaching writing, Calkins expands and deepens her ideas about writing and the writing process. She describes writing not only as a recording event, but more importantly as the "process of developing story or idea" (p. 8). Through a child-centered lens and examples of student work, the author offers suggestions on how to engage students in the writing process.

Cambourne, B., & Turbill, J. (1987). *Coping with chaos.* Portsmouth, NH: Heinemann.

> This book explores the ways in which classroom environment affects young learners. The authors describe the perceptions and performance of children, from a variety of cultural and linguistic backgrounds, who are students in process writing classrooms.

Cazden, C. (1988). *Classroom discourse: The language of teaching and learning.* Portsmouth, NH: Heinemann.

> In her study of student-teacher and student-student interactions, Cazden examines the discourse patterns and register of classroom language. The author discusses ways in which language use is tied to definitions of "knowledge" and of "learning." Cazden describes language as a process which unites the cognitive and the social. From this theoretical perspective, the author explores language use and identity, the link between students' ability to recognize and successfully engage in certain discourse patterns, and the inequalities of students' educational opportunities.

Cochran-Smith, M., Paris, C.L., & Kahn, J.L. (1991). *Learning to write differently: Beginning writers and word processing*. Norwood, NJ: Ablex.

> This book is based on results from a 2-year study of elementary school students' use of the computer as a tool for writing. The authors concluded that teaching writing by using the computer and word processing is qualitatively different from teaching writing using pen and paper. They found that teachers altered their instructional strategies for teaching writing, and students learned writing differently when using word processing.

Cooper, C.R., & Odell, L. (1977). *Evaluating writing: Describing, measuring, judging*. Urbana, IL: National Council of Teachers of English.

> Various means of evaluating the writing of secondary school and college students are described in the six chapters of this classic work, including change in intellectual and linguistic processes, holistic evaluation, primary trait scoring, goal setting, self-evaluation, and peer evaluation.

Dahl, K.L., & Farnan, N. (1996). *Children's writing: Perspectives from research*. Newark, DE: International Reading Association.

> The authors present the findings and views of researchers and teachers about classroom practice and children's writing process, highlighting several studies with classroom applications. The authors aim to engage teachers in research and to expand collaborations between classroom instructors and university researchers.

Delpit, L. (1995). *Other people's children: Cultural conflict in the classroom*. New York: The New Press.

> In a collection of essays, the author examines students' behaviors and teachers' expectations on a common theme, the politics of cross-cultural interactions. Delpit offers an examination of the ways in which minority students in the United States can be denied access to education. She also offers an ethnographic look at schools in Papua New Guinea.

Dixon, J. (1967). *Growth through English*. Reading, UK: National Association for the Teaching of English.

> In September 1966, a group of educators from the United Kingdom and the United States concerned with improving the teaching of English met at Dartmouth College to exchange ideas and experiences and to reach a

consensus on how best to improve English language teaching practices. Dixon outlines the major points of these discussions.

Dyson, A.H., & Freedman, S.W. (1991). Writing. In J. Flood, J.M. Jensen, D. Lapp, & J.R. Squire (Eds.), *Handbook of research on teaching the English language arts*. New York: Macmillan.

> Research on the complexities of writing and the complexities of teaching writing is reviewed in this chapter. The contexts in which writing is used, the process by which writing evolves, and the development of writing are discussed.

Ehri, L.C. (1992). Review and commentary: Stages of spelling development. In S. Templeton & D.R. Bear (Eds.), *Development of orthographic knowledge and the foundations of literacy: A memorial Festschrift for Edmund H. Henderson* (pp. 307–332). Hillsdale, NJ: Erlbaum.

> This volume presents chapters on theories and research on orthographic development. Ehri's chapter is a review with commentary on the works contained in the volume. She also proposes her own theory of spelling development in terms of the relationship between orthographic and phonological/morphemic units.

Elbow, P. (1973). *Writing without teachers*. London: Oxford University Press.

> Elbow offers a guide to writing effectively. The author provides exercises designed to help writers write more freely and powerfully, as well as guidelines by which to judge the quality of their own writing. Though it can be used in a classroom, the book is intended for those engaged in an independent study of their own writing.

Emig, J. (1971). *The composing process of twelfth graders*. Urbana, IL: National Council of Teachers of English.

> Case studies were used to investigate the writing processes of eight twelfth graders. In this study, Emig initiated the use of the think-aloud. Findings revealed that the subjects engaged in two types of writing—extensive and reflexive—and that there were differences in length of text and other features. The author concluded that changes needed to be made in teaching composition in order to assist students to develop both modes of writing.

Ferreiro, E., & Teberosky, A. (1982). *Literacy before schooling.* Exeter, NH: Heinemann.

> This book focuses on research on the developmental processes of young children (ages 4, 5, and 6) learning to read and write. The authors report on findings from longitudinal studies in which, following the Piagetian concept, children were interviewed to determine the knowledge they had acquired about reading and writing before formal instruction began.

Flower, L. (1990). The role of task representation in reading to write. In L. Flower, V. Stein, J. Ackerman, M.J. Kantz, K. McCormick, & W. Peck (Eds.), *Reading-to-write.* (pp. 35–75) New York: Oxford University Press.

> In a study of the interpretation of task representation in academic discourse, Flower found that task representation is a constructive process based on personal experiences and understandings. These individual interpretations can lead to misunderstandings between student and instructor. Strategic knowledge is seen as an important key to alleviating misunderstandings.

Flower, L., & Hayes, J.R. (1994). A cognitive process theory of writing. In R.B. Ruddell, M.R. Ruddell, & H. Singer (Eds), *Theoretical models and processes of reading* (4th ed., pp. 928–950). Newark, DE: International Reading Association.

> In this model, three major elements of writing are identified: task environment, writing processes, and the writer's memory. The authors suggest that writers define and set goals based on their knowledge of the writing task, the topic, their audience, and their experience with the writing process. According to this model, writers monitor the text they have produced, comparing it to their initial goals.

Freedman, S., Dyson, A., Flower, L., & Chafe, W. (1987). *Research in writing: Past, present, and future* (Technical Report No. 1). Berkeley, CA: Center for the Study of Writing.

> This report offers an overview of research conducted on writing during the 1970s and 1980s. Topics explored include uses of writing, the evaluation of written language, the nature of writing, and the acquisition of writing.

Gearhart, M., Herman, J.L., Baker, E.L., & Whittaker, A.K. (1992). *Writing portfolios at the elementary level: A study of methods for writing assessment.* Los Angeles: Center for Research on Evaluation, Standards, and Student Testing.

> A study of the effectiveness of portfolio assessment as a means of evaluating elementary student writing is reported. Thirty-five portfolios were rated using both holistic and analytic scoring rubrics. Results showed high interrater agreement. Concerns with differences in scoring a portfolio as opposed to scoring separate student samples, as well as concerns in organizing large-scale portfolio assessment, also are addressed.

Gee, J. (1996). *Social linguistics and literacies: Ideology in discourses* (2nd ed.). Bristol, PA: Taylor and Francis.

> The author presents a critical overview of classroom literacy instruction. Gee relies on the concept of "discourse" to examine interactions between teachers and students. Discourse is made up of both language and behavior and is embedded deeply in social context. The discourse in a mainstream classroom can be very different from the discourse in the homes of the students.

Gere, A. (Ed.). (1985). *Roots in sawdust: Writing to learn across the curriculum.* Urbana, IL: National Council of Teachers of English.

> A product of the Puget Sound Writing Program, this collection of essays examines the difference between "writing to show learning and writing to learn" (p. 1). High school teachers offer examples from their own classrooms to illustrate the use of the "writing to learn" approach in the teaching of art appreciation, German, social studies, science, math, and philosophy.

Goldman, S.R., & Trueba, H.T. (Eds.). (1987). *Becoming literate in English as a second language.* Norwood, NJ: Ablex.

> This book is a collection of articles in which authors explore second-language literacy development in children and adults. The chapters examine home/community settings as contexts for literacy learning, the transfer of cognitive skills from first to second language literacy, and the evaluation of students' reading and writing. Most of the chapters focus on Spanish-speakers whose second language is English.

Graves, D. (1983). *Writing: Teachers and children at work*. Portsmouth, NH: Heinemann.

> Graves provides the reader with strategies for teaching writing as a process in this book based on findings from a 2-year research study conducted in Atkinson, New Hampshire (1978–1980). Children's growth in the fluency of writing also is discussed, as well as ways of assessing and recording their progress. Examples and observations from the research sites are provided.

Haas, C. (1989). How the writing medium shapes the writing process: Effects of word processing on planning. *Research in the Teaching of English, 23*, 181–207.

> Haas presents a study that examines the effects of using pen and paper or word processing on planning. The study found that writers using word processing alone planned less overall, planned less before beginning to write, and engaged in less conceptual planning and more sequential or local planning.

Halliday, M.A.K., & Hasan, R. (1976). *Cohesion in English*. White Plains, NY: Longman.

> The authors discuss the importance of cohesion and cohesive devices for maintaining continuity in a text, as well as for recognizing and displaying the boundaries of a text. Various types of cohesion are explained. The final chapter offers suggestions for analyzing text cohesion.

Hanna, P.R., Hanna, J.S., Hodges, R.E., & Rudorf, E.H. (1966). *Phoneme-grapheme correspondences as cues to spelling improvement*. Washington, DC: U.S. Government Printing Office.

> The authors conducted an analysis of the relationship between phonemes and graphemes and how that relationship relates to spelling instruction. Based on their findings, the authors offer suggestions and strategies for effective spelling instruction.

Heath, S.B. (1983). *Ways with words: Language, life and work in communities and classrooms*. Cambridge, UK: Cambridge University Press.

> This book reports the findings of a 9-year ethnographic study of children's language development in two communities in the southeastern United States. Heath explores language use at home and at school in "Roadville," a white working-class community, and "Trackton," a black working-class community. Heath describes the ways that beliefs and practice surrounding

language and literacy can vary from one community to another. The study examines incongruities between home language and school expectations.

Hillocks, G. (1986). *Research on written composition: New directions for teaching.* Urbana, IL: ERIC Clearinghouse on Reading and Communication Skills.

A review of research conducted between 1963 and 1982 on written composition is presented. Topics in the meta-analysis include the composing process, the repertoire of the writer, experimental studies and meta-analysis, modes of instruction, grammar and syntax, and criteria for better writing and invention. Implications and recommendations for teaching are also included.

Hodges, R.E. (1991). The conventions of writing. In J. Flood, J.M. Jensen, D. Lapp, & J.R. Squire (Eds.), *Handbook of research on teaching the English language arts.* New York: Macmillan.

The author reviews research on writing conventions including spelling, handwriting, punctuation, segmentation, and capitalization, as well as research on teaching these conventions in schools. The author concludes that just as writing is a developmental process that is learned both in and out of the classroom, so too are learning and understanding the use of the conventions of writing.

Jensen, J. (1993). What do we know about the writing of elementary school children? *Language Arts, 20,* 290–294.

Thirty years after the publication of "The Braddock Report," a study of the teaching of writing, Jensen collected responses to the question, What is the single most important thing that we as a profession know now that we didn't know 30 years ago about the teaching and learning of writing in the elementary school? The author asked this question of 24 scholars cited most frequently in Dyson and Freedman's (1991) *Handbook of Research on Teaching the English Language Arts.*

Johnston, P. (1992). *Constructive evaluation of literate activity.* White Plains, NY: Longman.

Evaluation as a reflective practice and as a way of improving teaching and learning is the focus of this work. Johnston explores both theoretical and practical aspects of literacy evaluation, and offers suggestions on how schools can improve evaluation.

Kroll, B. (Ed.). (1990). *Second language writing: Research insights for the classroom*. Cambridge, UK: Cambridge University Press.

> This book provides both teachers and researchers with current theories and research about writing and the writing process in a second or foreign language. It is divided into two sections: in the first section, the authors present insights into aspects of the writing process for second-language learners; in the second section, research studies focusing on different aspects of second-language writing and writing instruction are presented.

Loban, W. (1976). *Language development: Kindergarten through grade twelve* (Research Report 18). Urbana, IL: National Council of Teachers of English.

> This book is the final in a series of progress reports of a study of 211 of the original sample of 338 students. The students' development was traced from kindergarten through twelfth grade. Data were gathered on reading, writing, listening, and other language behavior. The purpose of the study was to determine typical levels of proficiency for each grade level, speed, and stage of language development.

Martin, N. (1983). *Mostly about writing*. Upper Montclair, NJ: Boynton/Cook.

> Martin presents an anthology of her works on writing and the writing process. Essays include topics such as children's language and the language of education, transformation of experience in storytelling, writing and learning, and models of writing.

Matsuhashi, A. (1987). *Writing in real time: Modeling production process*. Norwood, NJ: Ablex.

> This eclectic collection offers a variety of perspectives on the production of written text. Part of the book explores the writing process, generation and revision, and writing and second-language learners and deaf students. The other chapters examine discourse and contexts in which text is produced: interactions during writing conferences and the use of computers in composing.

Moffett, J. (1968). *Teaching the universe of discourse*. New York: Houghton Mifflin.

> This book comprises essays the author wrote while preparing *A Student-Centered Language Arts Curriculum, Grades K–13: A Handbook for Teachers*. Mof-

fett examines dramatic and narrative discourse and argues that children learn about language by playing with and using it.

Moll, L., & Whitmore, K. (1993). Vygotsky in classroom practice: Moving from individual transmission to social transaction. In E. Forman, N. Minick, & C.A. Stone (Eds.), *Contexts for learning: Sociocultural dynamics in children's development* (pp. 19–42). New York: Oxford University Press.

Research on literacy activities of a third-grade Spanish bilingual class are described in this article. The research is framed in the idea that a classroom is a sociocultural environment in which students are actively involved in both teaching and learning from each other. The researchers provide examples of various ways in which the teacher engages the students in writing activities.

Mosenthal, P., Tamor, L., & Walmsley, S. (Eds.). (1983). *Research on writing: Principles and methods.* White Plains, NY: Longman.

This book provides an introduction to the principles and procedures used by a variety of researchers who study the writing process. Among the researchers included in this multidisciplinary collection are Bereiter and Scardamalia, Calfee, Freedman, and Flower and Hayes.

Murray, D. (1968). *A writer teaches writing: A practical method of teaching composition.* Boston: Houghton Mifflin.

Based on his experience as a published writer and practicing teacher, Murray describes the skills and behavior of a successful writer and a successful writing teacher. He explores the writing experience of most elementary and secondary school students and offers suggestions as to how to transform a classroom into a writing workshop. The final chapter offers techniques recommended for writing teachers.

Nelson, N., & Calfee, R. (Eds.). (1998). *The reading-writing connection* (NSSE 97th yearbook, Part 2). Chicago: The University of Chicago Press.

This volume focuses on the connection between reading and writing, as well as the importance of integrating the two in instruction. After an initial chapter on the historical context of the reading-writing connection, authors of the succeeding chapters discuss how reading and writing are integrated in other contexts, including the academic disciplines.

North, S. (1987). *The making of knowledge in composition: Portrait of an emerging field*. Portsmouth, NH: Heinemann.

> North offers an overview of the development of the field of composition in the 1970s and 1980s. The book introduces the scholars and the researchers who advanced the field: historians, philosophers, critics, experimentalists, clinicians, formalists, and ethnographers.

Purves, A.C. (1992). Reflections on research and assessment in written composition. *Research in the Teaching of English, 26*(1), 108–122.

> This article was written at the culmination of a 10-year international study of performance in writing. Purves explores three major issues that confronted the researchers: defining the domain of "school-writing," examining process versus product in writing, and establishing norms for "quality" in writing. The author suggests that this study illustrates the complexities of the assessment of writing.

Rosenblatt, L.M. (1978). *The reader, the text, the poem: The transactional theory of the literary work*. Carbondale, IL: Southern Illinois University Press.

> Rosenblatt presents her theory of the transactional relationship between the reader and the text. She proposes that readers are active participants in reading and that their transactions with the text are individualistic and personal. The type of transaction the reader has with the text lies on a continuum between an efferent response and an aesthetic response.

Shanahan, T. (1984). The nature of the reading-writing relationship: An exploratory multivariate analysis. *Journal of Educational Psychology, 76*, 466–477.

> Shanahan studied a group of second and fifth graders to determine the relationship between reading and writing. An analysis of multiple reading and writing measures showed that although some significant relationships were found between reading and writing, they accounted for no more than 46% of the variable. The study also found that the reading-writing relationship changed as students gained proficiency in reading, suggesting the importance of an integrated curriculum of reading and writing.

Shaughnessy, M. (1977). *Errors and expectations: A guide for the teacher of basic writing*. New York: Oxford University Press.

In this detailed study of writing produced by college students, Shaughnessy examines "errors" basic writers make in handwriting and punctuation, syntax, spelling, and vocabulary. The author suggests that students' oral language differs from the regularity of word forms and sentence structure expected in academic writing. Shaughnessy provides guidelines for helping all students become accomplished academic writers.

Spivey, N.N., & King, J.R. (1994). Readers as writers composing from sources. In R.B. Ruddell, M.R. Ruddell, & H. Singer (Eds.), *Theoretical models and processes of reading* (4th ed., pp. 668–694). Newark, DE: International Reading Association.

In this study of 60 sixth, eighth, and tenth graders in U.S. public schools, the authors examine students' written reports of information gathered through reading. Students' writing was measured by text (quantity, organization, connectivity, holistic quality) and by task (planning, retranscription, and composing time). The study revealed that older students and better readers showed more connectedness of discourse in their writing and were more likely to include important information in their syntheses.

Squire, J.R. (1999). Language arts. In G. Cawelti (Ed.), *Handbook of research on improving student achievement* (2nd ed., pp. 88–103). Arlington, VA: Educational Research Service.

Providing a review of research-based practices in reading and writing that will lead to improved student test scores, the author summarizes research findings in twelve areas.

Teale, W.H., & Sulzby, E. (Eds.). (1986) *Emergent literacy: Writing and reading*. Norwood, NJ: Ablex.

A series of research studies of the conceptual and developmental aspects of literacy of very young children are presented in this book. Common to all the studies is the finding that literacy development begins long before a child enters school, and this literacy is influenced by the social, psycholinguistic, conceptual, and developmental experiences of the child. The term *emergent literacy* is proposed to describe this developmental process of young readers and writers.

Wagner, B.J. (1991). Imaginative expression. In J. Flood, J.M. Jensen, D. Lapp, & J.R. Squire (Eds.), *Handbook of research on teaching the English language arts*. New York: Macmillan.

> Imaginative discourse in literacy is the focus of this chapter. Wagner reviews research that studied how poetry, drama, and fictional narrative are taught and learned. The author states that a curriculum, which is holistic and integrated, is needed to effectively teach students in this creative endeavor.

Winterowd, W.R. (1986). *Composition/rhetoric: A synthesis*. Carbondale, IL: Southern Illinois University Press.

> This book is both a historical guide to and a commentary on the evolution of the teaching of composition during the 1970s and 1980s. Through theoretical models of writing and biological research on the workings of the brain, Winterowd introduces the field of composition and rhetoric. The author explores the classroom applications of existing theories and research.

Author Index

Page references followed by *f* and *t* indicate figures and tables, respectively.

Farstrup, A.E., 327
Faw, H.W., 145, 158
Ferdman, B.M., 130, 134
Ferreiro, E., 48, 64, 78, 79, 80, 81, 86, 200, 203, 204, 205, 208, 331
Ferris, J.A., 123, 134
Fetterley, J., 130, 134
Filby, N.A., 313, 323
Fillmore, C.J., 114, 118, 134
Finn, J.D., 17, 41
Fischer, F.W., 80, 87
Fitzgerald, J., 324
Fivush, R., 71, 74, 75, 86
Flanders, N.A., 248
Fletcher, R., 177, 184
Fletcher-Flinn, C.M., 79, 88
Flihan, S., 2, *112-139*, 150
Flood, J., 3, 119, 134, 176, 184, *233-350*, 243, 249, 250
Flood, S., 243, 249
Flor Ada, A., 233, 237, 250
Flower, L.S., 7, 14, 18, 22, 26, 35, 40, 41, 42, 101, 108, 114, 116, 119, 120, 125, 126, 135, 178, 184, 255, 275, 332
Flude, B.M., 205, 208
Foertsch, M.A., 142, 157
Fowler, C., 80, 87
Frake, C., 114, 135
Francis, W.N., 163, 164, 165, 170, 172, 185
Frary, R.B., 285, 301
Freedman, A., 52, 53, 64
Freedman, S.W., 12, 13, 41, 233, 234, 249, 280, 285, 292, 301, 311, 323, 331, 332
Freeman, F., 204, 208
Freire, P., 58, 59, 64, 130, 135, 259
Friedlander, A., 36, 41
Friere, P., 256, 270, 275
Fries, C.C., 115, 135
Frith, U., 195, 208

Fulwiler, T., 218, 232
Fung, H., 71, 87

G

Gage, J.T., 141, 158
Garcia, G.E., 289, 301
Garrett, M.F., 35, 36, 41
Gaur, A., 191, 208
Gearhart, M., 280, 292, 294, 301, 332
Gee, J.P., 71, 76, 86, 104, 105, 108, 333
Geisler, C., 105, 108, 281, 301
Gentile, C.A., 143, 157, 178, 183
Gentry, J.R., 200, 208
Gere, A., 219, 228, 231, 333
Giacobbe, M.E., 203, 207
Gilligan, C., 130, 135
Gilmore, P., 55, 64
Gilyard, K., 60, 64
Giroux, H.A., 131, 135
Gitomer, D.H., 280, 302
Glaser, R., 21, 281, 300
Glass, G.V., 315, 316, 323, 324
Glasspool, D.W., 194, 209
Glatthorn, A.A., 313, 314, 323
Godshalk, F.I., 101, 103, 108
Goffman, E., 55, 64
Goldberger, N.R., 133
Goldman, S.R., 333
Goodman, K.S., 115, 117, 135, 289, 301
Goodman, Y.M., 117, 135, 289, 301
Goodnow, J.J., 117, 133
Gordon, C.J., 184
Goss, K., 243, 250
Goswami, U., 198, 199, 201, 208
Gough, P.B., 196, 198, 208, 209
Goulandris, N.K., 208
Gould, J.D., 13, 41
Gove, M., 215, 232

Horn, E., 170, 171, 172, 185, 193, 209
Hornberger, N.H., 249
Hotof, N., 209
Houghton, G., 194, 204, 209
Huckin, T., 105, 107
Hudelson, S., 249
Hudson, J., 71, 73t, 87
Hull, C.L., 16, 42
Hull, G., 13, 42
Hunt, B., 158
Hunt, K., 97, 109
Hutchins, E., 12, 42
Huxford, L., 207
Hymes, D., 46, 51, 59, 64, 114, 133
Hythecker, V.I., 12, 43

I

Indrisano, R., *1-4*, 242, 250, *305*, *306*
Inhelder, B., 115, 136
International Reading Association, 102, 109, 315, 323, *326-327*
Irwin, J.W., 98, 109
Isadore of Seville, 190

J

Jacobs, V.A., 118, 133
Jaeger, R.M., 280, 301
Janik, C., 38, 44
Jenkins, L.B., 142, 157
Jensen, A.R., 194, 209
Jensen, J.M., 4, 176, 184, 249, *307-325*, 335
Jeong, M., 76, 87
Jesso, B., 74, 88
John, V.P., 114, 133
Johnson, B.V., 167, 167f, 174, 185
Johnson, C.J., 145, 159
Johnson, D.D., 3, *162-186*, 167, 167f, 168, 173, 174, 185, 190
Johnson, D.W., 240, 250
Johnson, M., 314, 324

Johnson, P., 265, 274
Johnson, R.T., 240, 250
John-Steiner, V., 128, 136
Johnston, P., 335
Johnston, R.C., 320, 324
Jones, I., 241, 250, 253, 265, 275
Jones, R.J., 107
Jones, R.S., 146, 152, 158
Jordan, J., 59, 64
Juel, C., 80, 87
Just, M.A., 23, 42

K

Kahn, J.L., 241, 249, 329
Kalantzis, M., 100, 107, 130, 134, 256, 274
Kalman, J., 53, 64
Kamberelis, G., 239, 250
Kameenui, E.J., 176, 183
Kamil, M.L., 175, 183
Kamler, B., 79, 80, 87
Kane, M.B., 278, 280, 287, 302
Kane, M.S., 286, 302
Kaufer, D.S., 14, 35, 42
Keifer, K., 275
Kerek, A., 97, 107
Kerr, S., 253, 263, 275
Kiecolt-Glaser, R., 21, 43
Kiesler, S., 14, 44
Kilarr, G., 79, 80, 87
King, J.R., 126, 138, 150, 159, 339
King, M., 98, 110
Kintsch, W., 152, 158, 225, 231
Kinzer, C., 269, 276
Kirschner, B.W., 123, 137
Klaus, C., 96
Klein, A.F., 327
Klein, S., 280, 302
Klimenkoff, M., 284, 302
Knoblauch, C.H., 309, 310, 324
Koda, K., 250

Pierce, L.V., 281, 303
Pinker, S., 164, 168, 185
Pinsky, R., 1, 4
Pitcher, E.G., 68, 69t, 88
Plaut, D.C., 192, 195, 196, 197, 210
Poe, E.A., 182
Porwell, P.J., 316, 324
Poundstone, C.C., 158
Powell, W., 174
Prelinger, E., 68, 69t, 88
Pressley, M., 145, 159
Purves, A.C., 104, 109, 119, 137, 338

R

Rabinowitz, P., 131, 137
Ransom, K.A., 327
Raphael, T.E., 123, 137, 153, 154, 159
Razik, T., 170, 184
Read, C., 48, 65, 88, 98, 110, 117,
        137, 200, 210
Reddy, M., 263, 267, 274, 276
Redish, J., 20, 43
Reil, M., 258, 259, 274
Reitman, W.R., 32, 43
Rentel, V., 98, 110
Resnick, D.P., 285, 303
Resnick, L.B., 285, 303
Reyes, M. de la Luz, 51, 65
Rice, M.E., 158
Richards, J.C., 250
Richman, B., 164, 165, 173, 183
Richmond-Welty, E.D., 80, 88
Rinehart, S.D., 146, 152, 159
Ringgold, F., 60, 65
Rinsland, H.D., 162, 164, 165, 169,
        170, 171, 172, 185
Robinson, A., 203, 208
Robinson, F.P., 195, 210
Robinson, G., 316, 324
Robinson, S., 7, 42
Rock, D., 107

Rockhill, K., 131, 137
Rocklin, T., 12, 43
Rodale, J.I., 180, 185
Roen, D.H., 335
Roget, P.M., 185
Roget's Children's Thesaurus, 181, 185
Roget's Student's Thesaurus, 181, 185
Rogoff, B., 50, 65
Roosevelt, E., 177
Rosaen, C.L., 144, 159
Rose, M., 131, 137
Rosen, H., 90, 107, 217, 231
Rosen, L.M., 122, 123, 124, 133
Rosenblatt, L.M., 93, 110, 338
Rothkopf, E.Z., 30, 43
Rowe, D., 269, 276
Rubin, A., 120, 122, 123, 124, 137
Ruddell, M.R., 176, 185, 186
Ruddell, R., 174
Ruddell, R.B., 176, 186
Rudorf, E.H., 334
Rudorf, E.H., Jr., 198, 209
Rumelhart, D.E., 114, 137, 144, 159
Ruptic, C., 284, 302
Rush, R.T., 170, 185

S

Salomon, G., 264, 276
Santa, C.M., 223, 231, 327
Santa, J.L., 34, 43
Sayers, D., 258, 261, 274
Scardamalia, M., 27, 41, 98, 101,
        107, 114, 116, 119, 133, 237,
        248, 255, 263, 264, 267, 272,
        274, 276, 328
Schank, R.C., 114, 137
Schickedanz, J.A., 2, 66-89, 79, 80,
        88, 256
Schieffelin, B.B., 52, 65, 78, 88
Schilperoord, J., 14, 36, 43
Schoer, L., 309, 323

Velez, L., 13, 44
Venezky, R.L., 199, 211
Viadero, D., 319, 325
Vygotsky, L.S., 47, 48, 49, 50, 65, 66,
    89, 116, 138, 256, 267, 272,
    276, 295, 304

W

Wagner, B.J., 340
Walker, E.V.S., 51, 65
Wallace, D.L., 28, 44
Waller, T.G., 145, 158
Walmsley, S., 337
Walters, J., 280, 303
Warburton, J.T., 314, 325
Waterman, D., 7, 42
Waters, G.S., 211
Watson-Gegeo, K., 269, 274
Weber, R.M., 130, 139
Webster, L., 121, 139
Webster, S., 98, 107
Webster's Elementary Dictionary, 163,
    186
Weir, R., 117, 139
Weiser, I., 281, 304
Welch-Ross, M.K., 70, 89
Wellman, H.M., 70, 89
Whitmore, K., 53, 64, 337
Whittaker, A.K., 332
Wigfield, A., 158
Wiggins, G.P., 280, 304
Wilde, S., 203, 211
Wiley, A.R., 71, 87

Wiley, D.E., 286, 289, 304
Williams, C.K., 164, 327
Wing, A.M., 194, 204, 211
Winograd, P., 126, 137, 147, 152,
    159, 160, 220, 221, 222, 223,
    231, 285, 304
Winograd, T., 114, 139
Winterowd, W.R., 340
Winters, L., 281, 301
Wishbow, N., 39, 44
Wittebols, J., 316, 324
Wittrock, M.C., 117, 139, 145, 146,
    147, 160
Wolf, D.P., 280, 287, 300
Wolf, S.A., 280, 294, 301, 304
Wong-Fillmore, J., 130, 139
Woodlief, L., 53, 65
Woodruff, E., 255, 263, 267, 276
Woodward, V.A., 79, 87
Wright, E.N., 324
Wright, P., 20, 44

Y

Yancey, K.B., 281, 304
Yen, W.M., 304
Young, A., 205, 208, 216, 218, 224,
    228, 232
Young, R., 17, 43
Youngblade, L., 70, 86

Z

Zasloff, T., 28, 44
Zutell, J., 200, 211

Subject Index

Page references followed by *f* and *t* indicate figures and tables, respectively.

of fluency and control of written language, 98; in intermediate grades, 239; of mastery of diverse purposes for writing, 96; portfolio, 285; in primary grades, 236–238; Scholastic Aptitude Test, 286

ASSIGNMENTS: 5-minute essay, 216; authentic, 290; high-stakes, 218–219; low-stakes, 218–219

ATTEND, 7

AUDIENCE, 57; knowledge of, 37–38

AUTHENTIC WRITING: assignments, 290; portfolio as scaffold for, 289–293

AUTHOR'S THEATER, 59

AUTHORSHIP, 105

AUTOBIOGRAPHICAL MEMORY: parental scaffolding of, 71–74, 72t–73t

AWARENESS, 216

B

BAY AREA WRITING PROJECT, 223, 279, 289

BIOPOEMS, 228–229

BRITAIN: The National Curriculum, 189

BRONTË, CHARLOTTE AND EMILY, 207

C

CALIFORNIA: Council of Teachers of English, 307; Department of Education, 295; incentive to reduce class sizes, 320–321; Reading/Language Arts standards, 288, 291

CALIFORNIA LEARNING ASSESSMENT SYSTEM (CLAS), 294–295, 298; CLAS-Plus enhancements, 296–298, 299–300

C.A.R.S. (CENTER-ACTIVITY ROTATION SYSTEM), 244–247; in classroom, 244, 245f; Computer Center, 246–247; Conference Center, 246; Listening Center, 246; Resource Center, 246; Teacher-Sharing Center, 247; Viewing Center, 246; Writing Center, 245–246

CHILD TALK: excerpts, 47, 48–49. *See also* Talk

CHILDREN: alphabetic, phonological, and orthographic knowledge, 77–78; as apprentices, 50; autobiographical memory, 71–74, 72t–73t; parent-child interactions, 82–83; personal narrative productions, 71–75; primary grade, 241–242; social and cultural contexts that influence writing of, 238; stories produced by, 68, 69t; teaching writing to, 241–242; writing process, 236; young, 67–68, 78–80. *See also* Students

CLAS. *See* California Learning Assessment System

CLAS-PLUS, 296–298, 299–300

CLASS LOAD, 318, 322

CLASS SIZE: debate continuance, 321–322; elementary school, 317–318, 318–321; financial implications of, 321–322; general research on,

314–316; International Reading Association Resolution on Class Size Reduction, 326–327; recommendations for, 317; reducing in elementary school, 316–318; research on, 307–325; state initiatives to reduce, 318–321 models of, 193, 196–199; English, 188–189, 192–202; handwriting in models of, 203–205; historical context, 189–192; learning, 187–188; models and processes of, 192–202; punctuation in models of, 202–203; serial models of, 193–194

CORI. *See* Concept-Oriented Reading Instruction

COURSE MATERIAL: journal writing to support personal interactions with, 226–228

CREATIVITY: imaginative writing to encourage, 228–230

CRITICAL LITERACY, 58; communication technology requirements, 270–274

CRITICAL PRACTICES, 55–60

CSIW. *See* Cognitive Strategy Instruction in Writing

CULTURAL ISSUES: contexts that influence children's writing, 238; differences in socialization of narrative, 75–77; writing as object, 81

CURRICULUM: resources, 233–350. *See also* Writing across the curriculum

CYBERPLAY, 262–264

CYBERSPACE, 253, 257–264

CYBERWRITING, 257–262

D

DECISION MAKING, 32–33

DESCRIPTIVE RESEARCH, 68–71

DEVELOPMENT: of children's alphabetic, phonological, and orthographic knowledge, 77–78; of competence, 161–211; cyberplay process, 262–264; of fluency and control of written language, 96–98; proximal, 50; writing, 5–110, 240–241

DEVELOPMENTAL STAGE MODELS, 199–202; of written English conventions, 193

A *DICTIONARY OF THE ENGLISH LANGUAGE* (JOHNSON), 190

DIRECT STRATEGY INSTRUCTION, 155

DISCOURSE: social construction of, 71–77; synthesis of, 150

DISTORTIONS, 194

DISTRIBUTED COGNITION, 264–265

DISTRIBUTED COMPOSING, 264, 265–267

DUAL-ROUTE MODELS, 196–199; of written English conventions, 193

DYADIC INSTRUCTIONAL ENCOUNTERS, 52

DYADS, 49–51

E

EARLY MODERN ENGLISH, 190

EDUCATORS: vocabulary considerations, 179. *See also* Teachers

ELABORATION, 33, 125

ELEMENTARY SCHOOL: class load of teachers in, 318; NCTE interest in class sizes, 317–318; reducing class size in, 316–318; state initiatives to reduce class size in, 318–321

EMERGENT LITERACY, 129

EMERGENT WRITING, 66–89

ENGLISH: Early Modern English, 190; Modern English, 189; Old English, 189; orthography, 189–190, 192; vocabulary, 165–166; written conventions, 188, 189–192, 192–202

ENVIRONMENT: classroom, 240–241; physical, 13–14; social, 12–13; task, 8, 9f, 9–11, 10f, 12–14

ENVIRONMENTALLY ASSISTED CLASSROOMS, 240

ENVISIONMENT-BUILDING LITERATURE CLASSES, 128

ERIC/RCS DATABASE, 141

ERRORS: spelling, 193, 194; typing, 205; "word exchange," 36

ESSAY WRITING: to encourage analytical thinking, 230; 5-minute essays, 216

EVALUATION: external, 284–289. *See also* Assessment

EVENTS, 51–55; classroom, 53–55; learning within, 52–53; literacy, 51, 127–130; unofficial, 55–60

EXHIBITIONS, 289

EXPENDITURES, 321–322

EXPOSITION, 140

EXPOSITORY TEXT, 140

EXPRESSIVE LANGUAGE, 93

EXPRESSIVE WRITING, 217

F

FINANCES, 321–322

5-MINUTE ESSAY, 216

FLUENCY: assessing, 98; development of, 96–98

FRENCH, 165, 189

FUTURE DIRECTIONS, 130–132, 155–157, 205–207

G

GAP-FILLING DECISIONS, 32

GENERATING PRINCIPLE, 79

GENRES, 256

GERMAN, 165

GOALS, 17–18

GREAT VOWEL SHIFT, 189

GREEK, 190

GROUPING, 242–244

H

HANDWRITING, 189, 191–192; in models of writing conventions, 203–205

HAYES-FLOWER MODEL OF WRITING, 6; new, 9–11, 10*f*; as proposed in 1980, 7–9, 8*f*, 9*f*

HIGH SCHOOL STUDENTS: statements about communication technologies, 251–252

HIGH-STAKES WRITING ASSIGNMENTS, 218–219

HISTORICAL CONTEXT, 189–192

I

IMAGINATIVE WRITING: to encourage students to play with ideas and think creatively about subjects studied, 228–230

IN-SERVICE EDUCATION: recommendations for, 312–313

INDIANA: PRIME TIME, 319

INDIVIDUAL, 15–21

INFERENCING, 33–34

INFORMATIONAL WRITING: integrating, 225; to move beyond simple recall, 224–226

INFORMATIVE PROSE, 140; responding to, 140–160; writing in response to, 141–144, 144–151, 151–155

INSTRUCTION: arrangement and grouping in, 242–244; Cognitive Strategy Instruction in Writing (CSIW), 153–154; Concept-Oriented Reading Instruction (CORI), 154–155; critical factors affecting, 234–235, 235*f*; direct strategy, 155; dyadic encounters, 52; explicit, 155; methods for, 151–155; writing and reading and, 122–124; writing process, 234–235, 235*f*

INTERMEDIATE GRADES, 239; teaching writing with technology in, 242; writing strategies in, 239

INTERNATIONAL READING ASSOCIATION, 116, 174; Resolution on Class Size Reduction, 326–327

INTERNET, 254, 258

INVENTED SPELLING, 80

INVENTION, 310

IRISH MISSIONARIES, 189

ITEM-RESPONSE THEORY, 286

J

JAMES (FIRST GRADER), 214–215, 217

JOHNSON, SAMUEL: *A Dictionary of the English Language*, 190

JOURNAL OF READING, 174

JOURNAL WRITING, 226–228

K

KENTUCKY, 307

KNOWLEDGE: of audience, 37–38; children's alphabetic, phonological, and orthographic, 77–78; communicating, 124–127; strategic, 101–103; structural, 98–101; of words, 167–169

KNOWLEDGE RESTRUCTURING, 144

KNOWLEDGE TELLING, 101

KNOWLEDGE TRANSFORMING, 101

L

LANGUAGE: expressive function of, 217–218; expressive uses of, 93; of literature, 93; oral, 45–65; poetic, 93; transactional, 93; transactional function of, 217–218; written, 96–98, 98

LANGUAGE ARTS TEACHERS, 318. *See also* Teachers

LASTING BENEFITS, 319, 320

LATIN, 190

LAWRENCE, JACOB, 61

LEARNING: in events, 52–53; mode of, 140; processes of, 80–86; to read and spell, 201; teaching and, 131; types of, 144; from writing, 149; writing in response to informative prose and, 144–151; writing-to-learn, 141; writing-to-learn from multiple texts, 150–151; writing-to-learn from single texts, 144–150

LEARNING PORTFOLIO, 284

LEARNING WRITTEN CONVENTIONS, 187–188

LEXEMES, 163, 165; types of, 163–164, 164–165

LEXICAL ITEMS, 163

LEXICON: American school, 173; mental, 167

LISTEMES, 164

LISTENING CENTER (C.A.R.S.), 246

LITERACY: critical, 58, 270–274; emergent, 129; as political tool, 256–257; research, 116

LITERACY EVENTS, 51, 54, 127–130

LITERATURE: envisionment-building classes, 128; language of, 93

LOW-STAKES WRITING ASSIGNMENTS, 218–219

M

MANAGEMENT, 233–350

MATERIAL: journal writing to support personal interactions with, 226–228

MATURATIONISM, 66

MEMORY: autobiographical, 71–74, 72*t*–73*t*; long-term, 9, 9*f*, 10*f*, 11, 37–40; "phonological loop," 15; short-term buffer, 194; "sketchpad," 15; working,

OLD ENGLISH, 189
OMISSIONS, 194
ORAL LANGUAGE, 45–65
ORILLAS PROJECT, 261
ORTHOGRAPHY: children's knowledge of, 77–78; English, 189–190, 192

P

PARALLEL DISTRIBUTED PROCESSING (PDP) MODELS, 195
PARENT-CHLD INTERACTIONS, 82–83
PARENTS: scaffolding by, 71–75, 72t–73t; topic-extending, 71–74
PARTICIPATION POINTS, 227
PDP MODELS. *See* Parallel distributed processing (PDP) models
PERFORMANCE ERRORS, 194
PERSONA: representations of, 29–30
"PHONOLOGICAL LOOP", 15
PHONOLOGY: children's knowledge of, 77–78; visual, 199
PHYSICAL ENVIRONMENT, 13–14
PIAGETIAN FRAMEWORK, 66–67
PLANNING, 7, 31–34
PLAY: cyberplay, 262–264
POEMS, 229; biopoems, 228–229
POETIC LANGUAGE, 93
POETIC WRITING, 229–230
POLITICS: literacy as tool for, 256–257
PORTFOLIO ASSESSMENT, 285
PORTFOLIOS, 278–304; classroom, 281; as classroom activity, 283–284; as classroom assessment and external evaluation, 284–289; in contemporary practice, 283–300; design proposal, 293–300; future of, 293; ideal, 281; learning, 284; perspectives on, 281–283; as scaffolds for authentic writing, 289–293
PRACTICE: impact of, 39–40
PRESENTATIONAL SKILLS, 189
PREWRITING ACTIVITIES, 310–311
PRIMARY GRADES, 236–238; teaching writing with technology in, 241–242
PRIME TIME, 319
PRINT, 189
PROBLEM SOLVING, 31–32
PROJECT STAR. *See* Student/Teacher Achievement Ratio project
PROSE, INFORMATIVE, 140–160
PROTOCOL-AIDED REVISION, 38
PROXIMAL DEVELOPMENT, ZONE OF, 50

PSYCHOLOGICAL FACTORS: in intermediate grades, 239; in primary grades, 236–238

PUERTO RICO: Orillas project, 261

PUNCTUATION, 189, 190–191; in models of writing conventions, 202–203

PUNCTUATION PROJECT, 203

R

READING: affective responses in, 19–21; as central process in writing, 28–31; cognitive processes in, 23–25, 24f, 25f; Concept-Oriented Reading Instruction (CORI), 154–155; to define tasks, 28; learning, 201; processes of, 118–127; replacing revision with, 22–28; source text, 28–29; to understand task, 31; writing and, 111–160

READING/LANGUAGE ARTS STANDARDS (CALIFORNIA), 288, 291

REAL WRITERS, 289–290

RECALL, 224–226

REFLECTION, 22; scaffolding for, 49–51

REPRESENTATIONS: of text as spatial display, 30; of writer's persona, 29–30

RESEARCH: on class size, 307–325, 314–316; descriptive, 68–71; on development of alphabetic, phonological, and orthographic knowledge, 77–78; future directions, 130–132, 155–157, 248; literacy, 116; National Conference on Research in English Charter, 116; social interaction framework, 77; support for writing across the curriculum, 219–223; teaching and learning studies, 131; vocabulary, 169–173, 173–177, 179; writing and reading, 113–116

RESOURCE CENTER (C.A.R.S.), 246

RESOURCES: curriculum, 233–350, 240–241, 241–242; recommended reading, 328–340

RESPONSES: affective, 19–21; to informative prose, 140–160

REVISION, 7; control structure for, 26; model of, 26, 27f; process of, 22–23, 23f; Protocol-Aided Revision, 38; replacing with reading, 22–28

RHETORIC: Aristotelian, 113, 305; and research on class size, 307–325

ROGET'S THESAURUS, 180

ROMAN MISSIONARIES, 189

RULE BREAKING, 61–62

RUSSIAN, 165

S

SCAFFOLDING: parental, 71–75, 72t–73t; portfolio as, 289–293; reflective behavior, 49–51

SCHOLASTIC APTITUDE TEST, 286

SCHOOLS: American lexicon, 173; elementary, 316–318, 318–321; reducing class size in, 316–318; secondary, 90; urban, 233–350; U.S., 90–92; writing tasks in, 147. *See also* Classrooms

SEA OF TALK, 45, 60–63; solidification of, 46–55; writing and, 45–55

SECONDARY SCHOOLS: National Study of Writing in the Secondary School, 90; student statements about communication technologies, 251–252. *See also* Schools

SEEGER, PETE, 61

SENTENCES: length of parts, 36; topic, 225

SERIAL MODELS OF WRITTEN ENGLISH CONVENTIONS, 193–194

SERIAL POSITION EFFECT, 194

SHORT-TERM MEMORY BUFFER, 194

"SKETCHPAD", 15

SLIPS, 194; of fingers vs of pen, 205

SOCIAL CLASS DIFFERENCES, 75–77

SOCIAL ENVIRONMENT, 12–13; construction of narrative discourse, 71–77; influence on children's writing, 238; writing as participation in, 103–106

SOCIAL INTERACTIONISM, 66, 67; research framework effects, 77

SOCIALIZATION OF NARRATIVE, 75–77

SOCIOCULTURAL CONTEXT, 255–256

SODA ERRORS, 194

SOURCES, 66–89; text, 28–29

SOUTH CAROLINA, 279

SPANISH: Orillas project, 261

SPATIAL DISPLAY, 30

SPEECH: manipulating, 48–49; oral language, 45–65

SPELLING, 189; as bottom-up process, 195; competence errors, 194; connectionist models of, 195–196; convention errors, 194; developmental stage models of, 199–202; dual-route models of, 196–199; error types, 193, 194; invented, 80; learning, 201; parallel distributed processing (PDP) models of, 195; performance errors, 194; serial models of, 193–194; serial position effect, 194; SODA errors, 194

STATE INITIATIVES: to reduce numbers in elementary classes, 318–321. *See also* *specific states*

STEINBECK, JOHN, 206

STORIES: produced by children ages 2 to 5 years old, 68, 69t. *See also* Narrative

STRINGFIELD, KRISTIN, 59

STRUCTURAL KNOWLEDGE, 98–101; assessment of, 100–101

STUDENT/TEACHER ACHIEVEMENT RATIO PROJECT (PROJECT STAR), 319, 320

STUDENTS: high school, 251–252; primary grade, 242. *See also* Children

SUBSTITUTIONS, 194

SUMMARY WRITING, 225

SYNTACTIC ATOMS, 164

T

TALK: functions of, 47–49; internal, 218; as recruiting area, 48; sea of, 45–55, 46–55, 60–63; written, 61–62

TASK ENVIRONMENT, 8, 9*f*, 12–14; new model, 9–11, 10*f*

TASK SCHEMAS, 37

TASKS: reading to define, 28; reading to understand, 31; school writing, 147

TEACHER-SHARING CENTER (C.A.R.S.), 247

TEACHERS: class load of, 318, 322; elementary, 318; prototypal, 313; roles of, 57; teachers teaching, 223; vocabulary considerations, 179; work load, 311

TEACHING: and learning, 131

TEACHING TEACHERS, 223

TEACHING WRITING: to intermediate grade students, 242; to primary grade children, 241–242; with technology, 241–242, 242; in urban schools, 233–350

TEACHING WRITING IN RESPONSE TO INFORMATIVE PROSE, 151–155

TECHNOLOGY: communication, 251–276; teaching writing to intermediate grade students with, 242; teaching writing to primary grade children with, 241–242; thinking and composing with technological tools, 264–270

TENNESSEE: class reduction effort, 319; Lasting Benefits, 319, 320; Student/Teacher Achievement Ratio project (Project STAR), 319, 320

TEXT: expository, 140; genre forms, 256; reading for comprehension of, 23–25, 24*f*; reading for evaluation of, 23–25, 25*f*; representations as spatial display, 30; source, 28–29

TEXT INTERPRETATION, 22

TEXT PRODUCTION, 22, 35–36

THEORIES OF WRITING, 254–256

THESAURI, 180, 181

THINK SHEETS, 153

THINKING: with technological tools, 264–270; writing and reading and, 124–127

THINKING ALOUD ON PAPER, 218

TOPIC-EXTENDING PARENTS, 71–74

TOPIC SENTENCES, 225

TRANSACTIONAL LANGUAGE, 93

TRANSACTIONAL WRITING, 217

TRANSFORMATIONAL COMPOSING, 264

TRANSFORMATIVE COMPOSING, 267–270

TRANSLATING, 7

TUBMAN, HARRIET, 61

TYPING ERRORS, 205

U

UNDERSTAND, 7

UNITED STATES: Orillas project, 261; writing development in, 104; writing in schools in, 90–92. *See also specific states*

UNIVERSITY OF MARYLAND: Concept-Oriented Reading Instruction (CORI), 154–155

URBAN SCHOOLS, 233–350

UTTERANCES, 46, 56

V

VALIDITY, CONSTRUCT, 286

VIEWING CENTER (C.A.R.S.), 246

VIRGINIA, 307

VISUAL PHONOLOGY, 199

VOCABULARY, 162–186; active, 168, 169*f*; bogus words, 166; categories of, 167, 167*f*; considerations for, 179; early research, 169–173; English, 165–166; guidelines for helping expand, 182–183; known, 167–169; more recent interest in, 173–177; new, 166; passive, 168, 169*f*; recommendations for classroom, 182–183; and writing, 177–182

VOICES. *See* Talk

VYGOTSKIAN THEORY, 66, 67

W

WAC. *See* Writing across the curriculum

WALKER, JILL, 54

WEBSTER, NOAH, 190

"WHAT NEXT" STRATEGY, 237

"WORD EXCHANGE" ERRORS, 36

WORDS, 163–169; bogus, 166; creation of, 78–80; definition of, 163; English, 165–166; known, 167–169; new, 166; right, 162–186; types of, 164–165

WORKING MEMORY, 10*f*, 11, 15–16

WORKS PROJECT ADMINISTRATION (OKLAHOMA), 171

WRITERS: persona of, 29–30; real, 289–290

WRITING, 141; affective responses in, 19–21; assessment of, 236–238, 239, 277–304; authentic, 289–293; children's, 236, 238; cognitive processes in, 9, 9*f*, 10*f*, 11, 21–40, 255; communication technologies and, 251–276; conventions of, 187–211; as cultural object, 81; in cyberspace, 257–264; emergent, 66–89; essay, 230; expressive, 217; extensive practice and, 39–40; Hayes-Flower model of, 6, 7–9; imaginative, 228–230; informational, 224–226; in intermediate grades, 239; journal, 226–228; knowledge telling, 101; knowledge transforming, 101; learning from, 149; in lives of two learners, 214–217; as mode of learning, 140; motivation in, 17; National Study of Writing in the Secondary School, 90; new framework for understanding cognition and affect in, 6–44; new model, 9–11, 10f; oral language in, around, and about, 45–65; as participation in social action, 103–106; poetic, 229–230; portfolio as scaffold for, 289–293; in primary grades, 236–238; processes, 118–127; purposes of, 92–96; reading and, 28–31, 111–160; in response to informative prose, 141–144, 144–151, 151–155; school writing tasks, 147; and sea of talk, 45–55; as sociocultural context, 255–256; summary, 225; teaching, 233–350, 241–242, 242; theories of, 254–256; transactional, 217; in U.S. schools, 90–92; value of, 140–141; vocabulary and, 162–186, 177–182

WRITING ACROSS THE CURRICULUM (WAC), 141, 214–232; implications for classroom practice, 223–230; research support for, 219–223

WRITING ACTIVITIES, 148; in intermediate grades, 239; in primary grades, 236–238

WRITING ASSIGNMENTS: 5-minute essay, 216; authentic, 290; high-stakes, 218–219; low-stakes, 218–219

WRITING CENTER (C.A.R.S.), 245–246

WRITING CONFERENCES, 50

WRITING DEVELOPMENT, 5–110; alternative models of, 90–110; classroom environment and, 240–241; natural, 94; in United States, 104

WRITING INSTRUCTION. See Instruction

WRITING PORTFOLIOS, 278–304

WRITING STRATEGIES: 5-minute essay, 216; assessment of, 102–103; Cognitive Strategy Instruction in Writing (CSIW), 153–154; direct strategy instruction, 155; in intermediate grades, 239; knowledge of, 101–103; "what next" strategy, 237

WRITING-TO-LEARN, 141; from multiple texts, 150–151; from single texts, 144–150

WRITTEN CONVENTIONS. See Conventions of writing

WRITTEN TALK, 61–62

Y

YOUNG CHILDREN: development of narrative in, 67–68; understanding of word creation in alphabetic writing system, 78–80. See also Children

Z

ZONE OF PROXIMAL DEVELOPMENT, 50